SO-BVU-487

Readings in Behavior

Readings
in Behavior

Joseph M. Notterman
Princeton University

ASU WEST LIBRARY

RANDOM HOUSE New York

A15021 976435

BF
149
.N67
WEST

Copyright © 1970 by Random House, Inc.
All rights reserved under International and Pan-American
Copyright Conventions. Published in the United States by
Random House, Inc., New York, and simultaneously in
Canada by Random House of Canada Limited, Toronto.

Library of Congress Catalog Card Number: 71-99963

Manufactured in the United States of America.
Composed by H. Wolff Book Mfg. Co., Inc., N.Y.
Printed and Bound by Halliday Lithograph Corp., West Hanover, Mass.

Design by J. M. Wall

First Edition

987654321

BF
149
N67

BRIARCLIFF COLLEGE LIBRARY

6439

For my son Daniel

Introduction

In choosing the various writings included in this Readings book, a deliberate attempt has been made to capture the breadth of psychological inquiry. No particular formal approach has been urged upon the student; to the contrary—he is invited to accept, to modify, or to reject the points of view expressed by diverse contemplators of behavior.

Toward that end, the selections include philosophical as well as empirical articles. They also reflect both biological and sociological concerns, ancient and modern insights, and foreign as well as American positions.

If anything binds together these selections, it is an emphasis upon *behavioral adaptation*. Whether made explicit in the technical terminology of science and engineering, or the logical structure of philosophy, or the resonance of poetry, Man's wonder at Man's ability to accommodate the pressures of living has always sought expression. The following pages reflect to some extent the variety of ways in which this wonder has been brought under critical scrutiny.

Acknowledgments

Several individuals were kind enough to provide helpful suggestions concerning either the selection of readings, or the comments that introduce the readings. In particular, I am indebted to Stephen C. Fowler, Daniel A. Notterman, and Carl E. Sherrick.

Mrs. Jeanette Koffler supervised the clerical aspects of manuscript preparation; and Miss Elaine Rosenberg of Random House, the editorial problems of actual publication. I am grateful to both.

Contents

I

II

III

IV

MODIFYING RESPONSES THROUGH
CUE ESTABLISHMENT

V

COGNITIVE PROCESSES

VI

MODIFYING RESPONSES THROUGH DRIVE OPERATIONS

VII

PHYSIOLOGICAL AND NEUROLOGICAL CONCOMITANTS OF BEHAVIOR

VIII

EXTENSIONS TO THE INDIVIDUAL

IX

EXTENSIONS TO THE GROUP

X

EPILOGUE AND PROLOGUE

Foundations of Modern Psychology

1

Problems and Scope of Psychology

John B. Watson

Watson is usually viewed as being a "mechanistic" psychologist—one concerned with the individual's current acts, and little else. That his interests and perspectives went far beyond such limited analyses is indicated in this reading. It demonstrates that he also stressed the importance of knowing the past history of the organism, if the immediately observable behavior is to be properly interpreted. Watson, moreover, had considerable respect for nonexperimental insights, particularly those stemming from folklore and the arts.

This particular passage consists of the first few pages of the introductory chapter to Watson's 1919 text, *Psychology from the Standpoint of a Behaviorist.* It is revealing to discover how germane so many of his comments still are, especially those bearing upon the problems faced by society in its attempts to shape individual and group behavior.

PSYCHOLOGY A SCIENCE OF BEHAVIOR

Psychology is that division of natural science which takes human activity and conduct as its subject matter. It attempts to formulate through systematic observation and experimentation the laws and principles which underlie man's reactions. Every one agrees that man's acts are determined by something, and that, whether he acts orderly or not, there are sufficient grounds for his acting as he does act, if only these grounds can be discovered. In order to formulate such laws we must study man in action—his adjustments to the daily situations of life, and to the unusual situations which may confront him. When sufficiently worked out, the principles we obtain from such a study permit of two generalizations:

Reprinted by permission from *Psychology from the Standpoint of a Behaviorist* by J. B. Watson, published by J. B. Lippincott Company, pp. 1–8. Copyright © 1919 by J. B. Lippincott Company.

1. *To predict human activity with reasonable certainty.* It is sometimes asserted that we can never reach a point where such predictions can be made—that human activity is too variable; and determined by too many momentary conditions to permit us ever to reach such a goal. A little consideration shows that common-sense psychology is already, and has been since the social life of man began, making serviceable predictions. Every institution and custom we have depends upon it; for example, our savings banks, churches, and business. When it comes to the individual the facts are not different. We accept a man's note because we predict (not always or ordinarily in words) from our study of his character that he will pay it at the proper time. The wife cheerfully begins the rearing of a family because she predicts that her husband will remain attached to her, and provide herself and her children with bread. We can bring the matter still further down to a specific situation. If a man is walking in a wooded country when some one suddenly begins to fire at him with a revolver he will duck behind the nearest tree. Even that one who doubts most strongly our ability to predict human conduct will not willingly leave his purse in an unprotected place. The more constantly we are thrown with an individual the more accurately we can map out his program of activity for the day.

2. An equally important result coming from our psychological study is our *formulation of laws and principles whereby man's actions can be controlled by organized society.* Psychology endeavors to guide society as to the ways in which the environment may be modified to suit the group or individual's way of acting; or when the environment cannot be modified, to show how the individual may be moulded (forced to put on new habits) to fit the environment. It must be understood at the outset, though, that psychology at present has little to do with the setting of social standards of action, and nothing to do with moral standards. It does lie within her province to tell whether the individual man can act in accordance with such standards, and how we may control him or lead him to act in harmony with them. These laws of control or training must be general and comprehensive, since social standards are constantly changing.

Psychology, when looked at in this way, is seen to be something which every one has been using more or less all of his life without calling it by that name. We learn by failures and successes how to run our business, how to get along with our colleagues and associates. We teach our children to act in certain ways. They must eat with a fork, learn to dress themselves, to treat their playmates as they themselves like to be treated, to master the three R's, and then, later, a trade or profession. We skillfully or bunglingly steer them on their course from infancy until they no longer need our guidance.

THE ANCIENT ORIGIN OF PSYCHOLOGY

Indeed, a glance at the mythology, folk-lore, or history of any given race will show that the practical psychology of control began as soon as there were two individuals on the earth living near enough together for the behavior of one to influence the behavior of the other. The serpent controlled Eve's behavior by offering her the delectable apple. Eve learned her lesson quickly, and tempted Adam in the same way. Atalanta, the swiftest of runners, was beaten, not through the superior agility of Hippomenes, but by the fact that she could not resist the temptation to stop and pick up the golden apples thrown by her suitor. The taboo system, the initiation ceremonies, and the machinations of the medicine men all serve to illustrate progress towards the control of group and individual behavior.

COMMON-SENSE PROCEDURE IN SECURING
THE CONTROL OF BEHAVIOR

Long before the dawn of modern scientific psychology society found that by roundabout hit-and-miss methods she had secured a fairly serviceable body of data as to what man can do—his complement of acts; the appropriate situation for calling out any given act; and crude training methods whereby the repertoire of the acts themselves might be enlarged. A brief glance at the practical procedure in securing control of individuals and groups may serve to illustrate both how such data are obtained and how they are used.

The situations or devices for drawing crowds for whatever purpose show the greatest development of skill in practical psychology. If two or three individuals happen by chance to gather around a patent medicine vendor the vendor's momentary success is assured. The small crowd is an irresistible stimulus, and soon gathers unto itself a larger crowd. For this reason initial buyers, listeners, applauders, and, yes, even sometimes suitors and mourners are provided and paid for before the public is allowed to act. The advertisement of a "fire sale" is likewise an ancient and honorable device for gathering a crowd. The announcement at Jamestown of a shipload of virtuous women to be sold as wives apparently, if historical report can be trusted, brought out the whole of the unmarried able-bodied male population of Virginia.

After the crowd has collected, devices for controlling the individual are numerous. Chief among these we find the various lottery schemes. Many individuals will not give twenty-five cents for a charitable purpose, but at any charity gathering they will eagerly take one of a dozen twenty-five-cent chances on almost any object the total value of which need not be greater than the cost of a single chance. So uniform is the response to lottery schemes that they have oftentimes become national mediums for raising government funds.

Organized society displays much ingenuity in devising situations for the control of reaction; the clergyman, having found empty pews under an orthodox type of routine, and that the young people were not engaging in church activities, began to try out in a similar way what could be done by altering the old, austere situation, and by creating for the church entirely new situations. The exteriors of the churches were vastly modified, the interiors decorated, rest- and play-rooms added, as well as gymnasia and playgrounds. A certain type of action was expected, and the church arranged a situation for bringing it about. We see the same attempt at control illustrated in governing bodies: state legislatures, depressed by the prevalence of drunkenness and crime, establish a new situation for prohibiting the sale of drugs and spirituous liquors, in the hope that such legislation will prevent that type of conduct. Finally, mention may be made of recent changes in prison methods. The more advanced prisons, becoming dissatisfied with the amount of insubordination, vice, sloth, and ignorance of all forms of government among the inmates, are trying a new situation, with good results, *viz.*, that of letting them establish a miniature republic. This republic makes its own laws, and metes out its own punishments. Society has developed by hit-and-miss methods a *system of standards of action, but it does not know just what situations will produce the needed responses.* The situations are set up in the social field by trial and error; they are modified, changed, etc., until the desired reactions take place, or until they are despaired of.

WATCHING THE ACT OR RESPONSE TO OBTAIN
DATA ON THE STIMULUS OR SITUATION

We thus, as we see, get a part of our knowledge of the factors underlying behavior by the trial and error method of manipulating the situation, and noting the reactions that take place. This gives us a body of usable data on what to expect of men when they are placed in certain situations. We deal here with situations of our own contrivance. Equally serviceable results are obtained by taking an individual who is performing some act (action not regulated by the observer), and examining immediately into the situation which led to that act—the act is known, the situation which led to it must be investigated. This method is, of course, supplementary to the first. It extends our knowledge of situations, and what to expect from them, and at the same time adds to our knowledge of man's repertoire of acts. Illustrations of the results of this type of practical procedure are numerous; it is hard to convince a mother that she cannot predict* what the situation is which leads her baby to give a certain cry. Depending upon the variations in the cry, she will say that the "baby is hungry, wet, or has colic" (her conclusions are often wrong, be it said). Advancing somewhat in the age scale we see, in passing through a forest, a youth trained to hunt firing upward into a tree, and we note that the dog he has with him has "treed." An observer responds to this picture by telling his companion that the boy is hunting *squirrels*. But if he sees the boy fire in another way, say, horizontally, and sees a dog in the act of pointing, he will state that the lad is hunting *quail*. If the boy fires towards the ground, and has a hound with him, he is shooting *rabbits*. Finally, if he is seen in the hunting fields on horseback, with no gun, but accompanied by a pack of hounds in full cry, our observer remarks that the boy is hunting a *fox*. Watching his actions, and taking note of all attendant circumstances, enable any one to tell with some degree of probability what the immediate situation is leading to the boy's actions. Our ability to observe an act, and to tell what the possible or probable stimulus to that act is, depends upon the fact that often

---

* By prediction we mean nothing but the common-sense, scientific, and logical use of material gathered from observation and experimentation. The planet Neptune was predicted; coat-color or eye-color of animals can, within certain limits, be predicted before the birth of the animal.

during our past life, when we have seen individuals doing certain things, we have immediately investigated the situations which led to the acts. A good and well-trained observer becomes adept in predicting not only the more immediate stimulus leading to an act, but also in getting a serviceable notion of the range and variety of the performer's training and skill.

NEED OF ACQUAINTANCESHIP WITH AN INDIVIDUAL'S PAST

When we come to deal practically or scientifically with individuals, too much emphasis cannot be laid upon the extent to which acquaintanceship with their past life will gradually afford the basis for making serviceable predictions as to their probable ways of acting, and as to the situations which will call out any given act. This can possibly be most easily illustrated in the animal world. We soon come to the prediction stage with our horses and dogs, and can map out with some certainty what they would do under the various situations which might confront them. After watching two monkeys for some time I found after repeated observation that B would not touch food until J had finished and left the dish, and that J would eat and stuff three bananas into his cheek pouches, and drag off another with his right forefoot; that J would attack a problem-box rapidly and in a rough and harum-scarum way—pulling the box towards him, turning it over, and maltreating it generally; that B would approach cautiously, moving the parts slowly, and with no violence; but, as a rule, would solve the problem before J.

But with an organization so highly developed as man's, the prediction of his actions is not always so easy. An individual's actions in every-day situations depend upon such complex factors as his heredity, his past success in adjustments, and his failures of adjustment; the responses he has just had to make, as well as upon the permanent and temporary conditions of his organic mechanisms (digestion, circulation, sleep, etc.). A badly cooked dinner, an insufficient amount of food (as in the case of a person who is dieting), or extreme heat, may so change the state of the organism that the response reasonably expected is not forthcoming. An approaching marriage, graduation, separation, offer situations which, by their involvement of emotional factors, may almost completely disrupt for the time being the every-day systems of responses which are customary with a given individual. In such a complex setting a man may show a temporary breakdown; he may make blunders, or show a general inability to go through with his ordinary routine. A bad dream, or a slight rebuff at the hands of a friend, likewise may upset a man's reactions for a whole day. Further on we shall see that many of the habits formed in childhood and in adolescence, now long since discarded, such, *e.g.*, as attachments to early play-mates, to members of the family, early love affairs, may have had a potent influence in shaping the whole course of adult acquisitions.

If we are called upon to predict what a stranger of twenty-five years of age will do when confronted in a dark alley by a burglar, we are almost, but not quite, helpless so far as prediction is concerned. Now, give us an opportunity of systematically studying the make-up of the man, of knowing something of his reactions in past dangerous situations, the stability of his emotional tendencies, and we shall be able at least to make a crude but serviceable prediction, *viz.*, that he will quickly throw up his hands and let the burglar go through his pockets. He will neither become hysterical, attempt to attack the burglar, nor will he suffer any severe after-effects by reason of his experience. The chances are good that he will report his mishap to the police, confess to his wife or friends that he has been held up, and then will cease to be further troubled by the experience. In another type of individual, whose heredity is questionable, whose reactions are unstable, who is generally excitable and liable to overreaction, we venture the prediction that, even if he does throw up his hands (which he does not always do) and allow himself to be robbed, he will go to pieces after the experience, and may suffer some serious and lasting consequences.

COMMON-SENSE A CRUDE BUT GENUINE PSYCHOLOGY

Most of our illustrations have involved little or no technical psychology, and yet they do illustrate a genuine psychological procedure. The business man, the artist, and the artisan have built for themselves rather definite rules of psychological procedure, without ever calling it psychology. The church and the theatre illustrate this equally well. It is possibly even a debatable question whether common-sense has not kept closer to the fundamental truth underlying the psychology of reaction than has the too-detached psychology of the laboratory. But even those who are the best practical psychologists realize that common-sense methods can never produce universal or widespread progress in psychology. Our great military leaders, our great religious leaders, the demagogues and the politicians, have accomplished their results by their very wide acquaintanceship with the reaction tendencies in man, and by their happy accidents in creating the situations which will call out such reactions. By reason of the fact that occasional success has been obtained by crude methods and happy accidents, we must not conclude that psychology should not attempt to discover and analyze and bring under scientific control the factors which have occasionally made such successes possible. Because an occasional business leader has known how to pick out and keep good men, we are offered no reason why we should not seek to understand and control the processes involved in picking and keeping good men. The same may be said of the factors in keeping men out of crime, keeping them honest and sane, and their ethical and social life upon a high and well-regulated plane.

This brief summary of the every-day uses of psychology should convince us of two things: first, that common-sense, while a reasonable method so far as it goes, does not go far enough, and never can; and secondly, that in order to make progress, the phenomena of human behavior must be made an object of scientific study. We shall attempt next, then, to gain some impression of this systematic psychological procedure.

❋   ❋   ❋

2

The Limits of Science

Eugene P. Wigner

Professor Wigner, a Nobel Laureate in theoretical physics (1963), concerns himself in this essay with the development of science as a human endeavor. He wonders whether man's scientific achievements may not already have reached the point at which their scope is beyond any single person's intellectual capacity. He also inquires whether the character of science itself is not in the process of shifting emphasis from its traditional, increasingly intensive preoccupation with the physical world, to that of the mental world. The student of the future may turn—if only in frustration—from the physical sciences to the life sciences (including psychology). The future scholar may also be forced to work as a member of a research team. A major issue, then, will be whether "individuality"—which is so characteristic of the creative process—will be retained in the anonymity so often attendant upon identity with a group. In this connection, he comments briefly on the phenomenon of subconscious solutions of problems.

The present discussion is not put forward with the usual pride of the scientist who feels that he can make an addition, however small, to a problem which has aroused his and his colleague's interest. Rather, it is a speculation of a kind which all of us feel a great reluctance to undertake: much like the speculation on the ultimate fate of somebody who is very dear to us. It is a speculation on the future of science itself, whether it will share, at some very distant future, the fate of "Alles was entsteht ist wert dass es zu Grunde geht" [Everything worthwhile eventually perishes]. Naturally, in such a speculation one wishes to assume the best of conditions for one's subject and disregard the danger of an accident that may befall it, however real that danger may be.

From *Proceedings* (1950), Vol. 94, No. 5, pp. 422–427; reprinted by permission of the American Philosophical Society.

THE GROWTH OF SCIENCE

The most remarkable thing about Science is its youth. The earliest beginning of chemistry, as we now know it, certainly does not antedate Boyle's *Sceptical Chemist* which appeared in 1661. More probably, one would place the birthyear of chemistry around the years of activity of Lavoisier, between 1770 and 1790, or count its years from Dalton's law in 1808. Physics is somewhat older, Newton's *Principia*, a rather finished work, became available in 1687. Archimedes discovered laws of physics around 250 B.C. but his discoveries hardly can be called the real beginning of physics. On the whole one is probably safe in saying that Science is less than 300 years old. This number has to be compared with the age of Man, which is certainly greater than 100,000 years.

The number of people who devote years of their life to the acquisition of knowledge had an equally spectacular rise. Thus about ten per cent of the American youth are graduated from college, a percentage that has lately doubled in every twenty years. Harvard College was founded in 1636 and it was certainly not a scientific college at that time. The American Association for the Advancement of Science is one-hundred years old and had originally 461 members. Today, it has more than half a million and its membership increased by almost 10,000 in a single half year. The growth of college attendance was less spectacular in some other countries, probably more spectacular in Russia.

Man's increased mastery of the Earth can be directly traced to his increased knowledge of the laws of nature. The surface of the Earth, as a whole, has not been affected by Man for 99,700 years but vast areas were deforested or the surface's store of some minerals depleted since the birth of Science. For 99,700 years, a man equipped with a good telescope on the moon might not have discovered Man's existence on the Earth. He could not have overlooked it during the last three-hundred years. There is no natural phenomenon that is comparable with the sudden and apparently accidentally timed development of science, except perhaps the condensation of a supersaturated gas or the explosion of some unpredictable explosives. Will the fate of science show some similarity to one of these phenomena?

Actually, if one views detachedly the rapid growth of science, and of the power of man, one cannot help fearing the second alternative. Surely man has not been able to adjust his spiritual outlook to the responsibility which his increased power imposed on him and one has to fear a catastrophe as a consequence of this maladjustment. This has come to be so well recognized recently, particularly as a result of the development of atomic weapons and the subsequent failure of man to cope, or even to come to grips, with the problems created by these weapons, that it is almost a commonplace. Nevertheless, this possibility will be disregarded here, and the limits of the growth of science will be considered under the assumption that no cataclysmic effect will interrupt this growth. The following speculations therefore apply only if we should be able to avoid the cataclysm which threatens us, and science can develop in a relatively peaceful atmosphere. They will look for the inherent limitations of science, rather than the limitations imposed by external effects, whether or not these external effects are influenced by science.

WHAT CAN WE CALL "OUR SCIENCE"

What might be considered as the natural limit of our science will become perhaps best apparent if we try to define what "our science" is. It is our store of knowledge of natural phenomena. The question then is, what is "our" store? This question will be approached by giving both too broad and too narrow definitions and then attempting an acceptable compromise. A set of volumes, containing information and theories, certainly does not become our store of knowledge by our mere possession of it: the renaissance, or rather the preceding dark ages, teach us that physical possession is not enough. Is it then necessary that anybody know all the contents of those volumes before they can be called "our science"? This may be a defensible point of view but if it were accepted science would have reached its limits already, might have reached them quite some time ago. Is it then enough that there be, in our society, for every volume a person who is fully familiar with it? No, because there may be contradictions between the statements of the various volumes which would remain hidden if everyone knew only part of them. Science is an edifice, not a pile of bricks, valuable as such a pile may be.

I would say that a store of knowledge can reasonably be called "our science" if there are people who are competent to learn and use any part of it, who would like to know each part of it even if they realize that they cannot, and if one has good assurance that the parts are not contradictory but form a whole. The section on elasticity must use the same picture of the structure of iron on which the section on magnetism is based.

LIMITS OF "OUR SCIENCE"

If the above is accepted as a fair description of what may be called "our science" then its limitations are in the human intellect, in its capacity for interest and learning, in its memory and facilities for communication. All these are surely related to the finite span of the human life. In fact, if we accept the above, science is already changing not only by acquiring new territories, but partly also by shifting from older to new fields. We forget things and focus our attention on more recent developments. Right now, the older parts of science cease to be parts of our science not so much because we have no assurance that they fit into the new picture—I believe they do—but rather because nobody has a strong desire to know them, at least nobody who is interested in the new parts.

Surely, the possibilities of this type of growth are very far from being exhausted. Today, we are neglecting the theory of solids in which a student has to study perhaps six-hundred papers before he reaches the frontiers and can do research on his own; we concentrate instead on quantum electrodynamics in which he has to study six papers. Tomorrow, we may give up a whole science, such as chemistry, and concentrate on something that is less explored. These changes in interest are, furthermore, surely not arbitrary but in most cases well justified inasmuch as the new subject is deeper than the abandoned one, starts from more fundamental realizations, and embraces the old one. The properties of solids follow from the principles of quantum electrodynamics and this discipline is, in addition, able to deal with many phenomena besides those important for solids.

One should realize, nevertheless, that the embracing of the old subject by the new discipline is somewhat illusory. Thus the theory of solids is relinquished by the student of quantum electrodynamics in a very real sense because the human intellect is not powerful enough to derive the important properties of solids from quantum theory, unless it has made a particular, both experimental and theoretical, study to develop the idealizations and approximations which are useful for the description of solids. Only an unusual intellect could guess on the basis of the principles of ordinary quantum theory that there are solids and that they consist of regular lattice-like arrangements of the atoms. No human intellect could overlook, as a matter of course, the significance and role of the defects of these lattices. The equations of quantum theory may form the words of a magic oracle which describes the phenomena of crystal physics in a wonderfully condensed fashion. However, no human intellect can understand this oracle without using a commentary to its words, the length of this commentary being in the same proportion to the condensate of the oracle as is the whole Bible to Leviticus 19, 18 [. . . thou shalt love thy neighbor as thyself . . .]. There is clearly a limit beyond which condensation, elevating though it may be as a purpose *per se*, is not useful any more for storing information. Present-day condensation in physics has certainly reached this limit.

SHIFT OF THE SECOND TYPE

The question now comes up whether science will at least be able to continue the type of shifting growth indefinitely in which the new discipline is deeper than the older one and embraces it at least virtually. The answer is, in my opinion, no, because the shifts in the above sense always involve digging one layer deeper into the "secrets of nature," and involve a longer series of concepts based on the previous ones which are thereby recognized as "mere approximations." Thus, in the example above, first ordinary mechanics had to be replaced by quantum mechanics, thus recognizing the approximate nature and limitation of ordinary mechanics to macroscopic phenomena. Then, ordinary mechanics had to be recognized to be inadequate from another point of view and replaced by field theories. Finally, the approximate nature and limitation to small velocities of all of the above concepts had to be uncovered. Thus, relativistic quantum theory is at least four layers deep; it operates with three successive types of concepts all of which are recognized to be inadequate and are replaced by a more profound one in the fourth step. This is, of course, the charm and beauty of the relativistic quantum theory and of all fundamental research in physics. However, it also shows the limits of this type of development. The recognizing of an inadequacy in the concepts of the tenth layer and the replacing of it with the more refined concepts of the eleventh layer will be much less of an event than the discovery of the theory of relativity was. It will, furthermore, require a much more elaborate and a much longer study to arrive at an understanding of the roots of the evil than was the study needed to appreciate the discrepancies which were eliminated by the theory of relativity. It is not difficult to imagine a stage in which the new student will not be interested any more, perhaps will not be able any more, to dig through the already accumulated layers in order to do research at the frontier. The number of physics graduate students will then drop and the shift of science to new territories will be more drastic than the shifts we are accustomed to: the new discipline in fashion will not embrace physics any more in the same way, as, for instance, quantum theory embraces classical physics. I will call this type of shift the shift of the second type.

The above picture assumes that, in order to understand a growing body of phenomena, it will be necessary to introduce deeper and deeper concepts into physics and that this development will not end by the discovery of the final and perfect concepts. I believe that this is true: we have no right to expect that our intellect can formulate perfect concepts for the full understanding of inanimate nature's phenomena. However, the second type of shift will occur also if we do, because science does not seem to be viable if no research is being done on its outskirts and the interest will soon flag in a completed subject. It is possible also that neither of the two alternatives will come to pass, that it will never be decided whether the concepts of the tenth layer are adequate "in principle" for the understanding of the inanimate world. Absence of interest and the weakness of the human intellect may easily combine to postpone indefinitely the determination of the full adequacy of the nth layer of concepts. In that case physics will be left by the wayside, in a somewhat similar fashion to the way in which the phenomena connected with superconductivity are apparently being left by the wayside, most physicists not feeling an acute sense of unhappiness about it.

The second type of shift will not be all resignation. In fact, many feel nowadays that the life sciences and the science of the minds of both animals and men have been already neglected too long. Our picture of the world would surely be more rounded if we knew more about the minds of men and animals, their customs and habits. The second type of shift may mean, however, the acknowledgment that we are unable to arrive at the full understanding of even the inanimate world, just as, a few centuries ago, man came to the conclusion that he has no very good chance to foresee what will happen to his soul after the death of his body. We all continue to feel a frustration because of our inability to foresee our soul's ultimate fate. Although we do not speak about it, we all know that the objectives of our science are, from a general human point of view, much more modest than the objectives of, say the Greek science, were; that our science is more successful in giving us power than in giving us knowledge of truly human interest. The development of the natural sciences was, however, not less vigorous because of the ensuing sense of frustration. Similarly, the vigor of work in the fields to which the second type shifts will lead, will not be smaller because we shall have abandoned the full realization of our dreams concerning an earlier field.

However, the second type of shift will mean some new resignation and also mark a turning point in the existence of science, taking science in the sense of our definition. When shifts of the second type will have occurred in relevant numbers, science will lose some of the attraction on the young mind which it now holds. It will be something altogether different, a bit less fascinating. The wonderful elation which we scientists now are experiencing, and which comes from the new feeling of the power of our intellect, will be somewhat dampened by the recognition of the limits of that power. We will have to acquiesce in the fact that our intellect's toil cannot give us a satisfactory picture of the world such as the Greeks dreamed to attain in an effortless way, by easy speculation.

STABILIZING FORCES

Many of us will be inclined to make light of the preceding argument and say that science has a natural vitality by which it will overcome the limits which we, small minds of today, imagine to perceive in its path. There surely is much truth in this statement and we shall shortly turn to elements of elasticity in the whole picture which support it. However, I believe that the darker picture is the fundamentally correct one and that our instinctive desire not to believe it is the desire and ability of the human mind not to think of repugnant events in the future if their threat has no accurately foreseeable date. However, great changes, and often very unwanted changes, do take place and the elasticity of nature only delays them: buffaloes did die out as sources of food; the role of the individual warrior has vanished; the detailed explanation of the holy writings, once the only subject worthy of human studies, has ceased to be an element of our culture; Mathus' dire predictions are sure to come true at least in some respects. All the forecasts predicting these events were once resented by large groups just as we resent and resist the statement of the insufficiency of science.

Can we see even today signals of the crisis in science? Perhaps. The difficulty in penetrating to the frontiers of physics has been mentioned before. It is already so serious for the average human mind that only a negligible fraction of our contemporaries really feels the force of the arguments of quantum and relativity theories. Chemistry has grown so big that very very few people can keep an even loose acquaintance with all its ramifications. Shifts of the first type are going on in these sciences constantly, some of them being the butts of constant jokes.

The clearest sign of the growing realization that the capacity of our intellect limits the volume of science is the number of queries which we hear every day, whether this or that piece of research "is worth doing." In almost all such cases, the problem posed is interesting, the proposed method of attack shows elements of ingenuity, and the answer, whatever it may turn out to be, can be expected to be worth remembering. However, the questioner realizes how great is the number of problems of similar importance, how limited the time and memory of those to whom the results will be of interest. He wonders whether his proposed work would not remain submerged in the mass of literature, with nobody taking time and energy fully to understand and appreciate it. Hence the query. Similar doubts on the "worth" of some proposed research must have arisen at all times. It seems to me doubtful, however, that they ever were as deep as they are now, and concerned as intrinsically interesting problems. I believe I have observed an increase in the frequency of these queries and doubts even during my own short scientific life.

Recently, Mr. Fierz, in a very thoughtful article, has pointed to

what may well become in time a shift of the second type. He
pointed out that both physics and psychology claim to be all embracing disciplines: the first because it endeavors to describe all
nature; the second because it deals with all mental phenomena, and
nature exists for us only because we have cognizance of it. Fierz
points out that the pictures of the world which these two disciplines
project into us are not necessarily contradictory. However, it surely
is difficult if not impossible to recognize the two pictures as only
different aspects of the same thing. Furthermore, it is hardly an
exaggeration to say that no psychologist understands the philosophy
of modern physics. Conversely, only the exceptional physicist understands the language of the psychologist. Of course, psychology's
philosophy is as yet too vague to draw definite conclusions. However, it is not impossible that we, or our students, are going to
witness a real split of science right here.

It would be foolish to draw far-reaching conclusions from the
emergence of two sciences, both of which may claim to be all
embracing and between the concepts and statements of which one
cannot, at present, see any real similarity. Both may yet be united
into a deeper common discipline without overtaxing our mind's
capacity for abstraction. Altogether, there are many favorable stabilizing effects which can delay the balkanization of science for very
long periods. Some of these are methodological: as we understand
discoveries more fully, we will be able to explain them better. It is
certainly no accident that we have scores of excellent books on
thermodynamics but had surely until recently nothing comparable
in quantum theory. Relativity theory was understood, so it was
claimed, twenty-five years ago only by two—today we teach its
principles to undergraduates. Examples of improving teaching techniques by both minor simplifications and by spectacular "condensa-
tions" and generalizations are in fact too obvious to bear enu-
meration.

Another important stabilizing effect will be the reduction of the
size of disciplines by elimination of parts of it. An example which
must have struck everyone of my age is that the theory of ellyptic
functions—a theory as spectacular in its methods and successes as
any part of modern mathematics—is right now falling into oblivion.
This is a shift of the first kind to which even the queen of sciences is
not immune. As such it keeps mathematics more learnable.

Finally, it is not impossible that we'll breed during the coming centuries a human whose power of recollection, whose facility of abstraction, is greater than ours. Or at least that we make a greater and more aptly guided effort to select among the young those best suited for furthering science.

There is, on the other hand, a circumstance which will undoubtedly have an opposite effect. Thirst for knowledge, curiosity concerning the extent of one's mental faculties, and a healthy sense of rivalry, are strong stimulants of the young scientist and will continue to spur him along also in the future. They are, however, not his only motives: the desire to improve the lot of mankind, to extend its power, is also a traditional trait of scientists. These latter incentives are, however, waning, at least as far as the natural sciences are concerned, with the advent of man's full mastery of the element, with the increasing realization that the economic welfare of man is a question of organization rather than a problem of production. The effect of the loss of this incentive will certainly be present; its magnitude is unpredictable.

CO-OPERATIVE RESEARCH

If science is expected to grow so great, both in the comprehensiveness of its subject and also in depth, that the human mind will not be able to embrace it, that the life span of man will not be long enough to penetrate to its fringes in time to enlarge it, could several people not form a team and accomplish jointly what no single person can accomplish? Instead of returning with Shaw to Methuselah, can we find a new way to enlarge the capacity of human intellect by the juxtaposition of several individual intellects rather than by extending a single one? This is a possibility which is so little explored that all that one may say about it must remain highly speculative—much more speculative, I believe, than the rest of this article. The possibilities of co-operative research have to be explored, however, to a much greater extent than they have been so far because they form the only visible hope for a new lease on life for science when it will have grown too large for a single individual.

Most of us scientists are too individualistic to take co-operative research too seriously. As the founder of relativity theory once remarked, he cannot imagine how relativity theory could have been conceived by a group. Indeed, if we think of the present-day research groups, working under a group leader who received his assignment through a section chief, the idea becomes amusingly absurd. Clearly, no fundamental change in our way of thinking can come about that way and no such fundamental change is intended by the groups referred to.

The case against group research can be stated more rationally on the basis of Poincaré's keen analysis of the nature of mathematical discovery. It is, I believe, our intuitive awareness of the facts which he and Hadamard have expressed so aptly which makes us smile at the idea of group research. Poincaré and Hadamard have recognized that, unlike most thinking which goes on in the upper consciousness, the really relevant mathematical thinking is not done in words. In fact, it happens somewhere so deep in the subconscious that the thinker is usually not even aware of what is going on inside him.

It is my opinion that the role of subconscious thinking is equally important in other sciences, that it is decisive even in the solution of apparently trivial technical details. An experimentalist friend once told me (this was some twenty years ago) that if he could not find the leak in his vacuum system he usually felt like going for a walk, and very often, when he returned from the walk, he knew exactly where the leak was. The problem of group research is therefore to give free rein to the inventiveness of the subconscious of the individual but, at the same time, have available for him the whole store of knowledge of the group.

It is certainly impossible to tell now whether and how this can be accomplished. It will surely need a much more intimate symbiosis between collaborators than has been established to date. Part, but only part, of this more intimate symbiosis will be a higher faculty for the communication of ideas and information than we have developed so far. If group research is to be fully effective, it will also need a much deeper understanding of the functioning of the human mind than we now have. However, neither of these is impossible; in fact we may be closer to both than we suspect.

Meanwhile, we should keep two facts in mind. The first is that the difficulty in the future development of science, which we have envisaged before, is based in the first place on the limited capacity of the human mind, not on its limited depth. Even if the depth, which is more intimately based on subconscious thinking, could not be increased, the first obstacle, the limitation of the capacity, might well be cut back by teamwork. Second, we should not forget that while it is true that relativity theory could not have been conceived by teamwork, the structure of the George Washington Bridge, and probably even that of the Hanford nuclear reactors, could not have been thought out by a single individual. The problem of group research is to avoid suppressing the subconscious thinking of the individual but to make available for him the information and to some degree even the unfinished ideas of his collaborators. Success of this may mean that the limitations of "our science," which were described above, are limitations only for individualist science.

It is depressing for every scientist and for every person to have to conclude that his principal motive, or that of his epoch, is not here to stay. However, humanity's goals and ideals have shifted already several times during our known history. In addition, it must fill us with pride to believe that we are living in the heroic age of science, in the epoch in which the individual's abstract knowledge of nature, and, we may hope, also of himself, is increasing more rapidly and perhaps to a higher level than it ever has before or will afterwards. It is uncomfortable to believe that our ideals may pass as the Round Table's illusions disappeared. Still, we live in the heroic age of these ideals.

3

Significance of Significant

Franz Ingelfinger

"Significance of Significant" is uncommon in at least two ways: First, it was initially published as an editorial; and, second, it originally appeared in a medical journal.

This brief reading addresses itself in lucid terms to the distinction that needs to be drawn between the word "significance," used in its colloquial sense, and the same word used in statistical interpretation of data.

Because "significance" will be encountered frequently in the selections that follow, the reader—in coming to understand at an early stage the subtleties of its various meanings—will be in a better position to evaluate for himself which particular nuance was intended by the different writers.

Significance, being one of those words that mean everything or nothing, is too convenient for the medical writer. In its refined statistical sense, significance embodies mathematical precision. In its vulgar usage, unrelated to statistical manipulations, it comfortably serves ambiguity. It permits an author to describe his clinical findings as significant, or his patients as prospering significantly, and so to impute importance to his efforts without requiring him to use an acceptable measure of that importance. It affords him, moreover, with a mobile hedge against criticism. With the label of significance, he may circumvent the more direct immodesty of claiming importance, and he can safely insist that a given event is undeniably significant to him. A nosebleed, after all, may be significant to the laundryman who cannot quite remove the hemoglobin stains from the handkerchief, or to the patient so frightened that he calls his physician in the middle of the night, or to the otolaryngologist who has to pack a nose, or to the intern who has to transfuse a

From the *New England Journal of Medicine* (1968), Vol. 278, No. 22, pp. 1232–1233; reprinted by permission.

nearly exsanguinated patient. In this, its conventional usage, significant has become a word devoid of significance.

In contrast, the medical writer who uses significance to express a statistical analysis is being rigorously exact. Under these conditions, and unless otherwise specified, description of a finding as significant indicates a probability of less than 5 per cent that the finding is the result of pure chance. Often, the probability or p value is much smaller. Nevertheless, the role of chance can never be eliminated entirely. Nor does a p value have any meaning if it is derived from improperly designed experiments. It should also be noted that lack of a significant difference (that is, a p value exceeding 5 per cent) does not in itself establish identity. In spite of these caveats, significance used to summarize a statistical operation is fabulously useful for the clinical investigator. Few other words serve precision so well.

To have one popular word serve the extremes of both exactness and inexactness hardly furthers clarity in medical writing. The *Journal* therefore proposes to discourage the use of significance and its corresponding adjective and adverb in its scientific articles, except when the term is warranted by statistical backing. Writers and other editors, it is hoped, will be persuaded to do likewise. A variety of appropriately vague words, such as appreciable, considerable, definite and marked, are available to lend emphasis or to assign immeasurable importance. Predictably, a "significant" or so will find its way into our verbal ranks, and there is a good possibility that it might even infiltrate an editorial effort. Yet vigilant we must be, for the use of significance in any but its statistical sense not only confuses the reader but at times may mislead him ~~significa~~-egregiously.

Variables
of
Psychology

II

4

Introduction to an Objective
Theory of Behavior

Clark L. Hull

It is difficult to exaggerate the influence that Hull's *Principles of Behavior* has had upon the development of American psychology. In this—the introductory chapter to his major writing—Hull sets forth his views concerning the nature of psychological science.

Beginning with an elucidation of the adaptive qualities of behavior, he goes on to discuss the interrelations between physiology and psychology, the hazardous (but necessary) use of intervening variables and hypothetical constructs in the formulation of theories, the need for empirical research, the logical circularity of teleological explanations, and the dangers of anthropomorphic subjectivism.

The "Notes" to his chapter are particularly valuable for their concise statements concerning "operationism" and "subjectivism." His comments on the former seem to be pointed toward those psychologists who question the need for concepts such as the "intervening variable." For example, Skinner has argued that if the antecedent and consequent events of any assumed process are adequately described (Figure 1, on page 34), there is no real purpose served by introducing additional explanatory devices, such as hypothetical construct or intervening variable. To the rejoinder that theories of behavior cannot be built unless hypothetical constructs are used to generate premises, the rebuttal is, "Are theories of learning necessary?" (Skinner, B. F. *Psychol. Rev., 1950,* **57,** 193–216).

The debate continues to this day.

Having examined the general nature of scientific theory, we must now proceed to the elaboration of an objective theory as applied

From *Principles of Behavior* by Clark L. Hull, pp. 16–31. Copyright, 1943, © 1967. Reprinted by permission of Appleton-Century-Crofts, Educational Division, Meredith Corporation.

specifically to the behavior of organisms (10). Preliminary to this great and complex task it will be well to consider a number of the more general characteristics of organismic behavior, as well as certain difficulties which will be encountered and hazards which ought to be avoided.

THE BASIC FACT OF ENVIRONMENTAL-
ORGANISMIC INTERACTION

At the outset of the independent life of an organism there begins a dynamic relationship between the organism and its environment. For the most part, both environment and organism are active; the environment acts on the organism, and the organism acts on the environment (5, p. 2). Naturally the terminal phase of any given environmental-organismic interaction depends upon the activity of each; rarely or never can the activity of either be predicted from knowing the behavior characteristics of one alone. The possibility of predicting the outcome of such interaction depends upon the fact that both environment and organism are part of nature, and as such the activity of each takes place according to known rules, i.e., natural laws.

The environment of an organism may conveniently be divided into two portions—the internal and the external. The external environment may usefully be subdivided into the inanimate environment and the animate or organismic environment.

The laws of the internal environment are, for the most part, those of the physiology of the particular organism. The laws of the inanimate environment are those of the physical world and constitute the critical portions of the physical sciences; they are relatively simple and reasonably well known.

The laws of the organismic environment are those of the behavior of other organisms, especially organisms of the same species as the one under consideration; they make up the primary principles of the behavior, or "social," sciences and are comparatively complex. Perhaps because of this complexity they are not as yet very well understood. Since in a true or symmetrical social situation only organisms of the same species are involved, the basic laws of the activities of the environment must be the same as those of the organism under consideration. It thus comes about that *the* *objective of the present work is the elaboration of the basic molar* behavioral laws underlying the "social" sciences.*

ORGANISMIC NEED, ACTIVITY, AND SURVIVAL

Since the publication by Charles Darwin of the *Origin of Species* (2) it has been necessary to think of organisms against a background of organic evolution and to consider both organismic structure and function in terms of *survival*. Survival, of course, applies equally to the individual organism and to the species. Physiological studies have shown that survival requires special circumstances in considerable variety; these include optimal conditions of air, water, food, temperature, intactness of bodily tissue, and so forth; for species survival among the higher vertebrates there is required at least the occasional presence and specialized reciprocal behavior of a mate.

On the other hand, when any of the commodities or conditions necessary for individual or species survival are lacking, or when they deviate materially from the optimum, a state of *primary need* is said to exist. In a large proportion of such situations the need will be reduced or eliminated only through the action on the environment of a particular sequence of movements made by the organism. For example, the environment will, as a rule, yield a commodity (such as food) which will mediate the abolition of a state of need (such as hunger) only when the movement sequence corresponds rather exactly to the momentary state of the environment; i.e., when the movement sequence is closely synchronized with the several phases of the environmental reactions. If it is to be successful, the behavior of a hungry cat in pursuit of a mouse must vary from instant to instant, depending upon the movements of the mouse. Similarly, if the mouse is to escape the cat, its movements must vary from instant to instant, depending upon the movements of the cat.

Moreover, in a given external environment situation the behavior must often differ radically from one occasion to another, depending on the need which chances to be dominant at the time; e.g.,

---

* By this expression is meant the uniformities discoverable among the grossly observable phenomena of behavior as contrasted with the laws of the behavior of the ultimate "molecules" upon which this behavior depends, such as the constituent cells of nerve, muscle, gland, and so forth. The term *molar* thus means coarse or macroscopic as contrasted with molecular, or microscopic.

whether it be of food, water, or a mate. In a similar manner the behavior must frequently differ widely from one environmental situation to another, even when the need is exactly the same in each environment; a hungry man lost in a forest must execute a very different sequence of movements to relieve his need from what would be necessary if he were in his home.

It follows from the above considerations that *an organism will hardly survive unless the state of organismic need and the state of the environment in its relation to the organism are somehow jointly and simultaneously brought to bear upon the movement-producing mechanism of the organism.*

THE ORGANIC BASIS OF ADAPTIVE BEHAVIOR

All normal higher organisms possess a great assortment of muscles, usually with bony accessories. These motor organs are ordinarily adequate to mediate the reduction of most needs, provided their contractions occur in the right amount, combination, and sequence. The momentary status of most portions of the environment with respect to the organism is mediated to the organism by an immense number of specialized receptors which respond to a considerable variety of energies such as light waves (vision), sound waves (hearing), gases (smell), chemical solutions (taste), mechanical impacts (touch), and so on. The state of the organism itself (the internal environment) is mediated by another highly specialized series of receptors. It is probable that the various conditions of need also fall into this latter category; i.e., in one way or another needs activate more or less characteristic receptor organs much as do external environmental forces.

Neural impulses set in motion by the action of these receptors pass along separate nerve fibers to the central ganglia of the nervous system, notably the brain. The brain, which acts as a kind of automatic switchboard, together with the remainder of the central nervous system, routes and distributes the impulses to individual muscles and glands in rather precisely graded amounts and sequences. When the neural impulse reaches an effector organ (muscle or gland) the organ ordinarily becomes active, the amount of activity usually varying with the magnitude of the impulse. The movements thus brought about usually result in the elimination of the need, though often only after numerous unsuccessful trials. But organismic activity is by no means always successful; not infrequently death occurs before an adequate action sequence has been evoked.

It is the primary task of a molar science of behavior to isolate the basic laws or rules according to which various combinations of stimulation, arising from the state of need on the one hand and the state of the environment on the other, bring about the kind of behavior characteristic of different organisms. A closely related task is to understand why the behavior so mediated is so generally adaptive, i.e., successful in the sense of reducing needs and facilitating survival, and why it is unsuccessful on those occasions when survival is not facilitated.

THE NEUROLOGICAL VERSUS THE MOLAR APPROACH

From the foregoing considerations it might appear that the science of behavior must at bottom be a study of physiology. Indeed, it was once almost universally believed that the science of behavior must wait for its useful elaboration upon the development of the subsidiary science of neurophysiology. Partly as a result of this belief, an immense amount of research has been directed to the understanding of the detailed or molecular dynamic laws of this remarkable automatic structure. A great deal has been revealed by these researches and the rate of development is constantly being accelerated by the discovery of new and more effective methods of investigation. Nearly all serious students of behavior like to believe that some day the major neurological laws will be known in a form adequate to constitute the foundation principles of a science of behavior.

In spite of these heartening successes, the gap between the minute anatomical and physiological account of the nervous system as at present known and what would be required for the construction of a reasonably adequate theory of molar behavior is impassable. The problem confronting the behavior theorist is substantially like that which would have been faced by Galileo and Newton had they seriously considered delaying their preliminary formulation of the molar mechanics of the physical world until the micromechanics of the atomic and subatomic world had been satisfactorily elaborated.

Students of the social sciences are presented with the dilemma of waiting until the physico-chemical problems of neurophysiology have been adequately solved before beginning the elaboration of behavior theory, or of proceeding in a provisional manner with certain reasonably stable principles of the coarse, macroscopic or molar action of the nervous system whereby movements are evoked by stimuli, particularly as related to the history of the individual organism.

There can hardly be any doubt that a theory of molar behavior founded upon an adequate knowledge of both molecular and molar principles would in general be more satisfactory than one founded upon molar considerations alone. But here again the history of physical science is suggestive. Owing to the fact that Galileo and Newton carried out their molar investigations, the world has had the use of a theory which was in very close approximation to observations at the molar level for nearly three hundred years before the development of the molecular science of modern relativity and quantum theory. Moreover, it is to be remembered that science proceeds by a series of successive approximations; it may very well be that had Newton's system not been worked out when it was there would have been no Einstein and no Planck, no relativity and no quantum theory at all. It is conceivable that the elaboration of a systematic science of behavior at a molar level may aid in the development of an adequate neurophysiology and thus lead in the end to a truly molecular theory of behavior firmly based on physiology.

It happens that a goodly number of quasi-neurological principles have now been determined by careful experiments designed to trace out the relationship of the molar behavior of organisms, usually as integrated wholes, to well-controlled stimulus situations. Many of the more promising of these principles were roughly isolated in the first instance by the Russian physiologist, Pavlov, and his pupils, by means of conditioned-reflex experiments on dogs. More recently extensive experiments in many laboratories in this country with all kinds of reactions on a wide variety of organisms, including man, have greatly extended and rectified these principles and shown how they operate jointly in the production of the more complex forms of behavior. Because of the pressing nature of behavior problems, both practical and theoretical aspects of behavior science are, upon the whole, being developed according to the second of the two alternatives outlined above. For these reasons the molar approach is employed in the present work.

In this connection it is to be noted carefully that *the alternatives of microscopic versus macroscopic, and molecular versus molar, are relative rather than absolute.* In short, there are degrees of the molar, depending on the coarseness of the ultimate causal segments or units dealt with. Other things equal, it would seem wisest to keep the causal segments small, to approach the molecular, the fine and exact substructural details, just as closely as the knowledge of that substructure renders possible. There is much reason to believe that the seeming disagreements among current students of behavior may be largely due to the difference in the degree of the molar at which the several investigators are working. Such differences, however, do not represent fundamental disagreements. In the end the work of all who differ only in this sense may find a place in a single systematic structure, the postulates or primary assumptions of those working at a more molar level ultimately appearing as theorems of those working at a more molecular level.

THE RÔLE OF INTERVENING VARIABLES IN BEHAVIOR THEORY

Wherever an attempt is made to penetrate the invisible world of the molecular, scientists frequently and usefully employ logical constructs, intervening variables, or symbols to facilitate their thinking. These symbols or X's represent entities or processes which, if existent, would account for certain events in the observable molar world. Examples of such postulated entities in the field of the physical sciences are electrons, protons, positrons, etc. A closely parallel concept in the field of behavior familiar to everyone is that of *habit* as distinguished from habitual action. The habit presumably exists as an invisible condition of the nervous system quite as much when it is not mediating action as when habitual action is occurring; the habits upon which swimming is based are just as truly existent when a person is on the dance floor as when he is in the water.

In some cases there may be employed in scientific theory a whole series of hypothetical unobserved entities; such a series is presented by the hierarchy of postulated physical entities: molecule, atom, and electron, the molecule supposedly being constituted of atoms and the atom in its turn being constituted of electrons. A rough parallel to this chain of hypothetical entities from the physical sciences will be encountered in the present system of behavior theory. For the above reasons the subject of symbolic constructs, intervening variables, or hypothetical entities which are not directly observable requires comment (6, p. 3 ff.).

Despite the great value of logical constructs or intervening variables in scientific theory, their use is attended with certain difficulties and even hazards. At bottom this is because the presence and amount of such hypothetical factors must always be determined indirectly. But once (1) the dynamic relationship existing between the amount of the hypothetical entity (X) and some antecedent determining condition (A) which can be directly observed, and (2) the dynamic relationship of the hypothetical entity to some third consequent phenomenon or event (B) which also can be directly observed, become fairly well known, the scientific hazard largely disappears. The situation in question is represented in Figure 1. When a hypothetical dynamic entity, or even a chain of

$$A \longrightarrow f \longrightarrow (X) \longrightarrow f \longrightarrow B$$

FIGURE 1. Diagramatic representation of a relatively simple case of an intervening variable (X) not directly observable but functionally related (f) to the antecedent event (A) and to the consequent event (B), both A and B being directly observable. When an intervening variable is thus securely anchored to observables on both sides it can be safely employed in scientific theory.

such entities each functionally related to the one logically preceding and following it, is thus securely anchored on both sides to observable and measurable conditions or events (A and B), the main theoretical danger vanishes. This at bottom is because under the assumed circumstances no ambiguity can exist as to when, and how much of, B should follow A.

THE OBJECTIVE VERSUS THE SUBJECTIVE
APPROACH TO BEHAVIOR THEORY

If the circumstances sketched above as surrounding and safeguarding the use of hypothetical entities are not observed, the grossest fallacies may be committed. The painfully slow path whereby man has, as of yesterday, begun to emerge into the truly scientific era is littered with such blunders, often tragic in their practical consequences. A pestilence or a hurricane descends upon a village and decimates the population. The usual hypothesis put forward by primitive man (and many others who think themselves not at all primitive) to explain the tragic event (B) is that some hypothetical spirit (X) has been angered by the violation (A) of some tribal taboo on the part of one or more inhabitants of the village. Unfortunately this mode of thinking is deeply ingrained in most cultures, not excepting our own, and it even crops up under various disguises in what purports to be serious scientific work.

Perhaps as good an example of such a fallacious use of the intervening variable as is offered by recent scientific history is that of the *entelechy* put forward by Hans Driesch as the central concept in his theory of vitalism (3). Driesch says, for example:

> A *supreme* mind, conversant with the inorganic facts of nature and knowing all the intensive manifoldness of all entelechies and psychoids . . . would be able to predict the individual history of the latter, would be able to predict the actions of any psychoid with absolute certainty. *Human* mind, on the other hand, is not able to predict in this way, as it does not know entelechy before its manifestation, and as the material conditions of life, which alone the mind of man *can* know . . . in its completeness, are not the only conditions responsible for organic phenomena. (3, p. 249.)

Driesch's entelechy (X) fails as a logical construct or intervening variable not because it is not directly observable (though of course it is not), but because the general functional relationship to antecedent condition A and that to consequent condition B are *both* left unspecified. This, of course, is but another way of saying that the entelechy and all similar constructs are essentially metaphysical in nature. As such they have no place in science. *Science has no use for unverifiable hypotheses.*

A logically minded person, unacquainted with the unscientific foibles of those who affect the scientific virtues, may naturally wonder how such a formulation could ever mediate a semblance of theoretical prediction and thus attain any credence as a genuinely scientific theory. The answer seems to lie in the inveterate animistic or anthropomorphic tendencies of human nature. The entelechy is in substance a spirit or daemon, a kind of vicarious ghost. The person employing the entelechy in effect says to himself, "If I were the entelechy in such and such a biological emergency, what would I do?" Knowing the situation and what is required to meet the emergency, he simply states what he knows to be required as a solution, and he at once has in this statement what purports to be a scientific deduction! He has inadvertently substituted himself in place of the construct and naïvely substituted his knowledge of the situation for the objective rules stating the functional relationships which *ought* to subsist between A and X on the one hand, and between X and B on the other.

This surreptitious substitution and acceptance of one's knowledge of what needs to be done in a biological emergency for a theoretical deduction is the essence of what we shall call *anthropomorphism,* or the *subjective,* in behavior theory. After many centuries the physical sciences have largely banished the subjective from their fields, but for various reasons this is far less easy of accomplishment and is far less well advanced in the field of behavior. The only known cure for this unfortunate tendency to which all men are more or less subject is a grim and inflexible insistence that all deductions take place according to the explicitly formulated rules stating the functional relationships of A to X and of X to B. This latter is the essence of the scientifically *objective.* A genuinely scientific theory no more needs the anthropomorphic intuitions of the theorist to eke out the deduction of its implications than an automatic calculating machine needs the intuitions of the operator in the determination of a quotient, once the keys representing the dividend and the divisor have been depressed.

Objective scientific theory is necessary because only under objective conditions can a principle be tested for soundness by means of observation. The basic difficulty with anthropomorphic subjectivism is that what appear to be deductions derived from such formulations do not originate in rules stating postulated functional relationships, but rather in the intuitions of the confused thinker. Observational check of such pseudo-deductions may verify or refute these intuitions, but has no bearing on the soundness of any scientific principles whatever; such verifications or refutations might properly increase the reputation for accurate prophecy of the one making such intuitive judgments, but a prophet is not a principle, much less a scientific theory.

OBJECTIVISM VERSUS TELEOLOGY

Even a superficial study of higher organisms shows that their behavior occurs in cycles. The rise of either a primary or a secondary need normally marks the beginning of a behavior cycle, and the abolition or substantial reduction of that need marks its end. Some phase of the joint state of affairs resulting from the environmental-organismic interaction at the end of a behavior cycle is customarily spoken of as a goal. Our usual thoughtless custom is to speak of cycles of behavior by merely naming their outcome, effect, or end result, and practically to ignore the various movements which brought this terminal state about. Guthrie has expressed this tendency more aptly than anyone else (4, p. 1). We say quite naturally that a man catches a fish, a woman bakes a cake, an artist paints a picture, a general wins a battle. The end result of each angling exploit, for example, may be in some sense the same but the actual movements involved are perhaps never exactly the same on any two occasions; indeed, neither the angler nor perhaps anyone else knows or could know in their ultimate detail exactly what movements were made. It is thus inevitable that for purposes of communication we designate behavior sequences by their goals.

Now for certain rough practical purposes the custom of naming action sequences by their goals is completely justified by its convenience. It may even be that for very gross molar behavior it can usefully be employed in theory construction, provided the theorist is alert to the naturally attendant hazards. These appear the moment the theorist ventures to draw upon his intuition for statements concerning the behavior (movements) executed by the organism between the onset of a need and its termination through organismic action. Pseudo-deductions on the basis of intuition born of intimate knowledge are so easy and so natural that the tendency to make them is almost irresistible to most persons. The practice does no harm if the theorist does not mistake this subjective intuitional performance for a logical deduction from an objective theory, and attribute the success of his intuitions to the validity of the theoretical principles.

An ideally adequate theory even of so-called purposive behavior ought, therefore, to begin with colorless movement and mere receptor impulses as such, and from these build up step by step both adaptive behavior and maladaptive behavior. The present approach does not deny the molar reality of purposive acts (as opposed to movement), of intelligence, of insight, of goals, of intents, of strivings, or of value; on the contrary, we insist upon the genuineness of these forms of behavior. We hope ultimately to show the logical right to the use of such concepts by deducing them as secondary principles from more elementary objective primary principles. Once they have been derived we shall not only understand them better but be able to use them with more detailed effectiveness, particularly in the deduction of the movements which mediate (or fail to mediate) goal attainment, than would be the case if we had accepted teleological sequences at the outset as gross, unanalyzed (and unanalyzable) wholes.

"EMERGENTISM" A DOCTRINE OF DESPAIR

Perhaps the very natural and economical mode of communication whereby we speak of the terminal or goal phases of action, largely regardless of the antecedent movements involved, predisposes us to a belief in *teleology*. In its extreme form teleology is the name of the belief that the *terminal* stage of certain environmental-organismic interaction cycles somehow is at the same time one of the *antecedent* determining conditions which bring the behavior cycle about. This approach, in the case of a purposive behavior situation not hitherto known to the theorist, involves a kind of logical circularity: to deduce the outcome of any behavioral situation in the sense of the deductive predictions here under consideration, it is necessary to know all the relevant antecedent conditions, but these cannot be determined until the behavioral outcome has been deduced. In effect this means that the task of deduction cannot begin until after it is completed! Naturally this leaves the theorist completely helpless. It is not surprising that the doctrine of teleology leads to theoretical despair and to such pseudo-remedies as vitalism and *emergentism*.

Emergentism, as applied to organismic behavior, is the name for the view that in the process of evolution there has "emerged" a form of behavior which is ultimately unanalyzable into logically more primitive elements—behavior which cannot possibly be deduced from any logically prior principles whatever. In particular it is held that what is called goal or purposive behavior is of such a nature, that it cannot be derived from any conceivable set of postulates involving mere stimuli and mere movement (8, pp. 7–8; 7, pp. 26–27).

On the other hand, many feel that this defeatist attitude is not only unwholesome in that it discourages scientific endeavor, but that it is quite unjustified by the facts. The present writer shares this view. Therefore a serious attempt will ultimately be made to show that these supposedly impossible derivations are actually possible; in some cases they will be shown to be quite easy of accomplishment.

A SUGGESTED PROPHYLAXIS AGAINST ANTHROPOMORPHIC SUBJECTIVISM

As already suggested, one of the greatest obstacles to the attainment of a genuine theory of behavior is anthropomorphic subjectivism. At bottom this is because we ourselves are so intimately involved in the problem; we are so close to it that it is difficult to attain adequate perspective. For the reader who has not hitherto struggled with the complex but fascinating problems of behavior theory, it will be hard to realize the difficulty of maintaining a consistently objective point of view. Even when fully aware of the nature of anthropomorphic subjectivism and its dangers, the most careful and experienced thinker is likely to find himself a victim to its seductions. Indeed, despite the most conscientious effort to avoid this it is altogether probable that there may be found in various parts of the present work hidden elements of the anthropomorphically subjective.

One aid to the attainment of behavioral objectivity is to think in terms of the behavior of subhuman organisms, such as chimpanzees, monkeys, dogs, cats, and albino rats. Unfortunately this form of prophylaxis against subjectivism all too often breaks down when the theorist begins thinking what he would do if he were a rat, a cat, or a chimpanzee; when that happens, all his knowledge of his own behavior, born of years of self-observation, at once begins to function in place of the objectively stated general rules or principles which are the proper substance of science.

A device much employed by the author has proved itself to be a far more effective prophylaxis. This is to regard, from time to time, the behaving organism as a completely self-maintaining robot, constructed of materials as unlike ourselves as may be. In doing this

it is not necessary to attempt the solution of the detailed engineering problems connected with the design of such a creature. It is a
wholesome and revealing exercise, however, to consider the various
general problems in behavior dynamics which must be solved in the
design of a truly self-maintaining robot. We, in common with other
mammals, perform innumerable behavior adaptations with such
ease that it is apt never to occur to us that any problem of explanation exists concerning them. In many such seemingly simple activities lie dynamical problems of very great complexity and difficulty.

A second and closely related subjective tendency against which
the robot concept is likely to prove effectively prophylactic is that to
the *reification* of a behavior function. To reify a function is to give it
a name and presently to consider that the name represents a thing,
and finally to believe that the thing so named somehow *explains* the
performance of the function. We have already seen an example of
this unfortunate tendency in Driesch's entelechy. The temptation to
introduce an entelechy, soul, spirit, or daemon into a robot is slight;
it is relatively easy to realize that *the introduction of an entelechy*
would not really solve the problem of design of a robot because
there would still remain the problem of designing the entelechy
itself, which is the core of the original problem all over again. The
robot approach thus aids us in avoiding the very natural but
childish tendency to choose easy though false solutions to our
problems, by removing all excuses for not facing them squarely and
without evasion.

Unfortunately it is possible at present to promise an explanation of only a portion of the problems encountered in the infinitely
complex subject of organismic behavior. Indeed, it is no great
exaggeration to say that the present state of behavior theory re-
sembles one of those pieces of sculpture which present in the main a
rough, unworked block of stone with only a hand emerging in low
relief here, a foot or thigh barely discernible there, and elsewhere a
part of a face. The undeveloped state of the behavior sciences
suggested by this analogy is a source of regret to the behavior
theorist but not one of chagrin, because incompleteness is characteristic even of the most advanced of all theoretical sciences. From this
point of view the difference between the physical and the behavioral sciences is one not of kind but of degree—of the relative
amount of the figure still embedded in the unhewn rock. There is
reason to believe that the relative backwardness of the behavior

sciences is due not so much to their inherent complexity as to the difficulty of maintaining a consistent and rigorous objectivism.

SUMMARY

The field of behavior theory centers primarily in the detailed interaction of organism and environment. The basic principles of organismic behavior are to be viewed against a background of organic evolution, the success or failure of the evolutionary process being gauged in terms of survival. Individual and species survival depend upon numerous optimal physiological conditions; when one of these critical conditions deviates much from the optimum, a state of primary need arises. Need reduction usually comes about through a particular movement sequence on the part of the organism. Such sequences depend for their success jointly upon the nature of the need and the nature and state of the environment.

The condition of organismic need and the status of the environment evoke from specialized receptors neural impulses which are brought to bear jointly on the motor organs by the central ganglia of the nervous system acting as an automatic switchboard. The primary problem of behavior theory is to discover the laws according to which this extraordinarily complex process occurs. Students of behavior have resorted to the coarse, or "molar," laws of neural activity as revealed by conditioned-reflex and related experiments, rather than to the "molecular" results of neurophysiology, because the latter are not yet adequate.

Perhaps partly as the result of this molar approach, it is found necessary to introduce into behavior theory numerous logical constructs analogous to molecules and atoms long used in the physical sciences. All logical constructs present grave theoretical hazards when they are not securely anchored to directly observable events both as antecedents and consequences by definite functional relationships. Under conditions of unstated functional relationships the naïve theorist is tempted to make predictions on the basis of intuition, which is anthropomorphic subjectivism. The derivation of theoretical expectations from explicitly stated functional relationships is the objective method. Experimental agreement with expectations can properly validate theoretical principles only when objective procedures are employed.

Some writers believe that there is an impassable theoretical gulf between mere muscle contraction and the attainment of goals; that the latter are "emergents." This doctrine of despair grows naturally out of the doctrine of teleology. The present treatise accepts neither teleology nor its pessimistic corollary. Goals, intents, intelligence, insight, and value are regarded not only as genuine but as of the first importance. Ultimately an attempt will be made to derive all of these things objectively as secondary phenomena from more elementary objective conditions, concepts, and principles.

NOTES

OPERATIONAL DEFINITIONS AND INTERVENING VARIABLES

In 1938 Bridgman, a physicist whose chief research activities have been concerned with the empirical determination of various physical phenomena under very great pressures, wrote a book (1) in which he made an acute examination of the use of various concepts in current physical theory, particularly those representing intervening variables. The cure which he recommended for such abuses as he found was the scrupulous recognition of the operations carried out by the experimentalists as a means to the making of the observations and measurements of the observable events (A and B, Figure 1). This, as we saw above, has special significance for the science of behavior, which is so prone to the subjective use of intervening variables. Quite naturally and properly, Bridgman's work has greatly impressed many psychologists. Unfortunately his emphasis upon the operations which are the means whereby the observations and measurements in question become possible has led many psychologists to mistake the means for the end. The point here to be emphasized is that while observations must be considered in the context of the operations which make them possible, the central factor in the situation is *what is observed*. The moral of Bridgman's treatise is that the intervening variable (X) is never directly observed but is an inference based on the observation of something else, and that the inference is critically dependent upon the experimental manipulations (operations) which lead to the observations. An emphasis on operations which ignores the central importance of the dependent observations completely misses the virtue of what is coming to be known as operationism.

THE SUBJECTIVE VERSUS THE OBJECTIVE
IN BEHAVIOR THEORY

The critical characteristic of the subjective as contrasted with the objective is that the subjective tends to be a private event, whereas the objective is a public event, i.e., an event presumed to be independently observable by many persons. Thus the perceptual experience or conscious feeling of a person when stimulated by light rays of a certain wave length is said to be a private or subjective event, whereas the light rays themselves, or the overt behavior of another person in response to the impact of the light rays, is said to be a public or objective event.

A typical case of subjectivism in the field of theory, on the other hand, is one in which the alleged theorist asserts, and even believes, that he has deduced a proposition in a logical manner, whereas in fact he has arrived at it by mere anthropomorphic intuition. The subjectivism of behavior theory is thus dependent upon a kind of privacy, but one quite different from that of perceptual consciousness or experience. The subjective aspect of experience is dependent upon the private nature of the process hidden within the body of the *subject;* subjectivism in the field of behavior theory, on the other hand, is dependent upon the private nature of the processes within the body of the *theorist,* whereby he attempts to explain the behavior of the subject. A theory becomes objective when the primary assumptions and the logical steps whereby these assumptions lead to further propositions (theorems) are exhibited to public observation and so make possible a kind of repetition of the logical process by any other person. Propositions originating in private intuitions masquerading as unstated logical processes are, of course, not theoretical material at all, and have no proper place in science.

HISTORICAL NOTE CONCERNING THE CONCEPT OF MOLAR
BEHAVIOR AND OF THE INTERVENING VARIABLE

The important concept of molar, as contrasted with molecular, behavior was introduced into psychology in 1931 by E. C. Tolman. The present writer has taken over the concept substantially as it appears in Tolman's well-known book (8).

The explicit introduction into psychology of the equally important concept of the intervening variable is also due to Professor Tolman; its first and best elaboration was given in his address as President of the American Psychological Association, delivered at Minneapolis, September 3, 1937 (9).

REFERENCES

1. BRIDGMAN, P. W. *The logic of modern physics.* New York: Macmillan, 1938.
2. DARWIN, C. *Origin of species.* New York: Modern Library, 1936.
3. DRIESCH, H. *The science and philosophy of the organism,* second ed. London: A. C. Black, 1929.
4. GUTHRIE, E. R. Association and the law of effect. *Psychol. Rev.,* 1940, **47,** 127–148.
5. HULL, C. L. Conditioning: outline of a systematic theory of learning (Chapter II in *The psychology of learning,* Forty-First Yearbook of the National Society for the Study of Education, Part II). Bloomington, Ill.: Public School Publishing Co., 1942.
6. ———, HOVLAND, C. I., ROSS, R. T., HALL, M., PERKINS, D. T., and FITCH, F. B. *Mathematico-deductive theory of rote learning.* New Haven: Yale Univ. Press, 1940.
7. KOFFKA, K. *Principles of Gestalt psychology.* New York: Harcourt, Brace and Co., 1935.
8. TOLMAN, E. C. *Purposive behavior in animals and men.* New York: Century Co., 1932.
9. ———. The determiners of behavior at a choice point. *Psychol. Rev.,* 1938, **45,** 1–41.
10. WATSON, J. B. *Psychology from the standpoint of a behaviorist,* second ed. Philadelphia: J. B. Lippincott Co., 1924.

5

Behavior, Purpose and Teleology

Arturo Rosenblueth, Norbert Wiener, Julian Bigelow

"Behavior, Purpose and Teleology" is the product of collaborative efforts by an eminent neurologist (Rosenblueth), a primary progenitor of cybernetics (Wiener), and a scholarly engineer (Bigelow).

The first few paragraphs will be more readily understood, and thereby the remainder of the paper, if the reader grasps that the term "object," as used by the authors, is meant to include both biological and nonbiological entities. Their observations concerning the energy relations of an object with its environment are, accordingly, biophysical in character.

By "purpose," the authors mean "goal-directed." The main thrust of their argument is that all purposeful behavior requires some information from the goal itself, or from the object's relation to the goal. This information may or may not involve feedback, that is, a change in information available to the object as a consequence of prior behavior. If it does, then purposeful behavior may be described as being "teleological," and without any taint of logical circularity. If the behavior does not involve feedback, then— *although still purposeful*—it should not be described as being teleological. Put somewhat differently, the authors distinguish between guided versus ballistic, purposeful behavior. Reaching for a glass while looking at it falls into the former category; doing so while not looking at it (but having an idea of where it is) falls into the latter.

Having drawn these distinctions, the authors go on to discuss in non-mathematical terms what might be called a "calculus" of behavior; namely, how it is that predictions of the future course of behavioral events depend upon sensory and perceptual interpretation of the changing present.

This essay has two goals. The first is to define the behavioristic study of natural events and to classify behavior. The second is to stress the importance of the concept of purpose.

From *Philosophy of Science* (1943), Vol. 10, pp. 18–24. Copyright 1943, The Williams & Wilkins Company. Reprinted by permission of The Williams & Wilkins Company.

Given any object, relatively abstracted from its surroundings for study, the behavioristic approach consists in the examination of the output of the object and of the relations of this output to the input. By output is meant any change produced in the surroundings by the object. By input, conversely, is meant any event external to the object that modifies this object in any manner.

The above statement of what is meant by the behavioristic method of study omits the specific structure and the intrinsic organization of the object. This omission is fundamental because on it is based the distinction between the behavioristic and the alternative functional method of study. In a functional analysis, as opposed to a behavioristic approach, the main goal is the intrinsic organization of the entity studied, its structure and its properties; the relations between the object and the surroundings are relatively incidental.

From this definition of the behavioristic method a broad definition of behavior ensues. By behavior is meant any change of an entity with respect to its surroundings. This change may be largely an output from the object, the input being then minimal, remote or irrelevant; or else the change may be immediately traceable to a certain input. Accordingly, any modification of an object, detectable externally, may be denoted as behavior. The term would be, therefore, too extensive for usefulness were it not that it may be restricted by apposite adjectives—i.e., that behavior may be classified.

The consideration of the changes of energy involved in behavior affords a basis for classification. Active behavior is that in which the object is the source of the output energy involved in a given specific reaction. The object may store energy supplied by a remote or relatively immediate input, but the input does not energize the output directly. In passive behavior, on the contrary, the object is not a source of energy; all the energy in the output can be traced to the immediate input (e.g., the throwing of an object), or else the object may control energy which remains external to it throughout the reaction (e.g., the soaring flight of a bird).

Active behavior may be subdivided into two classes: purposeless (or random) and purposeful. The term purposeful is meant to denote that the act or behavior may be interpreted as directed to the attainment of a goal—i.e., to a final condition in which the behaving object reaches a definite correlation in time or in space with respect to another object or event. Purposeless behavior then is that which is not interpreted as directed to a goal.

The vagueness of the words "may be interpreted" as used above might be considered so great that the distinction would be useless. Yet the recognition that behavior may sometimes be purposeful is unavoidable and useful, as follows. The basis of the concept of purpose is the awareness of "voluntary activity." Now, the purpose of voluntary acts is not a matter of arbitrary interpretation but a physiological fact. When we perform a voluntary action what we select voluntarily is a specific purpose, not a specific movement. Thus, if we decide to take a glass containing water and carry it to our mouth we do not command certain muscles to contract to a certain degree and in a certain sequence; we merely trip the purpose and the reaction follows automatically. Indeed, experimental physiology has so far been largely incapable of explaining the mechanism of voluntary activity. We submit that this failure is due to the fact that when an experimenter stimulates the motor regions of the cerebral cortex he does not duplicate a voluntary reaction; he trips efferent, "output" pathways, but does not trip a purpose, as is done voluntarily.

The view has often been expressed that all machines are purposeful. This view is untenable. First may be mentioned mechanical devices such as a roulette, designed precisely for purposelessness. Then may be considered devices such as a clock, designed, it is true, with a purpose, but having a performance which, although orderly, is not purposeful—i.e., there is no specific final condition toward which the movement of the clock strives. Similarly, although a gun may be used for a definite purpose, the attainment of a goal is not intrinsic to the performance of the gun; random shooting can be made, deliberately purposeless.

Some machines, on the other hand, are intrinsically purposeful. A torpedo with a target-seeking mechanism is an example. The term servomechanisms has been coined precisely to designate machines with intrinsic purposeful behavior.

It is apparent from these considerations that although the definition of purposeful behavior is relatively vague, and hence operationally largely meaningless, the concept of purpose is useful and should, therefore, be retained.

Purposeful active behavior may be subdivided into two classes:

"feed-back" (or "teleological") and "non-feed-back" (or "non-teleological"). The expression feed-back is used by engineers in two different senses. In a broad sense it may denote that some of the output energy of an apparatus or machine is returned as input; an example is an electrical amplifier with feed-back. The feed-back is in these cases positive—the fraction of the output which reenters the object has the same sign as the original input signal. Positive feed-back adds to the input signals, it does not correct them. The term feed-back is also employed in a more restricted sense to signify that the behavior of an object is controlled by the margin of error at which the object stands at a given time with reference to a relatively specific goal. The feed-back is then negative, that is, the signals from the goal are used to restrict outputs which would otherwise go beyond the goal. It is this second meaning of the term feed-back that is used here.

All purposeful behavior may be considered to require negative feed-back. If a goal is to be attained, some signals from the goal are necessary at some time to direct the behavior. By non-feed-back behavior is meant that in which there are no signals from the goal which modify the activity of the object *in the course of the behavior.* Thus, a machine may be set to impinge upon a luminous object although the machine may be insensitive to light. Similarly, a snake may strike at a frog, or a frog at a fly, with no visual or other report from the prey after the movement has started. Indeed, the movement is in these cases so fast that it is not likely that nerve impulses would have time to arise at the retina, travel to the central nervous system and set up further impulses which would reach the muscles in time to modify the movement effectively.

As opposed to the examples considered, the behavior of some machines and some reactions of living organisms involve a continuous feed-back from the goal that modifies and guides the behaving object. This type of behavior is more effective than that mentioned above, particularly when the goal is not stationary. But continuous feed-back control may lead to very clumsy behavior if the feed-back is inadequately damped and becomes therefore positive instead of negative for certain frequencies of oscillation. Suppose, for example, that a machine is designed with the purpose of impinging upon a moving luminous goal; the path followed by the machine is controlled by the direction and intensity of the light from the goal. Suppose further that the machine overshoots seriously when it follows a movement of the goal in a certain direction; an even stronger stimulus will then be delivered which will turn the machine in the opposite direction. If that movement again overshoots, a series of increasingly larger oscillations will ensue and the machine will miss the goal.

This picture of the consequences of undamped feed-back is strikingly similar to that seen during the performance of a voluntary act by a cerebellar patient. At rest the subject exhibits no obvious motor disturbance. If he is asked to carry a glass of water from a table to his mouth, however, the hand carrying the glass will execute a series of oscillatory motions of increasing amplitude as the glass approaches his mouth, so that the water will spill and the purpose will not be fulfilled. This test is typical of the disorderly motor performance of patients with cerebellar disease. The analogy with the behavior of a machine with undamped feed-back is so vivid that we venture to suggest that the main function of the cerebellum is the control of the feed-back nervous mechanisms involved in purposeful motor activity.

Feed-back purposeful behavior may again be subdivided. It may be extrapolative (predictive), or it may be non-extrapolative (non-predictive). The reactions of unicellular organisms known as tropisms are examples of non-predictive performances. The amoeba merely follows the source to which it reacts; there is no evidence that it extrapolates the path of a moving source. Predictive animal behavior, on the other hand, is a commonplace. A cat starting to pursue a running mouse does not run directly toward the region where the mouse is at any given time, but moves toward an extrapolated future position. Examples of both predictive and non-predictive servomechanisms may also be found readily.

Predictive behavior may be subdivided into different orders. The cat chasing the mouse is an instance of first-order prediction; the cat merely predicts the path of the mouse. Throwing a stone at a moving target requires a second-order prediction; the paths of the target and of the stone should be foreseen. Examples of predictions of higher order are shooting with a sling or with a bow and arrow.

Predictive behavior requires the discrimination of at least two coordinates, a temporal and at least one spatial axis. Prediction will be more effective and flexible, however, if the behaving object can respond to changes in more than one spatial coordinate. The sensory receptors of an organism, or the corresponding elements of a machine, may therefore limit the predictive behavior. Thus, a bloodhound *follows* a trail, that is, it does not show any predictive behavior in trailing, because a chemical, olfactory input reports only spatial information: distance, as indicated by intensity. The external changes capable of affecting auditory, or, even better, visual receptors, permit more accurate spatial localization; hence the possibility of more effective predictive reactions when the input affects those receptors.

In addition to the limitations imposed by the receptors upon the ability to perform extrapolative actions, limitations may also occur that are due to the internal organization of the behaving object. Thus, a machine which is to trail predictively a moving luminous object should not only be sensitive to light (e.g., by the possession of a photoelectric cell), but should also have the structure adequate for interpreting the luminous input. It is probable that limitations of internal organization, particularly of the organization of the central nervous system, determine the complexity of predictive behavior which a mammal may attain. Thus, it is likely that the nervous system of a rat or dog is such that it does not permit the integration of input and output necessary for the performance of a predictive reaction of the third or fourth order. Indeed, it is possible that one of the features of the discontinuity of behavior observable when comparing humans with other high mammals may lie in that the other mammals are limited to predictive behavior of a low order, whereas man may be capable potentially of quite high orders of prediction.

The classification of behavior suggested so far is tabulated here:

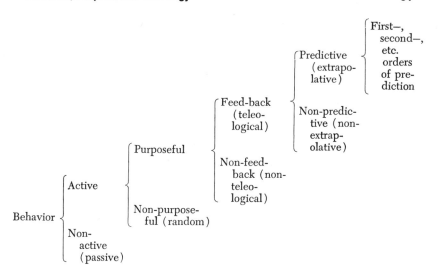

It is apparent that each of the dichotomies established singles out arbitrarily one feature, deemed interesting, leaving an amorphous remainder: the non-class. It is also apparent that the criteria for the several dichotomies are heterogeneous. It is obvious, therefore, that many other lines of classification are available, which are independent of that developed above. Thus, behavior in general, or any of the groups in the table, could be divided into linear (i.e., output proportional to input) and non-linear. A division into continuous and discontinuous might be useful for many purposes. The several degrees of freedom which behavior may exhibit could also be employed as a basis of systematization.

The classification tabulated above was adopted for several reasons. It leads to the singling out of the class of predictive behavior, a class particularly interesting since it suggests the possibility of systematizing increasingly more complex tests of the behavior of organisms. It emphasizes the concepts of purpose and of teleology, concepts which, although rather discredited at present, are shown to be important. Finally, it reveals that a uniform behavioristic analysis is applicable to both machines and living organisms, regardless of the complexity of the behavior.

It has sometimes been stated that the designers of machines merely attempt to duplicate the performances of living organisms. This statement is uncritical. That the gross behavior of some machines should be similar to the reactions of organisms is not surprising. Animal behavior includes many varieties of all the possible modes of behavior and the machines devised so far have far from exhausted all those possible modes. There is, therefore, a considerable overlap of the two realms of behavior. Examples, however, are readily found of man-made machines with behavior that transcends human behavior. A machine with an electrical output is an instance; for men, unlike the electric fishes, are incapable of emitting electricity. Radio transmission is perhaps an even better instance, for no animal is known with the ability to generate short waves, even if so-called experiments on telepathy are considered seriously.

A further comparison of living organisms and machines leads to the following inferences. The methods of study for the two groups are at present similar. Whether they should always be the same may depend on whether or not there are one or more qualitatively distinct, unique characteristics present in one group and absent in the other. Such qualitative differences have not appeared so far.

The broad classes of behavior are the same in machines and in living organisms. Specific, narrow classes may be found exclusively in one or the other. Thus, no machine is available yet that can write a Sanscrit-Mandarin dictionary. Thus, also, no living organism is known that rolls on wheels—imagine what the result would have been if engineers had insisted on copying living organisms and had therefore put legs and feet in their locomotives, instead of wheels.

While the behavioristic analysis of machines and living organisms is largely uniform, their functional study reveals deep differences. Structurally, organisms are mainly colloidal, and include prominently protein molecules, large, complex and anisotropic; machines are chiefly metallic and include mainly simple molecules. From the standpoint of their energetics, machines usually exhibit relatively large differences of potential, which permit rapid mobilization of energy; in organisms the energy is more uniformly distributed, it is not very mobile. Thus, in electric machines conduction is mainly electronic, whereas in organisms electric changes are usually ionic.

Scope and flexibility are achieved in machines largely by temporal multiplication of effects; frequencies of one million per second or more are readily obtained and utilized. In organisms, spatial multiplication, rather than temporal, is the rule; the temporal achievements are poor—the fastest nerve fibers can only conduct about one thousand impulses per second; spatial multiplication is on the other hand abundant and admirable in its compactness. This difference is well illustrated by the comparison of a television receiver and the eye. The television receiver may be described as a single cone retina; the images are formed by scanning—i.e., by orderly successive detection of the signal with a rate of about 20 million per second. Scanning is a process which seldom or never occurs in organisms, since it requires fast frequencies for effective performance. The eye uses a spatial, rather than a temporal multiplier. Instead of the one cone of the television receiver a human eye has about 6.5 million cones and about 115 million rods.

If an engineer were to design a robot, roughly similar in behavior to an animal organism, he would not attempt at present to make it out of proteins and other colloids. He would probably build it out of metallic parts, some dielectrics and many vacuum tubes. The movements of the robot could readily be much faster and more powerful than those of the original organism. Learning and memory, however, would be quite rudimentary. In future years, as the knowledge of colloids and proteins increases, future engineers may attempt the design of robots not only with a behavior, but also with a structure similar to that of a mammal. The ultimate model of a cat is of course another cat, whether it be born of still another cat or synthesized in a laboratory.

In classifying behavior the term "teleology" was used as synonymous with "purpose controlled by feed-back." Teleology has been interpreted in the past to imply purpose and the vague concept of a "final cause" has been often added. This concept of final causes has led to the opposition of teleology to determinism. A discussion of causality, determinism and final causes is beyond the scope of this essay. It may be pointed out, however, that purposefulness, as defined here, is quite independent of causality, initial or final. Teleology has been discredited chiefly because it was defined to imply a cause subsequent in time to a given effect. When this aspect of teleology was dismissed, however, the associated recognition of the importance of purpose was also unfortunately discarded. Since we consider purposefulness a concept necessary for the understanding of certain modes of behavior we suggest that a teleological study is useful if it avoids problems of causality and concerns itself merely with an investigation of purpose.

We have restricted the connotation of teleological behavior by applying this designation only to purposeful reactions which are controlled by the error of the reaction—i.e., by the difference between the state of the behaving object at any time and the final state interpreted as the purpose. Teleological behavior thus becomes synonymous with behavior controlled by negative feed-back, and gains therefore in precision by a sufficiently restricted connotation.

According to this limited definition, teleology is not opposed to determinism, but to non-teleology. Both teleological and non-teleological systems are deterministic when the behavior considered belongs to the realm where determinism applies. The concept of teleology shares only one thing with the concept of causality: a time axis. But causality implies a one-way, relatively irreversible functional relationship, whereas teleology is concerned with behavior, not with functional relationships.

Modifying
Responses
Through
Reinforcement
Operations

6

Soviet Psychology
and Psychophysiology

Gregory Razran

The title of this article is much too modest, for Razran goes well beyond what of and by itself would be an exacting task, namely, describing Soviet psychology and psychophysiology. What he actually accomplishes is a sophisticated comparison of Soviet and American distinctive interests in behavioral science.

The major point made by Razran is that what the Russians consider as "psychophysiology" is practically the equivalent of what Americans perceive as the entire field of experimental psychology; it is not synonymous with "physiological psychology." What the Russians call "psychology" is limited principally to problems of a pedagogical nature.

The influence of Pavlov and his students still dominates Soviet theorizing and experimentation. Their research into acquired visceral responses, for example, is much more advanced than ours. In general, psychophysiology has been relatively free to develop without political intereference. Such has not been the case, however, with Soviet psychology. Razran sees the latter as being used as an instrument of Communist ideology.

In the summer of 1934, I visited the Soviet Union, and among other things, I tried to interview Pavlov. I had just received my doctor's degree; I had no appointment with Pavlov, but he consented to talk to me in his laboratory. The first question he asked was: "Are you a physiologist?" Sensing trouble, I said: "Unfortunately, I am only a psychologist." He smiled and said: "Are you at least a behaviorist?" I said: "I was" (at that time I could say it more readily than now), and this saved, in part, the situation. Pavlov talked to me for about three hours, discussing his ape experiments, criticizing Gestalt psy-

From *Science* (November 14, 1958), Vol. 128, No. 3333, pp. 1187–1194; reprinted by permission of the American Association for the Advancement of Science.

chology and praising British associationism and the work of Thorndike, Loeb, and Jennings. I could not put in a word or question edgewise; he never asked me where I learned Russian or whether I was of Russian descent, but in the course of talking he remembered a review on conditioning I had written and remarked that we Russians must show the world that we can do more than make revolutions. His close collaborator and "aide-de-camp," M. K. Petrova, came in twice, ostensibly worried about the length of the interview (Pavlov was 85 at the time), and I, too, though obviously pleased, became concerned after a while. Pavlov, however, did not seem to heed our "conditioned" reactions, continuing his exposition with unusual and youthful vigor and lapsing, at one time, into a recital of a long passage from *Faust* to illustrate how the laws of conditioning operate in verbal associations. He promised to have his office send me a prepublished report of his ape experiments and several other publications, which, for some reason, I never received. Pavlov died a year and a half later.

I am telling this story not merely for reasons of rhetoric but as a substantive preface to a consideration of the special state of psychology in Soviet Russia and to my contention that no meaningful tracing and evaluation of Soviet psychology in terms of American psychology is possible without including Pavlovian physiology, which we may call psychophysiology but which Pavlov called, for years, "higher nervous activity." Let me illustrate. Suppose you take our two psychological journals of basic research, the *Journal of Experimental Psychology* and the *Journal of Comparative and Physiological Psychology*, and ask who in Russia would do this kind of research; the answer would be that in three out of four cases— surely in two out of three and possibly in four out of five—such research in Russia would be done by psychophysiologists (more correctly, "higher nervous activitists," but that is a clumsy term). If you take the *Journal of Abnormal and Social Psychology*, you will first find that a large portion of the work reported would not have been done in Russia at all, but then will discover that in this case too, Soviet psychologists trail their psychophysiologists and psychiatrists in whatever is done in the area. Even the kind of material published in the *Journal of Applied Psychology* and the *Journal of Educational Psychology*—again, whatever is done in the area— would as frequently come from a physiological as from a psychological laboratory. Likewise, whatever we have in our two evaluative journals, the *Psychological Bulletin* and the *Psychological Review*, would in Russia fall mostly within the bailiwick of physiology or psychophysiology or higher nervous activity.

GENERAL ORIENTATION

A few months ago Smirnov stated (1), with some pride, that the Soviets have now no less than 700 professional psychologists (the 1958 *Directory of American Psychologists* lists 16,644). I have not seen an estimate of the number of their psychophysiologists, but my files contain the names of about 60 publishing Soviet psychologists and about 500 publishing Soviet psychophysiologists. I recently checked the *Large Soviet Encyclopedia*—the 39-volume recent edition—for sketches of contemporary Soviet psychologists and psychophysiologists. I found sketches of 13 physiologists but of only one psychologist. At the recent convention of Soviet psychologists (2), the two longest and, by all tokens, most important papers, as well as a number of other papers, were by physiologists. Soviet psychological publications are published by the Academy of Pedagogical Sciences; psychophysiological publications are published by the General Academy of Sciences, which is a very restricted body—more restricted than our National Academy of Sciences—and the true Olympus of basic Soviet science. More than that, the only journal in the natural sciences that the General Academy publishes in German as well as in Russian is the psychophysiological *Journal of Higher Nervous Activity*. There are, in the Soviet Union, scores of research institutes in psychophysiology but there are only about half a dozen in psychology.

I think I have said enough to indicate that, vis-à-vis psychophysiology, psychology is a rather small enterprise as a basic science in the Soviet Union. I do not even know whether I should call it a junior partner or a younger brother: perhaps an "unsteady sputnik" might be more appropriate, or really a commensal organism, one that partakes of the food of another organism without being parasitic. And, finally, with respect to training, a Soviet physiologist is an American physiologist *plus*—that is, he has the training of an American physiologist plus special training in psychophysiology. A Soviet psychologist is an American psychologist *minus*—that is, he has a narrower spectrum; he is likely to know less physiology, be less familiar with brass instruments, and in general be less of a scientist. Of course he may say he knows dialectical materials. But what is that? Even if one grants that it is a tenable philosophy, its heuristic value to an independent hard-core psychology is, to use a Russian expression, that of *"toloch vodu"* (grinding water); at best it is merely declaratory and programmatic.

Yet within its own orbit, Soviet psychology as such is not without influence. Psychologists seem to dominate the Academy of Pedagogical Sciences and, together with the "methodists" (specialists in methods of teaching), seem to set the pattern of "how to do it" in Soviet education. Psychology was until very recently taught as a high-school subject in the Soviet Union, and, as a result, each year several million copies of elementary psychology textbooks were mastered by Soviet youngsters and reached Soviet homes; this, of course, is more than we do here. And psychologists participate, to some extent, in the work of mental institutions—though such participation is mostly confined to work with the handicapped (so-called "defectology") as distinguished from psychopathology (in Russian, usually "pathopsychology")—and are now beginning to plan to participate in Soviet industrial and agricultural adjustments. Again, while a good many of their publications are still more largely concerned with "what is to be done," and with "trying to do" rather than with "doing," I suppose their very "tryings" and "ways of tryings" are in themselves of special interest, particularly since there is no question of discontinuing psychology, as such, in the Soviet Union. The prevalent ideology is surely that, right or wrong, there must be a psychology on top of a psychophysiology, and about the worst accusation you can make against a Soviet psychophysiologist is to say that he wants to liquidate Soviet psychology (*liquidate* is an uncomfortable word). So, we have two disciplines to consider; let us begin with psychophysiology.

PSYCHOPHYSIOLOGY: IN PAVLOV'S FOOTSTEPS

The first significant point about Soviet psychophysiology that needs to be made is the fact that, unlike Soviet psychology, it has in itself, in the course of 40 years, been very little, if at all, interfered with by the Soviet state or Soviet philosophy. At no time was experimentation in Pavlovian conditioning and related phenomena in any way curtailed, and at no time was any Pavlovian doctrine per se—let us say, stimulus generalization or higher order conditioning—criticized as being in conflict with dialectical materialism. (Of course, it might well have been!) All that was said, at certain times (in fact, most of the time), was that Pavlovian psychophysiology does not exhaust psychology or, in Soviet lingo, that "it studies the material basis of the mind, but not the mind itself"—which was no doubt fine with the vast majority of the rank-and-file experimentalists, tired of extrapolating and stretching their research findings. It must be remembered that Soviet psychophysiologists, unlike American psychologists or even American behaviorists, are under no compulsion to explain mental phenomena—most of them seem to be well satisfied with the significance of their results at their own level (just as our own physiologists would be). Hence, the curve of production of Soviet psychophysiological research has been steady and continuous and, as a rule, positively accelerated—now very much so—from the very beginning of the Soviet era till the present day (3). I cannot detect in this curve any influence of the "new economic policy" or the "popular front" or the "Hitler pact" or of Stalin's changing and deteriorating personal predilections. The fact is that the philosophical basis of Soviet psychophysiology per se was questioned even less than that of Soviet physics—let us say, the physics of Mandelstamm and Kapitza. And no Soviet scientist was, by Soviet standards, more tolerated or more coddled than Pavlov, whose views were at times openly anti-Communist (4).

True, beginning with 1950 Pavlovian psychophysiology has, in a sense, fallen under state control (5). But these controls aimed to preserve its purity and extend its applicability and by no means to question its validity or interfere with its empirical continuity. Besides, these controls have in the last three or four years been mostly removed. Hence, by and large, the development of Pavlovianism per se has really been quite autochthonous and probably would not have been very different if Pavlov had lived in a free country (6). Indeed, an argument can be made to the effect that to some extent—or to a large extent—Soviet psychophysiology has in the last 30 years developed more normally, more evenly, and more efficiently than its familiar homolog or counterpart, American behaviorism. Let me explain what I mean in eight short summary statements, which will, I hope, also serve as short sketches of the present status and achievement of the Soviet psychophysiology and which will keep American behaviorism as a yardstick or frame of reference.

1. Soviet psychophysiology has continued to be strongly empiricistic and fact-collecting. The conceptualization and mathematicalization that has gripped a good portion of American behaviorism in the last two decades or so has not touched it. Lacking, in general, the benefit of our philosophy of science, it may also, perhaps, have benefitted from the lack of it. Soviet psychophysiologists seem to be little worried about having too many meaningless facts and not enough meaningful theoretical frames to pin the facts to and, as a result, have accumulated a staggering amount of experimental material (my bibliography of their experiments has now reached the 4000 mark). The extent to which the Russians go to get facts on conditioning, for instance, is surprising. There are four experiments in which dogs were conditioned, put to death, then revived after 3 to 15 minutes and retested for conditioning change [(7), the Soviet Academy of Medical Sciences has for some years maintained in Moscow a special "resuscitation" laboratory]. There are experiments in which dogs were conditioned dressed in jackets loaded with heavy weights (8). There are experiments on the relation of conditioning to dozens of diseases, scores of drugs, wide varieties of diets, and all kinds of tissue ablations (9), as well as to such special variables as sexual excitation (10), castration (11), ligation and cutting of spermatic cords (12), pregnancy (13), ligation of veins and arteries (14), ovarian implantation (15), operative rejuvenation (16), antibiotics (17), and radial acceleration (18). Indeed, the standard Soviet way of trying out a drug is to see its effect on conditioning; their equivalents of our studies of the psychological effects of, let us say, polio or lead poisoning would be studies of the effects of polio (19) or lead poisoning (20) on higher nervous activity—that is, conditioning. On the other hand, the Russians do not have—or, shall I say, do not waste experiments on "settling"— subtle problems of theoretical controversy: need reduction, nature of discrimination, cognition, and so on. In this respect they are really much like B. F. Skinner and American functionalists. But here is the second statement.

2. Unlike Skinner and a number of other behavioral positivists, however, the Russians have never given up investigating the neurology of learning. Their studies in brain extirpation, their searchings for anatomical and physiological loci and foci of learning and, in more recent years, for electroencephalographic—brain-wave—correlates of learning, are surely impressive in number. I would estimate

that Russian experimentation in the last-named area may well exceed American and English efforts combined; just a single issue of a recent Russian journal (21) reports 11 substantial studies on electroencephalographic correlates of conditioning—six with rabbits and five with human subjects. And it seems that this is the first area of Russian experimentation to begin to attract the attention of Americans. In the 1957 *Annual Review of Physiology*, Liberson reviews 140 Russian titles in a chapter entitled "Recent advances in Russian neurophysiology" (devoted mostly to the neurology of learning), and in a prepublication chapter for the forthcoming *Handbook of Neurophysiology*—a chapter entitled "The neural basis of learning," by Robert Galambos and Clifford Morgan—there are extensive quotations from more than twenty abstracts of Russian references. Moreover, both Liberson, and Galambos and Morgan, are complimentary in their appraisal of the Russian work. Liberson states, for instance, "In the field of electrographic correlates of conditioning, Russian neurophysiologists have been doing pioneering work," and, "It is in the field of comparative physiology of higher nervous functions that the most intriguing work has been turned out in Russia during recent years," while Galambos and Morgan say, "The use of microelectrodes in EEG is just beginning in non-Russian hands."

Galambos and Morgan do not, I assume from their references, read Russian and have had access only to some non-Russian abstracts, while Liberson, who reads Russian, complains that a good deal of the literature was not available to him. An All-Union Conference on Electrophysiology, at which 70 papers were read, was held in Leningrad 8–11 May 1957 (22). From the conference's abstracts as well as from the work on morphological neural changes during conditioning reported by the laboratories of Beritov (23) and of Sarkisov (24), I judge that the Russians feel that they are on the verge of real breakthroughs in the neurology of learning and that they are actually in the process of converting Pavlov's "conceptual nervous system" into a real one. And I notice that the French electrophysiologist Gastaut seems to share this view. He and his colleagues Rogers, Dongier, Naquet, and Regis (25) have been working hard on providing, in their own way, true neural underpinnings to Pavlov's brain theories, and they seem to feel that at least in part they have succeeded. The long-existing gap between Pavlovian and classical neurology may thus, it may be hoped, be bridged. I of course do not mean to minimize our own break-throughs in the area, such as those of Olds (26) and of Delgado, Roberts, and Miller (27). But the Russians have been at it all the time, while we are, to a large extent, Johnny-come-lately's. Our *positivism* may well have served us negatively.

3. My third statement pertains to psychopathology and psycho-pharmacology. Pavlov began applying his teachings to problems of psychopathology as early as 1918, while his interest in relating pharmacology to conditioning started around 1908 (Pavlov was a professor of pharmacology before he was one of physiology). And this initial work in experimental neurosis, special typology, func-tional pathological neural states (paradoxical and ultraparadoxi-cal), and differential conditioning effects of bromides and caffein has since multiplied, manifoldly and multifariously, and has added new empirical findings and concepts of verbal conditioning, intero-ceptive conditioning, sleep therapy, hypnotherapy, drug therapy, and the like, so that by now the Russians have quite a complete and complex system with respect to the etiology, understanding, and treatment of mental disorder. The clinical claims of Soviet psycho-pathology are difficult to evaluate, though the Russians' discharge rates from mental hospitals do not seem to be lower than ours, but their experiments, particularly the psychopharmacological ones, are too objective and too numerous (about 500 experiments) for us to ignore. One series of experiments, combining studies of the pharma-cology and the neurology of learning, by Anokhin (28), probably the most brilliant of all Soviet psychophysiologists, seems worth citing specifically. Three pairs of electrodes were implanted in the cortex, thalamus, and reticular system of rabbits, and the animals were conditioned to refuse food (carrots) in a hutch in which they had previously received electric shocks. The neurological effects of the conditioning were clear-cut electroencephalographic desynchro-nizations when the animals were placed in this hutch. But when the drug aminazine was administered, the conditioning was "washed out": electroencephalographic synchronization was restored, and the animals accepted avidly the proffered food in the hutch to which they were negatively conditioned.

4. Soviet psychophysiology has also made, in recent years, not-able—indeed striking—contributions to our knowledge of verbal conditioning—that is, conditioning reflexes to verbal stimuli (not verbal reinforcement). I have done a little work in this area myself,

but in general this sort of experimentation has been very scanty in this country, and until very recently the Russians, too, have not done much. However, after Stalin's 1950 pronunciamentos on linguistics, they dug up Pavlov's view on the second signal system, combined the two in some way, and started a mad rush, so that today verbal conditioning is probably their most intensively investigated single area—an area in which, incidentally, the psychologists have joined the psychophysiologists. Let me cite three recent experiments as samples. Markosyan, a psychophysiologist reporting at a psychological conference (29), conditioned blood coagulation, through electric shock, to the sound of a metronome and the flash of an electric lamp and found that this conditioning transferred to the words *metronome* and *lamp* as well as to semantically and phonetically related words. Elkin (30) conditioned the eyelid reflex of 25 school children to the sentences "it is a sunny day today" and "it is raining today" and found that the conditioning was very easy when the sentences corresponded to the prevailing weather but very difficult or impossible when the weather during the conditioning or testing, or both, was different from that described in the sentences. Volkova (31) discovered that the food-salivary reflexes of school children who had been conditioned positively to the word *right* and negatively to the word *wrong* carried over correctly to right and wrong sentences: for example, to "8 divided by 2 is 4" versus "10 divided by 2 is 3," and to "Snow melts in spring" versus "It is always cold in the South." I don't think the Russians have discovered a way of conditioning to truth! But obviously the experiments are of basic significance to both the theory and practice of human behavioral control.

5. One of the chief differences between Soviet and American conditioning studies is that we concentrate on one kind of reaction while they go in for variety. And of this variety of reactions, the most important one, and the one that we have never even touched, is that of interoceptive, or viscerovisceral and viscerosomatic, conditioning. You condition the uterus to respond when the ureter or urinary bladder is stimulated and vice versa, or you condition the pancreas to secrete when the gall bladder is stimulated or vice versa, or you simply teach the animal to withdraw its paw or lift its paw when the visceral changes occur (32). Most of these experiments are done through surgical exteriorization of the viscera, and their ramified theoretical and clinical significance could hardly be

overestimated. In fact, they are even important in animal space travel, inasmuch as Soviet animals could presumably be trained by means of conditioned interoception to signalize not only stimuli around them but also reactions within themselves. Bykov's book, which has just been translated into English by Gantt (33), contains some of these experiments; but the book was originally written in 1942, whereas 85 percent of these interoceptive experiments have been performed since (my bibliography of interoceptive conditioning has now reached the 200 mark). And here I am tempted to say something in general about viscera. Some American behaviorists have suggested that classical Pavlovian conditioning is confined to autonomic or visceral reactions and so is not too important. I do not agree to the formulation. But even if I agreed, I do not see why visceral conditioning is so unimportant. After all, our viscera are with us all the time, you can't get rid of them, and they keep on learning, whereas the Lord has not provided us with levers to pull or buttons to push—or even to peck at!

6. The Russians have several laboratories of what they call evolutionary physiology in which they compare conditioning throughout almost the entire animal kingdom, from hydras to horses and from ascidians to apes (34), whereas we, concentrating as we do on one or two species, are in danger of losing comparative psychology or comparative behavior as a separate discipline or area of knowledge. Liberson has praised Russian work in this area. I have space only to mention one other comparative area, which Liberson has not reviewed—namely, that of human ontogeny, comparative conditioning characteristics in infants and young children. The Russians have developed here what might be called Gesell-type or Kuhlmann-Anderson-type scales. While we have scales of capacity, they seem to have scales of modifiability (35).

7. Another significant area of Soviet psychophysiological research is that of sensory interaction. The field was surveyed by Ivan London in the November 1954 issue of the *Psychological Bulletin*. London's bibliography is quite complete, and his brief summary of the Russians' main findings is generally accurate. However, his doubts and disparagements of the findings are either unjustified or in need of definitive qualifications. He states, for instance, that there is "ready evidence of inadequate instrumentation" in the Russian experiments, but nowhere does he mention what the evidence is. The laboratories of Lazarev (36) and of Kravkov (37), the chief

interaction experimenters, appeared to me—and to others—quite well equipped in 1934, and recent diagrams and photographs of Soviet sensory apparatus surely reveal an advanced level of technical skill (38). Lazarev was a trained physicist as well as a physician, a physiologist, and a member of the Russian Academy of Sciences before the Revolution, while Kravkov, a corresponding member of the Academy, was the only psychologist to attain that rank, either before or after the revolution. Kravkov also had, as far as I could ascertain, special training in physics and engineering and is, incidentally, *the* psychologist mentioned in the *Large Soviet Encyclopedia*. If you doubt the work of these two, you might as well doubt everything about Soviet science.

London's criticisms of the Soviet experiments for "primitiveness in the statistical treatment of data" and poor reportage are largely well founded, but not basic with respect to the main validity of the findings. I recently subjected the data of 300 Russian experiments on salivary conditioning (the statistical level of which differs but little from that of experiments on sensory interaction) to tests of significance and found that in only 29 percent of the cases did the stated Russian results fail to reach the conventional 5-percent level of confidence. Likewise, my earlier and less extensive qualitative treatments of Russian data showed the behavioral findings to be *mostly* statistically reliable. Inadequate statistics is, as is known, a general characteristic of reports by physiologists, though the Russians are no doubt guiltier that the rest—a curious phenomenon in view of the advanced state of their mathematical statistics and electronic computing machines (the latter field was cited by E. Teller in a press statement as being among the few areas in which the Russians are superior to us).

Little need be said about reportage. Our practice of writing elegant reports, of often spending more time on writing up an experiment than on doing it, and of stressing strict editorial supervision of style and organization is, by all tokens, not shared by the Russians, and they may be right.

8. Finally, it might be worth while to mention Soviet practical animal training. To realize its highly advanced level, one would have to see the commercial film *Animal Theatre*, with its complete animal orchestras, animal trains, elephants ringing bells, dogs selling tickets, chickens punching the tickets, flustered rabbits missing the train, cat conductors, and the like (39). Animal training is, in

the Soviet Union, as a rule under the supervision of leading scientists; their animal space training is, for instance, according to the *New York Times,* under the direction of Vladimir Chernigovsky, whom I recognize as the head of the Laboratory of Receptor Physiology of the Pavlov Institute of Physiology and as an outstanding student of interoception and interoceptive conditioning. And, incidentally, the training is carried on in operant or reward fashion, which, of course, the Russians simply call conditioning (40). "Conditioning reflexes and patience is all you need" says one of their animal-film commentators.

PSYCHOLOGY: IN SEARCH OF A SYNTHESIS
WITH MARXISM-LENINISM

Turning now to the development of psychology proper in the Soviet Union, we are confronted with a totally different picture—with few achievements and lots of trials, woes, and tribulations. Unlike Soviet psychophysiology, Soviet psychology has been in its very core Communist-constricted all the way along, the degree of constriction being a monotonic function of the degree of Stalinism, and having lessened only in the last three or four years. And unlike the steady curve of research and thought production of Soviet psychophysiology, the curve of production of Soviet psychology has been spotty, at times quite scanty, and at other times practically "nilly." And surely the course of underlying systematics of Soviet psychology has, unlike that of Soviet psychophysiology, been very uneven, very nonautochthonous, typically tortuously zigzagging, and not uncommonly paroxysmally self-destroying.

I shall divide the Communist constriction into three periods: 1917 to 1930, 1930 to 1936, 1936 to the present. The constriction that existed between 1917 and 1930 might be called self-constriction. There is no evidence that the Communist party or state actually told psychologists what to think or do or what not to think or do during that period. It was the psychologists themselves who tried very hard to accommodate their views and work to Communist thinking and to the objectives of the Soviet state. And since Communist thinkers —Marx, Engels, and Lenin—had few, if any, specific thoughts on systematic psychology, and since the objectives of the state were also more or less seesawing in the '20's, there was an almost free-for-all fight among the psychologists for the final common path or final

Communist path: Which psychology should become the Marxian psychology? (Of course the idea of possibly letting more than one flower bloom never occurred to their minds, I suppose. Or did it?)

The constriction of the period between 1930 and 1936 I would designate as Communist-psychologist constriction or interference. It begins with the Communist cell of the Moscow Psychological Institute initiating a series of discussions of the basic premises for a Marxian psychology, primarily a criticism of the then-established Kornilov reactology. What happened was that Lenin's *Philosophical Notes* were published in 1929 and some treasured commandments of dos and don'ts for psychology were presumably disinterred; hence there followed an era of self- and other chastisement, name-callings, accusations, imprecations, recriminations, and related such and sundry niceties. The periodicals *Psikhologiya, Pedalogiya, Psikhotekhnika,* and *Psikhonevrologiya* of the period teem, as it were, with Gaston-Alphonse compliments of mechanistic, idealistic, biologistic, sociologistic, and fatalistic geneticism, fatalistic environmentalism, abstractionistic functionalism, and so on and on.

Finally, the period of mere words passed and the period of real action and full-powered Communist control was ushered in—the purge of pedology, psychotechnics, and mental testings, in 1936. And this control continued unabated—at times augmented—during Stalin's lifetime, relented somewhat after his death, but has by no means disappeared even now, the course of the control following indeed in all respects the course of Communist control and "partyization" of related intellectual endeavors. Why should psychology be different?

SYSTEMATIC VIEWS: REFLEXOLOGY

On the other hand, with respect to systematic views, four periods seem to stand out in the Soviet era: 1917 to 1923, the "reflexological" period (41); 1923 to 1931, the "reactological" one (42); 1931 to 1950, which I shall call "unanchored cognition" (43); and 1950 to the present, "anchored cognition" (44). The reflexological period is the one in which Bekhterev's reflexology, coupled with American behaviorism, came pretty close to becoming the official Soviet psychology. Pavlov's experiments and views were used in the enterprise, but Bekhterev and his disciples were the moving spirits,

Pavlov himself being indeed not at all involved. True, Pavlov became interested during the revolution in experimental neurosis, the concept of sleep as inhibition, and psychopathology in general. But these interests were, I presume, results of accidental circumstances and not of ideological influences. Pavlov could not take, in 1918, his summer vacation in the country, he did not want to experiment during the summer (he never did), so he decided to spend two months working in a clinic, just about the time when the semistarved condition of his dogs made them lethargic and demented and neurotic—and supplied Pavlov with new ideas and pursuits.

On the other hand, Bekhterev set out, right after the revolution, to inweave his reflexology into the Soviet system. He published a monograph on *Psychology, Reflexology, and Marxism* and an article, with Dubrovsky, on "Reflexology and dialectical materialism" (45), trying to show that reflexology is the proper Marxian and dialectical psychology. He became the editor of a periodical, *Problems of Studying and Training Personality* (*Problemy Izucheniya i Vospitaniya Lichnosti*), in 1919, and set up in his Brain Institute divisions of genetic reflexology, pathological reflexology, collective reflexology, pedagogical reflexology, and "what-not" reflexology. His associate Sorokhtin developed theories on associative sex tensions to replace Freudianism (46), and he and his associate Polonsky experimented with mutative or emergent characteristics of associative reflexes (47), presumably as substitutes for *Gestalt* principles. The reflexologists were very active in research and, in their own way, very fruitful in hypotheses. Had they continued unhampered, they no doubt would have made significant contributions and probably would have developed a psychology not very different from what some of our behaviorists would like to have. But the school was declared too mechanistic for Communist philosophy and slowly passed out of existence.

REACTOLOGY

Kornilov's reactology was a school of psychology that let the physiologists study the reflex while keeping to itself the study of voluntary reactions or voluntary behavior. Its methodology was primarily objective, but it did not completely disdain introspections—particularly introspection of the Würzburg variety—as a method of preliminary private survey. The school also contained a principle of *wholeness*—that total behavior dominates individual reaction behavior and social behavior dominates individual behavior—and a principle of *socioeconomic prepotency*—that, while the form of reactions may be determined biologically, their content is social, specifically economic, and man in general is a variate or function of a particular economic class. The school was certainly wider in scope than reflexology and no less experimental and, if permitted to exist, would no doubt have been of considerable significance. [A good example of a reactological approach to psychology is Luria's studies of affective reactions (48). Both Luria and Vygotsky (49) were students of Kornilov (50), though they later founded a school of their own.] But, as already indicated, reactology, like reflexology, was declared undialectical and inadequately Marxist-Leninist, in 1931, and its fate, too, was, naturally, thereby sealed. The charges were: Man as a mere reacting organism is too passive a concept for Leninist activism; reactology leads to psychophysical parallelism on the one hand and to epiphenomenalism on the other, either of which is at variance with dialectical materialism; and, in simpler terms, reactology fails to accord consciousness its directing, controlling role in transforming man, society, and nature (51).

UNANCHORED COGNITION

Whatever it had been, from there on Soviet psychology became what we might call a cognitive psychology. However, it came to be a very special kind of cognitivism, rejecting as it did Gestalt psychology, phenomenology, functionalism, psychoanalysis, the Würzburg school, and, indeed, whatever cognitivists had worked at. What it most resembled was a very naive, common-sense 18th- and 19th-century-vintage cognitivism, bordering on scholasticism, and it is for this reason that I called it "unanchored." Man is controlled by his goals, wills, purposes, conscious needs, thoughts, duties, and so on, but these categories are in no way empirically delineated, measured, or even adequately described. One student of Soviet psychology (52) calls this period "the New Man in Soviet Psychology" and stresses its rational aspects. But it is really an old-man, or, better, a new old-man, period—the old rational "faculty psychology" of the German Christian Wolff (whose book *Rational Psychology* appeared in 1734) Marxistically peppered. The acid test of productivity reveals an extreme sterility, a near absence of any significant psychological research and any specific psychological thought between 1936 and 1950, and present-day Soviet historical surveys and bibliographies reflect a glaring hiatus in psychological publications of that period. Perhaps, this will demonstrate to our own extreme cognitionists that, to succeed, a cognitive approach in psychology must be tied to something empirical and isolably concretizable—must reach beyond its own circularity.

ANCHORED COGNITION

I designated the current (since 1950) systematic position of Soviet psychology as one of "anchored cognition." By this I mean that, while present-day Soviet psychologists continue to accord supraphysiological status to traditional psychological cognitive categories, they nonetheless insist that these categories are wholly unviable—indeed hopelessly sterile and reactionary—if there is no study and understanding of their material basis, Pavlovian physiology. Thinking and imagination are thus, for instance, tied to Pavlov's concept of language as a "second-signal system," and perception is tied to Pavlov's investigatory or "what-is-it" reflexes. The tie-up does not represent, as is known, a natural evolution of theoretical-experimental views but has come about as a rather forced affair. From 28 June to 4 July, 1950, the Soviet Academy of Sciences met jointly with the Soviet Academy of Medical Sciences and resolved "that psychology, psychiatry and a number of related fields be reconstructed on the basis of Pavlov's teachings" (53).

Just what this forced marriage of Pavlovian physiology and cognitive psychology will lead to it is as yet, perhaps, too soon to gauge. So far, however, the benefits seem to be only unilateral, benefiting physiology or psychophysiology but not psychology or cognitive psychology. After a few years of trying, Soviet psychologists are beginning to contribute significantly to such areas as verbal conditioning and physicalistic studies of perception (54), but, except for formal lip service, they do not seem to manage to relate their contributions, and the contributions of their physiologists, systematically to key problems of cognitive controls. The task is of course generally difficult. But in the case of Soviet psychologists there is the additional handicap of needing cognitive formulations that counter traditional and "bourgeois" equivalents. As already indicated and as might be suspected, in Soviet ideology cognitive psychology (not unlike literature, art, philosophy, and the social sciences) is much more class-construed and class-angled than are psychophysiology, physics, and engineering. Soviet psychology must constantly prove its Marxist-Leninist nature, whereas Soviet psychophysiology need not do so—at least not to the same degree—its very advancement being assumedly in itself the right unfolding of the Soviet physicalistic (or materialistic) world view. There is thus much more freedom for research and thought in the latter discipline than in the former, and even in the Soviet Union students and scientists are drawn to freedom. In fine, the incomparably greater progress of Soviet psychophysiology as compared with Soviet psychology is not just a matter of differences in subject matter and of the Pavlovian traditions but also (and perhaps more so) of the different relations of the two to the Soviet state and philosophy.

IDEOLOGICAL CORRELATES

Viewed differently, one might say that, while Soviet psychophysiology is a "learn from" area, Soviet psychology is, so far, mostly one of "learn about" (that is, we may learn from Soviet psychology more about the Soviets than about psychology); or that, while Soviet psychophysiology may provide us with knowledge, Soviet psychology furnishes us mostly with only a "sociology of knowledge." One must avoid, however, temptingly facile generalization about the relation of general Soviet ideology to specific works and views in psychology without considering psychology's autochthonous development and its basis of psychophysiology—such generalization, for example, as the suggestion that Soviet psychologists had not been interested in the "law of effect" because the "law of effect" means "tension reduction" and "tension reduction" is too passive a concept for Soviet activism (55). Obviously, the "law of effect" may also mean "reward-getting" or "pleasure-seeking" and thus may be a very active concept. The simpler, and historically and systematically truer, explanation is the fact that Pavlov's associationism is not a "law of effect" type. Neither is the associationism of Guthrie or Tolman, whose views we don't tie up, I hope, to their ideology or politics.

In fact, the very adoption, in the Soviet Union, of a particular school of psychology may well be based on other than an intrinsic relationship to Marxian ideology or Soviet objectives. Psychologists in East Germany, under the leadership of Kurt Gottschaldt, are at the present time mostly *Gestalt*-oriented, and one of them, Hans Hibsch, argues in a recent Russian periodical that the concepts of *Gestalt* and *Ordnung* are Marxian and dialectical (56). Yet East Germany is otherwise very much in the orbit of orthodox communism. Again, it is known that Leon Trotsky had in the early 20's advocated the adoption of psychoanalysis, indeed a synthesis of Pavlov and Freud. In picturesque language, Trotsky is quoted by Shemyakim and Gershonovich to have said: "In the well of knowledge, Pavlov sits at the bottom of the well minutely probing its contents and topography, whereas Freud uncovers the same well's contents and topography by penetratingly gazing from the top" (57)—and I might add that the Marxist-Leninists of Israel are deeply involved in Freud-Marx-and-Lenin syntheses (58). There is no doubt that the chief reason for the dominance of reflexology in the Soviet Union of the early '20's, and for the resurgence of Pavlovianism in 1950, is the fact that Pavlov and Bekhterev were Russians. It could have been otherwise. (A lot of things could have been otherwise in the Soviet Union: It could have been Beria or Molotov instead of Malenkov, or Malenkov or Zhukov instead of Khrushchev, and even Trotsky instead of Stalin.) Of course, when "thiswise" is adopted, "otherwise" gets condemned and "thiswise" gets coordinated; hence, Gestalt psychology is probably not likely to hold out long even in East Germany. Pavlovianism has now already become the official psychology of Czechoslovakia, of the Balkan countries, and, to a considerable extent, also of China and Poland (59). The iron curtain brooks no unclosured loopholes in its *Gestalt*.

BEHAVIORAL SCIENCES IN THE U.S.S.R. AND THE U.S.

Permit me now to end this long article by a short word on the relative status of behavioral sciences and of scientific knowledge of behavioral control in the Soviet Union and in this country, with particular reference to the recent statement in the press by a group of behavioral scientists that the behavioral sciences in the Soviet Union are Communist-constricted and lagging behind. As I have pointed out, this is surely true with respect to psychology proper, and it is even truer—much truer—with respect to several social behavioral sciences. But it is not true—not at all true—for Soviet psychophysiology, which has kept up a steady record of significant achievements and a steady and consistent non-Communist—rather, supra-Communist, supra-everything—wholly empirical point of view and orientation. And it is this psychophysiology which is— most of you may agree—the scientific core of the behavioral sciences, and which, with its drug effects, its interoceptive and verbal conditioning, its neurology, pathology, and pharmacology of learning, may hold within itself the possibilities of real breakthroughs in the scientific control of human thought and action. So, it is sad and disconcerting to have to state that American psychologists and behavioral scientists know so little about Soviet psychophysiology, know indeed less—much less—than American physicists know about Soviet physics (60). And then there is also the consideration that, in general, the Soviets possess a readier and more responsive machinery for transforming behavioral knowledge into behavioral applications; that they control their applied psychologists and behavioral scientists more completely than we do, or want to do, ours, not letting them, shall we say, become too "diluted" by popular client-orientation; and that, while they may suffer from a too-orthodox theoretical rigidity, we, on the other hand, may suffer from a too heterodox theoretical fragmentation and individual-system aggrandizement. The situation as a whole thus contains elements of concern and calls for more knowledge and work; greater familiarity with, and duplication and verification of, the Russian work; and less complacency and ethnocentricity. The need to catch on, catch up, and surpass in vital areas of psychophysiology and the control of men may not be very different from the related requisite in physics and the control of missiles.

SUMMARY

Pavlov's experiments, begun long before the revolution, have always been generously supported by the Soviet state. However, their far-reaching ontological and methodological implication gained an official and commanding position to Soviet biomedical and psychosocial (as distinct from socioeconomic) sciences only in 1950 with the Resolution of the 28 June–4 July Joint Pavlovian Session of the Soviet Academy of Sciences and Academy of Medical Sciences. In the biomedical sciences, present-day Soviet Pavlovianism may best be conceived of as (i) a doctrine of *nervism* (a Russian term)—the ubiquity of neural control of bodily reactions (neural, neurosomatic, neurovisceral, and neurohumoral) and (ii) a doctrine of what might be called *concomitantism* (my term)—the ready and radical modification of these reactions by concomitant reactions; or, viewed more generally and somewhat differently, as (iii) a far-reaching *physicalistic psychosomaticism* or, rather, a *neuroviscerosomaticism*. Psychophysiology—or higher nervous activity—is the key discipline here. With scores of research institutes, it is indeed a very well-established, wide-scoped, and far-advanced science that, in both present achievements and future capabilities, is a challenge to American and Western equivalents.

On the other hand, in the psychosocial sciences and the key discipline of psychology proper, unmitigated Pavlovian physicalism and objectivism is met head on by (i) the unbending postulate of dialectical materialism of "the specific emergent efficacy of consciousness and subjective conscious categories" as well as by (ii) the simple consideration that a consistent Pavlovianism is a fully autarchic psychology and needs no other science of psychology on top of it. A large portion of current Soviet psychological theory in psychology proper is thus primarily a textual and exegetic collation and conciliation of the views of Pavlov with those of Marx, Engels, and Lenin (until recently and, to some extent even now, also of Stalin), just as most current Soviet psychological experimentation in psychology proper is primarily a duplication of what Soviet psychophysiology could do as well, if not better. Moreover, there is the long-standing drastic ban on intelligence testing, psychoanalysis, Gestalt psychology, and other to-be-shunned "bourgeois-psychological" thought-and-practice systems, so that, in all, psychology proper is a much constricted and, per se, more ancilliary than basic discipline of Soviet empirical research—a state of affairs plainly reflected in the fact that the number of its research institutes and publications (as well as the number of psychologists proper) is but a small fraction of the number in psychophysiology. Yet, in evaluating our efforts in the area vis-à-vis those of the Soviets, we must, obviously, take full account of both disciplines, Soviet psychophysiology being in all respects a psychology in American terms (61). Indeed, it is Soviet psychophysiology, and not Soviet psychology proper, that is the homolog not only of American behavioristics but also, to a large extent, of all American experimental psychology.

REFERENCES

1. A. A. Smirnov, *Voprosy Psikhol.* **3**, No. 5, 9 (1957).
2. *Materials of the Conference on Psychology* (Akad. Pedagog. Nauk S.S.S.R., Moscow, 1957).
3. G. Razran, *Psychol. Bull.* **54**, 1 (1958). Non-Russian readers may gain some knowledge of current Soviet psychophysiology from (i) the current English translations of the *Fiziol. Zhur. S.S.S.R.* and the *Zhur. Eksptl. Biol. i Med.*, (ii) the German edition (in East Germany) of the *Pavlov Journal of Higher Nervous Activity* (*Pawlow-Zeitung der höheren Nerventätigkeit*), (iii) the "Abstracts of Soviet medicine" published by *Excerpta Medica*, and (iv) the four mimeographed volumes of translated "Selected Russian Articles on CNS and Behavior" available in the National Library of Medicine, Washington 25, D.C., as well as from transactions of recent international congresses of physiology, electrophysiology, neurology, psychology, and the like.
4. ———, *Science* **126**, 1107 (1957).
5. *Scientific Session on the Problems of the Physiological Teachings of Academician I. P. Pavlov. 28 June–4 July 1950* (Akad. Nauk S.S.S.R., Moscow, 1950).
6. I. P. Pavlov, *Complete Works* (Akad. Nauk S.S.S.R., Moscow, 1951), vols. 1–5; *Pavlov's Wednesday Seminars* (Akad. Nauk S.S.S.R., Moscow, 1949), vols. 1–3; *Pavlov's Clinical Wednesday Seminars* (Akad. Nauk S.S.S.R., 1954), vols. 1 and 2.
7. V. A. Negovsky et al., *Zhur. Vysshey Nervnoy Deyatel'nosti im. I. P. Pavlova* **6**, 584 (1956). (As a rule, only one Russian reference to a topic will be given.)
8. I. S. Aleksandrov, *Arkh. Biol. Nauk* **32**, 292 (1932).
9. G. Razran, *Psychol. Bull.* **54**, 1 (1951).
10. F. P. Mayorov, *Arkh. Biol. Nauk* **38**, 223 (1935).
11. A. M. Pavlova, *Trudy Fiziol. Lab. Pavlova* **7**, 781 (1937); K. M. Petrova, *ibid.* **7**, 231 (1937).
12. V. M. Arkhangelsky, *Russ. Fiziol. Zhur.* **14**, 255 (1931).
13. V. Y. Katinas, *Zhur. Vysshey Nervnoy Deyatel'nosti im. I. P. Pavlova* **4**, 376 (1954).
14. E. Asratyan, *Fiziol. Zhur. S.S.S.R.* **18**, 739 (1935); G. T. Sakhiulina, *Zhur. Vysshey Nervnoy Deyatel'nosti im. I. P. Pavlova* **5**, 76 (1955).
15. E. I. Gekker, *Kazan Med. Zhur.* **27**, 487 (1931).
16. D. I. Soloveychik, *Trudy Fiziol. Lab. Pavlova* **4**, 13 (1930).
17. Nestruyeva, *Zhur. Vysshey Nervnoy Deyatel'nosti im. I. P. Pavlova* **8**, 272 (1958); V. K. Krasusky, *ibid.* **7**, 575 (1957).
18. V. V. Usachev, *ibid.* **6**, 555 (1956).
19. P. M. Pratusevich and K. M. Shteyngart, *ibid.* **7**, 666 (1957); A. E. Alekseyeva and G. P. Shishulina, *ibid.* **7**, 381 (1957).

20. G. GRINBERG, *Zhur. Eksptl. Med.* **3**, 38 (1928).
21. *Trudy Inst. Vysshey Nervnoy Deyatel'nosti im. I. P. Pavlova, Ser. Fiziol.* (1955).
22. M. Y. RABINOVICH, *Zhur. Vysshey Nervnoy Deyatel'nosti im. I. P. Pavlova* **8**, 148 (1958).
23. *Fiziol. Zhur. S.S.S.R.* **43**, 1021 (1957).
24. *Zhur. Vysshey Nervnoy Deyatel'nosti im. I. P. Pavlova* **7**, 868 (1957).
25. A. GASTAUT *et al., ibid.* **7**, 185 (1957).
26. J. OLDS AND P. MILNER, *J. Comp. and Physiol. Psychol.* **47**, 419 (1954).
27. J. M. R. DELGADO, W. W. ROBERTS, N. E. MILLER, *Am. J. Physiol.* **179**, 587 (1954).
28. *Fiziol. Zhur. S.S.S.R.* **43**, 1072 (1957).
29. *Materials of the Conference on Psychology* (Akad. Pedagog. Nauk S.S.S.R., Moscow, 1957), p. 152.
30. *Op. cit.*, p. 370.
31. V. D. VOLKOVA, *Zhur. Vysshey Nervnoy Deyatel'nosti im. I. P. Pavlova* **7**, 525 (1957).
32. *Voprosy Fiziologii Interotseptsii* (Akad. Nauk S.S.S.R., Moscow, 1952); E. S. AYRAPETYANTS, *Higher Nervous Activity and the Receptors of the Internal Organs* (Akad. Nauk S.S.S.R., Moscow, 1952); I. A. BULYGIN, *Trudy Inst. Fiziol. S.S.S.R.*, **1**, 7 (1956).
33. K. M. BYKOV, *The Cerebral Cortex and the Internal Organs* (Chemical Publishing Co., New York, 1957).
34. L. G. VORONIN, *Zhur. Vysshey Nervnoy Deyatel'nosti im. I. P. Pavlova* **7**, 831 (1957); I. A. BARYSHKIN, *Fiziol. Zhur. S.S.S.R.* **43**, 1045 (1957).
35. N. I. KASATKIN, *Conditioned Reflexes in Early Human Ontogeny* (Akad. Med. Nauk, Moscow, 1948); *Zhur. Vysshey Nervnoy Deyatel'nosti im. I. P. Pavlova* **7**, 805 (1957).
36. P. P. LAZAREV, *Research on Adaptation* (Akad. Nauk S.S.S.R., Moscow, 1947).
37. S. V. KRAVKOV, *The Eye and Its Functions* (Akad. Nauk S.S.S.R., Moscow, ed. 4, 1950).
38. *Problems of Physiological Optics* (Akad. Nauk S.S.S.R., Moscow), vol. 11.
39. I am describing the film from memory, and some details about which animals did what may be somewhat inexact. There is, however, no doubt in my mind that each of the animals mentioned performed one or another of the enumerated acts.
40. M. A. GERD, in *Materialy Soveschaniya po Psikhologii* (Akad. Pedagog. Nauk S.S.S.R., Moscow, 1950), pp. 683–89.
41. V. M. BEKHTEREV, *Ob'yektivnaya Psikhologiya* (Soikin, St. Petersburg, 1907); *Objektive Psychologie oder Psychoreflexologie* (Teubner, Leipzig and Berlin, 1913); *General Principles of Human Reflexology* (GIZ, Moscow, 1917).

42. K. N. KORNILOV, *The Study of Man's Reactions or Reactology* (GIZ, Moscow, 1922); *Textbook of Psychology from the Standpoint of Dialectical Materialism* (GIZ, Moscow, 1926).
43. ——— *et al.*, Eds., *Psikhologiya* (GIZ, Moscow, 1948).
44. A. A. SMIRNOV *et al.*, Eds., *Psikhologiya* (GIZ, Moscow, 1956).
45. V. M. BEKHTEREV, *Psychology, Reflexology, and Marxism* (GIZ, Leningrad, 1925); V. M. BEKHTEREV and A. V. DUBROVSKY, *Pod. Znam. Marksizma*, No. 7–8, **85** (1926).
46. G. N. SOROKHTIN, *Voprosy Izuch i. Vospit Lichnosti* 6, No. 1–2, **64** (1927).
47. V. M. BEKHTEREV AND Y. A. POLONSKY, *ibid.* 5, No. 2–3, **115** (1926).
48. A. R. LURIA, *The Nature of Human Conflicts* (Liveright, New York, 1932).
49. L. S. VYGOTSKY, *Thought and Speech* (GIZ, Moscow, 1934).
50. KORNILOV died 10 July 1957. An obituary article about him and his school appeared in *Science* [128, **74** (1958)], and his portrait appeared in *Contemporary Psychology* [**3**, 85 (1958)].
51. G. RAZRAN, *Science* 128, **74** (1958).
52. R. A. BAUER, *The New Man in Soviet Psychology* (Harvard Univ. Press, Cambridge, Mass., 1952).
53. G. RAZRAN, *Science* **126,** 1101 (1957).
54. ———, *Contemporary Psychol.* 3, 85 (1958).
55. R. BAUER, *ibid.*, p. 165.
56. H. HIBSCH, *Voprosy Psikhol.* 3, No. 3, 131 (1957).
57. F. SHEMYAKIM and L. GERSHONOVICH, *Psikhologiya.* No. 1–2, 3 (1932).
58. Y. GOTTHELF, *Freud's Theory and Marxism* (in Hebrew) (Hamerkaz L'Tarbut Mitkademet, Tel Aviv, 1953); *Ofakim* (Hebrew periodical), 7–10 (1953–56).
59. G. RAZRAN, *Am. Psychologist* 13, 177 (1958).
60. Only 28 percent of the reports of Russian experiments on salivary conditioning have been abstracted in *Psychol. Abstr.* [G. RAZRAN, *Psychol. Bull.* **43,** 19 (1957)]. In 1929, *Psychol. Abstr.* contained 7 percent Russian abstracts: in 1954, 0.5 percent [C. M. LOUTTIT, *Am. Psychologist* **12,** 20 (1957)].
61. Reported Soviet successes in education should be attributed, however, to their special educational practices and to special sociohistorical factors, rather than to a possession of special psychological or psychophysiological knowledge. Whatever Soviet special knowledge in the area is, it is certainly, by all tokens, as yet in a prodromal-basic and not in an applied-conclusive state. The same holds for Soviet successes with respect to propaganda and so-called "brainwashing."

7

Operant Behavior

B. F. Skinner

In writing this essay, Skinner appears to have had two major objectives:
(1) to maintain that the concept of "reinforcement" is more valuable to the
researcher and to the theoretician than is the concept of "purpose," and
(2) to explain why it is that rate of responding, as a key attribute of behavior, has yet to gain universal acceptance among psychologists.

Skinner believes that Thorndike's Law of Effect eliminated the need for
"purpose" as an explanatory device, one vital to an adequate understanding
of behavior. He feels so because of Thorndike's assumption that the consequences of reinforcement left their mark in one way or another upon the
organism. The sources of previously reinforced, *current* behavior could
therefore be anchored to the past (as called for by determinism), and not to
the future (as "purpose" or "intent" would demand). The reader should compare this view of "purpose" with that offered by Rosenblueth, Wiener, and
Bigelow in Chapter 5, particularly in the last three paragraphs of their article.

The following are among the principal reasons given by Skinner in
accounting for what he senses to be resistance among psychologists toward
acceptance of rate as a measure of behavior: (1) rate disregards traditional
assumptions concerning the importance to learning theory of hypothecated
inner processes; (2) it places emphasis upon individual, as opposed to
average, data; and (3) it examines the behavior of human subjects without
the customary emphasis upon verbal reports.

We are interested in the behavior of an organism because of its
effects on the environment. (One effect on the social environment is,
of course, the arousal of our interest.) Some effects seem to throw
light on the behavior which produces them, but their explanatory
role has been clouded by the fact that they follow the behavior and,
therefore, raise the specter of teleology.

From *American Psychologist* (1963), Vol. 18, pp. 503–515; copyright 1963 by the American Psychological Association, and reproduced by permission. A chapter in Werner Honig
(Ed.), *Operant behavior and psychology.* New York: Appleton-Century-Crofts, 1966.

An attempt has been made to solve the problem by creating a contemporary surrogate of a given effect. A quality or property of purpose is assigned to behavior to bring "what the organism is behaving for" into the effective present, or the organism is said to behave in a given way because it intends to achieve, or expects to have, a given effect, or its behavior is characterized as possessing utility to the extent that it maximizes or minimizes certain effects. The teleological problem is, of course, not solved until we have answered certain questions: What gives an action its purpose, what leads an organism to expect to have an effect, how is utility represented in behavior?

The answers to such questions are eventually to be found in past instances in which similar behavior has been effective. The original problem can be solved directly in the same way. Thorndike's Law of Effect was a step in that direction: The approximately simultaneous occurrence of a response and certain environmental events (usually generated by it) changes the responding organism, increasing the probability that responses of the same sort will occur again. The response itself has passed into history and is not altered.

By emphasizing a change in the organism, Thorndike's principle made it possible to include the effects of action among the causes of future action without using concepts like purpose, intention, expectancy, or utility. Up to that time, the only demonstrable causes of behavior had been antecedent stimuli. The range of the eliciting stimulus was later to be extended by Pavlovian conditioning, and the concept could be broadened to include the releasers of the ethologists, but only a small part of behavior can be predicted or controlled simply by identifying or manipulating stimuli. The Law of Effect added an important new class of variables of which behavior could be shown to be a function.

Thorndike's solution was probably suggested by Darwin's treatment of phylogenetic purpose. Before Darwin, the purpose of a well developed eye might have been said to be to permit the organism to see better. The principle of natural selection moved "seeing better" from the future into the past: Organisms with well developed eyes were descended from those which had been able to see better and had therefore produced more descendants. Thorndike was closer to the principle of natural selection than the above statement of his law. He did not need to say that a response which had been followed by a certain kind of consequence was more likely to occur again but simply that it was not less likely. It eventually held the field because responses which failed to have such effects tended, like less favored species, to disappear.

Thorndike was concerned with how animals solved problems rather than with the concept of purpose, and his Law of Effect did not end purposive formulations. The devices used for the study of behavior during the next quarter of a century continued to emphasize an intentional relation between behavior and its consequences. The relation was represented spatially. In mazes, runways, and open fields, for example, organisms ran *toward* their goals. In discrimination apparatuses they chose the door which led *to* food. They escaped *from* the dangerous side of shuttle boxes or pulled *away from* sources of dangerous stimulation. They drew objects *toward* them with rakes or strings. The experimenter could see the purpose of an action in the spatial relation of the organism and the objects toward which it was moving or from which it was receding. It was even asserted that the organism itself should see a purposive relationship in some such form in order to behave effectively. Köhler, for example, criticized Thorndike on just this score.

The spatial representation of purpose, expectancy, or intention obscured one of the most important features of the relation emphasized by Thorndike. The process he identified remained unexplored for 30 years, and during that time was confused with rote habit formation and with various formulations of Pavlovian conditioning. In the late 1920s, however, the consequences of behavior began to be studied with devices of another sort. Pavlov's technique for the study of conditioned reflexes contributed to their development, even though Pavlov himself was not primarily concerned with consequences as such. In his basic studies, indeed, it might be said that the organism did not receive food *for* doing anything; the salivation elicited by the conditioned stimulus did not produce the food which followed. The experimental design, however, called for food to be introduced at a given moment automatically. Once the procedure was familiar, it was no great step to arrange devices in which a response "produced" food in a similar fashion. Ivanov-Smolensky (1927), one of Pavlov's associates, studied an experimental arrangement, close to Thorndike, in which a child squeezed a rubber bulb and delivered candy into his mouth. Miller and Konorski (1928) devised an apparatus in which a shock to the foot of a dog elicited flexion of the leg, and the resulting movement was followed by the presentation of food; the leg eventually flexed even when the foot was not shocked. In America D. K. Adams (1929) used a similar arrangement with cats, and in England Grindley (1932) with guinea pigs. The essential features may be seen in an apparatus in which depression of a lever operates a food dispenser (Skinner, 1932). Pressing a lever is not a natural or unconditioned way of getting food. The response produces food only in the sense that food follows it—a Humean version of causality. Behavior is nevertheless altered. The consequences of action change the organism regardless of how or why they follow. The connection need not be functional or organic—as, indeed, it was not in Thorndike's experiment.

PRACTICAL ADVANTAGES

These early devices were not designed to eliminate spatial representations of purpose, but they all did so, and the fact had far-reaching consequences. Some of these were practical. The experimenter could choose a response which was conveniently recorded, or one which the organism could execute rapidly and without fatigue for long periods of time, or one which minimized the peculiarities of a species and thus furthered a comparison between species with respect to properties not primarily related to the topography of behavior. In particular, it was possible to choose a response which was relatively free of extraneous variables and not likely to be confused with responses elicited or evoked by them. When a shuttle box, for example, is used to study the effect of the postponement or termination of a shock, the behavior affected (running or jumping from one side to the other) is topographically similar to unconditioned responses to the shock, such as startle or jumping into the air, and to more elaborate patterns of escape from a space in which shocks have been received. It may also resemble response of both these sorts conditioned in the Pavlovian manner and elicited by the warning stimuli. The inevitable confusion can be avoided by making the postponement or termination of a shock contingent on an arbitrary response, such as pressing a lever in the Sidman arrangement, which is not otherwise related to the variables at issue (Sidman, 1953).

A response which is only temporally related to its consequences could also be conveniently studied with automatic equipment.

Instruments were developed which permitted the investigator to conduct many experiments simultaneously, particularly when unskilled technical help was available. It is true that automatic mazes and discrimination boxes had been or were soon to be built, but most modern programing and recording equipment can be traced to research on responses with arbitrarily arranged consequences for the very good reason that the conditions are easily instrumented. The availability of automatic equipment has helped to standardize experiments and has facilitated the study of relations between responses and consequences too complex to be arranged by hand or followed by eye.

Another practical result was terminological. The concept of the reflex made no reference to the consequences of a response. Reflexes were often obviously "adaptive," but this was primarily a phylogenetic effect. The term "operant" was introduced to distinguish between reflexes and responses operating directly on the environment (Skinner, 1937). The alternative term "instrumental" suggests the use of tools. To say that a rat "uses a lever to obtain food" has purposive overtones, and where nothing can be identified as an instrument, it is often said that the organism "uses a response" to gain an effect. For example, verbal behavior is interpreted as "the use of words," although the implication that words exist as things apart from behavior unnecessarily complicates an analysis (Skinner, 1957). Another change was from "reward" to "reinforcement." Reward suggests compensation *for* behaving in a given way, often in some sort of contractual arrangement. Reinforcement in its etymological sense designates simply the strengthening of a response. It refers to similar events in Pavlovian conditioning, where reward is inappropriate. These changes in terminology have not automatically eliminated purposive expressions (such as, "The pigeon was reinforced *for* pecking the key"), but a given instance can usually be rephrased. Comparable teleological expressions are common in other sciences, as Bernatowicz (1958) has pointed out.

RATE OF RESPONDING AS A DATUM

A more important result of studying an arbitrary connection between a response and its consequences, together with the simplified procedures which then become available, has been to emphasize rate of responding as a property of behavior. Earlier devices were almost always used to study responses from trial to trial, where rate of responding was controlled by the experimenter and hence obscured as a datum. When the organism can respond at any time, its rate of responding varies in many subtle ways over a wide range. Changes in rate comprise a vast and previously largely unsuspected subject matter. (The changes are made conspicuous with a cumulative recorder, the ubiquity of which in the study of operant behavior is no accident. In a cumulative record, rate and changes in rate are visible at a glance over substantial periods of time. The "on-line" record permits the experimenter to note changes as they occur and take appropriate steps.)

Rate of responding is important because it is especially relevant to the principal task of a scientific analysis. Behavior is often interesting because of what might be called its character. Animals court their mates, build living quarters, care for their young, forage for food, defend territories, and so on, in many fascinating ways. These are worth studying, but the inherent drama can divert attention from another task. Even when reduced to general principles, a narrative account of *how* animals behave must be supplemented by a consideration of *why*. What is required is an analysis of the conditions which govern the probability that a given response will occur at a given time. Rate of responding is by no means to be equated with probability of responding, as frequency theories of probability and comparable problems in physics have shown. Many investigators prefer to treat rate of responding as a datum in its own right. Eventually, however, the prediction and control of behavior call for an evaluation of the probability that a response will be emitted. The study of rate of responding is a step in that direction.

Rate of responding is one of those aspects of a subject matter which do not attract attention for their own sake and which undergo intensive study only when their usefulness as a dependent variable has been discovered. Other sciences have passed through comparable stages. The elements and compounds studied by the chemist also have fascinating characters—they exist in many colors, textures, and states of aggregation and undergo surprising transmutations when heated, dissolved, combined, and so on. These are the characteristics which naturally first attract attention. They were, for example, the principal concern of the alchemists. In contrast, the mere weight of a given quantity of a substance is of little interest in its own right. Yet it was only when the weights of substances entering into reactions were found to obey certain laws that chemistry moved into its modern phase. Combining weight became important because of what could be done with it. Rate of responding has emerged as a basic datum in a science of behavior for similar reasons—and, hopefully, with comparable results.

Rate of responding differs from the measures derived from earlier devices and procedures, such as the time required to complete a task or the effort expended or the number of errors made in doing so, and the two kinds of data have led to different conceptions of behavior as a scientific subject matter. We like to believe that basic processes are orderly, continuous, and significant, but the data obtained from mazes, memory drums, shuttle boxes, and so on, vary "noisily" from trial to trial and depend for their dimensions on particular tasks and apparatuses. Orderly and significant processes are therefore sought elsewhere—in some mental, physiological, or merely conceptual inner system which by its nature is neither directly observed in, nor accurately represented on any given occasion by, the performance of an organism. There is no comparable inner system in an operant analysis. Changes in rate of responding are directly observed, they have dimensions appropriate to a scientific formulation, and under skillful experimental control they show the uniformity expected of biological processes in general. Those accustomed to the older formulation have nevertheless found them difficult to accept as an alternative subject for analysis.

BEHAVIORAL PROCESSES

One difficulty is that changes in rate do not closely resemble the behavioral processes inferred from earlier measures. A few examples may be cited from the field of learning. By arranging a reinforcing consequence, we increase the rate at which a response occurs; by eliminating the consequence, we decrease the rate. These are the processes of operant conditioning and extinction. Topographical properties of the response depend on the contingencies. The force with which a lever is pressed, for example, is related to the force required to operate the food dispenser. An initial moderate force can be increased indefinitely, within physiological limits, by progressively requiring greater forces. A complex topography can be "shaped" with a series of changing contingencies, called a program, each stage of which evokes a response and also prepares the organism to respond at a later stage. A shaping program can be mechanically prescribed in advance, but the process is most easily demonstrated when the experimenter improvises contingencies as he goes.

The behaviors evoked by mazes, puzzle boxes, memory drums, and so on, are also shaped, but almost always without specific programing of contingencies. The organism is usually exposed at once to a set of *terminal* contingencies, for which it possesses no adequate behavior. Responses occur, however—the rat explores the maze, the subject guesses at the next nonsense syllable—and some of these may be reinforced in ways which lead at last to a terminal performance. What can we conclude from the series of stages through which this comes about?

Such data are usually plotted in so-called learning curves showing, let us say, the times required to complete a task or the number of errors made in doing so, by trials. These are facts and in some sense quantifiable. From such a curve we may predict within limits how another organism will behave in similar circumstances. But the shape of the curve tells us little or nothing about the processes of conditioning and extinction revealed in an operant analysis. It merely describes the rather crude overall effects of adventitious contingencies, and it often tells us more about the apparatus or procedure than about the organism.

Similar discrepancies appear in the analysis of stimuli. In so-called stimulus-response theories, a stimulus is broadly defined as something which customarily precedes a response—the eliciting stimulus in a conditioned reflex, the "cue" to more complex behavior, or even an internal "drive state." The term is little more than a synonym for cause, and various relations between cause and effect are usually not distinguished. The stimulus control of an operant, on the other hand, has been carefully analyzed. Although we can shape the topography of a response without identifying or manipulating any anterior stimulus, stimuli enter into a more complex type of contingency in which a response is reinforced in the presence of a stimulus and is therefore more likely to be emitted in its presence. The relations among the three terms in this contingency—stimulus, response, and reinforcement—comprise a substantial field for investigation.

One property of the control acquired by a stimulus when a response is reinforced in its presence is shown in the so-called stimulus generalization gradient. Hypothetical gradients in mental, neurological, or conceptual inner systems have been discussed for years, but thanks to the work of Guttman (1963) and his students, and others, behavioral gradients are now directly observed. A pigeon, reinforced when it pecks a circular key of a given color and size, will peck keys of other shapes, colors, or sizes at lower rates depending upon the differences in the properties. When the response is reinforced in the presence of one property and extinguished in the presence of others—the well-known process of discrimination—a very sensitive and powerful control is established. In a classroom demonstration a response is brought under the control of a red as against a green key. So long as the key is green, no response is made; when it turns red, the pigeon pecks it immediately. The power of the stimulus can be dramatically shown by changing from red to green just as the pigeon's beak moves toward the key. The pecking response will be interrupted in mid-air, even though stopping probably requires more energy than following through. Stimulus control can also be shaped by changing relevant stimuli in a program which leads the organism into subtle discriminations, often without "errors," as Terrace (1963) has recently shown. Very little of this is seen in traditional studies of sensory learning, however. In using a classical multiple-choice apparatus, for example, the organism is exposed at once to a set of terminal contingencies. Its progress toward an appropriate performance is represented in a curve showing, say, the number of errors made or the times required to reach a criterion, over a series of trials, but the dimensions of these measures are again arbitrary, and the behavior is obviously the product of shifting, largely adventitious contingencies.

Classical studies of learning have emphasized the process of *acquisition,* presumably because one can easily see that an organism is doing something new or is responding to a new stimulus, but reinforcement is also responsible for the fact that an organism goes on responding long after its behavior has been acquired. The fact has usually been attributed to motivational variables, but an experimental analysis has shown that various schedules of intermittent reinforcement are usually involved. The nature or quantity of reinforcement is often much less important than the schedule on which it is received. Programing is again important, for many schedules can take effect only when the organism has passed through intervening contingencies. To take a very simple example—an apparatus which reinforces every hundredth response will have no effect at all if 100 responses are never emitted, but by reinforcing every second, then every fifth, then every tenth response, and so on, waiting until the behavior is well developed at each stage, we can bring the organism under the control of the more demanding schedule. The pathological gambler and the dedicated scientist both show terminal behavior resulting from a special history of reinforcement on a related ("variable-ratio") schedule—a history which society attempts to prevent in the former case and encourage in the latter.

The history which brings a complex terminal schedule into control is not, of course, visible in the terminal performance. A scientist once borrowed an apparatus to demonstrate the use of a multiple fixed-interval fixed-ratio schedule in assessing the effects of certain drugs. When one of the pigeons lent with the apparatus was accidentally killed, he purchased another, put it into the apparatus, and was surprised to find that nothing happened. We make the same mistake when we attempt to explain conspicuous effects of reinforcement on human behavior by examining only *current* schedules.

Complex terminal contingencies involving multiple stimuli and responses, in sequential or concurrent arrangements, are often called problems. An organism is said to have solved such a problem when it comes under the control of the terminal contingencies. Its capacity to respond appropriately under such contingencies must, however, be distinguished from its capacity to reach them through a given series of intervening stages. Whether an organism can solve a problem in this sense is as much a question of the program through which it passes—and the skill of the programmer who constructed it—as of any so-called problem solving ability. Whether an organism can solve a problem without the help of a prepared program depends on the behavior initially available and the more or less accidental contingencies which follow from it. Apparent differences in problem solving ability among species or among organisms of different ages or other properties within a species must be interpreted accordingly. Solving a problem, like learning, is again often attributed to an inner system, although the supposed inner processes, like the facts they explain, are more complex. Those committed to sequestered faculties and thought processes are not likely to feel at home in an analysis of the behavior itself and may, therefore, find it inacceptable as an alternative enterprise.

STATISTICS

Another difficulty is methodological. Processes taking place in some inner system can usually be investigated only with "statistics." If learning is never accurately represented in one performance, performances must be averaged. If statements about the inner system cannot be directly confirmed, hypotheses must be set up, and theorems deduced and tested, following established practices in logic and scientific method. If some properties of the inner system are meaningful only with respect to larger sets of facts, a procedure such as factor analysis may be needed. It is not surprising that research on this pattern has come to be judged by the sophistication of its statistical and logical techniques. Confidence in an experiment is proportional to the number of subjects studied, an experiment is good only if properly "designed," and results are significant only at a level determined by special tests.

Much of this is lacking in the experimental analysis of behavior, where experiments are usually performed on a few subjects, curves representing behavioral processes are seldom averaged, the behavior attributed to complex mental activity is analyzed directly, and so on. The simpler procedure is possible because rate of responding and changes in rate can be directly observed, especially when represented in cumulative records. The effect is similar to increasing the resolving power of a microscope: A new subject matter is suddenly open to direct inspection. Statistical methods are unnecessary. When an organism is showing a stable or slowly changing performance, it is for most purposes idle to stop to evaluate the confidence with which the next stage can be predicted. When a variable is changed and the effect on performance observed, it is for most purposes idle to prove statistically that a change has indeed occurred. (It is sometimes said in such a case that the organism is "used as its own control," but the expression, borrowed from a basically different methodology, is potentially troublesome.) Much can be done in the study of behavior with methods of observation no more sophisticated than those available to Faraday, say, with his magnets, wires, and cells. Eventually the investigator may move on to peripheral areas where indirect methods become necessary, but until then he must forego the prestige which attaches to traditional statistical methods.

Some traditional uses must also be questioned. Learning curves remain inadequate no matter how smooth they are made by averaging cases. Statistical techniques may eliminate noise, but the dimensions are still faulty. A curve which enables us to predict the performance of another organism does not therefore represent a basic process. Moreover, curves which report changes in variables having satisfactory dimensions can often not be averaged. The idiosyncracies in a cumulative record do not necessarily show caprice on the part of the organism or faulty technique on the part of the experimenter. The complex system we call an organism has an elaborate and largely unknown history which endows it with a certain individuality. No two organisms embark upon an experiment in precisely the same condition nor are they affected in the same way by the contingencies in an experimental space. (Most contingencies would not be representative if they were precisely controlled, and in any case are effective only in combination with the behavior which the organism brings to the experiment.) Statistical techniques cannot eliminate this kind of individuality; they can only obscure and falsify it. An averaged curve seldom correctly represents any of the cases contributing to it (Sidman, 1960).

An analysis which recognizes the individuality of the organism is particularly valuable when contact is made with other disciplines such as neurology, psychopharmacology, and psychotherapy, where idiosyncratic sets of variables must also be considered. The rigor of the analysis is not necessarily threatened. Operant methods make their own use of Grand Numbers: Instead of studying 1,000 rats for 1 hour each, or 100 rats for 10 hours each, the investigator is likely to study 1 rat for 1,000 hours. The procedure is not only appropriate to an enterprise which recognizes individuality, it is at least equally efficient in its use of equipment and of the investigator's time and energy. The ultimate test of uniformity or reproducibility is not to be found in method but in the degree of control achieved, a test which the experimental analysis of behavior usually passes easily.

The study of operant behavior also seldom follows the "design of experiments" prescribed by statisticians. A prior design in which variables are distributed, for example, in a Latin square may be a severe handicap. When effects on behavior can be immediately observed, it is most efficient to explore relevant variables by manipulating them in an improvised and rapidly changing design. Similar practices have been responsible for the greater part of modern science. This is not, however, the tenor of R. A. Fisher's *Design of Experiments,* which, as Lancelot Hogben (1957) has said, gives the reader

> the impression that recourse to statistical methods is prerequisite to the design of experiments of any sort whatever. In that event, the whole creation of experimental scientists from Gilbert and Hooke to J. J. Thomson and Morgan has been groaning and travailing in fruitless pain together; and the biologist of today has nothing to learn from well-tried methods which have led to the spectacular advances of the several branches of experimental science during the last three centuries [p. 29].

Statistics, like logic and scientific methodology in general, emphasizes the verbal behavior of the scientist: How reliable are his measures, how significant are the differences he reports, how confident can we be that what he says is true? His nonverbal behavior is much less easily codified and analyzed. In such considerations, what the scientist *does* takes second place to what he *says.* Yet the a priori manipulation of variables, guided by directly observed effects, is superior to the a posteriori analysis of covariation in many ways. It leads more rapidly to prediction and control and to practical recombinations of variables in the study of complex cases. Eventually, of course, the experimenter must behave verbally. He must describe what he has done and what he has seen, and he must conduct his research with this obligation in mind. But a compulsive preoccupation with validity or significance may be inimical to other, equally important obligations.

A nonstatistical strategy may also be recommended for its effect on the behavior of the investigator, who is perhaps as strongly reinforced during a successful experiment as the organism he studies. The contingencies to which he is submitted largely determine whether he will continue in similar work. Statistical techniques often inject a destructive delay between the conduct of an experiment and the discovery of the significance of the data—a fatal violation of a fundamental principle of reinforcement. The exceptional zeal which has often been noted in students of operant behavior is possibly attributable to the immediacy of their results.

THE CIRCUMVENTION OF AN OPERANT ANALYSIS

By accepting changes in rate of responding as basic behavioral processes and by emphasizing environmental variables which can be manipulated with the help of automatic equipment, research on operant behavior has been greatly simplified. But it has not been made easy. Technical advances have been offset by the demand for increasing rigor, by the problems which arise in studying one organism at a time, and by the attack on more and more complex arrangements of interrelated operants. Behavior—human or other-wise—remains an extremely difficult subject matter. It is not surpris-ing that practices which seem to circumvent or simplify an operant analysis are common. In particular, verbal communication between subject and experimenter is widely used in lieu of the explicit arrangement of contingencies of reinforcement and the objective recording of behavior. The practice goes back to the study of mental life and is still favored by psychologists who formulate their subject matter in mental terms, but it survives as if it were a labor-saving device in many essentially behavioristic formulations.

The manipulation of independent variables appears to be cir-cumvented when, instead of exposing an organism to a set of contingencies, the contingencies are simply described in "instruc-tions." Instead of shaping a response, the subject is told to respond in a given way. A history of reinforcement or punishment is re-placed by a promise or threat: "Movement of the lever will some-times operate a coin dispenser" or ". . . deliver a shock to your leg." A schedule of positive or negative reinforcement is described rather than imposed: "Every response to the right lever postpones the shock but increases the number of responses to the left lever re-quired to operate the coin dispenser." Instead of bringing the behavior under the control of a stimulus, the subject is told to behave as if a discrimination had been established: "Start when the light goes on, stop when it goes off." Thus instructed, the subject is asked either to behave appropriately or to describe behavior he might emit under such circumstances. The scope of the verbal substitute can be estimated by considering how a nonverbal orga-nism, human or otherwise, could be similarly "instructed."

Descriptions of contingencies are, of course, often effective.

Hypothetical consequences are commonly used for practical purposes ("Will you do the job if I pay you $50?" or "How would you
feel about going if I told you that X would be there?"), and the
subject is worth studying. Verbal instruction may be defended
when the resulting behavior is not the primary object of interest; for
example, the experimenter may show a subject how to operate a
piece of equipment rather than shape his behavior through reinforcement so long as he is not concerned with the acquisition of the
response but with what happens to it later. Verbal communication is
not, however, a substitute for the arrangement and manipulation of
variables.

There is no reason why a description of contingencies of reinforcement should have the same effect as exposure to the contingencies. A subject can seldom accurately describe the way in which
he has actually been reinforced. Even when he has been trained to
identify a few simple contingencies, he cannot then describe a new
contingency, particularly when it is complex. We can scarcely expect him, therefore, to react appropriately to descriptions by the
experimenter. Moreover, the verbal contingencies between subject
and experimenter must be taken into account. Instructions must in
some way promise or threaten consequences not germane to the
experiment if the subject is to follow them.

The other major task in an operant analysis may seem to be
circumvented when, instead of recording behavior so that rate or
probability of response can be observed or inferred, the experimenter simply asks the subject to evaluate his tendency to respond
or to express his preference for responding in one way rather than
another. The subject may do so by describing his "intentions" or
"plans" or by reporting "expectations" regarding the consequences
of an action. Such behavior may be worth investigating, but it is not
a substitute for the behavior observed in an operant analysis. Only
in the simplest cases can a person correctly describe his ongoing
behavior. The difficulty is not linguistic, for he may be given an
operandum and permitted to "model" the behavior—for example, to
generate a cumulative record. It is practically impossible to construct a curve closely resembling the curve one would generate if
actually exposed to a specified set of contingencies, or even a curve
one has already generated when so exposed. Changes in rate of
responding are not easy to describe. They necessarily take place in
time, and even a second observer cannot "see" them until they have

been reduced to graphic form. The subject's own behavior presents other difficulties, which are not overcome by permitting him to be less specific. If we ask him to say simply whether he will be more or less likely to respond or will respond more or less rapidly, we have increased his chances of being right only by asking him to say less. Any report, no matter how specific, is also subject to the verbal contingencies which induce him to describe his behavior and possibly by similar contingencies elsewhere which may classify his behavior, for example, as right or wrong.

Verbal substitutes for arranged or observed variables may be used at different points in an investigation: Contingencies may be described and the subject's behavior then actually observed, the subject may be exposed to a set of contingencies and then asked to evaluate the nature or probability of his responses, and so on. Similar practices are used to evaluate the reinforcing or aversive properties of a given event or procedure, to predict the outcome of several variables operating at once, and so on, and are subject to the same criticism.

To those interested primarily in mental processes, verbal communication may not be an attempted circumvention or shortcut. On the contrary, an operant analysis may seem to be the long way around. The position is sometimes defended by insisting that the student of behavior always begins with an interest in mental life—possibly his own—and designs his experiments essentially to test hypotheses about it. Whatever the case may once have been, operant research has long since passed the point at which the experimenter can be guided by considering possible effects of variables on himself. The introspective vocabulary used in circumventing an experimental analysis is hopelessly inadequate for the kinds of facts currently under investigation. If one field is to borrow from the other, the debt will henceforth almost certainly be in the other direction: From the study of the behavior of other organisms, the experimenter is most likely to come to understand himself. In some theories of knowledge, introspective observations may be regarded as primary data, but in an analysis of behavior they are a form of theorizing which is not required or necessarily helpful (Skinner, 1963).

❊　　❊　　❊

THE CONTINGENCIES OF REINFORCEMENT

The Law of Effect specifies a simple temporal order of response and consequence—the relation implied by the term operant. The contingencies of reinforcement currently under investigation are much more complex. Reinforcement may be contingent, not only on the occurrence of a response, but on special features of its topography, on the presence of prior stimuli, and on scheduling systems. An adequate analysis must also reach into the traditional fields of motivation and emotion to determine what is reinforcing and under what conditions. Interrelated systems of operants raise other problems.

The techniques of an experimental analysis have fortunately remained commensurate with the increasing complexity of the subject. Rate of responding has come to be examined over a much wider range and in much greater detail. Cumulative records have been supplemented by distributions of interresponse times and, very recently, by "on-line" computer processing. Better measures of topographical properties have become available. Independent variables have been effectively controlled over a wider range and in more complex patterns. Arrangements of operants resembling many of the behaviors attributed to higher mental processes have been successfully constructed and studied.

The experimental space has been improved. Brief daily experimental periods have given way to continuous observation for many hours, days, weeks, or even months. More of the behavior exhibited in the experimental space has been controlled, recorded, and analyzed. Total control of the environment from birth is within range. As in the study of animal behavior in general, the hundreds of thousands of extant species are still far from adequately sampled, but problems of instrumentation have been solved for a fairly wide range of anatomical and behavioral differences.

The contingencies of reinforcement which define operant behavior are important in the analysis of variables of other sorts. The stimulus control of behavior is central to a kind of nonverbal psychophysics, where interest may be primarily in the action of receptor mechanisms. Operant techniques are important in defining the behavioral effects of physiological variables—surgical, electrical, and chemical—in specifying what aspects of behavior are to be attributed to hereditary endowment, in tracing features of mature behavior to early environment, and so on. They are important in clarifying the nature of defective, retarded, or psychotic behavior. As Lindsley (1963) has pointed out, the important thing about a psychotic is often not what he is doing but what he is not doing, and in such a case it is important to be able to predict normal performances under standard conditions.

Contingencies of reinforcement are also valuable in interpreting behavior not easily submitted to a laboratory analysis. Verbal behavior, for example, can be defined just in terms of its contingencies: Its special characteristics are derived from the fact that reinforcement is mediated by other organisms. In education the instructional programing of reinforcement is the *raison d'être* of teaching machines, the future of which is much brighter than current activities may suggest. It is too early to predict the effect of comparable analyses in other branches of the social sciences—for example, economics and government—but if the history of physical technology is any guide, the knowledge and skills derived from an experimental analysis will become increasingly important.

In short, in the field of human behavior as a whole, the contingencies of reinforcement which define operant behavior are widespread if not ubiquitous. Those who are sensitive to this fact are sometimes embarrassed by the frequency with which they see reinforcement everywhere, as Marxists see class struggle or Freudians the Oedipus relation. Yet the fact is that reinforcement *is* extraordinarily important. That is why it is reassuring to recall that its place was once taken by the concept of purpose; no one is likely to object to a search for purpose in every human act. The difference is that we are now in a position to search effectively. In its very brief history, the study of operant behavior has clarified the nature of the relation between behavior and its consequences and has devised techniques which apply the methods of a natural science to its investigation.

REFERENCES

ADAMS, D. K. Experimental studies of adaptive behavior in cats. *Comp. Psychol. Monogr.*, 1929, **6** (1, Whole No. 27).

BERNATOWICZ, A. I. Teleology in science teaching. *Science*, 1958, **128**, 1402–1405.

GRINDLEY, G. C. The formation of a simple habit in guinea pigs. *Brit. J. Psychol.*, 1932, **23**, 127–147.

GUTTMAN, N. Laws of behavior and facts of perception. In S. Koch (Ed.), *Psychology: A study of a science.* Vol. 5. New York: McGraw-Hill, 1963. Pp. 114–178.

HOGBEN, L. *Statistical theory.* London: Norton, 1957.

IVANOV-SMOLENSKY, A. G. On methods of examining conditioned food reflexes in children and in mental disorders. *Brain*, 1927, **50**, 138–141.

LINDSLEY, O. R. Direct measurement and functional definition of vocal hallucinatory symptoms. *J. nerv. ment. Dis.*, 1963, **136**, 293–297.

MILLER, S., and KONORSKI, J. Sur une forme particulière des réflexes conditionnels. *CR Soc. Biol., Paris*, 1928, **99**, 1155–1157.

SIDMAN, M. Avoidance conditioning with brief shock and no exteroceptive warning signal. *Science*, 1953, **118**, 157–158.

———. *Tactics of scientific research.* New York: Basic Books, 1960.

SKINNER, B. F. Drive and reflex strength: II. *J. gen. Psychol.*, 1932, **6**, 38–48.

———. Two types of conditioned reflex: A reply to Konorski and Miller. *J. gen. Psychol.*, 1937, **16**, 272–279.

———. *Verbal behavior.* New York: Appleton-Century-Crofts, 1957.

———. Behaviorism at fifty. *Science*, 1963, **134**, 566–602.

TERRACE, H. S. Discrimination learning with and without "errors." *J. exp. Anal. Behav.*, 1963, **6**, 1–27.

8

Satiation Effects Under Fixed-Ratio Schedules of Reinforcement

Murray Sidman · William C. Stebbins

The experiment reported in this paper draws attention to the fact that response-induced stimuli (that is, internal stimuli generated by feedback from the response itself) serve as almost irresistible cues for ensuing behavior. The data show that for rats, cats, and monkeys, rate of responding under fixed ratio is independent of degree of satiation. Once the animals start responding, they keep right on until reinforcement appears. After receiving their reinforcement, the animals characteristically "pause" (that is, do not respond). Sidman and Stebbins demonstrate that the prevalence of such pauses is related either to the length of a session (presumably because of the number of reinforcements obtained), or to the amount of prefeeding. Rate of responding—after the animals enter a given FR cycle—is remarkably constant, regardless of satiation level. As noted elsewhere, however, force of responding is not constant—it increases progressively within FR cycles (Notterman, J. M., *Behavior: A Systematic Approach,* 1970, Random House).

In a fixed-ratio schedule the reinforcing stimulus appears only after a fixed number of responses has been emitted. Skinner (3, p. 385) has pointed out three consequences of such a schedule:

a. The probability that a reinforcement will appear during a rapid burst of responses is high. As a result, rapid responding is selectively strengthened.

b. Rapid responding produces more frequent reinforcements. This in turn increases the rate of responding still more. A cyclic process is set up which culminates in a maximal rate.

c. The fixed number of responses becomes a discriminative

From the *Journal of Comparative and Physiological Psychology* (April 1954), Vol. 47, No. 2, pp. 114–116; copyright 1954 by the American Psychological Association, and reproduced by permission.

occasion for reinforcement. Each successive response, as this number is approached, sets up a stronger occasion for reinforcement. This has the effect of making the behavior "self-generating." As successive responses are emitted, there is an increasing probability that the run will be completed.

Skinner has presented data illustrating these phenomena in rats (2) and pigeons (4), and has indicated the importance of ratio size and amount of reinforcement (3, pp. 103, 386). The present experiments were designed to investigate the effects of partial satiation upon food-reinforced fixed-ratio responding, and to determine whether the phenomena observed could be extended to cats and monkeys.

Method

Subjects. Four male Wistar rats, two male stock cats, and one female rhesus monkey served as Ss. All animals had extensive previous experience with lever pressing on regular and fixed-ratio schedules of reinforcement.

Apparatus. Skinner boxes of sizes appropriate to the different species were used. A system of relays and timers automatically controlled the scheduling, recording, and reinforcement delivery. Responses were recorded on a Harvard Cumulative Recorder.

The cats, monkey, and two rats received liquid reinforcement. This consisted of water for the rats, a 50 per cent mixture of evaporated milk and water for the cats, and water sweetened with table sugar for the monkey. Two rats were reinforced with food pellets, .045 gm. in weight and manufactured from Purina Laboratory Chow.

Procedure. Partial satiation was accomplished first by running the animals for long sessions, during which a large number of reinforcements was secured, and second, by feeding the animals before running. The experiment was conducted in two phases. In the first phase, the liquid-reinforced rats were deprived of water for 48 hr. before running; the cats were kept at 70 per cent of their ad libitum body weight; and the monkey was deprived of food and water for 40 hr. The two food-reinforced rats received all their food in the experimental situation and were run every day. The Ss ran for 60 to 150 hr. at various fixed ratios in phase 1.

Only the monkey and the two liquid-reinforced rats were used in the second phase. Prior to phase 2, these animals were placed on a ratio of 25 responses per reinforcement for three sessions. They were kept on this ratio for three sessions in the second phase. Immediately prior to running, the rats had access to water for ½ hr., and the monkey was fed approximately 500 cc. of the sugar solution.

RESULTS

Sample records from the first phase are presented in Figure 1 for one rat, one cat, and the monkey. The rate for a given individual is

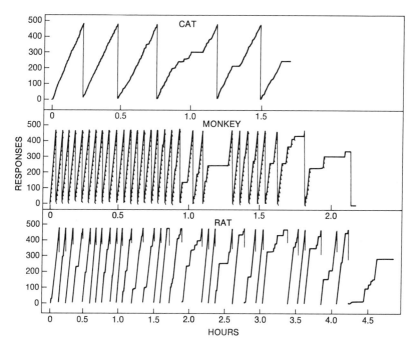

FIGURE 1. Sample cumulative response records under fixed-ratio schedules of reinforcement. Ratio of responses to reinforcements is 25:1 for the rat and monkey, and 20:1 for the cat. The short diagonal strokes indicate reinforcements. Some strokes may not appear because of photographic reduction.

essentially two-valued, with a zero rate occasionally appearing just after a reinforcement and a high, constant rate prevailing at other times. In the case of the cat, short pauses follow each reinforcement, even at the beginning of the record. These, however, are independent of the experimental procedure, resulting from a small residue of milk around the rim of the liquid dispenser. Following each reinforcement, the cats spent 5 to 10 sec. licking this residue. With the exception of this artifact, the rates are generally regular at the start of the sessions, with breaks of varying lengths beginning to appear as the period progresses. With few exceptions these breaks appear immediately after a reinforcement. Even at the end of the session, however, when long periods of no responding have become frequent, the same rate is maintained when the animal does respond.

After subtracting the time taken for pauses following reinforcement, the response rate was determined over the first, middle, and last 30 min. of each session at a given schedule. This did not include the first session, during which the animal adjusted its rate from the previous schedule. The initial rate ranged from a low of 51 responses per minute for one of the rats to a high of 167.7 responses per minute for the monkey. No variation greater than 1 per cent of the initial rate was observed within or between sessions for a given animal at a given ratio.

Figure 2 shows sample records from the monkey and the same

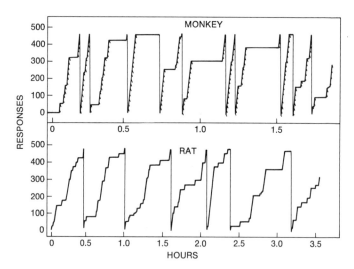

Figure 2. Sample records following prefeeding. Animals and schedules are the same as those in Figure 1.

rat as in Figure 1 after they had been prefed. The only effect of the partial satiation appears to be an earlier and more frequent appearance of the periods of no responding. As a consequence, the total number of responses emitted during the experimental period is less. However, when the animals do respond, their rates are the same (within 1 per cent) as those observed at any time during the first phase.

DISCUSSION

The general features of the fixed-ratio curves are in agreement with those previously observed by Ferster and Skinner. With respect to the pauses following reinforcement, they write, "With short enough ratios—under 60 or so for the pigeon—there is no pause following the reinforcement. With larger ratios the pause increases as a function of the size of the ratio" (personal communication). The present findings indicate that these pauses are also under the control of deprivation and satiation operations.

Of greater interest, perhaps, is the independence of the response rate from the feeding operation. If total responses had only been summated with a counter, and then divided by the length of the experimental session, it would have appeared as though feeding produced a lower rate. Examination of the moment-to-moment record, however, indicates that when the animals do respond, their rate is always the same.

Connected with this is the observation that once the animal began to respond, it always continued without a break until the next reinforcement was received. When the animal responded, its own behavior set up a powerful discriminative occasion for reinforcement, each response generating a successor until the reinforcement appeared. Evidence for such a discrimination, or "count," has been presented by Skinner (4) and Ferster (1). The present data indicate that degree of satiation alters only the probability of occurrence of the first response in the run, but has no effect upon the discrimination responsible for the stable rate.

SUMMARY

Four rats, two cats, and one rhesus monkey were trained to press levers under fixed-ratio schedules of reinforcement. The effects of satiation were observed (a) after a considerable number of reinforcements had been received in the experimental situation and (b) after feeding the animals prior to running them.

Characteristics of the cumulative response curves were similar to those previously obtained by Skinner and Ferster from rats and pigeons.

The effect of satiation was to introduce periods of no responding immediately following reinforcements. However, when the animals did respond, their rates were constant and independent of the degree of satiation. Prefeeding simply produced an earlier and more frequent appearance of the periods of no responding.

REFERENCES

1. FERSTER, C. B. Use of the blackout in the investigation of temporal discrimination in fixed-interval reinforcement. *J. exp. Psychol.*, 1954, **47**, 69–74.
2. SKINNER, B. F. *The behavior of organisms.* New York: Appleton-Century, 1938.
3. ———. *Science and human behavior.* New York: Macmillan, 1953.
4. ———. Some contributions of an experimental analysis of behavior to psychology as a whole. *Amer. Psychologist*, 1953, **8**, 69–78.

9

Conditioning of Mental-Hospital Patients to Fixed-Ratio Schedules of Reinforcement

R. R. Hutchinson · N. H. Azrin

The investigation described in this article shows that the properties of fixed-ratio responding manifested by human subjects are the same as those displayed by a variety of other organisms (see Chapter 8). In this particular study, the subjects were schizophrenic patients in a mental hospital, and their behavior was reinforced with either cigarettes or candy. The research is representative of a number of similar endeavors. These efforts have in common the attempt to bring under control the otherwise unmalleable behavior of psychotics.

The present investigation is an analysis of the responding of mental-hospital patients to fixed-ratio schedules of reinforcement.

SUBJECTS

The subjects in these experiments were seven male patients of a mental hospital who were diagnosed as schizophrenic. Their ages ranged from 26 to 69 years, with a median of 47 years. These subjects were long-term or "chronic" patients; with only one exception, they had been hospitalized for at least 14 years. Their length of hospitalization ranged from 2 to 36 years, with a median of 19 years. Aside from the usual hospital medication, none of the subjects was undergoing formal therapy during this study; nor did medical diagnosis indicate organic involvement. In order to insure regular

From the *Journal of the Experimental Analysis of Behavior* (1961), Vol. 4, pp. 87–95. Copyright 1961 by the Society for the Experimental Analysis of Behavior, Inc. Reprinted by permission of the Society for the Experimental Analysis of Behavior, Inc.

participation by the subjects, no patients were selected who had frequent visitors to the hospital, who were allowed home visits, or who had grounds passes or jobs in the hospital. Only those patients were selected who accepted cigarettes and candy, since those reinforcers could be most easily programmed with available equipment. Each patient was receiving thorazine regularly as treatment.

APPARATUS

Experimental Chamber

The experimental room was a sound-attenuated and temperature-controlled enclosure 7 feet wide, 10 feet long, and 12 feet high. The door to this room could be closed securely, but was never locked. The subjects could be observed through a window of one-way glass which was effectively concealed from the patient by a ventilator grill and which allowed no mirrored reflection. The manipulandum and vending magazine were placed on the wall opposite this window. An electric cigarette lighter and ashtray were mounted nearby.

Response and Reinforcement Apparatus

The manipulandum was of the type designed by Lindsley (1956), and consisted basically of a brass knob mounted on a shaft. When a subject pulled this knob through a distance of 1 centimeter with a force of 300 grams, a concealed switch closed. Closure of this switch constituted the measured response. An enclosed magazine with a capacity of 100 reinforcements was located above the response knob. Reinforcement consisted of the delivery of a single cigarette or piece of candy into a tray that was located 7 inches from the response knob. At the time of reinforcement, the delivery tray was lighted and a soft buzzer sounded for 3 seconds. Typically, the reinforcer was obtained by the patient within a second or two after its delivery into the tray. In other instances, the reinforcers were simply allowed to accumulate in the tray until the end of the session. In both instances, the receipt of reinforcement required negligible time and produced little or no interruption of the ongoing responding. For this reason, all of the programming apparatus as well as the recorders and counters remained functional during the delivery of reinforcement. The response panel and vending magazine appeared self-contained to the subject, but in fact were connected by a concealed cable with the controlling and recording apparatus located in another room.

PROCEDURE

Patient Handling and Programming Procedure

The experimental sessions for a given patient were conducted daily, Monday through Friday, and at the same time each day. The sessions ended after the delivery of a fixed number of reinforcements. Assistants who were naive about the purposes, objectives, or expectations of the study escorted the patients to and from the experimental room. When the door of the experimental room was closed, an electrical switch automatically started the session. The use of this door switch to initiate the sessions proved to have two advantages. First, no extinction period could occur between the time the patient entered the room and the time the "authorized" session began. Second, the patient considered the reinforcement schedule to be less under the control of the experimenter because no waiting period was necessary while the assistant was starting the session.

Instructions to Subjects

On the first occasion that a patient was brought to the experimental room, he was asked, "Would you like some candy and cigarettes?" The assistant would obtain a cigarette or piece of candy for himself by moving the response knob and would encourage the subject to do the same, saying: "You can get as many as you want to take back to the ward with you." He then left the room saying, "Get all you want; I'll be back in a little while." If the subject did not respond within 20 or 30 minutes, the assistant again entered the room and further demonstrated the apparatus. If necessary, he even placed the subject's hand on the manipulandum. Although minimal instruction had been desired, in some cases responding began only if the above instructions were used.

RESULTS AND DISCUSSION

Of the seven patients initially selected for these experiments, five were studied for a period of over 3 months. The response curves of two of the subjects, shown in Fig. 1, demonstrate the typical changes in performance which occurred during the initial weeks of conditioning. At the start of conditioning, every response was rein-

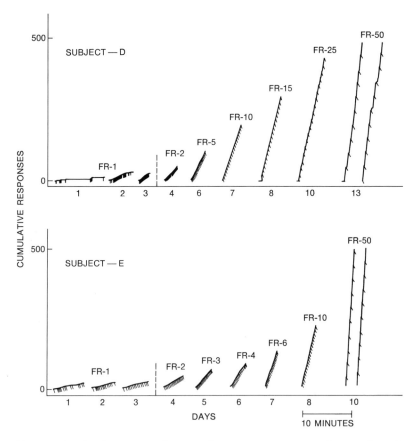

FIGURE 1. Performance of two subjects on successive days and with progressively higher numbers of responses required for reinforcement. Each diagonal mark on the cumulative-response curves indicates the delivery of a reinforcement. Each curve represents the response record of one entire session (except for FR 50, which contains two curves).

forced. To the extent that responding was sustained under this continuous reinforcement, progressively larger numbers of responses were required. Both subjects in Fig. 1 had an extremely low response rate of only 4 or 5 responses per minute during the first several experimental sessions. Gradually, however, responding increased to a level greater than 100 per minute at the higher ratio requirements. All five subjects initially showed these same low rates of less than 6 responses per minute during the first two experimental sessions. The time required to produce high rates of responding varied among subjects. Indeed, with two subjects, over 40 experimental sessions were required before response rates above 100 per minute were observed. All subjects consistently maintained the level of final performance such as that shown in Fig. 1 over consecutive experimental sessions.

The reason for the day-to-day increase in responding is not clear from the above data. Possibly, responding was increased because of the successively higher number of responses required for reinforcement. On the other hand, the same increase might have been simply a function of time. This question is partially answered by Fig. 2, which presents the average rate of responding of Subject

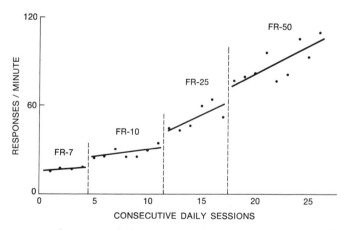

FIGURE 2. Changes in daily response rate for one subject over 26 days.

C over a 26-day period. The response rate appears to increase moderately each time the number of responses required for reinforcement increases. An even more evident effect is in the day-today increase in the rate of responding when the number of responses required for reinforcement is not changed. This increase in time is particularly noticeable at the higher ratios. Boren (1956) and Skinner (1938), using animal subjects, have also found that the over-all rate of responding increases as the number of responses required for reinforcement is raised. On the other hand, the observed increase in response rate over time has not been found in studies with animals, but has been noted by Ellis *et al.* (1960) in a study of mental defectives.

Figure 3 illustrates the typical performance of each subject on

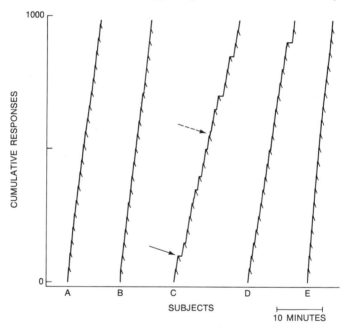

FIGURE 3. Typical performance by each of five subjects during an FR 50 schedule of reinforcement. The solid arrow indicates the characteristic pause following reinforcement. The dashed arrow indicates one of the rare instances in which the pause occurs after responding has begun.

an FR 50 schedule. Responding under fixed-ratio schedules of reinforcement was observed to take place in a characteristic temporal pattern. The pattern of responding was essentially bi-valued:

either responding occurred at a high rate or not at all. Pausing, or the absence of responding, occurred immediately after reinforcement (solid arrow). Pauses occurred only rarely once responding had begun (dotted arrow); the frequency of such pauses was found to be no greater than is commonly observed with animal subjects in this laboratory. As is also true of animal subjects, the differences observed among subjects in over-all response rates appear largely due to differences in the duration of pausing following reinforcement. These findings are quite similar to those reported by other investigators in work with normal humans (Holland, 1958), mental defectives (Ellis, 1960), psychotic children (Lindsley, 1956), as well as with animal subjects (Ferster and Skinner, 1957).

Ordinarily, the number of responses required for reinforcement was increased only when a stable pattern of responding was well-established. Under this procedure, fixed-ratio requirements as great as 300 were maintained with no disruption of performance. In several cases, however, the ratio requirement for a particular subject was raised to a value much greater than had previously been programmed. Figure 4 illustrates the effect of such "ratio strain" for one subject. Responding was successfully maintained as the number of responses required for reinforcement was raised from 50 to 100 on Day 2, and then to 200 on Day 3. On Day 4 the ratio was further increased to 300, where it was held through Day 7. The performance deteriorated severely on Day 5, although pausing was still partially localized after reinforcement. However, the subject ceased responding entirely after 15 reinforcements (not shown). By the fourth day at FR 300 (Day 7 in Fig. 4), deterioration was even more severe, and the subject stopped responding entirely after only 11 reinforcements (also not shown). On Days 8 and 9 the ratio requirement was reduced to 150. Even though performance was previously sustained at a ratio of 200, responding at FR 150 was now very erratic and terminated after 10 reinforcements. When the ratio requirement was lowered to the original value of 50 (Day 10), sustained performance was again observed. However, pausing did not immediately localize after reinforcement, but it appeared at many points in the ratio. Over a period of 14 experimental sessions, normal performance gradually returned (Day 23). It may be noted that before the ratio requirement produced disturbance in normal performance, no increase was evident in the pause following re-

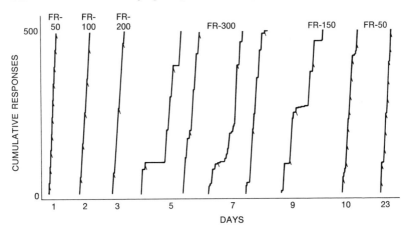

FIGURE 4. Ratio strain resulting from rapid increases in the number of responses required for reinforcement and subsequent recovery when the ratio requirement is reduced to the former value. Typical segments of the response record are shown for each day.

inforcement as a function of the ratio requirement. This absence of pausing at higher ratios is characteristic of the results observed throughout this investigation but differs from the results obtained with animals (Boren, 1956; Ferster and Skinner, 1957). However, this same absence of increased pausing at higher fixed ratios can be noted in Holland's (1957) study of normal humans as well as in Ellis' (1960) study of mental defectives.

Occasionally, reinforcement was deliberately withheld. Figure 5 illustrates the typical pattern of responding which resulted during this extinction procedure. Prior to extinction, every 50th response had been reinforced. The reinforcements were then withheld for the remainder of the session (starting at A). The subject continued to respond at the usual high fixed-ratio rate for over 2000 responses before any pausing occurred. Periods of responding then began to alternate with progressively more frequent periods of no responding. The same bi-valued rate was obtained during extinction as was seen during reinforcement (Ferster and Skinner, 1957). Eventually, responding ceased entirely and the patient often left the room at this time. Extinction was attempted with all subjects, each showing this same response pattern and the same eventual cessation of responding.

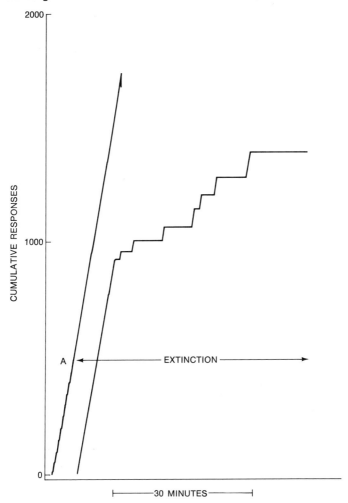

FIGURE 5. Responding during extinction following fixed-ratio conditioning. Extinction begins at *A*.

Figure 6 shows the control of behavior exerted by conditioned reinforcement. Reinforcement was withheld beginning at *A*. As in Fig. 5, the responses during this extinction procedure continue at the same rate as during reinforcement. The first major disruption in responding occurred at *B*. Occasionally, intermediate rates of responding appeared, such as at *C*, and the performance ceased

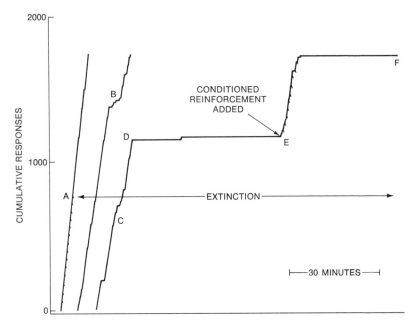

Figure 6. Responding induced by conditioned reinforcers. The diagonal marks on the response record up to A indicate the delivery of the reinforcer and its accompanying stimuli. At E the conditioned-reinforcing stimuli were scheduled alone. Typical changes in rate during extinction are indicated at B, C, and D. (See text.) Neither the reinforcement nor conditioned reinforcement was delivered from A to E.

almost entirely at D. The controlling apparatus was then set (prior to E), so that the next response and every 50th response thereafter would be followed by the buzzer sound and light change that normally accompanied the delivery of reinforcement. A response occurred at E which resulted in the rapid emission of over 600 more responses before responding again extinguished. The behavioral control exerted by these conditioned reinforcers is quite similar to that obtained in studies of animal behavior (Skinner, 1938).

It had been anticipated that great variability from day to day, as well as within each day, would characterize the performance of these chronic patients. As has been noted above, however, responding consistently occurred at the high rates that normally characterize fixed-ratio performance. Even more surprising is the consistency that was observed in the over-all rate of response from day to day.

In no case did the over-all rate on any one day differ by more than 20% from that of the previous day. Typically, the over-all rate did not change by more than 10%.

SUMMARY

Five mental-hospital patients, diagnosed as schizophrenic, were conditioned under fixed-ratio schedules of reinforcement. Low rates of responding were initially observed in all subjects. Over a period of from 5 to 40 experimental sessions and at progressively larger ratio requirements, all subjects came to respond much more rapidly.

Much less day-to-day variation was present than might be expected of the behavior of psychotic patients. The over-all response rate for a given patient usually varied less than 10% from one day to the next.

The temporal pattern of responding which developed was found to be essentially bivalued: the subjects either responded at a very high rate or they did not respond at all. Periods of no responding typically occurred after reinforcement and only rarely at any other time. When the number of responses required for reinforcement was drastically increased, the usual pattern of performance was disrupted severely and responding ceased entirely after a short period. When the ratio requirement was then reduced to the original value, the disruption persisted for a number of experimental sessions. During extinction, responding was reduced, because of progressively more frequent periods of no responding, with little change in the local response rate. It was found that responding could be reinstated temporarily through the use of conditioned reinforcers.

The results of these experiments are highly similar to those obtained in studies of infrahumans and normal humans. The one exception to this essential similarity is the extended period of time necessary to produce high rates of responding.

REFERENCES

BOREN, J. Response rate and resistance to extinction as functions of the fixed ratio. Diss. Abst., 1956, Vol. 14, 8, 1261.

ELLIS, N. R., BARNETT, C. D., and PRYER, M. W. Operant behavior in mental defectives: exploratory studies. *J. exp. anal. Behav.*, 1960, **1,** 63–69.

FERSTER, C. B., and SKINNER, B. F. *Schedules of reinforcement*. New York: Appleton–Century–Crofts, 1957.

HOLLAND, J. G. Human vigilance. *Science*, 1958, **128,** 61–67.

LINDSLEY, O. R. New techniques of analysis of psychotic behavior. Annual Technical Report No. 3 to the Group Psychology Branch, Office of Naval Research, September 1955–November 1956.

SKINNER, B. F. The behavior of organisms. New York: Appleton-Century Co., 1938.

Modifying Responses Through Cue Establishment

IV

10

Effect of a Secondary Reinforcing Agent in Black-White Discrimination

David Ehrenfreund

One of the major problems faced by reinforcement theorists is how to explain the acquisition and maintenance of behavior in the absence of primary reinforcers, such as food, water, or a sex object. During the 1930s and 1940s Hull, Skinner, Spence, and others became increasingly interested in the concept of secondary reinforcement. They perceived that such a construct is necessary if the behavior of mature human beings is eventually to be adequately understood.

The experiment here described by Ehrenfreund is in that tradition, and calls attention to the relation between secondary reinforcement and discrimination training. The central point is this: Discrimination between two sets of conditions is established most efficiently when there is as little overlap as possible between the stimuli associated with the respective reinforcing and nonreinforcing contingencies. This situation occurs probably because stimuli associated with the reinforced condition become secondary reinforcers. If these secondary reinforcers are then presented in the *nonreinforced* condition, they tend to sustain behavior that would otherwise be more rapidly extinguished.

The present investigation has its background in the recent experimental studies concerned with the role of secondary reinforcement in learning and the theoretical interpretations of this phenomenon. A number of investigators have demonstrated with a variety of organisms and in different types of learning situations that, under certain conditions, a previously neutral stimulus will acquire the capacity to act as a reinforcing agent.

From the *Journal of Comparative and Physiological Psychology* (February 1949), Vol. 42, No. 1, pp. 1–5; copyright 1949 by the American Psychological Association, and reproduced by permission.

One of the first of these experiments was reported by Skinner (6). This investigator presented sixty click-food combinations to a group of four naive rats and then later confronted them with a situation in which the depression of a horizontal bar by the animal led to the sounding of a click. The individual curves of the animal exhibited a fairly rapid rate of learning, and the attainment of a high level of performance indicated that the click had acquired reward value. Similarly, Cowles (1) in a more complicated learning situation found that chimpanzees were able to learn new and difficult discrimination tasks when rewarded only by poker-chips which had previously been associated with food. Recent experiments by Denny (2), Perkins (5), and Grice (3) have provided further detailed evidence as to the efficacy of secondary reinforcement in reference to such problems as intermittent reinforcement, gradients of reinforcement, and delay of reward.

As the principle of secondary reinforcement is stated by Hull (4), stimulus cues that are closely and consistently associated with a reinforcing state of affairs themselves acquire reward value. Theoretically, under the proper conditions, any stimulus cue can thus become a substitute or surrogate reward.

In most learning situations, various cues presumably have secondary reinforcing properties. In the typical maze or discrimination experiment the animal is first given a period of preliminary training. However, each time the animal is rewarded during this *preliminary* stage, cues that are closely and consistently associated therewith would, according to Hull's principle, acquire reward value. According to reinforcement theory, the presence or absence of such cues in the *learning* situation should differentially affect the rate of learning. For example, in many situations it is assumed, often implicitly, that the mere failure to provide the goal object for which the animal is motivated constitutes a non-reinforcing state of affairs. However, if, following an erroneous response, there are stimulus cues present which had previously acquired reward value, either by direct association with a primary rewarding object or by generalization, these cues will provide some amount of reinforcement. Thus, the full effect of the failure to provide the motivated goal object would be somewhat vitiated. In situations involving the competition between two or more responses, the acquisition of the correct response would thereby be retarded. Furthermore, the extent of such retardation is assumed to be some positive function of the strength of the secondary reinforcing agent.

The present paper presents data on the effect of such an agent in the negative goal box, on the learning of a black-white discrimination.

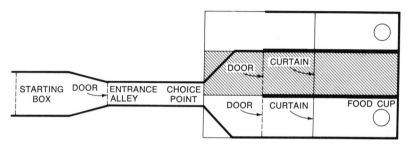

FIGURE 1. Diagram of apparatus.

Table 1. Data on Learning of Discrimination Problem

	ERRORS		TRIALS	
	Mean	σ_M	Mean	σ_M
Group II	17.50	2.09	42.20	3.70
Group I	7.16	1.44	24.40	4.18
Difference	10.34		17.80	
t	3.70		3.17	
P	.01		.01	

Method

Subjects. The subjects were 24 female albino rats from the colony maintained by the Psychology Department at the State University of Iowa. They ranged in age from 100 to 130 days.

Apparatus. Figure 1 shows a floor plan of the apparatus, which was essentially the same as that employed by Grice (3). It was so arranged that the animal went from a starting box into a narrow entrance alley from which he could, by turning slightly, continue forward and enter either a white or black stimulus alley. There were three such alleys or goal boxes, the middle one black, and the two outside ones white. On any one trial, two of these alleys were visible to the rat. They were arranged on a base which permitted moving them at right angles to the direction of the entrance alley, thus reversing the spatial position of the goal boxes. Guillotine-type doors prevented correction, and black and white cloth curtains prevented the animal from seeing the food cup before the door closed behind him. The food cup consisted of a clear glass furniture coaster about 2½″ in diameter. During preliminary training, gray boxes with gray curtains were used.

Procedure. All Ss were first placed on a one week feeding schedule during which they were fed 8 gr. per day in individual feeding cages at the same hour as their experimental session. The preliminary training occupied four days, during which all Ss were treated alike.

Day 1. Each S was placed in a gray goal box and allowed to eat 10 pellets from the food cup. Each pellet weighed approximately .25 gr.

Day 2. Each S was given four rewarded runs from the starting box to one of the gray goal boxes.

Days 3 and 4. On each of these days the Ss were given 10 rewarded runs to the gray goal boxes.

Thus, at the completion of this training, each animal had received 24 rewarded trials, forced equally often to the left and right in neutral goal boxes. Since on each of these trials the animal was rewarded with a pellet of food from the glass food cup, the latter should have acquired secondary reinforcing properties. On the following day, the animals were divided into two litter-matched groups of 12 animals each and trained to white positive versus black negative. All animals were given 10 massed trials per

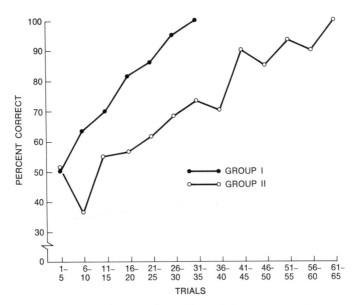

FIGURE 2. Showing the retarding effect of the presence of a secondary reinforcing agent (empty food cup) in the negative goal box.

day until the criterion of 90 per cent correct in 20 trials was attained. Correction of an erroneous response was never allowed.

Group I constituted what we shall describe as the non-secondary reinforcement group. In this group, the food cup was never present in the negative goal box. Thus, the possibility that an empty food cup would serve as a secondary reinforcer to the response to the negative stimulus was eliminated.

Group II constituted what we shall refer to as the secondary re-inforcement group. In the case of this group, a food cup similar to the one in the positive box was always present in the negative box, although it never contained food. If the empty food cup served as a reinforcing agent, the learning by this group should be retarded as the incorrect response to the negative black stimulus would be receiving a certain amount of secondary reinforcement. The effect would be to retard the development of a difference in the strength of the two competing responses.

RESULTS

Table 1 [p. 121] presents data on the learning of the discrimination problem in terms of errors and trials. In the case of both measures, that group was retarded in which the responses to the negative, black, stimulus received secondary reinforcement in the form of the empty food cup. The mean number of errors to learn for this group was 17.5 as compared with a mean of 7.16 for the group in which the food cup was not present in the negative goal box. The means of the trial scores were 42.2 and 24.4 respectively. These were computed in terms of the total number of trials taken up to the point at which no further errors were made.

On the average, then, Group II exhibited more than twice as many errors and required almost twice as many trials to reach this criterion as the non-secondary reinforcement group. That these differences are significant is revealed by a t value of 3.70 for errors and one of 3.17 for trials. For 22 degrees of freedom, a t of 2.819 is significant at the 1 per cent level of confidence. The hypothesis that these differences can be attributed to chance is thus rejected.

Figure 2 compares the acquisition curves for both groups. In this graph, the percentage of correct responses is plotted against successive blocks of five trials. The first thing to note is that both groups start out at about the 50 per cent point. The actual values are 50 and 51.6, which indicates that no initial preference existed for either the black or white stimulus. The curve for the non-secondary reinforcement group rises fairly rapidly, reaching 100 per cent at 35 trials or 3½ days of training. The retarding effect of the secondary reinforcing agent in the negative box is again revealed in the lower curve. This group required 65 trials, or 6½ days to reach 100 per cent.

DISCUSSION

The theory of discrimination learning as developed by Spence (7) assumes that each reinforced response results in an increment in the tendency to respond to the cues present at the time that response was made. Each non-reinforced response results in the development of an inhibitory factor which tends to decrease the tendency to respond to the accompanying cues. These hypothetical increments and decrements are assumed to accumulate. As training proceeds, the response tendencies to the two relevant cue stimuli become differentiated until the tendency to respond to the positive or rewarded cues is so much greater than its competing tendency that the animal comes to choose the positive cue consistently. According to this schema, successful discrimination depends upon the development of a certain difference between the competing response tendencies. As this difference becomes larger, the probability of occurrence of the correct response increases. The faster this difference develops, the faster will the animal come to respond consistently to the positive cue stimuli.

The optimum conditions for this differential development require the consistent reinforcement of one response and the consistent non-reinforcement of the other. If, however, the erroneous response is rewarded by the presence of secondary reinforcing cues, then this response will also acquire some habit strength, though presumably not quite so much as does the correct response. The result will be to delay the development of the difference between the competing tendencies necessary for the consistent choice of one over the other. The present experiment demonstrated that the food cup used in preliminary training can serve as a strong enough reinforcing agent to delay this development and thus retard learning.

SUMMARY

Two groups of rats were trained to respond to white positive versus black negative in a simple discrimination situation. One group had a secondary reward present in the negative box in the form of a food cup which had previously been associated with a reinforcing state of affairs.

The other group found this food cup only in the positive box. The latter group learned significantly faster both in terms of errors and of trials. The principle of secondary reinforcement was invoked to account for the difference, and some implications in terms of Spence's theoretical formulation of discrimination learning were noted.

REFERENCES

1. COWLES, J. T.: Food-tokens as incentives for learning by chimpanzees. *Comp. Psychol. Monogr.*, 1937, **14**, No. 71, 96 pp.
2. DENNY, R. M.: The role of secondary reinforcement in a partial reinforcement learning situation. *J. exp. Psychol.*, 1946, **36**, 373–389.
3. GRICE, G. R.: The relation of secondary reinforcement to delayed reward in visual discrimination learning. *J. exp. Psychol.*, 1948, **38**, 1–16.
4. HULL, C. L.: *Principles of Behavior*. New York: Appleton-Century, 1943, ix + 422.
5. PERKINS, C. C.: The relation of secondary reward to gradients of reinforcement. *J. exp. Psychol.*, 1947, **37**, 377–392.
6. SKINNER, B. F.: *The Behavior of Organisms, an Experimental Analysis*. New York: Appleton-Century, 1938, ix + 457.
7. SPENCE, K. W.: The nature of discrimination learning in animals. *Psychol. Rev.*, 1936, **43**, 427–449.

11

The Future of
Secondary Reinforcement

Edward L. Wike

In what is essentially an overview of the experiments on secondary reinforcement included in his book, Wike points out that two critical problems still exist: (1) how to go about determining the necessary and sufficient conditions for the establishment of a stimulus as a secondary reinforcer, and (2) how to enhance the durability of secondary reinforcers.

He believes that the first problem can be resolved only through meticulous, parametric investigations. The second problem might lend itself to solution by means of research that is initially an amalgam of several variables; the purpose is just to demonstrate—if possible—the mere fact of secondary-reinforcement "durability." Among the variables that could be selected for deliberate mixture are these: (1) variety of tasks and variety of drives under which the same stimulus is established as a secondary reinforcer; (2) intermittent pairing of the secondary reinforcer with primary reinforcement; and (3) age of organism at the time of initial exposure to the secondary reinforcing stimulus. If durability is thus demonstrated, controlled parametric investigation would next be in order.

TWO PERSISTING PROBLEMS

A survey of the history of secondary reinforcement reveals that two crucial questions have, so far, remained unanswered: (1) What are the necessary and sufficient conditions for the establishment of a stimulus as a secondary reinforcer? (2) How may highly durable secondary reinforcers be developed? Many writers (e.g., McClelland, 1951; Harlow, 1953b; Razran, 1955; Zimmerman, 1957, 1959; Mowrer, 1960a; Hall, 1961) have stressed the evanescent character

From pp. 474–478 in *Secondary Reinforcement: Selected Experiments* by Edward L. Wike. Copyright © 1966 by Edward L Wike. Reprinted by permission of Harper & Row, Publishers.

of secondary reinforcers. Our position is that, while both questions are of great importance, the first, regarding the establishment of secondary reinforcement, is the more fundamental. First, if secondary reinforcement is to occupy a focal position in behavior theory, it is essential that the precise conditions for the development of secondary reinforcers be specifiable. Otherwise, secondary reinforcement will remain in the category of "loose" concepts which may be applied in a capricious manner to "explain" everything. Second, a solution to the first problem might expedite the achievement of an answer to the second question. For example, a knowledge of the necessary and sufficient conditions for establishing secondary reinforcement would enable us to decide whether or not a proposed experiment on durable secondary reinforcement would provide evidence for *any* secondary reinforcement. On the other hand, a few isolated demonstrations of durable secondary reinforcement probably would not be especially informative with respect to determining the necessary and sufficient conditions for secondary reinforcement. Third, it is conceivable that even if no answer could be discovered to the second question, secondary reinforcement might still be a valuable concept for the analysis of some behavioral phenomena. For these reasons we regard the first question as more basic.

We can offer no remarkable suggestions for an experimental attack upon the problem of isolating the essential conditions. Obviously, the techniques of secondary reinforcement training must be subjected to detailed experimental inquiry. For example, in Skinner-box studies of secondary reinforcement, in which lever-pressing or key-pecking serves as a learning test, the secondary reinforcement training is accomplished in the context of magazine-training. General procedures for magazine-training have been described for the rat (Michael, 1963, 2) and the pigeon (Ferster and Skinner, 1957, 31). The Ferster-Skinner technique embodies three stages: (1) getting the bird to eat from the magazine, (2) getting the bird to approach the magazine only when the magazine stimuli are activated, and (3) preventing the bird from hovering about the magazine by reinforcing its approach in the presence of the magazine stimuli from all sectors of the box. When the bird will respond promptly from all sectors and will not respond in the absence of the magazine stimuli, then it is presumed that these stimuli have become strong secondary reinforcers. Just what details of this procedure are essential to the endowing of a stimulus with measurable secondary reinforcing properties? For example, if we deleted the third stage of this magazine-training procedure, would the magazine stimuli acquire any secondary reinforcing value? It is evident that the Ferster-Skinner technique conditions the magazine stimuli as S^D's. Yet numerous instances have been reported in which stimuli functioned as conditioned reinforcers when differential reinforcement was not part of the secondary reinforcement training. Consequently, the magazine-training situation must be fractionated in order to detect the minimal conditions necessary for secondary reinforcement.

These same questions can be raised with respect to all other secondary reinforcement training procedures. For example, Reynolds *et al.* (1961) fed .10-gm. food pellets to rats 60 times directly in a goal box. In a subsequent T-maze learning test clear evidence for secondary reinforcement was displayed. But other workers have not observed that direct feedings will endow a goal box with reinforcing properties. Is some detail of the Reynolds *et al.* procedure crucial here? The possibility exists, of course, that other aspects of the experimental situation, such as the massing of test trials, may have been crucial in the previous failures rather than the direct feeding procedure itself.

The issue in question would seem trivial if all investigations of secondary reinforcement had yielded secondary reinforcement effects. Unfortunately, there have been studies with no evidence whatsoever for secondary reinforcement; what is more serious, the reasons for the lack of secondary reinforcement are not obvious. For example, Girardeau (1962) intermittently presented an .86-sec. buzzer followed by candy for 210 times to mentally defective subjects who had to approach a food dish, pick up the candy, and eat it. These subjects did not make more buzzer-reinforced bar presses in test than control subjects who were trained with the buzzer but had delayed primary reinforcement. In another study, by Fort (1961), children were tested with the clown apparatus devised by Myers (1960). The children heard a buzzer upon pushing the clown's nose, and this was followed by candy. Under these conditions no evidence of secondary reinforcement was found. Myers (1960), however, with the same situation secured secondary reinforcement effects when the response produced a token. Failures like these provide support for our contention that the basic unresolved question is that of isolating the necessary and sufficient conditions for secondary reinforcement.

It is possible that leads for future research on this question may be gained from a collation and examination of secondary reinforcement studies which have failed and those which have succeeded. It might be instructive, also, to repeat studies such as Fort's and to determine what kind of modifications in the training procedure would be required to generate secondary reinforcement effects. Other helpful leads may emerge from new theories. . . .

While the solution to the first problem demands careful, highly controlled investigations, another research tactic might be attempted in studying the second question. The durable secondary reinforcers in everyday life, e.g., certain words, grades, and money, appear to have had a long history of conditioning, beginning in childhood, in various situations under diverse drive conditions with different schedules of reinforcement. A well-designed experiment, with all of the necessary control groups, to assess these variables would be a formidable undertaking. Accordingly, we would propose that some *deliberately confounded,* long-term experiments on secondary reinforcement should be executed in which one cue, e.g., a light, serves as a secondary reinforcer for a small group of rats in a variety of experimental tasks, e.g., T-maze, runway, Skinner box, and so on, under different drives and reward schedules. How durable would this secondary reinforcer be in the absence of primary reinforcement for these rats in adulthood in some test situation as contrasted with control subjects for whom the light did not have a long history of conditioning? If a series of such deliberately confounded studies did not disclose any durable secondary reinforcement, then we might be tempted to abandon the notion of durable secondary reinforcers. However, if durable secondary reinforcers were found, then controlled studies would be required to untangle the deliberately confounded experiments. In brief, deliberately confounded experiments are being suggested as a short-cut strategy for providing an answer to the question: Can durable secondary reinforcers be developed? These proposed experiments are based on the assumptions that (1) durable secondary reinforcers have had a long history of conditioning; (2) they are generalized reinforcers in the Skinner sense; and (3) irregular training conditions are important in their development (McClelland, 1951; McClelland and McGown, 1953).

Let us now look at the problem of durable secondary reinforcement from a radically different point of view and see what directions this viewpoint might impart to future research. Suppose we assume that *secondary reinforcers are not durable* even in everyday life. How, then, can we account for the instances of apparent durable secondary reinforcement? Two conditions might be operating to convey this impression: (1) durable secondary reinforcers are being maintained by their infrequent reconditioning with primary reinforcement and/or (2) the "tests" for secondary reinforcement are widely distributed in time. The first consideration leads directly to investigations upon the reconditioning of secondary reinforcers and the maintenance of secondary reward value. What kinds of reconditioning arrangements are necessary if a secondary reinforcer is to retain its reward value? Is it possible to maintain a secondary reinforcer indefinitely by certain reconditioning procedures? The structure of such secondary reinforcement experiments would depart from the usual two-stage (training and test) paradigm by the intermittent imposition of reconditioning procedures during test. Furthermore, the focus of interest would be primarily upon the nature of the reconditioning procedures rather than upon the influence of the initial secondary reinforcement training.

If this analysis of durable secondary reinforcers is valid, then the work on chained schedules and token rewards assumes new importance. Are durable secondary reinforcers analogous to token rewards in which token exchange is only rarely permitted? This view implies that token-reward studies should have a high priority in research and especially that the token-exchange procedure should be thoroughly investigated. In addition, research on extended chains (e.g., Findley, 1962) would appear to be of great significance.

The second possible condition pertaining to durable secondary reinforcers in everyday life, i.e., widely distributed tests, could be investigated directly. Instead of the usual massed secondary reinforcement tests, tests could be spread over much longer periods. Suppose that a buzzer were conditioned by magazine-training and that only one or two test trials (e.g., bar press followed by buzzer) were held in each session, with the sessions being separated by weekly intervals. Would the buzzer keep its reward value under these conditions? This idea is not a new one (see Zimmerman, 1957; Reynolds *et al.*, 1961), but it warrants greater attention than it has been accorded to date. Another possibility is that both conditions, i.e., infrequent reconditioning and widely separated tests, occur conjointly in everyday life to present the appearance of durable secondary reinforcement.

REFERENCES

FERSTER, C. B., AND SKINNER, B. F. *Schedules of reinforcement.* New York: Appleton-Century-Crofts, 1957.

FINDLEY, J. D. An experimental outline for building and exploring multi-operant behavior repertoires. *Journal of the Experimental Analysis of Behavior,* 1962, **5,** 113–166.

FORT, J. G. Secondary renforcement with preschool chldren. *Child Development,* 1961, **32,** 755–764.

GIRARDEAU, F. L. The effect of secondary reinforcement on the operant behavior of mental defectives. *American Journal of Mental Deficiency,* 1962, **67,** 441–449.

HALL, J. F. *Psychology of motivation.* Chicago: Lippincott, 1961.

HARLOW, H. F. Mice, monkeys, men, and motives. *Psychological Review,* 1953b, **60,** 23–32.

McCLELLAND, D. C. *Personality.* New York: Dryden Press, 1951.

————, AND McGOWN, D. R. The effect of variable food reinforcement on the strength of a secondary reward. *Journal of Comparative and Physiological Psychology,* 1953, **46,** 80–86.

MICHAEL, J. *Laboratory studies in operant behavior.* New York: McGraw-Hill, 1963.

MOWRER, O. H. *Learning theory and behavior.* New York: Wiley, 1960a.

MYERS, N. A. Extinction following partial and continuous primary and secondary reinforcement. *Journal of Experimental Psychology,* 1960, **60,** 172–179.

RAZRAN, G. A note on second-order conditioning—and secondary reinforcement. *Psychological Review,* 1955, **62,** 327–332.

REYNOLDS, W. F., FREEDMAN, P. E., AND RICHTER, M. L. Secondary reinforcement effects in a T-maze test following direct placement training. *Psychological Reports,* 1961, **8,** 345–349.

ZIMMERMAN, D. W. Durable secondary reinforcement: Method and theory. *Psychological Review,* 1957, **64,** 373–383.

————. Sustained performance in rats based on secondary reinforcement. *Journal of Comparative and Physiological Psychology,* 1959, **52,** 353–358.

12

Gestalt Psychology

Wolfgang Köhler

This manuscript was to have been delivered by Wolfgang Köhler as a speech before the American Psychological Association in 1967; unfortunately, his death intervened.

In what turned out, then, to be his last overview of Gestalt psychology, Köhler describes—as only the master of one's own specialty can—its historical origins and basic premises. Both are strikingly shown to be interwoven with Köhler's own life experiences: his six-year sojourn in Africa, studying chimpanzees; his exposure to the teachings of two great physicists, Planck and Maxwell; and his migration to the United States when the Nazis came into power.

His principal premise is that the phenomena of field psychology rest upon the phenomena of field physics, and that the brain—acting as a volume conductor rather than as a collection of independent wires—translates the physical events into the psychological.

In his closing paragraphs he speaks with the enthusiasm of a young man, although he was in his eighties at his death. He never lost the feeling of excitement that is a part of what he terms in this paper "the atmosphere of adventure in science."

What we now call Gestalt psychology began to develop in 1910. At the time, there was not much psychology anywhere in Germany. People were doing experiments on memory with the technique introduced by Ebbinghaus and on the problems of psychophysics. Fechner, a physicist-philosopher, somewhat optimistically regarded difference limens, as investigated by Weber, and the quantitative relation between stimulus and sensation from his own studies, as the beginning of a real science of the mind. Max Wertheimer, in

From *Psychologische Forschung* (1967), Vol. 31, pp. XVIII–XXX; reprinted by permission of Springer-Verlag, Heidelberg.

1910, was disturbed by the narrowness of such enterprises. He tried to study more interesting psychological facts and, as a first example, he chose "apparent movement," the movement seen when two objects appear in fairly rapid succession, one in one place and another in a different location.

Apparent movement as such was known; but many psychologists regarded it as a mere cognitive illusion. Since no real objective movement occurs under these conditions, it was believed that apparent movement could not be a real perceptual fact. Rather, it was felt, it must be a product of erroneous judging. The explanation went like this: First, I see one object; immediately afterwards I see an object of the same kind in a somewhat different place. Naturally, I regard this second object as identical with the first, and conclude that the first has simply moved from the one place to the other.

This is a tranquillizing explanation. No longer need we worry about apparent movement. But this is also what we would now call a case of "explaining away." A striking perceptual fact is observed we cannot immediately explain. Then we invent an explanation for which there is no factual evidence, an explanation according to which there simply is no perceptual fact that has to be explained, but only a curious cognitive blunder.

"Explaining away" has not entirely disappeared from psychology even now, although such extraordinary constructions as the one just mentioned are no longer used for the purpose. The procedure may kill important problems. When tempted to do this kind of thing, we therefore ought immediately to test our proposed explanation in experiments.

This is what Wertheimer did. He studied the conditions under which apparent movement is seen. He varied the spatial locations of the objects involved, and the rate at which they followed each other; he observed the variations of the movement itself which occurred under such conditions, and so on. He also showed his subjects optimal apparent movement and similar movement of a real object, side by side and simultaneously. He found that the two could not be distinguished by the observer. Eventually he added a most important test, which—it was afterwards discovered—had once before been done by a physiologist. First, a great many repetitions of apparent movement are shown in a given place. Later, when a stationary pattern is shown in the same place, subjects clearly see a negative after image of the apparent movement, just as negative after images are seen after repeated presentations of a physically real movement.

Wertheimer's was a masterpiece of experimental investigation in the field of perception. It was also the beginning of extremely fruitful studies in general Gestalt psychology. Much thinking and many discussions followed. The number of basic questions which Wertheimer now began to consider increased rapidly. At the time, he did not publish what he found; rather, he told Koffka about his questions and his tentative answers, and Koffka in turn began to tell his students what he had learned from Wertheimer and about further ideas that he himself had developed in the same productive spirit. These students investigated one interesting possibility after another in the new field. For a brief time I was able to take part in this development. It was Koffka who, realizing that Wertheimer hesitated to write down what he was thinking, formulated first principles of Gestalt psychology in an excellent article which was published in 1915*.

Similar questions had begun to be discussed in Austria. Years before Wertheimer began his work, von Ehrenfels had called attention to a serious omission in the customary treatment of perceptual facts. We are accustomed, he said, to regard perceptual fields as collections of local sensations whose qualities and intensities are determined by corresponding local physical stimuli. This simple assumption, he added, cannot explain a large number of particularly interesting perceptual phenomena. For, quite apart from such local sensations, we often find in perceptual fields phenomena of an entirely different class—Gestalt qualities such as the specific shapes of objects, the melodic properties of this or that sequence of tones, and so forth. These Gestalt qualities remain practically unaltered when the stimuli in question are transposed. They seem to depend upon relations among the stimuli rather than upon the individual stimuli as such.

From these, and other obvious perceptual facts, the Austrian psychologists developed an interpretation of perception which differed radically from the views developed by Wertheimer. Since the Gestalt qualities could not be derived from the properties of

* Koffka, K.: Zur Grundlegung der Wahrnehmungspsychologie. Eine Auseinandersetzung mit V. Benussi. Z. Psychol. 73, 11–90 (1915). See particularly pp. 56–59.

individual sensations, the psychologists in Austria felt that they must be products of higher mental operations which the mind constantly imposes on mere sense data. This theoretical approach, the so-called "production" theory, did not seem particularly inviting to Wertheimer and Koffka. Nevertheless one has to admit that at least one member of the Austrian School, Benussi, sometimes seemed to forget the curious production theory, and then invented most original experiments.

At this point, I have to say a few words about my own experiences during this period. I was aware of what Wertheimer was trying to do and found it not only objectively interesting but also most refreshing as a human endeavor. He observed important phenomena regardless of the fashions of the day and tried to discover what they meant. I had a feeling that his work might transform psychology, which was hardly a fascinating affair at the time, into a most lively study of basic human issues. My own work, however, was not yet related to Wertheimer's investigations, although I did write a fairly energetic paper against the tendency of others to invent explanations which served to get rid of many most interesting facts. Just when Wertheimer's work came near its most decisive stage, I became separated from my friends in Germany when I was sent to Spanish Africa by the Prussian Academy of Science. They wanted me to study a group of chimpanzees, just captured for the purpose in western parts of the African continent.

The chimpanzees proved to be extremely interesting creatures. I studied their sometimes strangely intelligent behavior and also the curious restrictions to which such achievements were often subject. Somewhat later, I occasionally interrupted these studies and investigated the perception of chimpanzees and, for the sake of comparison, that of chickens. It soon became clear that in the visual field of both species constancies of size and of brightness are almost as obvious as they are in humans. In further experiments these animals, particularly the chimpanzees, learned to choose between two objects of different size or brightness. I was able to show in tests of transposition that what they had learned was relationally determined. (I later discovered that experiments of the same kind had been done, a short time before, by American psychologists.)

I was kept in Africa for more than six years by the first World War. During that long period I did not always feel inclined to continue my work in animal psychology. Ideas with which I had become acquainted in Europe would come back to me, most often the changes in psychological thinking which Wertheimer had just introduced. But I was also very much aware of what I had learned as a student of Max Planck, the great physicist. He had just discovered the quantum of electromagnetic radiation, but at the time taught us mainly what physicists called field physics. Under Planck's influence I had dimly felt that between Wertheimer's new thinking in psychology and the physicist's thinking in field physics there was some hidden connection. What was it? I now began to study the important works on field physics. The first discovery I made was that, fifty years before Wertheimer, some of his basic questions had already been asked not by psychologists but by physicists, first of all by Clerk Maxwell, the greatest physicist of that period. The Gestalt psychologists, we remember, were always disturbed by a thesis which was widely accepted by others. One psychologist, strongly influenced by traditional convictions, had formulated it in the following words: "I do not know whether perceptual fields actually consist of independent local elements, the so-called sensations. But, as scientists, we have to proceed as though this were true." An extraordinary statement—an *a priori* general conviction about the right procedure in science is assumed to be more important than the nature of the facts which we are investigating.

From its very beginning, Gestalt psychology ignored this thesis and began its work with simple and unbiased observations of facts. Independent local sensations? Consider again what happens in apparent movement. After a first visual object has appeared in one place, a second visual object does not appear in its normal location but nearer the place where the first has just disappeared, and only then moves towards what I just called its normal location. Clearly, therefore, the process corresponding to the second object has been deflected, has been attracted by a remnant of what has just happened in another place, the place of the first object, and has only then approached its "normal" location. Consequently, under the conditions of such experiments, the second object does not behave as though it were an independent local fact at all. The statement, quoted earlier, that perceptual fields must be assumed to consist of independent local sensations, is therefore at odds with the behavior of percepts even under such fairly simple conditions. Or take any of the well known perceptual illusions, say, the Müller-Lyer illusion. Can there be any doubt that in this case two lines of objectively equal length become lines of different length under the influence of the angles added at the ends of the distances to be compared? And so on, in a long list of examples, all of them incompatible with the statement about the nature of perceptual fields.

Ours was an uphill fight. I felt greatly relieved, as mentioned above, to find so fundamentally similar an approach from the side of physics. In his great treatise, *Electricity and Magnetism,* Clerk Maxwell had remarked that we are often told that in science we must, first of all, investigate the properties of very small local places one after another, and only when this has been done can we permit ourselves to consider how more complicated situations result from what we have found in those elements. This procedure, he added, ignores the fact that many phenomena in nature can only be understood when we inspect not so-called elements but fairly large regions. Similarly, in 1910, Max Planck published lectures which he had just delivered in New York. In one of these, when discussing the second principle of thermodynamics, the entropy-principle, the author states emphatically that those who try to build up physics on the assumption that a study of local elements has to precede any attempt to explain the behavior of larger systems will never understand the entropy-principle, the principle which deals with the direction of physical processes. Or take Eddington, the astronomer, who once wrote the following sentences: "In physics we are often invited to inspect all tiny elements of space in succession in order to gain a complete inventory of the world." But, the author objects, if we were to do this, "all properties of the physical world would be overlooked which cannot be found or understood as matters of tiny elements in space."

I was greatly surprised by these statements of eminent scientists which so obviously agreed with statements made by Gestalt psychologists. Did these great physicists merely add further mysteries to the mysteries in which, according to many critics, the Gestalt psychologists were mainly interested? Actually, these physicists did not refer to mysteries at all. Rather, they studied a great many specific physical situations and did so in an extraordinarily clear fashion. They handled these situations as wholes rather than as collections of small, local, independent facts; they had to because of the nature of such situations, the parts of which are all functionally related (or interdependent) so that what happens at a given moment at a place happens only so long as conditions and events everywhere else in the system are not altered, so long, that is, as all interactions within the whole system remain the same.

Most of us are probably familiar with Kirchhoff's laws which describe the distribution of a steady electric flow in a network of wires. When looking at the fairly simple expression which indicates what occurs within a particular local branch of the network, we see at once that this expression refers to the conditions of conduction not only in this particular local branch but also to conditions in all other branches. This is, of course, necessary because, in the steady state, the local currents throughout the network must balance one another—which means that, while a current develops in the local branch, its flow is influenced by the flow in all other branches as much as by the condition in the interior of its branch. What could be more natural when function is balanced everywhere within the system as a whole? Obviously, there is no mystery in this behavior of physical system. And there would be no mystery either if the same kind of thing happened in a brain rather than in a network of wires. To be sure, networks of wires are exceptionally simple examples; other systems in which functional interrelations determine local facts in a far more radical fashion are not so easy to handle.

I was much impressed by such facts in physics. They offered a striking lesson to psychology in general and seemed to give Gestalt psychology a most welcome justification. I wrote, in Africa, a book about this part of exact physics and its possible application to psychology and to the understanding of brain function. The book has remained practically unknown in this country, partly, I think, because it uses the language and the logic of field physics, a part of physics with which not all of us are familiar.

When the book was published in 1920, both Wertheimer and Koffka greatly enjoyed its content. It showed that the alleged mysteries of Gestalt psychology agreed with perfectly clear procedures and facts in natural science. In a sense, Gestalt psychology has since become a kind of application of field physics to essential parts of psychology and of brain physiology.

When I was able to return to Germany, I found a most lively group of students just appearing at the Psychological Institute of the University of Berlin. They were attracted by Wertheimer, by Kurt Lewin, and, to a degree, by what I had discovered when experimenting with chimpanzees and reading physics in Africa. Not all our work referred to Gestalt psychology. For instance, we managed to prove that the famous moon illusion is by no means restricted to situations in which the sky and the moon play the decisive rôle. But Gestalt psychology remained the central issue. A few simple examples. One student, Scholz, examined the distance between two successively shown parallel lines when the rate of their succession was varied. He found that the second line appeared clearly too near the first line long before the rate of the succession approached that needed for apparent movement. Hence, the second line was attracted by some remnant of the first, just as Wertheimer had said. Or again: in an attempt to investigate time-errors in the comparison of shapes, and the connection of such errors with the fate of young memory traces, Lauenstein did some beautiful experiments. Also, just about the same time, von Restorff and I applied Gestalt principles of perception to problems of memory, and in doing so discovered the so-called isolation effect. Kurt Lewin, too, did experiments in memory. But his main achievements were experiments in which he boldly transferred psychological situations from ordinary life to the laboratory and thus enlarged the range of psychological investigations in a highly productive fashion.

The most important person of our group, however, remained Wertheimer, who at the time was completing his most significant study in perception, his investigation of the way in which objects, figures and patches are segregated from their environment as circumscribed entities. Perhaps it was not emphasized at the time, but for most of us it became the main result of his observations that, in this fashion, he gave a perfectly clear meaning to the term "perceived wholes"—which, before, had sounded so mysterious to many colleagues. Obviously, the appearance of wholes of this kind is just as much a matter of division or separation within the visual field as it is of their coherence, their unitary character.

So long as Wertheimer's observations referred only to well-known unitary things, many authors were inclined to believe that it was merely learning ("previous experience") which makes them appear as firm units detached from their environment. But Wertheimer continued his investigation of perceptual wholes when the units in question were unitary groups of individual objects rather than simple things. In such situations one can often demonstrate that the formation of specific group units is not a matter of prior learning. Wertheimer did not deny that sometimes past experience does influence perceptual grouping. But, on the other hand, one should not forget what Gottschaldt once demonstrated: that, in many cases, purely perceptual organization is too strong to be affected by past experience, even when this past experience is, as such, most powerful.

In the meantime, several European and American psychologists who were not members of the Gestalt group became intensely interested in its work. They had begun independently to work on similar problems. One such person was Edgar Rubin who concentrated on what he called the relation of "figure" and "ground" in perception. For instance, even when an object is part of a large frontal-parallel plane, this object appears slightly separated from the ground and stands out in the third dimension. We now know that this separation is not only a qualitative curiosity but a real perceptual depth effect which can easily be varied in a quantitative fashion, and may then establish quite specific shapes in three-dimensional space.

Other psychologists who turned in the same direction were David Katz and Albert Michotte in Europe, Lashley, Klüver and, to a degree, Gibson in America. I wish more people would study Michotte's marvelous publications, and also a lecture which Lashley delivered in 1929, when he was president of the American Psychological Association. The spirit of this lecture was throughout that of Gestalt psychology; later, it is true, Lashley became a bit more sceptical. Once, when we discussed the main tenets of Gestalt psychology, he suddenly smiled and said: "Excellent work—but don't you have religion up your sleeve?"

Time is too short for a discussion of the great achievements of Wertheimer and Duncker in the psychology of thinking. Their work in this field may be regarded as the last great development in Gestalt psychology that occurred in those years. Since then almost all members of the old school have died, and only a few younger psychologists are left whose investigations are clearly related to those of the earlier period. Solomon Asch is the most important person among them; I wish Mary Henle would add some further publications to the excellent specimens already available. Arnheim, Wallach and Heider are all well known to us.

When the Nazi regime became intolerable I emigrated to the United States which I knew well from earlier visits. In America, I tried to continue the investigations which had been started in Berlin. For instance, when actual perceptions have disappeared, traces of them must be left in the nervous system. They are supposed to be the factual condition which makes recall of those perceptions possible. My first question was: traces of what in perception? Perceptual fields contain not only individual objects but also other products of organization such as segregated groups, sometimes groups which contain only two members. Grouping of this kind may be just as obvious in perception as are the individual members of the groups. Now, this means a perceptual unification or connection within the group, and there is no reason why, in the realm of memory traces, this connection or unification should not be just as clearly represented as are the members of the group. Consequently, when the group has only two members, we must expect these members to be connected not only in perception but also as traces. How would this fact manifest itself in memory?

Among the concepts used in the psychology of memory, the concept "association" may mean, for instance, that two items in a perceptual field are functionally so well connected that, when one of them is reactivated, the same happens also to the other item. This is precisely what one has to expect if, in perception, the two items form a pair-group, and if the unitary character of the perceived pair is represented as a correspondingly unitary entity in the realm of traces. If this were true, the concept of association would be directly related to the concept of organization as applied to pairs in perception.

This assumption can be tested in simple experiments in the following manner. The formation of pairs in perception depends upon the characteristics of the objects involved; it is, for instance, most likely to occur when these objects resemble each other—or when both belong to the same class of objects. Consequently, if association is an after-effect of pair-formation in perception, association must be most effective precisely when the objects are similar or at least obviously members of the same general class. Tests of this conclusion could be quite easily arranged and showed, for instance, that association of members of a given class is far more effective than association of objects dissimilar in this sense. I fully realize—and some, Postman in particular, have emphasized—that this result may still be explained in another fashion; therefore, I have just begun to do further experiments which ought to tell us whether or not the organizational interpretation of our results is correct. Work in a young science is an exciting affair. It becomes particularly

exciting when new functional possibilities have just been introduced. I am grateful to those who make the present issue even more
exciting by their objections. They force me to do further experiments which will decide whether the concept of organization is
applicable to basic facts in memory.

Objections have also been raised against the Gestalt psychologist's organizational explanation of the isolation-effect, or the Restorff-effect. Here again, some investigators, including Postman,
believe that the intrusion of dangerous concepts developed in the
study of perception may be avoided and replaced by older, well-
known, and therefore (according to them) healthier ideas. I recently constructed sets of experiments which had to have one result
if the Restorff-effect can be understood in the conservative way but
just the opposite result if this effect must be interpreted as a consequence of organization in perception and in memory. The results
clearly prove that, in this case, the unhealthy organizational explanation is undoubtedly correct.

Another more recent investigation referred to a problem in perception. Wallach and I tried to discover whether, after prolonged
presentation of visual objects in a given location, these objects (or
others) show any after-effects such as changes of size or of shape.
When numerous objects and combinations of objects had been used
for the purpose it became perfectly clear that prolonged presence of
a visual object in a given place not only causes distortion of this
object but also displacements of other test-objects, displacements
away from the previously seen inspection-objects. Practically any
visual objects may serve as inspection-objects in such experiments.
Eventually it became obvious that the well-known distortions observed by Gibson in the case of some particular figures such as
curves and angles were special examples of a veritable flood of what
we now call figural after-effects.

When we had studied the figural after-effects which occur in a
frontal-parallel plane before the observer, Wallach and I asked ourselves whether there are not similar distortions and displacements in
the third dimension of visual space. These experiments clearly
showed that there are displacements of test-objects in the third
dimension, and that these are often even more conspicuous than the
displacements which occur in the first two dimensions. Next, I tried
another perceptual modality, namely kinesthesis, where Gibson had
already observed a figural after-effect. We could not only corrobo-

rate Gibson's findings but also observe such effects in further kinesthetic situations. Again, not only in the kinesthetic modality but also in simple touch were examples of figural after-effects immediately observable. Once, when I tried auditory localization, displacements of the same kind seemed to occur. Obviously, then, figural after-effects can be demonstrated in most parts of the perceptual world. This made us look with some suspicion at facts in perception which had generally been regarded as facts of learning. The Müller-Lyer illusion, for instance, can be abolished or greatly reduced when the pattern is shown repeatedly. This fact had previously always been regarded as a matter of learning how to observe the pattern better and better. But one look at this pattern suggests that it is most likely to develop considerable after-effects, effects which would surely reduce the size of the illusion under conditions of continued or often-repeated observation. Fishback and I found that such after-effects, not learning in the usual sense, were probably the right explanation of the reduction of the illusion so often found by other psychologists.

Now, what kind of change in the nervous system is responsible for all these after-effects? Or, what kind of process occurs in so many parts of the nervous system and always has about the same result? This question I regarded as particularly important because it seemed probable that the very process which is responsible for normally organized perception also causes the figural after-effects when perception continues to occur in a given place for some time.

The nature of figural after-effects in the visual field made it fairly easy to discover a good candidate for this fundamental rôle. The candidate must be able to explain the following facts:

1. The figural after-effects are the result of an obstruction in the nervous system. Why else should test-objects recede from the places where inspection-objects have been seen for some time?

2. The process in question and the obstruction which it causes cannot be restricted to the circumscribed area in which the inspection-object is seen. Otherwise, why does even a fairly remote test-object recede from that area?

3. The intensity of the process which causes the obstruction has to be particularly great near the boundary between the inspection-object and its background. For simple observa-

tions show that the displacements of test-objects are particularly conspicuous just inside and outside this contour, in
both cases, of course, away from the contour.

These simple statements almost tell the physiologist what kind
of process occurs in the brain when we see visual objects, and which
then produces the figural after-effects. Among the processes possible
in the brain only steady electrical currents spreading in the tissue as
a volume conductor have the functional characteristics just mentioned. Such currents would originate when a circumscribed area
with certain characteristics is surrounded by a larger area with
different properties. The currents would pass through the circumscribed area in one direction, and would then turn and pass through
its environment in the opposite direction so that a closed circuit and
current result. Consequently all together just as much current
would pass through the environment as flows through this circumscribed area, a behavior which fits our condition (2). The current
would be most intense near the boundary of the two regions, because here the lines of flow will be shortest and thus the resistance
lowest—a behavior which fits our condition (3). Condition (1), the
fact that the processes in question must cause an obstruction in the
tissue, is satisfied by any currents which pass through layers of cells.
In fact, the flow has several kinds of effects on the tissue, all of them
well known to the electrophysiologists. When the flow continues for
some time, these effects are obstructions. Physiologists in Europe
call these obstructions electrotonus, a name which (for unknown
reasons) has not become popular in the United States. The term
means that where currents enter cells, a kind of resistance or, better,
obstruction develops in to the surface layers of the cells, and this
reduces the local flow—whereupon the current is forced to change
its own direction and distribution. Thus the current has precisely
the effects which appear in perception as distortions and displacements, in other words, as figural after-effects.

We have now returned to field physics, but field physics applied to the neural medium. I need not repeat that which I
explained in the beginning of my report. What happens locally to a
current that flows in a volume conductor is not an independent local
event. What happens locally is determined and maintained within
the total distribution of the flow. Actually, our explanation is so
natural that when I once showed figural after-effects to the great

British physiologist Adrian, he turned to me after a few demonstrations, and said with a smile: "Nice demonstrations of electrotonus, aren't they?" He had never seen figural after-effects before, and did not know at all that his suggestion agreed entirely with our own explanation.

Although this explanation seemed plausible enough, could we be sure that the brain is really pervaded by quasi-steady currents when we perceive? We could not, and therefore I tried to record such brain-currents when visual objects appeared before human subjects or animals. This was not an easy task. To be sure, several physiologists (again in England) had recorded steady currents from other active parts of the nervous system, but not from the striate area, the visual center of the brain. After initial attempts made in order to discover optimal conditions for what we planned to do, we did succeed, and could record many such currents not only from the visual but also from the auditory cortex. I am surprised to see that, so far, no physiologists have repeated or continued our work. Too bad: the micro-electrode inserted in an individual cell seems to have abolished all interest in more molar functions of the nervous system.

Our observations lead to one question after another. For instance, how do currents of the visual cortex behave when the third dimension of visual space is conspicuously represented in what we see? Or also, are currents of the brain capable of establishing memory traces in the brain?—And so forth. The situation is exciting. What we now need more than anything else are people who get excited. Sooner or later there will be some people who enjoy the atmosphere of adventure in science, the atmosphere in which we lived when Gestalt psychology just began its work. If that could develop in Germany, why should it not also happen in America, the country which once produced so many pioneers?

13

Force Differentiation in Human Subjects

Donald E. Mintz · Joseph M. Notterman

The experiment described in this paper has the following objectives: (1) to test the premise that response differentiation is a special instance of ordinary stimulus discrimination; (2) to extend traditional psychophysical procedures in such a way that they permit examination of this premise.

The typical Weber ratio (or stimulus-discrimination) curve shown in Figure 1 (page 150) was obtained from four human subjects. Their task was to exert (with the right forefinger) required levels of force on an essentially immobile "lever." Visually displayed feedback—giving in numbers the actual force emitted—followed each response, and presumably served as reinforcement.

Apart from yielding the $\Delta F/F$ functions, the data also indicate that the rate of responding decreased as the force required of the subjects was increased.

ABSTRACT

Force of response was differentiated in four human Ss using a quantitative visual feedback procedure. Variations in the force required produced systematic changes in rate of response and in the precision with which the response was made.

INTRODUCTION

In a series of experiments with Wistar rats reported elsewhere (Notterman and Mintz, 1965), the proposition is advanced that the ordinary bar press relies to a greater extent than is ordinarily recognized upon proprioceptive and cutaneous feedback for its successful

From *Psychonomic Science* (1965), Vol. 2, pp. 289–290; reprinted by permission.

emission. In this sense, the precision with which an organism comes to meet a specific force requirement depends just as much upon cue discrimination as does the occurrence of a response to exteroceptive-stimulus cues (Notterman and Mintz, 1962). If discriminative processes do indeed underly the phenomenon of response differentiation, then the conventional analytic techniques of psychophysics should facilitate their description.

The study reported here extends the earlier work to consideration of a simple, differentiated response emitted by adult human Ss (two males and two females), and attempts to describe their behavior in terms of the well-known Weber ratio.

METHOD

The apparatus consisted of an operant force measuring system essentially identical to that described in greater detail by Notterman and Mintz (1965). The manipulandum was a strain gauge lever with a ½ in. diameter horizontal contact surface which each S was instructed to press with his right forefinger. Displacement of the lever was negligible under the range of forces used in the experiment; there were no audible correlates of response emission. A Hewlett-Packard 405 AR Digital Voltmeter was placed at eye level approximately 36 in. distant from the S. The voltmeter provided an arabic numeral readout of response peak force in gm to unit values. A panel containing five white christmas tree lamps in horizontal array was placed on top of the voltmeter. Immediately above each lamp was a printed label reading "25," "50," "100," "150," and "200," from left to right. The test chamber was sound-insulated.

A force of 10 gm was required to activate the system and to count as a response. The digital voltmeter registered the peak force of response approximately 200 msec. after response termination. This value remained until the next response was recorded.

Each S was given 10 training sessions on successive weekdays. Prior to each session the following instructions were read by the Ss:

"Your task is to learn to press the lever with a precise force. In front of you is a visual display of five lights directly above the illuminated numbers on the digital voltmeter. The numbers on the voltmeter will tell you the exact force of your response immediately after you have terminated the response. The numbers above the five lights give you the target force. For instance, when the light below

"100" is lit, you are to try to press the lever with a force of 100 gm. Immediately after the response the voltmeter will indicate the peak force you exerted. The forces required are as indicated: 25, 50, 100, 150, and 200 gm.

"Your responses are to be made with the right index finger. The hand support and arm rest may be positioned in whatever way you find comfortable. You may press the lever as frequently as you wish, using only the right index finger.

"The force requirement will change periodically. The change will be preceded by a loud audible click and the new requirement will be indicated by the appropriate light. Each target force will be in effect for one minute before changing. Every fifth minute none of the lights will be lit, giving you a one-minute rest.

"It is emphasized that you should try to come as close to the required force value as you can. The entire session will last 23 minutes; four minutes with each force requirement, and three one-minute rests."

Each session began with the 25 gm force requirement, with subsequent ascending and descending sequences of the five force criteria.

RESULTS AND DISCUSSION

The data presented are averages for the last two of the 10 daily sessions. No systematic performance changes across these two sessions were apparent. For all measures except response rate, the first five responses following a change in force criterion were omitted from the computations, since the objective of the experiment was to assess stable discriminative performance.

Table 1 provides the mean and standard deviation of peak force, and mean response rate for each S performing under the five force criteria. A small, though significant underestimation is evident in the mean peak force (sign test, 5% level). Rate of response shows a systematic inverse relation to force required (and emitted) for all Ss.

Figure 1 gives the ratio of the standard deviations to the required values for response peak force ($\Delta F/F$), plotted as a function of peak force criterion (F). These measures are comparable to the familiar Weber ratio, and provide an index of the relation between response variability and required magnitude of the force emission.

Table 1. Mean and standard deviation of response force, and mean response rate for each subject.

CRITERION (grams)	SUBJECTS			
	NK	JK	RF	DM
Mean Peak Force (grams)				
25	24.6	24.9	24.9	24.6
50	49.6	51.6	49.1	50.0
100	98.3	101.2	98.3	100.1
150	147.5	152.6	147.7	149.7
200	198.0	200.9	193.8	198.6
Standard Deviation (grams)				
25	3.6	4.3	2.7	2.1
50	6.1	5.3	5.7	4.4
100	10.4	7.5	9.0	7.9
150	15.6	11.5	11.6	10.4
200	20.3	15.7	13.5	13.2
Response Rate (responses per min.)				
25	35.0	30.5	38.9	49.3
50	32.3	28.5	35.6	47.4
100	30.0	26.5	33.0	45.1
150	28.8	25.4	31.3	42.9
200	27.8	23.9	30.8	42.5

The form of the obtained function suggests that $\Delta F/F$ is approaching the range of constancy.

The results of this experiment bear a striking resemblance to psychophysical data although the procedure is fundamentally that of a free-operant response differentiation. Reinforcement may be assumed implicit in the visual feedback (force readout) following the response. In addition, the visual feedback serves as a discriminative stimulus for the subsequent response. Part of this cueing function is presumably shared by the S's cutaneous and proprioceptive sensations during response emission. During the course of a given response, the S "adjusts" the response-feedback stimuli concomitant with force emission until they match the "standard," the sensations accompanying previously reinforced responses. Upon response termination, the quantitative nature of the visual feedback provides a cue for change in response force on the next response. An indication of supra-criterion force is the cue for subsequent force

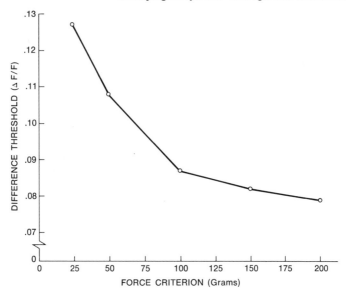

FIGURE 1. Ratio of standard deviation of peak force to peak force required as a function of the latter. Points are averages for four Ss.

decrement, and vice versa.

The foregoing analysis suggests that response differentiation is in essence a discriminative process. Reinforcement establishes the implicit "standard" against which subsequent behavior is matched.

Effort expenditure may also influence the results. This is indicated by both the regular decrement in response rate with a higher force criterion, and the general tendency toward underestimation in force emission.

REFERENCES

NOTTERMAN, J. M., AND MINTZ, D. E. Dynamics of response. New York: Wiley, 1965.
————, AND ————. Exteroceptive cueing of response force. *Science,* 1962, **135**, 1070–1071.

NOTE

1. This research was supported at Princeton University by the Office of Naval Research, Physiological Psychology Branch, under contract NONR 1858 (19).

Cognitive
Processes

V

14

Language and Behavior

Robert Cohn

The writer of this thought-provoking commentary on verbal behavior is a neurologist with extensive interest in language function.

He begins by tracing the origins of various alphabets. Initially, these were pictorial signs, representative of ordinary objects in Homo sapiens' early environment. Through the process of concept formation, the symbols depicting specific objects were eventually generalized to other objects having similar stimuli or functions in common. These generalized graphic symbols subsequently acquired characteristic names or sounds, leading—in turn—to the phonetic components of alphabets, and the formation of written words.

Cohn pursues the argument, originally advanced by Sapir and Whorf, that modern man's behavior—even to the way he perceives his environment—has become captive of his verbal processes. He closes on a pessimistic note; namely, that verbal communication can—in the long run—lead to society's destruction. Such maladaptation may be the consequence of verbal practices that accentuate, rather than minimize, differences within loosely structured cultural groups.

At its most complex level, language may be viewed as a means whereby goal-directed, social-adaptive and appetitive functions are performed. Under these conditions behavior and language become equivalents.

It seems quite unavailing to inquire directly into the specific origin of phonetic verbal language, as by its nature sound phenomena are retained only as memory traces in the brain of the recipient and speaker. However, through a study of the origin of graphic forms, some insight into all verbal forms may be achieved. This derives from the fact that brain function, as nearly all other biological phenomena, is basically repetitive and conservative.

Since the earliest *known* presentations of graphic verbal forms were indelibly inscribed in, or on, stone, clay, and other relatively indestructible material, they are particularly well-suited for studies

From *American Scientist* (1961), Vol. 49, pp. 502–508; reprinted by permission.

on the origin of language. These graphic verbal symbols appear to have arisen through generalizations of pictures which originally represented figures of common objects of the environment; i.e., as a direct representational form. In Fig. 1, an extremely early picture

FIGURE 1.

writing in stone is shown: a foot, asteroid, and circle are depicted. The meaning of this inscription is not known, but it has been suggested that the symbols were an astronomical marker and that the action indicated might have been, "Stand here to see the stars and moon"(1). More evidence of the pictorial origin of the symbols of verbal communication is observed in the material comprising Fig. 2. This is adapted from W. F. Albright's *Archeology of Palestine* (2). In this figure only the most obviously related pictures and symbols were included. Among these symbols are configurations that are similar to those extant in the Egyptian hieroglyphic writings.

Evidence that man's brain operates in a similar way, irrespective of the wide disparity of the geographic regions of productivity, is shown in the uses of pictures, particularly stylized heads, in Mayan and other Meso-American writings. Figure 3 is from Förstemann's paper in the Bulletin of Ethnology (1911); it shows a portion of the glyphs in the famous Cross of Palenque. The elaborate forms of heads, hands, and other ornamental objects are noteworthy. In the Far East strong elements of early pictographic forms have persisted in the graphic verbal language of the modern era.

From pictographic representations having sign value, or the

SINAITIC SCRIPT	DESCRIPTION OF SIGN	CANAANITE SCRIPT OF 13th CENT. B.C	CANAANITE SCRIPT OF c. 1000 B.C.	SOUTH ARAB SCRIPT OF IRON AGE	HEBREW NAME	PHOENICIAN SCRIPT OF 8th CENT. B.C. BAAL LEBANON	KARATEPE	OLD GREEK SCRIPT OF 8th CEN. B.C.	HEBREW CURSIVE OF c. 600 B.C.
	OX-HEAD				ALEPH				
	FENCE?				HETH				
	PALM OF HAND				KAPH				
	"OX-GOAD"				LAMEDH				
	WATER				MEM				
	SERPENT				NUN				
	EYE				AYIN				
	HUMAN HEAD				RESH				
	BOW				SHIN				
	MARK OF CROSS				TAW				

FIGURE 2.

property of denoting, written language developed to the phase where a picture no longer represented a specific object, but became related to a class of objects, or to a class of ideas. That is, the graphic form became an equivalent ideographic symbol able to generate particular responses in a particular culture. Later these ideographic forms as shown in Fig. 2 were utilized only for their phonetic characteristics to produce words. The precise time required for this latter development, of course, cannot be definitely determined, but it probably differed greatly in various cultures. In general, the earliest known graphic verbal and phonetic verbal equivalents had syllabic relationships; that is, there was a multi-consonantal rather than a monoconsonantal relation (as in alphabetic symbols) between the spoken and written media. A good example of the change in a representational symbol to phonetic correlates is afforded by the "water" symbol of Fig. 2. In ancient Egyptian the water symbol was called by its name "mem" and only later did it become a syllabic designator in complex phonetic combinations. With the law of parsimony of effort applying its relentless pressure, single signs were necessarily invented for particular sounds to generate the alphabets such as are in use today in nearly all major cultures.

The earliest extant written materials appeared to be practical in that they pertained to the listing of kings' names and genealogies, to

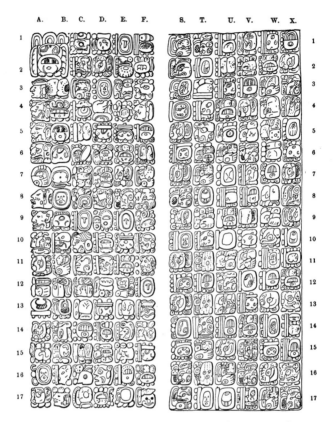

FIGURE 3. Inscription on the tablet of the Cross-Palenque.

the designation of commercial accounts, to the execution of rituals, to the propounding of astronomical and mensuration tables, as well as other data that required a relatively minimal amount of descriptive conceptualization and feeling. In a relatively short time from the first pictographs, legal documents, and even sagas appeared in Egyptian, Babylonian, Hebraic, Minoan Greek, and Hittite literature (3, 4). Language thus appeared to develop rapidly from pragmatism to a purveyor of esthetics. In the wake of this phenomenon, descriptive modes became more precise; through these media accurate description of environmental changes, as well as other changes in physical state, could be precisely chronicled and the milieu in which science could flourish was established.

It is worthy of special emphasis that man, who as Homo sapiens is presumed to have had his origin approximately 50,000 years ago, or around the end of the Mousterian cultural period (5), required nearly 40,000 years of acculturation before a definite written mode of expression was developed. Having invented this mode, it required only approximately 1000 more years to generate written language forms that could basically express his acquired properties; and within certainly much less than another 1000 years man utilized graphic verbal language to express highly complex descriptive material. This overwhelmingly rapid development of written verbal language is remarkable as an expression of the need and material importance of this cultural attribute—and of man's ingenuity.

To cap this explosive growth of man's instrumentalities of expression, a new horizon has been achieved with the introduction of digital computer systems. These not only perform prodigious mathematical computations, but may be programmed to read, to translate foreign languages, and even more pervading, to activate the performance of a stupendously versatile set of mechanical operations (6). This output makes obsolete many human mechanical and intellectual skills, except, of course, *Programming;* that is, the *art* of task-orienting the machine.

To emphasize the phenomenal growth of expression through graphic systems, Fig. 4 shows time plotted against arbitrarily defined achievement as determined by content, amount, and complexity of written material. The dashed line represents the relatively known growth; the dotted line shows the extrapolation based on the same rate of growth [the two are separated by an arrow]. If such linear extrapolations are valid, graphic writing may have had its origin around 7000 or 8000 years ago.

Insidiously, man's invented verbal communication modalities exerted restrictive forces through their *formality* and because of the relative paucity of expression forms in equating sense impressions with physical change. The divergence of sense-data from language results from the fact that even under optimum conditions the organism samples only segments of the impinging energy spectrum generated by the environment; that is, vision, hearing, and so on, represent only punctuate bands of energy in the continuous energy spectrum. Moreover under conditions of existence as goal-directed systems, the organism does not respond with maximal efficiency to

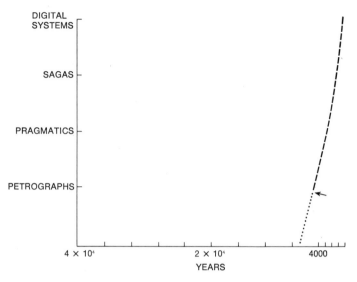

Figure 4.

any *single modality* of stimulation. The living organism responds to that which, through past experience, is immediately significant. In clinical settings this significance is demonstrated by response to multiple simultaneous stimuli; under these conditions responses are dependent on the integrity of the nervous system, the instantaneous sentiency and the regions of the organism stimulated (7). Even more compelling, in times of stress an individual who is sorely hurt may be unaware of the crippling injury until the *immediate significant* event has spent its force.

With the dominating forces of formality and expression-sense-data disparity operative, an even stronger relation necessarily developed between thinking° and language particularly as intra- and intercultural functions became more complex. As a consequence, the Sapir-Whorf hypothesis (8) developed the concept that language was a primary determinant of man's actions; i.e., man's ability to observe and respond to his observations was dependent to a high degree on the language forms in which the patterns of observations were made, and the actions executed. This is a particularity of the

° Where thinking may be defined as the process whereby immediacy is correlated with past experience in such a way that actions *can* take place.

general theory of Spengler (9) who stated that man's behavior is influenced and controlled by the general milieu in which the action takes place.

That the culture determines the observations and actions of individuals in a group is demonstrated by many behaviors of man. A homely example is demonstrated in the so-called "pagan" worship practiced by particular groups in certain areas; the outlander sometimes feels a sense of superiority or even pity for the deluded practitioner, but the individual in *his* culture sees no reasons for special interest by the onlooker as he berates, cajoles, or thanks his material God.

As another example of the relation of culture to actions might be the response to a mute unresponsive individual, who is not dead. The "unlearned" man may suspect that the person is possessed by malevolent forces (demons, etc.); to the sophisticate of a culture, similar mute behavior might be indicative of a disturbance of certain natural processes. In the former culture the treatment may be by scourge, by coercion, or by expiation of the offended demons. The sophisticated culture on the other hand aims to rectify the disordered natural processes.

With language playing such a decisive role in our conceptualization of sense impressions, may it not be that language, which to date has been such a dynamic, explosive force in the ascendancy of Homo sapiens, will place this same Homo sapiens at a biological disadvantage for further evolution? This possibility arises from: (1) A lessened ability to recognize and hence respond to important fundamental sense impressions; and (2) to an all-pervasive use of language to influence large language-coherent groups.

With respect to the precision response to sense impressions, if the disparity between sense impression and conceptualization via language does not become too great, the operating "inborn error probability" (10), that is, the inability precisely to change with past experience, would actually render services to man by forcing changes in observations, method, and behavior. However, if the disparity between sense impressions and concepts should become very great, then there is the strong possibility of a dreamlike, loose-coupled "reality."

The large-scale influence of peoples by means of radio, television, and cinema constitutes a potential for the welding of megalic public opinion and mass action that is prodigious. This extends from political propaganda to the selling of any commercial product or subtle idea.

It is most impelling to observe how verbal language, which evolved as an instrument to describe, to define, to sing, to acquaint man with the thoughts of another, which binds time and makes each man heir to the efforts of his brother (and a potential slave to the past) can destroy its maker. There seems to be a widespread belief that many of the social ills that beset man at the present time are the result of imperfect communication. The implication is that if Homo sapiens could really express himself in an understandable idiom he could rationally settle all arising differences of opinion. Such an idea is controverted by many biological phenomena. In simple societies, such as at a bird feeding station, it is observed that the greatest interaction as evidenced by pecking, threatening gestures and actual "fighting" occurs as an intraspecies phenomenon. Outside of the species, size, or power, alone appears to determine the feeding order.

In more highly organized societies, the idea of similar language meaning similar thought, and therefore more rational reactions, also falls down, as exemplified by the intensity and frequency of civil wars. The generality derived from such observations appears to be that when the operants are *commensurate* one can anticipate a strong interplay of forces. It is, therefore, my hypothesis that a major cause of tension among different large language groups is the *similarity* and *commensurateness* of the basic operating cultures. Thus, grossly similar, unwelded cultures allow minimal, but sufficient, differences to be accentuated by propaganda (verbal language) and other persuasive means to the level at which anxiety, distrust, and eventual belligerency become manifest. Under these conditions, language operates to destroy the beauties which it has helped to create.

It is easy for our culture to recognize how the massively armed, thick-skinned, over-sized megalosaurs and mastodons met their doom by progressive overloading of a particular attribute, mass. Is it possible that language (logos) too can develop so rapidly at the expense of all else that it may become destructive of the race? Are we to be known as the extinct "magalogogae" who were destroyed by a single hypertrophied attribute: language?

REFERENCES

1. CHEIRA, E. They Wrote on Clay. Edited by George G. Cameron. The University of Chicago Press, Chicago, Illinois, 1938.
2. ALBRIGHT, W. F. The Archeology of Palestine. Penguin Books, London, Melbourne, Baltimore, 1954.
3. GLANVILLE, S. R. K. Editor, The Legacy of Egypt. Clarendon Press, Oxford, 1941.
4. KRAMER, S. N. From the Tablets of Summer. The Falcon's Wing Press, Indian Hills, Colorado, 1956.
5. WELLS, H. G. The Outline of History. Garden City Books, Garden City, New York, 1949.
6. LOCKE, W. M., AND BOOTH, A. D. Editors, Machine Translation of Languages. Technology Press of MIT and John Wiley & Sons, Inc., New York, 1955.
7. COHN, R. On Certain Aspects of the Sensory Organization of the Human Brain. *J. Nerv. and Ment. Dis.*, 113, 471–484 (1953).
8. HOIJER, H. Editor, Language in Culture. The University of Chicago Press, Chicago, Illinois, 1954.
9. SPENGLER, O. The Decline of the West. Form and Actuality. Alfred A. Knopf, New York, 1944.
10. LANGER, S. K. Philosophy in a New Key. Mentor Book, New York, 1954.

15

The Functioning of Knowledge of Results in Thorndike's Line-Drawing Experiment

Harold Seashore · Alex Bavelas

Scientific journals generally insist that authors include actual data in their reports of original research. Such a policy assures that the findings are subject to the test of replication, or that different methods of analysis can be attempted by others.

The paper by Seashore and Bavelas is noteworthy in at least three respects. First, it reminds us of the fact that scientists occasionally find it necessary to refute a major conclusion drawn by an eminent authority (here, Thorndike). Second, it is illustrative of how simple statistics can be used to develop sophisticated conclusions. And, third, it draws attention to the importance of implicit cues, functioning as knowledge of results in learning situations.

One wonders whether the authors, after having so carefully scrutinized Thorndike's original data (presented in Table 1), were ever made aware of the error contained in their own Table 2! (Hint: The mistake is located in the row labeled "Deviation of medians.")

In his book *Human Learning*[1] Professor Thorndike reports a line drawing experiment as follows:

> You sit at your desk with a large pad of paper and a pencil, close your eyes, say, "Draw a four-inch line with one quick movement," and again and again draw with one quick shove a line intended to be four inches long. You keep your eyes closed throughout. Day after day you do this until you have drawn 3,000 lines, no one of which you have ever seen (p. 8).

From *Psychological Review* (1941), Vol. 48, pp. 155–162; copyright 1941 by The American Psychological Association, and reproduced by permission.

Table 1 shows the results of such an experiment. It illustrates two general truths or principals: (1) that of multiple response or variable reaction, and (2) that of the failure of repetition of the situation to cause learning (p. 10).

Table 1.[a] Distribution of the Responses at Each Sitting in Drawing Lines to Equal 4 Inches with Eyes Closed: Subject _T_

RESPONSE	1	2	3	4	5	6	7	8	9	10	11	12
3.7									1			
3.8								2				
3.9												
4.0			3						3			
4.1			4	1				1	3			2
4.2		4	8			1		3	6	1	2	1
4.3		3	9	1				4	5	3		4
4.4		13	12	6			3	4	12	2	4	3
4.5	3	18	18	14	2	7	3	15	14	8	7	11
4.6		20	23	23	3	7	8	13	14	8	14	11
4.7	6	20	14	22	11	14	16	25	13	9	14	21
4.8	6	22	15	18	14	27	17	16	18	15	19	26
4.9	13	17	24	24	22	28	18	21	16	10	18	30
5.0	25	20	16	24	26	21	29	25	14	24	19	20
5.1	27	10	16	12	25	32	14	15	14	22	31	22
5.2	24	11	8	12	24	21	23	25	16	18	28	16
5.3	30	8	2	11	21	13	17	8	18	18	16	12
5.4	17	4	2	8	10	10	7	8	12	12	7	7
5.5	12	1		4	13	8	7	3	10	13	4	3
5.6	7			2	4	7	4	1	4	5	2	2
5.7	3		7	1	4	2	5	2	6	4	3	1
5.8				1				1		2		
5.9	1			1						1	2	
6.0												
6.1												
6.2	1						1					
Total	175	171	174	183	181	198	172	192	200	175	190	192
Median	5.23	4.83	4.77	4.93	5.15	5.07	5.07	4.96	4.97	5.13	5.09	4.96
Q[b]	.16	.22	.23	.22	.19	.19	.21	.24	.33	.24	.21	.20

[a] This is Thorndike's Table 1 as found on page 9 of _Human Learning._
[b] Q is the half of the range required to include the middle 50 per cent of the responses.

Repetition of the situation 3000 times caused no learning. The lines drawn in the eleventh and twelfth sittings are not demonstrably better than or different from those drawn in the first and second (p. 10).

Our question is whether the mere repetition of a situation in
and of itself causes learning, and in particular whether the more
frequent connections tend, just because they are more frequent, to
wax in strength at the expense of the less frequent. Our answer is
No (p. 13).

The repetition of a situation may change a man as little as the
repetition of a message over a wire changes a wire. In and of itself, it
may teach him as little as the message teaches the switchboard. In
particular, the more frequent connections are not selected by their
greater frequency (p. 14).

The further analysis of Thorndike's data which will be given in
this paper was instigated by the sentence, "The lines drawn in the
eleventh and twelfth sittings are not demonstrably better than or
different from those drawn in the first and second," and by the first
sentence in the last quoted excerpt. The writers will demonstrate
that there is a progressive change in behavior of Subject *T* which
can be determined from data in Table 1 and will further argue that
a satisfactory explanation must be inconsistent with the statement,
"The repetition of a situation may change a man as little as the
repetition of a message over a wire changes a wire." According to
the mass of our psychological and physiological principles a subject
who draws about 3000 lines under conditions of high motivation to
make them just four inches long *will be different* as the experiences
multiply. The wire analogy is overdrawn and dangerous.

The writers have no disagreement with the whole of Thorndike's data and argument as presented in *Human Learning* and in
more experimental detail in the *Fundamentals of Learning*.[2] Thorndike set out to establish the relationship between repetition of a
situation and the waxing and waning of those "connections" which
appeared early in the learning process. The broad conclusion given
in the fourth quoted excerpt is obviously sustained by his research.
Further, the writers are supposing that the idea they are about to
elaborate is not unknown to Thorndike; his research program did
not require this further interpretation of the data.The ideas in the
two sentences to which the writers take exception do not seem to
have been raised in the extended presentation in the *Fundamentals
of Learning,* although Thorndike is inclined to believe the shifts in
central tendency from sitting to sitting are essentially chaotic.[3]

Since the sentences were made in relation to a set of data on
Subject *T,* one can assume that Thorndike considered this per-

formance a prototype of data from several subjects. The analysis in this paper is of Subject *T*. In an appendix similar analyses, with brief notes, are made of data from two other subjects.

The principle that knowledge of results facilitates learning has been demonstrated too often to need further discussion here. This principle implies, however, that various amounts of knowledge of results must lead to various degrees of learning, at least when the learner is well-motivated and recognizes his goal. If Subject *T* in Thorndike's line-drawing experiment was an alert and reasonably well-motivated person, the experimental situation as described above can be regarded as one in which Subject *T* had some kind and degree of knowledge of results. Obviously *T* did not know the measured lengths of the lines he was drawing, but the data in the table verify the common-sense observation that *T* must have been aware of the fact that he was not drawing lines twelve inches long or one inch short. If we assume that *T* did have some knowledge of results, then analysis of the data should reveal some trend toward modification of *T*'s behavior during the 2203 lines drawn by *T* during the twelve sittings. Contrary to Thorndike's statement, the lines drawn during the eleventh and twelfth sittings should be demonstrably "different from" the lines drawn in the first and second sittings. If the demonstrated difference is to be considered as learning it must also have the characteristic of being an orderly trend.

These observations may be stated as propositions:

a. Knowledge of results facilitates learning.

b. Subject *T* had some knowledge of results.

c. The knowledge of results which *T* had and his currently increasing body of "past experience" must have modified his responses.

d. The modification of responses would have to be in terms of the knowledge available to *T*. (In other words, the lines drawn would not necessarily tend to change in terms of an objective four inches, but in terms of the experiences of line-length which *T* was having.)

If these four propositions are correct, Table 1 should reveal a tendency for succeeding lines to vary less and less from the central tendency of the lines previously drawn. The following discussion and data are the result of an analysis of Thorndike's table to discover this predicted modification of behavior.

1. *T*'s concept of a four-inch line, in terms of his behavior, was not a standard four inches; all we know is that at the end of his 2203 trials his mean performance was 5.01 inches. This may be defined as *T*'s "experiental 'four-inch' line." Therefore, evidences of learning will have to be found in the modification of behavior which both depends upon and determines this personal norm.

2. Following is a table of the means for each sitting, the standard deviation of each mean, the deviation of each mean from the mean of the total (5.01), and the deviation of each median from the median of the total (5.02) [Table 2].

Table 2

MEANS	5.23	4.85	4.76	4.94	5.16	5.08	5.10	4.95	4.97	5.12	5.05	4.96
Sigma	.26	.29	.31	.30	.27	.28	.34	.34	.43	.34	.31	.29
Deviation of means	.22	.16	.25	.07	.15	.07	.09	.06	.04	.11	.04	.05
Deviation of medians	.21	.23	.25	.09	.13	.05	.05	.06	.05	.11	.07	.06

These data indicate an increasing stability of performance from sitting to sitting when the average of all the responses is considered as the reference point. This does not mean that the subject had a conscious goal of 5.01 inches as his concept of a "four-inch line."

Strictly speaking, the increase in stability which this analysis suggests can only be explained as the effect of preceding trials on succeeding trials. Therefore, a different type of calculation was made.

3. When *T* drew the *first* of his 2203 lines, he must have been governed by his *then existing* concept of a four-inch line. Every succeeding line-drawing act not only progressively changed his concept of a four-inch line, but was in part determined by the cumulative effect of his preceding experiences. If this is so, the mean and median of each sitting from 2 to 12 should deviate less and less from the mean and median, respectively, of the total number of lines drawn previously to that sitting. The results of this analysis are given in Table 3.

4. Let us now divide the 12 sittings into 4 groups of 3 sittings each: group 1 (sittings 1, 2, 3) is an early stage of *T*'s concept formation, while group 4 (sittings 10, 11, 12) is a later stage of concept formation. If *T* is forming an increasingly stable concept,

Table 3

DEVIATION OF SITTING:	FROM:	MEANS	MEDIANS
2	1	.38	.49
3	1– 2	.28	.19
4	1– 3	.01	.04
5	1– 4	.21	.19
6	1– 5	.09	.06
7	1– 6	.09	.05
8	1– 7	.07	.07
9	1– 8	.04	.05
10	1– 9	.12	.12
11	1–10	.03	.06
12	1–11	.05	.07

however factually erroneous, the three sittings *within* group 4 should vary less from each other than those in group 1. The average length of all the lines in sittings 1, 2, 3 was calculated and the mean deviations of the three sittings, from that figure, were in turn averaged; similar computations were made for all the groups. The data are in Table 4.

Table 4

	AVERAGE DEVIATION OF THE THREE MEANS
Group 1 (1, 2, 3)	.216
Group 2 (4, 5, 6)	.080
Group 3 (7, 8, 9)	.070
Group 4 (10, 11, 12)	.050

This evidence presented indicates that *T*'s responses were modified. These modifications were not random but systematic in character and can, therefore, be regarded as evidences of learning. This learning occurred because *T* had knowledge of results.

While Thorndike was correct in concluding that under the given experimental conditions the subject would not improve his performance in terms of an objective four inches and that repetition would not in and of itself fixate the initially predominant line-lengths, he was not correct in concluding that ". . . the lines drawn in the eleventh and twelfth sittings are not demonstrably better than or different from those drawn in the first and second." To be sure, they were not *better* in terms of four inches on a ruler, but that they were *different* it is impossible to deny.

DISCUSSION

This paper was begun because of a statement by Thorndike which does not seem to emerge from the data given to support it. The faulty statement, however, is not of crucial significance in the main line of argument in *Human Learning* and *Fundamentals of Learning*. Through this further analysis of the data attention is called to a need for clarification of the role of knowledge of results in learning.

The writers feel that in the line-drawing experiment, as in other situations in which conscious, motivated subjects are placed for observation of their trends of behavior, we have no basis for asserting or assuming that the subject has no knowledge of results and therefore learning will not occur. A conscious, motivated subject must know something about what he is doing. Even erroneous conceptions of what is occurring in his performances constitute part of his knowledge of results. The accuracy of his private body of knowledge of results depends upon his previous experiences in similar, or even quite remote, situations and upon the sensory cues which are now available to him. Remembered experiences (ideational or motor) and current sensory data, operating in an alert, well-motivated person, are variables which should enable him to learn, even though he has no objective evidence from other persons or by self-measurement with which to check himself.

Ordinarily, as in classrooms, we include under the caption "knowledge of results" only the external applications by other persons of verbal or physical approval or disapproval, with or without details of the successes and failures. Sometimes we permit the learner to gain knowledge of results by self-measurement; we give him physical helps such as rulers, answer books, etc. It is common practice in learning experiments to assert that knowledge of results is not a factor unless introduced in either of these ways. Our main interest, as experimental educational psychologists, in the effects of tutelage, guidance, and knowledge of correct solutions on learning in everyday and school situations has caused us to neglect the study of more subtle knowledge.

However, learning theory must consider other sources of knowledge of results even if these minor sources lead to little learning or even to learning of faulty responses. The psychological analysis of the formation of concepts and of the establishment of motor habits requires that we inspect what the subject himself contributes in the way of analyzing his own performance. The contributions to learning which come from these cues and the interpretations of them by alert, motivated subjects may not always be great; on the other hand they may be considerable. Explanations of transfer of training, positive and negative, must include the variables here indicated. The more passive the learner the less his personally derived knowledge of results will be; the more his past experience is applicable and the more he aggressively seeks to interpret the multitude of sensory cues currently available, the greater the role of this sort of knowledge of results.

The foregoing argument does not demand that performances increase in goodness. It only asserts that, given some knowledge of results, faulty or accurate, derived either from objective, external sources or from internal manipulation of memories and current stimulations of a limited nature, there will be changes in behavior which tend to become stabilized.[4] Individual differences in alertness, motivation, past experience, and sensory acuity will be observed.[5]

Experiments to analyze more precisely the functioning of these lesser sources of knowledge of results should not be too difficult to plan and should contribute to a general theory of learning. The writers have done a preliminary study with only a few subjects which indicates differentials in learning in groups with different degrees of knowledge of results ranging all the way from passive guidance of the subjects through the act to be learned to the conventional reporting of measured error to the subject.

REFERENCES

[1] E. L. THORNDIKE, *Human Learning*, New York: Century Co., 1931. Pp. 200.
[2] ——, *Fundamentals of Learning*, New York: Bureau of Publications, Teachers College, 1932. Pp. 638.
[3] *Fundamentals of Learning*, p. 501.
[4] Some of this stabilization may be in other aspects of the situation than the precise task being studied. Thorndike (*Fundamentals of Learning*,

p. 14) mentions some such changes. Doubtless emotional reactions to the whole situation change too.

5 While the foregoing analysis has indicated an increasing stability of performance from sitting to sitting, it also shows that the standard deviations, as well as the interquartile ranges, do not show a tendency to decrease. In agreement with Thorndike (*Fundamentals of Learning*, p. 499) a tentative explanation may be that the measure of variability within each sitting is a measure of T's kinesthetic acuity and motor control.

16

The Origins of Intellect: Piaget's Theory (Introduction)

John L. Phillips, Jr.

Piaget is a nonconformist. His technique of investigation is insufficiently rigorous for the purists among experimenters, and his mode of therapy is insufficiently conventional for the purists among clinicians. Yet Piaget, in taking his own path, has made brilliant contributions to our understanding of cognitive and perceptual processes, particularly as they develop in the young.

Although brief, Phillip's summary of Piaget's work is sufficiently detailed to provide the reader with some understanding of his basic philosophy and approach. The Swiss psychologist's concepts of "organization," "adaptation," and "function" have much in common with similar ideas advanced by Rosenblueth, Wiener, and Bigelow (Chapter 5); Köhler (Chapter 12); Rosenblith (Chapter 21); and even Hull (Chapter 4). His emphasis upon the biological foundations of behavior is also feedback-oriented and (as shown in the reading) is quite in accord with advanced neurological theorizing, particularly that of Hebb. Piaget uses the word "structure" to refer to the systematic organization of cognitive representations of sensation and response.

The discussion of the preoperational child's conception of velocity will perhaps be clearer if some terms are elaborated. By "preoperational," Piaget refers to a stage of development (between two and seven years) at which the child cannot very readily conceptualize ideas such as quantity, weight, volume, or movement. The last is a particularly difficult concept, since it involves a combination of space and time. For example, it is apparent (at least to the adult) that the faster of two objects will traverse the same distance in less time. Similarly, in a constant interval of time, the faster of two objects must cover a greater distance. These temporal and spatial cues are

From *The Origins of Intellect: Piaget's Theory* by John L. Phillips, Jr. W. H. Freeman and Company. Copyright © 1969, pp. 3–11.

used by the adult when he is called upon to make judgments of velocity (cf.
F. J. Mandriota, D. E. Mintz, and J. M. Notterman. Visual velocity discrimination: Effects of spatial and temporal cues. *Science,* 1962, **138,** 437–438). The
child, however, apparently has to *learn* to respond appropriately to the physics of the situation. Piaget has been eminently successful in describing how
this learning takes place.

PIAGET AND HIS METHODS

Jean Piaget is a Swiss psychologist who was trained in zoology and
whose major interests are essentially philosophical. He and his associates have been publishing their findings on the development of
cognitive processes in children since 1927, and have accumulated
the largest store of factual and theoretical observations extant
today.

Piaget is often criticized because his method of investigation,
though somewhat modified in recent years, is still largely clinical.
He observes the child's surroundings and his behavior, formulates a
hypothesis concerning the structure that underlies and includes
them both, and then tests that hypothesis by altering the surroundings slightly—by rearranging the materials, by posing the problem
in a different way, or even by overtly suggesting to the subject a
response different from the one predicted by the theory.

An example of the method is the investigation of the preoperational child's conception of velocity. The child observes the movement of an object through points *A, B, C,* and *D.* He reports that
the object passed through point *D* "after" point *A* and that it took
"more time" to get from *A* to *C* than from *A* to *B.* From this it might
reasonably be inferred that the child's conception of temporal succession and duration is the same as that of an adult. But the investigation doesn't stop there. The subject is then presented with the
simultaneous movements of *two* objects. The investigator systematically varies the actual distance through which each of the objects move, their time in transit, and their initial and terminal positions relative to one another. When that is done, the child no longer
responds as an adult would in similar circumstances. For example,
if two objects move simultaneously—i.e., if they start simultaneously and stop simultaneously—but at different velocities, the child

will deny their simultaneity of movement. To him, each moving object has a different "time," and one that is a function of the *spatial* features of the display.

The systematic manipulation of variables illustrated by that example is certainly in the tradition of classical experimental science. The example, however, is drawn from one of the more rigorous of the studies done by Piaget and his colleagues. Their investigations often begin with naturalistic observations and continue as an interaction between the child and the "experimenter"— an interaction in which each varies his behavior in response to that of the other.

Another example may serve to illustrate the point: it is an "experiment" designed to reveal the child's conception of number. The child is presented with an assemblage of coins and a large number of flowers; he is asked to tell how many flowers he can purchase with the coins if the price of each flower is one coin. Here is a transcript of one such encounter:

> Gui (four years, four months) put 5 flowers opposite 6 pennies, then made a one-for-one exchange of 6 pennies for 6 flowers (taking the extra flower from the reserve supply). The pennies were in a row and the flowers bunched together: "What have we done?—*We've exchanged them.*—Then is there the same number of flowers and pennies?—*No.*—Are there more on one side?—*Yes.*—Where?—*There* (pennies). (The exchange was again made, but this time the pennies were put in a pile and the flowers in a row.) Is there the same number of flowers and pennies?—*No.*—Where are there more?—*Here* (flowers).—And here (pennies)?—*Less.*[1]

This shifting of experimental procedures to fit the responses of a particular subject makes replication difficult, and the results may be especially susceptible to the "experimenter effect."[2] The reader who feels impelled to criticize Piaget's method is in good company. But before becoming too enthusiastic a critic, he should be sure to note the deliberate effort that is made to give the child opportunities for responses that would *not* fit the theory. He should also keep in mind Piaget's epistemological position that knowledge is action.[3] The subject is continually acting. His actions are structured, and they are also to some extent autonomous. The investigator must therefore continually change his line of attack if he is to follow those actions and to discern their underlying structure.

RELATION TO OTHER THEORIES

The early work of Piaget's Geneva group was given considerable attention in the scholarly press, but because psychology, especially in the United States, was at that time dominated by associationistic theories of learning and by content-oriented psychometrics, their work generated little interest.

The current explosion of interest in Piaget's work is an expression of the same concern that produced Hebb's neurological theory and the various contemporary models of the brain as an information-processing system. That concern was probably occasioned not so much by a sudden increase in dissatisfaction with existing theories as by the advances that have taken place recently in neurophysiology and computer engineering.

In any case, Piaget's observations and formulations are today a definite focus of theoretical and professional interest in psychology. The theory is cognitive rather than associationistic;[4] it is concerned primarily with structure rather than content—with *how* the mind works rather than with *what* it does. It is concerned more with understanding than with prediction and control of behavior.

These remarks can of course only be made by way of emphasis, for we can never know the *how* except through the *what;* we can only infer central processes from the behaviors that they organize. An affirmation of one kind of analysis does not necessarily imply a negation of the other. There are conflicts between them, but often the dissonance is more apparent than real, and a careful reading of both kinds of analysis often reveals a harmony that could not be seen at first glance. Hebb's work especially has shown us the way here, and his *magnum opus*[5] is highly recommended to the serious student of psychological theory.

Before turning to the first of Piaget's periods of development, let us take a quick overview of the theory. . . .

OVERVIEW OF PIAGET'S THEORY

Structure and Function

The basic underlying idea is that *functions* remain invariant but that *structures* change systematically as the child develops. This change in structures is development.

Another term found often in Piaget's writing is *content,* by which he means observable stimuli and responses. We may talk in abstract terms about "function" and "structure," but as soon as we cite an actual example, we must deal also with content.

Such an example might be: "A baby looks at a rattle and picks it up." The structure of this event includes the means (looking, reaching, grasping) and the end (stimulation from the object in hand). Each of these is related to the other, and it is this related-ness that Piaget calls "structure."[6] The function of the baby's act is *adaptation*—i.e., the reception and registration of inputs, and the accommodation of each element to the others. "Content" refers to the patterns of input and output.

The term "structure" refers to the systemic properties of an event; it encompasses all aspects of an act, both internal and ex-ternal. "Function," however, refers to biologically inherited modes of interacting with the environment—modes that are characteristic of such integrations in all biological systems. With reference to intelligence, this inherited "functional nucleus" imposes "certain necessary and irreducible conditions"[7] on structures. There are two basic functions: *organization* and *adaptation.* Every act is orga-nized, and the dynamic aspect of organization is adaptation.

. . . Throughout the developmental period, functions are per-manent. But structures are transitory; if they weren't, there would be no development.

ASSIMILATION

If we think of the human brain as a machine for processing information, we must realize not only that it is an exceedingly com-plex machine, but also that its internal structure is continually changing. We are reminded of Hebb's notion that the precise pattern of cortical activity initiated by an incoming stimulus is a function not only of the pattern of that stimulus, but also of what is already going on in the brain. . . . This is close to what Piaget means by assimilation.

Assimilation occurs whenever an organism utilizes something from its environment and incorporates it. A biological example would be the ingestion of food. The food is changed in the process, and so is the organism. Psychological processes are similar in that the pattern in the stimulation is changed and, again, so is the organism.

In introductory psychology courses it is demonstrated that even the perception of an object is not a faithful reproduction of a stimulus pattern. For example, our perception of objects remains the same even though changes in distance, angle of view, and amount of light produce rather striking differences in the size, shape, brightness, and hue of the image that is actually projected onto the retina. (This is, of course, the phenomenon known as "object constancy.") Beyond that, objects are invested with meaning—i.e., they are categorized in terms of such dimensions as familiarity, threat, and beauty. In sum, the input is changed to fit the existing "mediating" processes. The organism is always active, and its cognitions—even perceptions of its immediate surroundings—are as much a function of this activity as they are of the physical properties of the environment.

ACCOMMODATION

But at the same time that the input is being changed by the mediating processes, the mediating processes are being changed by the input. Object constancy, which was just used to illustrate the former, can also be used to illustrate the latter. Each "correction" that is applied by the brain to a retinal image had to be learned—i.e., the mediating processes that act upon the input have themselves been shaped by that input.

Take size constancy, for example. Think of the thousands upon thousands of times that the size of an image on your own retina has covaried with distance from you to the object. Other inputs, such as proprioceptive ones that arise as you have approached the object, and the temporal relations among these, all have contributed to the changing of patterns of mediation.[8] The mechanism by which these changes occur Piaget calls accommodation.

FUNCTIONAL INVARIANTS: ASSIMILATION AND ACCOMMODATION

Accommodation and assimilation are called "functional invariants" because they are characteristic of all biological systems, regardless of the varying contents of these systems. They are not, however, always in balance, one with the other.

Temporary imbalances occur when a child is imitating (accommodation over assimilation) and when he is playing (assimilation over accommodation). Behavior is most adaptive when accommodation and assimilation are in balance, but such a balance is always temporary, because the process of adaptation reveals imperfections in the system. (See the section below on *Equilibration*.)

SCHEMATA

As I mentioned previously, cognitive development consists of a succession of changes, and the changes are structural.

The structural units in Piaget's system are called *schemata*, which is the plural of *schema*. Schemata are roughly equivalent to the "mediating processes" of Hebb and others.[9] They form a kind of framework onto which incoming sensory data can fit—indeed must fit; but it is a framework that is continually changing its shape, the better to assimilate those data.

Figure 1 summarizes some of these relationships.

EQUILIBRATION

One concept that is *not* represented by the diagram is that of *equilibration*. The word will not be used again in this book, but the idea to which it refers should be kept constantly in mind while studying Piaget's theory in subsequent chapters, for it was the inspiration for the theory in the first place and remains its overarching principle.

The idea is that structures continually move toward a state of equilibrium, and when a state of relative equilibrium has been attained, the structure is sharper, more clearly delineated, than it had been previously. But that very sharpness points up inconsistencies and gaps in the structure that had never been salient before. Each equilibrium state therefore carries with it the seeds of its own destruction, for the child's activities are thenceforth directed toward reducing those inconsistencies and closing those gaps.

The process by which structures change from one state to an-

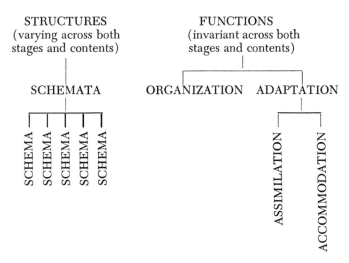

FIGURE 1.

other is called *equilibration,* and the result of that process is a state of *equilibrium.* Equilibrium is always dynamic and is never absolute. . . .

Developmental Units

Piaget conceives intellectual development as a continual process of organization and reorganization of structure, each new organization integrating the previous one into itself. Although this process is continuous, its results are discontinuous; they are qualitatively different from time to time. Because of that, Piaget has chosen to break the total course of development into units called *periods, subperiods,* and *stages.* Note carefully, however, that each of these cross sections of development is described in terms of the *best* the child can do at that time. Many previously learned behaviors will occur even though he is capable of new and better ones.

✿   ✿   ✿

REFERENCES

[1] JEAN PIAGET AND ALINA SZEMINSKA, *The Child's Conception of Number,* translated by C. Gattegno and F. M. Hodgson, New York: Humanities Press, 1952. (Original French edition, 1941.)

[2] Sometimes called the "Rosenthal effect," after R. Rosenthal, who in several recent studies has demonstrated that even in apparently objective experimental situations, the experimenter can influence the subject's behavior in a number of subtle and unacknowledged ways (facial expression, tone of voice, etc.). Even rat subjects perform better for experimenters who expect them to do so, presumably because of differences in handling by different experiments (R. Rosenthal and K. L. Fade, "The Effect of Experimenter Bias on the Performance of the Albino Rat," *Behavioral Science,* 1963, pp. 183–189, and R. Rosenthal and R. Lawson, "A Longitudinal Study of Experimenter Bias on the Operant Learning of Laboratory Rats," *Journal of Psychiatric Research,* 1964). An interesting study of the experimenter effect in humans is R. Rosenthal and L. Jacobson, *Pygmalion in the Classroom,* 1968.

[3] "Action" need not necessarily be motor.

[4] A cognitive theory is concerned especially with central organizing processes in higher animals, and it recognizes a partial autonomy of these processes, such that the animal becomes an actor upon, rather than simply a reactor to its environment. Actually, the opposite of all this, the so-called associationist doctrine, is to some extent a straw man; for excepting B. F. Skinner, who abjures all theories, there is probably no prominent psychologist today who does not explicitly recognize the importance of mediating processes. But there is a difference in emphasis, and like most straw men this one serves the purpose of accentuating that difference.

[5] D. O. HEBB, *The Organization of Behavior,* New York: John Wiley & Sons, Inc., 1949.

[6] Each by itself has its own structure, too. See also footnote 9.

[7] PIAGET, *The Origins of Intelligence in Children,* translated by Margaret Cook, New York: International Universities Press, 1952, p. 3. (Original French edition, 1936.)

[8] There is recent evidence that some of this organization is innate (T. G. R. Bower, "The Visual World of Infants," *Scientific American,* vol. 215, no. 6 (December 1966), pp. 80–92, and "Phenomenal Identity and Form Perception in an Infant," *Journal of Perception and Psychophysics,* 1967, pp. 74–76).

[9] Actually, Piaget's schemata include also the stimulus that triggers the mediating processes and the overt behavior that presumably is organized by them. Moreover, this whole process can involve interactions among schemata; i.e., they can assimilate each other. Schema, then, is the generic unit of structure. The earliest schemata are relatively simple, but with continued functioning, it becomes increasingly appropriate to consider such synonyms as "strategies," "plans," "transformation rules," "exceptancies," etc.

Modifying Responses Through Drive Operations

VI

17

The Descent of Instinct

Frank A. Beach

Beach traces the concept of instinct as far back as the writings of the early Greek philosophers. It was incorporated as part of Church doctrine during the Middle Ages, and—in one form or another—has found its way into modern, scientific thought.

In essence, the idea of instinct originates in the belief that man's behavior is governed by reason, and that the behavior of lower forms of life is controlled by inborn reflexes. However, Darwin's theory—in that it expounded a continuum between man and lower forms—required, in turn, that man's behavior be viewed as being less governed by reason, and animal's as being less controlled by instinct.

Despite the argument for biological continuity, the theory of evolution did not challenge the existence of the basic dichotomy, one which distinguishes between reason and instinct as wellsprings of behavior. The distinction was made in the early twentieth century by the radical behaviorists, who rejected entirely any explanatory need for the concept of instinct.

Beach points out that in the debate which followed, positions taken pro and con instinct were rarely based upon careful field observation, let alone empirical laboratory data. His own thought is that instinct, as such, is an unduly restrictive concept. He presents evidence which indicates that often what is taken to be entirely unlearned behavior can be influenced by a number of factors, ranging from dietary considerations to social variables. He concludes that instinct, as a scientific construct, is vague, and that it has outlived whatever heuristic value it might once have had.

> The delusion is extraordinary by which we thus exalt language above nature:—making language the expositor of nature, instead of making nature the expositor of language (Alexander Brian Johnson, *A Treatise on Language*).

From *Psychological Review* (November 1955), Vol. 62, No. 6, pp. 401–410; copyright 1955 by the American Psychological Association, and reproduced by permission.

The basic ideas underlying a concept of instinct probably are older than recorded history. At any rate they are clearly set forth in the Greek literature of 2,500 years ago. They have been controversial ideas and they remain so today. Nevertheless, the instinct concept has survived in almost complete absence of empirical validation. One aim of the present article is to analyze the reasons for the remarkable vitality of a concept which has stood without objective test for at least two millennia. A second objective is to evaluate the concept as it relates to a science of behavior.

ORIGINS IN PHILOSOPHY AND THEOLOGY

The concept of instinct evolved in relation to the broad problems of human destiny, of Man's place in nature, and his position in this world and the next. From the beginning, instinct has been defined and discussed in terms of its relation to reason and, less directly, to the human soul.

During the fourth century B.C. the Greek philosopher Heraclitus declared that there had been two types of creation. Men and gods were the products of rational creation, whereas irrational brutes comprised a separate category of living creatures. Heraclitus added the observation that only gods and men possess souls. The close relation between rational powers and possession of a soul has been reaffirmed time and again during the ensuing 2,500 years. Heraclitus did not advance the concept of instinct but he laid the groundwork for its development.

Stoic philosophers of the first century A.D. held that men and gods belong to one natural community, since they are rational beings. All animals were specifically excluded since they are not creatures of reason and even their most complex behavior takes place "without reflection," to use the words of Seneca. This stoical taxonomy was both flattering and convenient since, according to the tenets of this school, members of the natural community were forbidden to harm or enslave other members.

It is significant that neither Heraclitus nor the Stoics based their conclusions upon objective evidence. Their premises concerning the psychology of animals were not derived from empirical observation; they were demanded by assumption of the philosophical position that animals lack a rational soul.

Aristotle, who was more of an observer than a philosopher, was of a different mind. In *Historia Animalium* Man is placed at the top of Scala Natura (directly above the Indian elephant), and is accorded superior intellectual powers, but none qualitatively distinct from those of other species.

In the thirteenth century Albertus Magnus composed *De Animalibus*, based chiefly upon the writings of Aristotle but modifying the Aristotelian position where necessary to conform to Scholastic theology. Albertus removed Man from the natural scale, holding that he is unique in possessing the gift of reason and an immortal soul. Animals, lacking reason, "are directed by their natural instinct and therefore cannot act freely."

St. Thomas Aquinas, student of Albertus, supported his teacher's distinction between men and animals. Animals possess only the sensitive soul described by Aristotle. The human embryo is similarly endowed, but the rational soul is divinely implanted in the fetus at some time before birth.* The behavior of man therefore depends upon reason, whereas all animals are governed by instinct. Like the Stoic philosophers, the Scholastics were unconcerned with factual evidence. Their emphasis upon instinctive control of animal behavior was dictated by a need of the theological system, and in this frame of reference instinct was a useful concept.

Roughly four centuries after the time of St. Thomas Aquinas, René Descartes and his followers aggressively restated the existence of a man-brute dichotomy. The bare facts of the Cartesian position are common knowledge, but for the purpose of the present argument it is important to ask why Descartes felt so strongly about the matter—felt compelled to hold up man as the Reasoner, at the same time insisting that all other living creatures are only flesh-and-blood machines. The explanation stands out in the following quotation:

> After the error of atheism, there is nothing that leads weak minds further astray from the paths of virtue than the idea that the minds of other animals resemble our own, and that therefore we have no greater right to future life than have gnats and ants (René Descartes, *Passions of the Soul*).

From Albertus to Descartes the argument runs clear. The theological system posits a life after death. Hence the postulation of the soul. But mere possession of a soul is not enough. Each man

---

* It is not irrelevant to point out that weighty disputation concerning the exact age at which the soul enters the fetus retarded the advancement of embryological knowledge during its seventeenth century beginnings.

must earn the right of his soul's salvation. This in turn depends upon reason, which man exercises in differentiating good from evil, behavior which is sinful from that which is not. An afterlife is man's unique prerogative; no animals share it. They have no souls and therefore no need to reason. But how are the complex and adaptive reactions of subhuman creatures to be explained if not by reason, foresight, volition? They are comfortably disposed of as products of instincts with which the Creator has endowed all dumb brutes.

That the thirteenth-century point of view persists today is shown by the following quotation:

> In animals there are only instincts, but not in man. As St. Thomas points out, there cannot be any deliberation in a subrational being (even though we may get the impression that there is). . . . Instincts in animals seem to operate according to the pattern of physical forces, where the stronger always prevails; for animals are utterly devoid of the freedom which characterizes man. . . . That is why when one studies human behavior one must rise above the purely animal pattern and concentrate upon those two faculties, intellect and will, which separate man from animal (Msgr. Fulton J. Sheen, *Peace of Soul*).

To summarize what has been said thus far, it appears that the descent of the instinct concept can be traced from early philosophies which set man apart from the rest of the living world and sought for him some divine affinity. This was achieved by claiming for man alone the power of reason. By a process of elimination the behavior of animals was ascribed to their natural instincts. During the Middle Ages this dichotomous classification became a part of Church doctrine, with the result that possession of reason and of a soul were inextricably linked to the hope of eternal life. Prescientific concepts of instinct were not deduced from the facts of nature; they were necessitated by the demands of philosophical systems based upon supernatural conceptions of nature.

EARLY SCIENTIFIC USAGE

When biology emerged as a scientific discipline, there was a general tendency to adopt the prescientific point of view regarding instinct. Some exceptions occurred. For example, Erasmus Darwin's *Zoonomia* expressed the theory that all behavior is a product of experience, but this point of view was subsequently disavowed by the grandson of its sponsor. Charles Darwin made the concept of instinct one cornerstone of his theory of evolution by means of natural selection.

To bridge the gap of the Cartesian man-brute dichotomy, and thus to establish the evolution of mind as well as structure, Darwin and his disciples amassed two types of evidence. One type purported to prove the existence of human instincts; the other pertained to rational behavior in subhuman species. The idea of discontinuity in mental evolution was vigorously attacked, but the dichotomy between instinct and reason was never challenged.

The nineteenth-century literature on evolution shows plainly that the concept of instinctive behavior was accepted because it filled a need in the theoretical system, and not because its validity had been established by empirical test.

Contemporary psychologists such as Herbert Spencer were influenced by the evolutionary movement, and the idea of an instinctive basis for human psychology became popular. William James, in Volume II of his *Principles,* insisted that man has more instincts than any other mammal. McDougall's widely read *Social Psychology* listed human instincts of flight, repulsion, parental feeling, reproduction, self-abasement, etc. Woodworth, Thorndike, and other leaders agreed that much of human behavior is best understood as an expression of instinctive drives or needs.

One of the difficulties with such thinking is that it often leads to the nominal fallacy—the tendency to confuse naming with explaining. Some psychological writers were guilty of employing the instinct concept as an explanatory device, and the eventual result was a vigorous revolt against the use of instinct in any psychological theory.

THE ANTI-INSTINCT REVOLT

Dunlap's 1919 article, "Are there any instincts?" (5), was one opening gun in the battle, but the extreme protests came from the most radical Behaviorists as represented by Z. Y. Kuo, who wrote on the subject, "A psychology without heredity" (18). For a while the word "instinct" was anathema, but the revolt was abortive, and there were three principal reasons for its failure.

First, Kuo denied instinct but admitted the existence of unlearned "units of reaction." By this phrase he meant simple reflexes, but in using it he set up a dichotomy of learned and unlearned behavior which was fatal to his basic thesis. It merely shifted the debate to arguments as to the degree of complexity permissible in an unlearned response, or the proportion of a complex pattern that was instinctive. The second error consisted essentially of a return to the position taken by Erasmus Darwin at the close of the eighteenth century. Having averred that the only unlearned reactions consist of a few simple reflexes, the opponents of the instinct doctrine invoked learning to explain all other behavior. This forced them into untenable positions such as that of maintaining that pecking behavior of the newly-hatched chick is a product of head movements made by the embryo in the shell, or that the neonatal infant's grasp reflex depends upon prenatal exercise of this response. The third loophole in the anti-instinct argument derived from a dualistic concept of the hereditary process. Admitting that genes can affect morphological characters, and simultaneously denying that heredity influences behavior, opponents of instinct were hoist by their own petard. If the physical machinery for behavior develops under genetic control, then the behavior it mediates can scarcely be regarded as independent of inheritance.

It is important to note that this war over instinct was fought more with words and inferential reasoning than with behavioral evidence. It is true that a few individuals actually observed the behavior of newborn children or of animals, but most of the battles of the campaign were fought from the armchair in the study rather than from the laboratory.

CURRENT THOUGHT IN PSYCHOLOGY

Although there are militant opponents of the instinct doctrine among present-day psychologists, it is undoubtedly correct to say that the concept of instincts as complex, unlearned patterns of behavior is generally accepted in clinical, social, and experimental psychology. Among experimentalists, Lashley suggested that instinctive behavior is unlearned and differs from reflexes in that instincts depend on "the pattern or organization of the stimulus," whereas reflexes are elicited by stimulation of localized groups of sensory endings (19).

Carmichael (3) expressed agreement with G. H. Parker's statement that human beings are "about nine-tenths inborn, and one-tenth acquired." Morgan (20) studied food-hoarding behavior in rats, and concluded, "since it comes out spontaneously without training, it is plainly instinctive." The following quotation reveals that some modern psychologists not only embrace the concept of instinctive behavior, but consider it a useful explanatory device.

> Of the theories of hoarding which have been advanced, the most reasonable one in terms of recent data is that the behavior is instinctive . . . (28).

At least three serious criticisms can be leveled against current treatment of the problem of instinctive behavior. The first is that psychologists in general actually know very little about most of the behavior patterns which they confidently classify as instinctive. In his paper, "The experimental analysis of instinctive activities," Lashley mentions the following 15 examples:

1. Eating of Hydra by the Planarian, Microstoma.
2. Nest-building, cleaning of young and retrieving by the primiparous rat.
3. Restless running about of the mother rat deprived of her litter.
4. Homing of pigeons.
5. Web-weaving of spiders.
6. Migratory behavior of fishes.
7. Nest-building of birds, including several species.
8. Mating behavior of the female rat in estrus.
9. Dancing reactions of the honeybee returning to the hive laden with nectar.
10. Visual reactions of rats reared in darkness.
11. Responses of the sooty tern to her nest and young.
12. Reactions of the seagull to artificial and normal eggs.
13. Sexual behavior of the male rat.
14. Mating responses in insects.
15. Mating responses in domestic hens.

It is a safe guess that most American psychologists have never observed any of these patterns of behavior. At a conservative estimate, less than half of the reactions listed have been subjected to even preliminary study by psychologically trained investigators. The significance of this criticism lies partly in the fact that those psychologists who *have* worked in the area of "instinctive" behavior tend to be more critical of the instinct concept than are those who lack first-hand knowledge of the behavioral evidence.

Relevant to the criticism of unfamiliarity is the fact that the degree of assurance with which instincts are attributed to a given species is inversely related to the extent to which that species has been studied, particularly from the developmental point of view. Before the development of complex behavior in human infants had been carefully analyzed, it was, as we have seen, a common practice to describe many human instincts. Longitudinal studies of behavior have reduced the "unlearned" components to three or four simple responses not much more complex than reflexes (4).

The second criticism is that despite prevailing ignorance about the behavior which is called instinctive, there is strong pressure toward premature categorization of the as yet unanalyzed patterns of reaction. The history of biological taxonomy shows that the reliability of any classificatory system is a function of the validity of identification of individual specimens or even populations. Unless the systematist is thoroughly familiar with the characteristics of a given species, he cannot determine its proper relation to other groups. Similarly, until psychologists have carefully analyzed the salient characteristics of a given pattern of behavior, they cannot meaningfully classify or compare it with other patterns.

The third criticism of current treatment of instinctive behavior has to do with the classificatory scheme which is in use. When all criteria which supposedly differentiate instinctive from acquired responses are critically evaluated, the only one which seems universally applicable is that instincts are unlearned (21). This forces psychology to deal with a two-class system, and such systems are particularly unmanageable when one class is defined solely in negative terms, that is, in terms of the absence of certain characteristics that define the other class. It is logically indefensible to categorize any behavior as unlearned unless the characteristics of learned behavior have been thoroughly explored and are well known. Even the most optimistic "learning psychologist" would not claim that we have reached this point yet. At present, to prove that behavior is unlearned is equivalent to proving the null hypothesis.

Perhaps a more serious weakness in the present psychological handling of instinct lies in the assumption that a two-class system is adequate for the classification of complex behavior. The implication that all behavior must be determined by learning or by heredity, neither of which is more than partially understood, is entirely unjustified. The final form of any response is affected by a multiplicity of variables, only two of which are genetical and experiential factors. It is to the identification and analysis of all of these factors that psychology should address itself. When this task is properly conceived and executed there will be no need nor reason for ambiguous concepts of instinctive behavior.

GENES AND BEHAVIOR

Experimental investigation of relationships between genetical constitution and behavior was exemplified by the pioneering studies of Yerkes (30), Tryon (27), and Heron (12). Interest in this area has recently increased, and a large number of investigations have been summarized by Hall (11) who anticipates a new interdisciplinary science of psychogenetics.

As Hall points out, the psychologist interested in examining gene-behavior relations has several approaches to choose from. He can compare the behavior of different inbred strains of animals currently available in the genetics laboratory. He can cross two strains and study the behavior of the hybrids. Selective breeding for particular behavioral traits is a well-established technique. The behavioral effects of induced mutations have as yet received very little attention but should be investigated.

It is known that selective breeding can alter the level of general activity (23), maze behavior (12), emotionality (9), and aggressiveness (17) in the laboratory rat. Inbred strains of mice differ from one another in temperature preference (13), aggressiveness (24), and strength of "exploratory drive" (26).

Various breeds of dogs exhibit pronounced differences in behavioral characteristics. Some are highly emotional, unstable and restless; whereas others are phlegmatic and relatively inactive (7). Special breeds have been created by selective mating to meet certain practical requirements. For example, some hunting dogs such as the foxhound are "open trailers." While following a fresh trail they vocalize in a characteristic fashion. Other dogs are "mute trailers." The F_1 hybrids of a cross between these types are always open trailers although the voice is often that of the mute trailing parent (29).

Inbreeding of domestic chickens for high egg production has

produced behavioral deficiencies of various kinds. Although hens of some lines are excellent layers, they have almost totally lost the normal tendency to brood the eggs once they have been laid (15). The maternal behavior of sows of different inbred lines of swine is strikingly different. Females of one line are so aggressively protective of their young that they cannot be approached during the lactation period. Sows of a second genetical line possess such weak maternal interest that they frequently kill their litters by stepping or lying on the young (14).

Study of the effects of controlled breeding cast doubt upon the validity of any classificatory system which describes one type of behavior as genetically determined and another as experientially determined. For example, by manipulating the genotype it is possible to alter certain types of learning ability. As far as present evidence can show, the influence of genes on learning is as important as any genetical effect upon other behavior patterns commonly considered instinctive. There is no reason to assume that so-called instinctive reactions are more dependent upon heredity than noninstinctive responses; hence genetical determination is not a differentiating criterion.

THE MEANING OF GENETICAL DETERMINATION

Behavior which is known to vary with the genotype is often incorrectly defined as "genetically determined" behavior. Although we can show a correlation between certain genes and particular behavior patterns, this is of course no proof of a causal relationship. Many other genes and nongenic factors are always involved in such correlations. This point is nicely illustrated by a series of experiments on audiogenic seizures in mice.

Susceptibility to fatal seizures is high in some inbred strains and low in others (10). When a high-incidence and low-incidence strain are crossed, the susceptibility of the F_1 generation is intermediate between those of the parental strains. So far the evidence strongly supports the conclusion that seizure incidence is genetically determined. However, the incidence of seizures can be altered without changing the genetic constitution.

This is accomplished by modifying the prenatal environment. Fertilized eggs recovered from the tubes or uterus of a female of one strain and introduced into the uterus of a female of a different strain will sometimes implant normally and produce viable young. This has been done using seizure-susceptible females as donors and seizure-resistant females as hosts. Under such conditions the genetical characteristics of the young are unaltered, but their susceptibility to fatal seizures is lower than that of their own genetic strain and higher than that of the "foster" mothers in whose uteri they developed (8).

Studies of this sort emphasize the important but often neglected fact that postnatal behavior is affected by factors acting upon the organism before birth. As Sontag has pointed out, this is true of human beings as well as lower species.

> Fetal environment may play a part in determining characteristics of the physiological behavior of any newborn infant. We are too often inclined to neglect this source of modification of physiological potential. Too frequently we think of the individual as beginning life only at birth. Yet because it is during the period of intrauterine life that most of the cells of the vital organs are actually formed, it is during this period that "environmental" factors such as nutrition, oxygen, mother's hormones, etc., are most important in modifying their characteristics (**25**, p. 482).

Another fundamental principle illustrated by the results of transplanting fertilized ova is that the uniformity of behavior which characterizes highly inbred strains of animals cannot be ascribed solely to homozygosity, but depends as well upon *minimal variability of the prenatal environment*. More broadly conceived, this principle implies that behavioral similarities and differences observable at birth are in part a product of intrauterine effects.

If forced to relinquish the criterion of genetical control, proponents of the instinct doctrine fall back upon the criterion of the unlearned nature of instinctive acts. Now learning is a process occurring through time, and can only be studied by longitudinal analysis. If instinctive acts are unlearned, their developmental history must differ in some significant fashion from that of a learned response.

THE ONTOGENY OF BEHAVIOR

No bit of behavior can ever be fully understood until its ontogenesis has been described. Had psychologists always recognized this fact, much of the fruitless debate about unlearned behavior could have been avoided.

Perhaps the most widely cited psychological experiment on development and instinctive behavior is that of Carmichael, who studied the swimming behavior of larval amphibians (2). He reared embryos in a solution which paralyzed the striped muscles but permitted normal growth. Animals that were thus prevented from practicing the swimming response were nevertheless capable of normal swimming when placed in pure water. These findings are often offered as proof of the claim that swimming is instinctive. However, to demonstrate that practice is not essential for the appearance of a response is only the beginning of the analysis. This point is clearly illustrated by certain observations of insect behavior.

Gravid female moths, *Hyponomenta padella,* lay their eggs on the leaves of the hackberry plant and die shortly thereafter. The eggs hatch, the larvae eat the leaves and eventually become mature. Females of this new generation in turn select hackberry leaves on which to deposit their eggs. Another race of moths prefers apple leaves as an oviposition site. The difference between the two races has been perpetuated, generation after generation, for many centuries. It would appear to be the example par excellence of a genetically controlled behavior trait. But such an explanation is insufficient.

When eggs of the apple-preferring type are transferred to hackberry leaves, the larvae thrive on the new diet. Thirty per cent of the females developing from these larvae show a preference for hackberry leaves when it comes time for them to deposit their eggs (16).

The evidence is of course incomplete. Why only 30 per cent of the insects show a reversal of preference is not clear. It would be illuminating if the same experimental treatment could be repeated on several successive generations. Nevertheless it appears likely that the adult moth's choice of an oviposition site is influenced by the chemical composition of the food consumed during the larval period (6). If this interpretation is correct, the data illustrate the fact that a complex behavior pattern may be "unlearned" and still depend upon the individual's previous history.

Comparable examples can be found in the behavior of vertebrates. Stereotyped patterns of behavior appear with great regularity in successive generations under conditions in which practice plays no obvious role. Nonetheless such "species-specific" responses may be dependent upon previous experience of the organism.

The maternal behavior of primiparous female rats reared in isolation is indistinguishable from that of multiparous individuals. Animals with no maternal experience build nexts before the first litter is born, clean the young, eat the placenta, and retrieve scattered young to the nest (1). However, pregnant rats that have been reared in cages containing nothing that can be picked up and transported do not build nests when material is made available. They simply heap their young in a pile in a corner of the cage. Other females that have been reared under conditions preventing them from licking and grooming their own bodies fail to clean their young at the time of parturition (22).

There are undoubtedly many adaptive responses which appear *de novo* at the biologically appropriate time in the absence of preceding practice, but the possibility remains that component parts of a complex pattern have in fact been perfected in different contexts. Whether or not this is the case can only be determined by exhaustive analysis of the ontogeny of the behavior under examination. Nonetheless, to define behavior as "unlearned" in the absence of such analysis is meaningless and misleading.

SUMMARY AND CONCLUSIONS

The concept of instinctive behavior seems to have originated in antiquity in connection with attempts to define a clear-cut difference between man and all other animals. Human behavior was said to be governed by reasoning, and the behavior of animals to depend upon instinct. In his possession of the unique power of reason, man was elevated above all other creatures, and, incidentally, his use of them for his own purposes was thus morally justified.

Christian theologians adopted this point of view and averred that man was given the power of reason so that he could earn his own salvation. Similar privileges could not logically be accorded to lower animals. Therefore they were denied reason and their behavior was explained as a product of divinely implanted instincts. In both sacred and secular philosophies the concept of instinct served a practical purpose, although in no instance was there any attempt to validate it by examination of the empirical evidence.

The concept gained a central position in scientific thinking as a result of the Darwinian movement. Proponents of the evolutionary theory accepted uncritically the assumption that all behavior must be governed by instinct or by reasoning. Their aim was to demonstrate that animals can reason and that men possess instincts. The same dichotomy has persisted in experimental psychology. Attempts to eliminate the instinct concept were unsuccessful because those who made the attempt accepted the idea that all behavior is either acquired or inherited.

No such classification can ever be satisfactory. It rests upon exclusively negative definitions of one side of the dichotomy. It obscures the basic problems involved. It reflects an unnaturally narrow and naive conception of factors shaping behavior.

To remedy the present confused situation it is necessary first to refrain from premature classification of those kinds of behavior that are currently defined as unlearned. Until they have been systematically analyzed it will remain impossible to decide whether these numerous response patterns belong in one or a dozen different categories.

The analysis that is needed involves two types of approach. One rests upon determination of the relationships existing between genes and behavior. The other consists of studying the development of various behavior patterns in the individual, and determining the number and kinds of factors that normally control the final form of the response.

When these methods have been applied to the various types of behavior which today are called "instinctive," the concept of instinct will disappear, to be replaced by scientifically valid and useful explanations.

REFERENCES

1. BEACH, F. A. The neural basis of innate behavior. I. Effects of cortical lesions upon the maternal behavior pattern in the rat. *J. comp. Psychol.*, 1937, **24**, 393–436.
2. CARMICHAEL, L. The development of behavior in vertebrates experimentally removed from the influence of external stimulation. *Psychol. Rev.*, 1927, **34**, 34–47.
3. ———. The growth of sensory control of behavior before birth. *Psychol. Rev.*, 1947, **54**, 316–324.

4. DENNIS, W. Infant development under conditions of restricted practice. *Genet. psychol. Monogr.*, 1941, **23**, 143–189.
5. DUNLAP, K. Are there any instincts? *J. abnorm. Psychol.*, 1919–20, **14**, 35–50.
6. EMERSON, A. E. Ecology, evolution and society. *Amer. Nat.*, 1943, **77**, 97–118.
7. FULLER, J. L., AND SCOTT, J. P. Heredity and learning ability in infrahuman animals. *Eugenics Quart.*, 1954, **1**, 28–43.
8. GINSBURG, B. E., AND HOVDA, R. B. On the physiology of gene controlled audiogenic seizures in mice. *Anat. Rec.*, 1947, **99**, 65–66.
9. HALL, C. S. The inheritance of emotionality. *Sigma Xi Quart.*, 1938, **26**, 17–27.
10. ———. Genetic differences in fatal audiogenic seizures between two inbred strains of house mice. *J. Hered.*, 1947, **38**, 2–6.
11. ———. The genetics of behavior. In S. S. Stevens (Ed.), *Handbook of experimental psychology*. New York: Wiley, 1951.
12. HERON, W. T. The inheritance of maze learning ability in rats. *J. comp. Psychol.*, 1935, **19**, 77–89.
13. HERTER, K. Die Beziehungen zwischen Vorzugstemperatur und Hautbeschaffenheit bei Mausen. *Zool. Anz. Suppl.*, 1938, **11**, 48–55.
14. HODGSON, R. E. An eight generation experiment in inbreeding swine. *J. Hered.*, 1935, **26**, 209–217.
15. HURST, C. C. *Experiments in genetics.* Cambridge: Cambridge Univer. Press, 1925.
16. IMMS, A. D. *Recent advances in entymology.* Philadelphia: Blakiston's Sons, 1931.
17. KEELER, C. E. AND KING, H. D. Multiple effects of coat color genes in the Norway rat, with special reference to temperament and domestication. *J. comp. Psychol.*, 1942, **34**, 241–250.
18. KUO, Z. Y. A psychology without heredity. *Psychol. Rev.*, 1924, **31**, 427–451.
19. LASHLEY, K. S. Experimental analysis of instinctive behavior. *Psychol. Rev.*, 1938, **45**, 445–471.
20. MORGAN, C. T. The hoarding instinct. *Psychol. Rev.*, 1947, **54**, 335–341.
21. MUNN, N. *Psychological development.* New York: Houghton Mifflin, 1938.
22. RIESS, B. F. The isolation of factors of learning and native behavior in field and laboratory studies. *Ann. N.Y. Acad. Sci.*, 1950, **51**, 1093–1102.
23. RUNDQUIST, E. A. The inheritance of spontaneous activity in rats. *J. comp. Psychol.*, 1933, **16**, 415–438.
24. SCOTT, J. P. Genetic differences in the social behavior of inbred strains of mice. *J. Hered.*, 1942, **33**, 11–15.
25. SONTAG, L. W. The genetics of differences in psychosomatic patterns in childhood. *Amer. J. Orthopsychiat.*, 1950, **20**, 479–489.

26. THOMPSON, W. R. The inheritance of behaviour: behavioural differences in fifteen mouse strains. *Canad. J. Psychol.*, 1953, **7**, 145–155.
27. TRYON, R. C. Genetics of learning ability in rats. *Univer. Calif. Publ. Psychol.*, 1929, **4**, 71–89.
28. WADDELL, D. Hoarding behavior in the Golden Hamster. *J. comp. physiol. Psychol.*, 1951, **44**, 383–388.
29. WHITNEY, L. F. Heredity of trail barking propensity of dogs. *J. Hered.*, 1929, **20**, 561–562.
30. YERKES, R. M. The heredity of savageness and wildness in rats. *J. anim. Behav.*, 1913, **3**, 286–296.

18

Escape and Avoidance Conditioning in Human Subjects Without Their Observation of the Response

**Ralph F. Hefferline · Brian Keenan ·
Richard A. Harford**

This experiment in escape and avoidance conditioning makes two major contributions to an understanding of behavior. First, the procedure emphasizes the existence of "behavior without awareness," and illustrates how phenomena of this sort can be examined in the laboratory. Second, the data from one of the groups (Group 4) underline the importance of exteroceptive support (feedback from visual meter read-out) of kinesthetic information (feedback from the unconscious avoidance response).

(Note that the text refers to subjects 1, 2, and 3 in each of four groups. The figure, however, numbers the same subjects consecutively, from 1 to 12.)

Abstract. An invisibly small thumb-twitch increased in rate of occurrence when it served, via electromyographic amplification, to terminate or postpone aversive noise stimulation. Subjects remained ignorant of their behavior and its effect. Their cumulative response curves resembled those obtained in similar work with animals. Other subjects, informed of the effective response, could not produce it deliberately in a size small enough to qualify for reinforcement.

When the human subject has "voluntary control" of the response to be conditioned, experimental results are in general less predictable and reproducible than those obtained from animals. This is commonly attributed to "self instruction"—that is, to variables experimentally uncontrolled. In the study reported here this problem was circumvented by working with a response so small as to preclude a history of strengthening through discriminable effect upon the environment—in fact, so small as to occur unnoticed by the subject.

From *Science* (November 13, 1959), Vol. 130, pp. 1338–1339; reprinted by permission of the American Association for the Advancement of Science.

The electromyographic setup employed was a modification of the previously reported (1). The subject sat in a shielded enclosure in a reclining chair. Recording electrodes were attached to the palmar base of the left thumb and to the medial edge of the left hand. Three additional sets of dummy electrodes were applied in some instances, to suggest that a comprehensive study of body tensions was being conducted. Muscle-action potentials across the left hand were amplified by a factor of 1 million and rectified and their average momentary values were displayed on a meter. They were also permanently recorded by an Esterline-Angus recording milliammeter.

Twenty-four adults served as subjects. Records from 12 were ruined by apparatus failure, excessive artifact, or failure of the subject to sit still. Results are reported from eight men and four women ranging in age from 18 to 50 and divided into four groups of three each.

Group 1, with four sets of electrodes attached, were told that the study concerned the effects on body tension of noise superimposed on music. Their task was to listen through earphones and, otherwise, do nothing. Group 2, also with all electrodes attached, were told that a specific response, so small as to be invisible, would temporarily turn off the noise or, when the noise was not present, postpone its onset. Their task was to discover and make use of the response. Group 3 (with recording electrodes only) were informed that the effective response was a tiny twitch of the left thumb. Group 4 were given the same information as group 3 but had, in addition, a meter before them during the first half-hour of conditioning, which provided a potential basis for them to use the visual presentation of their response as a "crutch" for proprioceptive observation of the response.

Experimental procedure was identical for all groups. While the subject relaxed and listened to tape-recorded music through earphones, the experimenter watched the meter on his panel for 5 to 10 minutes to select for later reinforcement a response of a size occurring not more than once in 1 or 2 minutes. It was a ballistic swing of the pointer up and back over a few scale divisions. This represented, for a particular subject, a momentary voltage increment at the electrode of 1, 2, or 3 μv.

After the operant level for this response had been recorded for 10 minutes (*OL 1* in Fig. 1), conditioning was begun by super-

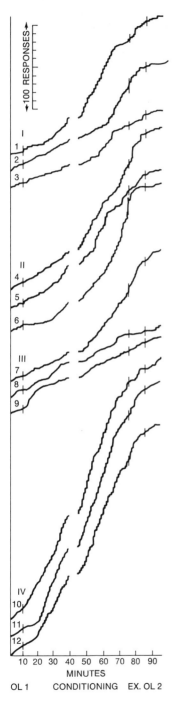

imposing on the music an aversively loud, 60-cycle hum. Whenever the experimenter saw on the meter an instance of the selected response, he pressed a key. This turned off the noise for 15 seconds or, when it was already off, postponed noise resumption for 15 seconds. [This type of avoidance schedule, mentioned in 1950 (2), has been extensively employed by Sidman in animal work (3).]

After an hour of conditioning, with a 5-minute intermission at the half-hour point, 10 minutes of extinction occurred during which the subject's response was ineffective in terminating continuously present noise. During final 10 minutes of music only, the extent of recovery of the original operant level was recorded.

Figure 1 presents cumulative response curves for each subject. Conditioning is clearly indicated by the positive acceleration in the rate of responding for all subjects except subjects 2 and 3 in group 3. These two kept so busy producing voluntary thumb-twitches that the small, reinforceable type of response had little opportunity to occur.

FIGURE 1. Cumulative response curves for adult human subjects in a situation where an invisibly small and unnoticed thumb-twitch either terminated or postponed noise stimulation. *OL 1* and 2, initial and terminal operant level determinations, respectively; *ex.*, extinction.

When interviewed later, all members of group 1 still believed that they had been passive victims with respect to the onset and duration of noise, and all seemed astounded to learn that they themselves had been in control. Subjects 1 and 2 of group 2 reported that they early gave up searching for an effective response and thus, in effect, transferred themselves to group 1. Subject 3 of group 2 professed to have discovered an effective response sequence, which consisted of subtle rowing movements with both hands, infinitesimal wriggles of both ankles, a slight displacement of the jaw to the left, breathing out—and then waiting. Subject 1 of group 3 gave evidence of conditioning perhaps because he misconstrued the instructions. Instead of making the response a quick contraction, he spent his time very gradually increasing pressure on an imaginary switch button. This may have kept deliberate activity at a level low enough for the correct response to break through and be reinforced.

Group 4 subjects, provided with their own meter, obtained many more reinforcements than the others, an effect which continued through the second half-hour of conditioning, with the meter removed. While the meter did not enable them to achieve direct control of the discrete response, it seems to have provided a basis for rapid responding within a range which included the reinforced size. This showed on the meter as rapid oscillation.

The technique employed in this study (4) offers possibilities for investigating human behavior, in a sense, at the animal level. Research now in progress is concerned with attempts to clarify the circumstances under which the human subject may come to discriminate verbally—that is, to become conscious of—his small responses.

REFERENCES

1. R. F. HEFFERLINE, *Trans. N.Y. Acad. Sci.* **20**, 739 (1958).
2. ————, *Genet. Psychol. Monographs* **42**, 231 (1950).
3. M. SIDMAN, *Science* **118**, 157 (1953).
4. This investigation was supported by research grant M-2961, National Institutes of Health, U.S. Public Health Service, and by grants from the Higgins Fund and the Columbia University Council for Research in the Social Sciences.

Physiological and Neurological Concomitants of Behavior

VII

19

Adaptive Stress Behavior

George E. Ruff · Sheldon J. Korchin
(with commentary by George Mandler)

In view of the great risk and expense involved in space flight, both United
States and Russian government laboratories have conducted extensive
research dealing with the consequences of psychological stress upon performance. In this review of Project Mercury (the program that culminated in
America's first successful manned orbital flight), Ruff and Korchin describe
the stress-related considerations that entered into the selection, training, and
postflight examination of the astronauts.

The article is taken from their contribution to an interdisciplinary
Conference on Psychological Stress held at York University in 1965. George
Mandler, in his invited commentary on Ruff and Korchin's paper, calls attention to what he terms the "organization-interruption paradigm." His main
point is that the emotional consequences of an interrupted plan can be
avoided, if other means are found to complete the sequence of behavior
called for by the original plan.

Stress occurs when an organism is forced into strenuous effort to
maintain essential functions at a required level. Because a load is
placed upon the organism, it must modify its activities. This involves the concept of adaptation—a compensatory response which
permits continued functioning in spite of the load.

Adaptation can be described in terms of a model of the organism as a system with inputs and outputs of energy and information. Each system tends to maintain steady states of many variables
through homeostatic mechanisms. These confine within a limited
range the variables which are crucial for continued existence of the
system. Inputs which force the variables beyond this range are

From *Psychological Stress*, Edited by Mortimer H. Appley and Richard Trumbull. Copyright © 1967 by Meredith Corporation. Reprinted by permission of Appleton-Century-
Crofts.

stressors. Adjustments made to restore equilibrium constitute the process of adaptation. This involves the reorganization of certain subsystems to prevent failure of other subsystems required for survival.

Stress can be defined by inputs, outputs, or both. *Input* definitions involve underloads or overloads of energy or information which produce stress within the system. In a sleep-deprivation study, for example, stress could be defined by total hours of wakefulness. *Output* definitions are based upon variables which are displaced from equilibrium under stress. Performance tests are commonly used for this purpose, with a decrement beyond a certain level being taken as an index of stress.

When used alone, each of these approaches has disadvantages. Input definitions involve either past experience, which demonstrates that certain conditions are stressful, or *a priori* decisions about what conditions are expected to be stressful. They may be inadequate in biological research, where responses to the same input vary from individual to individual and from occasion to occasion. On the other hand, output definitions may also be misleading. For one thing, performance decrements may occur without stress—as when motivation decreases. And, if compensatory responses are effective, performance may be maintained at a high level even while the subject is under a heavy load.

While definitions based on adaptive mechanisms avoid many of these problems, they also have disadvantages. Most involve a psychophysiological approach, where physiological variables are used as indices of the organism's state of activation. However, these variables may give contradictory results and may change in response to conditions not considered stressful. For example, many occur with stimuli which simply attract the attention of a resting subject. Unless the concept of stress is broadened to include all instances of increased arousal, demonstration of the adaptive mechanisms alone may not be sufficient to establish the presence of stress.

The most complete definition of stress is given by the combined use of input, output, and adaptive considerations. First, the experimenter specifies which inputs are the stressors and describes as well as he can the mechanism by which they produce their effects. Next, he measures one or more output variables which fall within a specified range under ordinary conditions but cannot be maintained under stress conditions. Whenever possible these variables should be part of the subject's natural, ongoing activities. Finally, indices of adaptive or compensatory processes are chosen. Insofar as possible, patterns of autonomic change are selected which have been found to characterize stress responses under the specific experimental conditions employed.

It would appear desirable to conceptualize all of these steps according to a single frame of reference. In psychological stress research, input, output, and adaptation should be presented in behaviorally-relevant terms. For example, if the input is information that a subject has failed at some task, the output could be a psychological function displaced from its usual range, such as the affect state or performance, and adaptation should be described as a psychological defense mechanism. Physiological processes measured concurrently may be of interest, but should be conceptualized on a separate level. In experiments where inputs are described psychologically, and outputs are described physiologically, the contribution to our understanding of the psychological processes may be minimal.

SOME PROBLEMS OF STRESS RESEARCH

Of more practical concern are the problems of a suitable experimental setting. The investigator usually has the choice of two broad strategies: either to study stress where it is naturally encountered or to create a model in the laboratory. Unfortunately, this choice may amount to a dilemma. Where conditions are naturally stressful, the possibilities for controlled investigation are often limited. Studies carried out under field conditions may be hampered by the exigencies which make these conditions stressful in the first place. On the other hand, constraints binding the investigator who seeks to create stress in the laboratory often give rise to procedures which approach his problem tangentially, at best.

Among the natural stress experiences which lend themselves to systematic study are those of military training, students before examinations, and patients awaiting surgery. Although many military training situations are not notably stressful, an exception is airborne training. Thus, Basowitz, Persky, Korchin, and Grinker (1955) studied psychological and physiological responses of paratrooper trainees while jumping from towers and planes. Students taking examinations are readily available, at least to those of us who live with the "natural stress" of academic life, but this may not be the kind of stress the investigator seeks to explore. The many factors which make an examination stressful for the student may or may not, for example, overlap the many factors which force the psychiatric patient into a psychosis. Another group which is often accessible consists of surgical patients. However, the focus here is inevitably on threats of bodily harm—a vitally important source of stress, but not necessarily the one the investigator prefers to explore. No one kind of experience can serve in the exploration of all stress behaviors.

Where the chosen interest of the investigator is matched by a natural experience involving the proper set of threats and amenable to systematic study, there should be no impediment to productive research. Naturally-occurring stressful events, particularly where controllable measures can be made, make possible "natural experiments," which combine many of the advantages of field and laboratory research. The paratrooper studies just mentioned and the work with the astronauts described below are cases in point, but such opportunities for stress research are rare. For this reason, or because of a desire to achieve better control over relevant variables, many workers choose to develop an artificial stress procedure in the laboratory. Unfortunately, this task is seldom approached with a firm notion of the kind of stress which is to be studied. The investigator chooses to do research on stress and attempts to devise a procedure which should be stressful. All too often he achieves a gimmick which alters subject behavior in some fashion but contributes little to our understanding of the psychology of stress. For example, a rigged situation in which the subject is convinced he has failed in a simple task may be an appropriate means to test a formulation regarding self-esteem. But simply as a means to produce stress in some nonspecific sense, it accomplishes little.

A problem for a particular type of stress research is the difficulty of producing laboratory analogs of the stress processes which are seen in psychiatric patients. The belief is commonly held that although external conditions may precipitate mental disorder, they do so by producing internal conflict. Although it is recognized that psychoanalytic and other formulations centering around this impression should be subjected to experimental study, it has proven difficult to devise a method which will consistently arouse inner conflict. The experimenter usually employs a laboratory procedure which confronts a subject with an external threat. This has been done by various methods, including fear-producing motion pictures or stress interview techniques, where threats can be "custom-made" to arouse whatever conflict appears important for a given subject. However, unless a procedure is included which demonstrates that the desired conflict *was* elicited, interpretation of results may be ambiguous.

A STUDY OF THE MERCURY ASTRONAUTS*

Many of these concepts and problems are illustrated by a study of the Project Mercury astronauts. From a research standpoint, Project Mercury had many advantages. First, it offered a chance to study men who had demonstrated particularly effective modes of adaptation to stress. Because the astronauts had been extensively tested at the time of selection (Ruff and Levy, 1959) and would be followed for a period of several years, it would be possible to study each individual carefully over time. Most important, they would be facing real stress which could not be simulated in the laboratory and which would be encountered under conditions allowing systematic observation.

The Project Mercury study involved simultaneous measurement of psychological, physiological, and biochemical variables in response to training and flight activities. It was carried out in three phases: (1) personality assessment; (2) repeated measurements during training; and (3) evaluation of response to flight.

Phase 1: Personality Assessment

This stage involved reevaluation of each of the seven astronauts to investigate personality mechanisms relevant to stress behavior. The

* We are grateful to the National Aeronautics and Space Administration and to the National Institute of Mental Health for making this study possible. However, the opinions and conclusions expressed in this article are those of the authors and do not necessarily represent the views of the National Aeronautics and Space Administration or any other governmental agency. Portions of the work reported here were presented to the American Association for the Advancement of Science, Philadelphia, December 28, 1962, and published in a volume reporting the proceeding of a symposium jointly sponsored by AAAS and American Psychiatric Association (Korchin and Ruff, 1964; Ruff and Korchin, 1964).

data consisted principally of interviews with the astronauts individually. In addition, the extensive material from the original assessment program was included in the analyses. To make it possible for the men to speak frankly without compromising their chances to be chosen for future flights, it was understood that details of the study data would remain confidential until selection was no longer an issue. To maximize reliability and the coverage of different areas, each of us interviewed all men in two one-hour sessions. All interviews were tape-recorded and transcribed for later study. The analysis and findings based on this material derive from independent study of the tapes and transcripts by the two psychological investigators and the convergence of their clinical judgments.

In the initial interviews, and amplified throughout the subsequent course of the study, the following general areas were investigated:

MOTIVATION FOR PROJECT

Each man's motivation for joining Project Mercury, and the needs subsequently served by participation, were explored. His goals and aspirations for the future were examined.

SELF-CONCEPT AND CONCEPT OF THE ASTRONAUT ROLE

Self-esteem and self-attitudes, in general and in connection with the astronaut role, were considered. Concepts of the "ideal astronaut," and the competence, values, and other aspects of behavior believed relevant were discussed.

EMOTIONAL ACTIVATION AND CONTROL

The variety, intensity, conditions for activation, and control of various emotional states were studied by examining behavior in situations of psychological threat and objective danger. The somatic representation and behavioral consequences of anxiety, anger, and depression were described. On the positive side the sources of pleasure, feelings of competence, mastery, achievement, and other conditions of well-being were also determined.

TYPE AND STRENGTH OF DEFENSES

Efforts were made to discover the typical modes of dealing with threats to psychological equilibrium. The efficiency of these mechanisms in coping with stress was assessed.

SOCIAL BEHAVIOR

Relations to family, to the other astronauts, to management, and to other persons were examined. The social organization of the group, as a group, was described.

OTHER ASPECTS OF PERSONALITY

Impulsivity and lability, energy level and fatigue, reactions to potentially disruptive agents, such as alcohol, and other qualities were reviewed. These included such dimensions as activity-passivity, dependence-independence, trust-distrust, and needs for affiliation, achievement, and autonomy.

Phase 2: Repeated Measurements During Training

During training, a small battery of psychological tests was given on repeated occasions over a two-year period. Paired measurements were made before and after centrifuge simulations of suborbital and orbital flights, environmental control system runs, and selected prelaunch activities. In addition, the battery was used during more relaxed control occasions. The primary purpose of this phase was to develop a baseline against which the same measures made at the time of flight could be evaluated. A "P-technique" model was used, where comparisons were made across occasions for each man individually. The areas of psychological functioning assessed and the measures used included:

MEASURES OF PERSONALITY AND EMOTION

The emotional state on each occasion was described by self-administered adjective check list (Clyde, 1959), self-rating scales, and a brief questionnaire which inquired into the astronaut's perception of the adequacy of his performance and asked him to describe any special circumstances which might have influenced his behavior on that occasion. Where scheduling permitted, interviews exploring these matters were also included.

PERFORMANCE MEASURES

In order to assess possible changes in psychomotor and intellectual functioning caused by training or flight stress, three tests developed for studies requiring repeated testing of the same individuals were used (Moran and Mefferd, 1959). These procedures had been administered to the astronauts at the time of the original selection program. The tests were (1) Aiming, which requires that the subject dot the center of connected circles as rapidly as possible; (2) Number Facility, a mental arithmetic task; and (3) Perceptual Speed, a number-cancellation procedure. All of these are timed tests of familiar-overlearned functions, which should be stable in repeated testing, except for changes resulting from stress or states of disorganization.

Phase 3: Study of Flight Behavior

The third phase of the study consisted of more intensive evaluation of five of the men who made suborbital or orbital flights. The battery of measures described above was administered immediately before and after each flight. At the same time, there were brief interviews evaluating the astronaut's condition just prior to and following the flight. There was a longer interview two days earlier to review each man's experiences since the last contact, to explore in greater depth his feelings and anticipations and to determine fears or doubts he may have had. Similarly, two days after flight, there was another long interview to review the flight experience itself. Observations were also made during debriefing sessions and other less formal contacts. In addition to the primary and back-up pilots, interviews were held with all other astronauts who were available during the pre- and post-flight periods.

Personality Qualities of the Mercury Astronauts

In order to understand the pattern of adaptive response observed, it is necessary to know something about the men who were studied. Although each of the astronauts has distinct and separate personality traits, certain features were found to be common to all. Some of the more salient personality characteristics which are relevant to the understanding of stress behavior are summarized:

GENERAL CHARACTERISTICS

The Mercury astronauts had high levels of intelligence, were concerned with problem solving, and had the ability to focus on the essentials of issues which confronted them. They tended not to be abstract or speculative but to think concretely. Facts rather than theories were emphasized. What was unknown and uncertain was handled by efforts to make it known. Details irrelevant to their areas of primary concern were avoided.

These men were not introspective and tended to have limited fantasy lives. However, they could describe their inner processes when asked to direct their attention toward them. They were oriented toward action rather than thought, preferred action to inaction, and disliked assuming a passive role. At the same time, they were not overly impulsive, and could refrain from action when it was not appropriate. In most of their behavior, evidence of emotional stability was apparent.

Although attachments within the group itself were not intense, the men shared a common purpose. The most important bond between them was their common background as test pilots. Strong emphasis was placed by each man on values related to professional competence.

MOTIVATION

All the men were professionally motivated to contribute to the space program. This was part of their strong drive toward mastery and achievement. In each case, this tendency became apparent early in life and was eventually expressed in a desire to fly. Not infrequently, the heightened drive toward mastery once served to reduce self-doubts. However, in most cases it later functioned independently of the need for such reassurance.

The astronauts felt the challenge of their work and enjoyed the opportunity to use all their capacities. They derived a sense of satisfaction from participating in something they considered important—something on the frontier of their field. Along with this, all had the conviction that they were making an important contribution to the national interest.

The men had no special wish to face danger, although they were willing to accept the risks demanded by their job. Where danger was present, it was not a motivation for their work. Although a few men enjoyed certain types of risks, this had little to do with volunteering for Project Mercury.

FRUSTRATION TOLERANCE

Since the astronauts' drive for achievement was strong, their potential for disappointment was great. Nevertheless, they displayed striking resilience in the face of frustration. The most important sources of disappointment were delays in the schedule and failure to be selected for a particular flight. In general, both were dealt with by looking beyond the immediate obstacle and deciding that the problem would be resolved in the future. Whenever a course of action suggested itself, they embarked upon it as quickly as possible.

Psychological Response to Training and Flight

EFFECTS OF TRAINING AND FLIGHT STRESS ON PERFORMANCE

Each of the three performance tests yielded two scores: (1) the number of items correctly completed within the time limit; and (2) the number of errors made. Since these two scores are essentially independent (Moran and Mefferd, 1959), both were considered separately as measures of behavioral efficiency. On all these tests, each man showed improved functioning after the training events, such as centrifuge runs and simulator trials. By contrast, from before to after flight there was a drop in total trials and a rise in errors. But in general, pre- to post-differences were small.

One finding is worthy of special comment. The preflight scores for all tests were above the general level of performance. The reverse might have been expected, since this measure was made at a time when preflight anxiety might be highest. Furthermore, preflight testing was done in the early morning hours, when most subjects are less efficient. That performance was so good at this point suggests a state of activation. The anticipatory anxiety such as might exist not only did not lessen but seems to have facilitated psychological functioning in the immediate preflight hours.

EMOTIONAL REACTION

As part of the test battery, along with the psychometric procedures, a mood scale consisting of 53 adjectives was administered. The astronaut was asked to what degree—on a four-point scale—each adjective described his mood at that moment. On factor analysis, Clyde (1959) had extracted six factor variables from this list: (1) "Friendly"; (2) "Energetic"; (3) "Clear-Thinking"; (4) "Aggressive"; (5) "Jittery"; and (6) "Depressed." The score for each of these is the sum of the ratings for the adjectives found loaded on the factor. Since each factor score is based on the sum of a different number of adjective ratings in the original scoring system, they were recalculated on a mean-per-adjective basis to simplify comparison.

On all occasions, the men described themselves more in terms of the positive than the negative emotional states. Thus, the highest ratings were obtained for Friendly, Energetic, and Clear-Thinking; the lowest ratings were for Aggressive, Jittery, and Depressed. As with the performance variables, pre- to post-changes were greater than those produced by training events. Following flight, there was a general tendency for the "Energetic" and "Clear-Thinking" scores to drop and for greater anxiety to be admitted. There was a parallel increase in "Friendly." Thus, compared to their state prior to launch, after flight they tended to be somewhat less energetic and clear-thinking, somewhat more anxious, and to feel more warmly related to people. However, it should be noted that most of these change scores are small, and that both before and after flight the men described themselves as alert and attentive and generally without fear or disturbing affect.

CLINICAL SUMMARY OF STRESS BEHAVIOR

Throughout the study, adaptive behavior was observed under various potentially disturbing conditions. As in any job, there were day-to-day problems. But because of the particular qualities of the project, the number of delays and frustrations was necessarily large. These were often enhanced by a sense of functioning in an unfamiliar organization. Procedures and responsibilities were often unlike those in the military services in which the men worked for years. Furthermore, the national importance of the project focused public attention on the astronauts and their work, none of whom could continue to live in accustomed anonymity. Both the novel technology and the unusual social conditions were potential sources of difficulty.

In spite of such considerations, few adverse reactions were noted during the development and training phases of the program. The astronauts were usually able to maintain a level-headed, realistic approach to their problems. For most, not being chosen for the first flight was the greatest threat to their self-esteem, since it carried the implication that they had somehow failed and were not functioning as well as they had assumed. In response, they analyzed possible faults in their performance and worked the harder to overcome them. Eventually each was able to believe that his day could come. Once chosen for a flight, schedule changes and delays had little impact, despite fears voiced by the press. Once decided, the issue of "when" was secondary.

Until the day of flight, the astronaut's major concern was with achieving a state of readiness. Discomfort was evident until the man felt "on top" of things. In the days and hours before flight, all of the men felt ready to go and competent for the job. Conscious thoughts of danger and possible death were infrequent, and suppressed as they arose. The men were preoccupied with operational details and showed little anticipatory anxiety. When it appeared, it was experienced as mild tension or "edginess." It was similar to that felt in combat or other earlier stress and, being familiar, was not disturbing. In most cases, anxiety seemed more related to an intense concern with the success of the mission than to fear of injury or death.

All of the astronauts had considered the risks. They were convinced that their past experiences and intensive training in the project had prepared them for any emergency. Much of the ability to control anticipatory anxiety resulted from confidence in their preparation. Considering every eventuality and doing all possible to prepare for it, they saw little point in worrying further. When thoughts of danger did arise, they were displaced by review of the flight plan or other technical aspects of the flight. In one man's words, "Whenever I think of something that may go wrong, I think of a plan to take care of it."

In the period just before lift-off, men reported being on edge and interpreted this as a positive sign. There was excitement, anticipation, and readiness to go, of the sort athletes describe before the race, but no instances of severe or potentially disabling anxiety. If tensions mounted, the response was to stop, take stock, and decide what to do to bring matters under control. Conscious mechanisms of self-control—a quality valued by these men—were available in all cases during the immediate prelaunch period.

So, too, during flight, thoughts centered on procedures needing execution and on the experiences of being in orbit. Successful launch and well-executed flight induced feelings of exhilaration, which were further reinforced by the pleasant sensation of weight-lessness. Anxiety never went to excessive levels, and even when objective dangers arose, functioning was effective and disturbing affect held in check.

After flight, there was uniform elation coupled with fatigue. Elation came from both a sense of a difficult job well done and from a sense of relief that the long-anticipated flight was over.

In conclusion, it might be said that the most striking finding of this study is the effectiveness of adaptive responses based on past experience and professional competence. Given a group of men with repeated success in accomplishment of hazardous duties, followed by training which led to highly organized, efficient patterns of behavior, evidence of disruptive stress behavior was minimal.

INVITED COMMENTARY

George Mandler: I am particularly pleased by the methodological stance which this paper represents. For many years, one dominant attitude in psychology has been that the way to learn about human beings is to study the abnormal, the hyponormal. The trend has been: "Let's find out about the schizophrenic, and then we'll know all about basic processes of human behavior." Very rarely have we been given data on the hyper-normal. This paper gives us an opportunity to see what adaptive behavior looks like when the organism has not been deliberately selected because he cannot adapt to stress. The subjects here were specifically chosen because they could adapt to stressful situations. Before discussing some general problems of adaptation to stress, I would like to make two specific comments.

First of all, I found Drs. Ruff's and Korchin's outline and discussion of the stress paradigm most helpful. Rather than waving some particular theoretical flag, they have given us an overview which, for a change, most of us can adopt. I think all of us can live with such a basis for discussion without having to worry whether we really do agree with this or that definition of stress.

Secondly, one general comment on the interpretation of the data. Psychologists have only recently been concerned with the demand characteristics of test and experimental situations. What are the subject's hypotheses about the test situation, and how do these expectations affect his behavior? What does he think is expected of him and why? Particularly in the kind of situation that has been described here, such problems may be quite important and should be carefully considered.

What I would like to discuss at greater length is the question of how the human organism adapts to stress and the relevant alternatives that may be available to him. I believe this problem is related to the general problem of planning, to the cognitive structures that the organism has available at the time he is placed in an unusual, stressful, or unexpected situation. Recently I have been much concerned with the organization of behavior, the development of organized labor sequences, and the effect of interruption of organized responses on behavior in general (Mandler, 1964; Mandler and Watson, 1966).

By organization I refer to the development of unitary sequences of behavior which, once they are initiated, run off smoothly and present an inevitability of completion. Some organized sequences—which we usually call consummatory responses—are built into the organism and need not be acquired. These include swallowing, drinking, sexual behavior, and so forth. Other, learned organized sequences include—at a very simple level—walking, typing, rowing. Exactly the same kinds of sequences develop at a more complex level. We may, for example, execute a very well integrated or organized sequence of driving or walking to the office. Organized behavior not only occurs at the overt level—in terms of observable behavior—but once behavior has been organized it is cognitively represented. The cognitive representation of organized behavior is equivalent, I believe, with what Miller, Galanter, and Pribram (1960) have called "plans."

Parenthetically I might note that within such a system it is not particularly useful to talk about goals or about organisms striving toward goals. Behavior sequences, once initiated, persist and end up with responses at a point which is usually called a goal. But the goal is part of the sequence and can be considered as a stop rule for a particular sequence. Rather than organisms striving toward a goal we may say that they execute a particular path with the goal at the end, a "goalpath."

Where does all this become relevant to stress? Stress results in a condition—or is one of the conditions—which interrupts these organized behavior sequences. Any event that prevents completion of an initiated sequence produces ANS arousal, which in turn sets the stage for emotional behavior (cf. Schachter and Singer, 1962; Mandler, 1962).

Now, to turn to the problem of adaptation. What can the organism do when a plan or an organized sequence has been interrupted? I have suggested three general reactions: persistence, increased vigor, and substitution. One well-organized sequence most of us have available is that of putting a key in a lock and opening a door. If it does not work the first time, we try again. Persistence frequently will complete the sequence and therefore undo the interruption. If it does not, we might try a little harder and increased vigor also may short-circuit the effects of interruption. Or we might break the key, in which case the effect of interruption would be more intense and prolonged. More central to the problem of adaptation is the third choice—substitution.

If a particular plan or sequence has been interrupted, one can avoid the emotional consequences by finding an alternative sequence or response which will complete the original plan that was laid down. The problem of substitution was effectively discussed years ago by Kurt Lewin and his students (1935).

The major point I want to make for present purposes is that interruption produces emotional arousal and that this arousal will, under certain circumstances, produce anxiety or distress. A subjective state of distress will be the emotion of choice if no successful alternate sequence is available, if the organism is helpless. In the animal literature, Mowrer and Vieck (1948) for example have shown that rats who were able to control the onset of shock were much less anxious than those could not do so. Watson and I (Mandler and Watson, 1966) have discussed the problem of control, and Dr. Watson has shown that subjects in a simple task will perform much better if they can control the sequence of tasks than if they cannot. We also know that the control of onset and offset of shock is much less disturbing to human subjects than lack of control. Dr. Haggard (1943) presented data to that effect some years ago, and more recently Elliot (1966) has replicated some aspects of his findings.

Stressors are stimuli which frequently fit very neatly into the organization-interruption paradigm. They interrupt a plan or an ongoing behavior sequence. And the most adaptive response to stress is to have alternate responses available.* There is something that the subject can do with the situation in which his plan is interrupted.

The astronaut, as cited by Drs. Ruff and Korchin, illustrates our theoretical notions very well: "Whenever I think of something that may go wrong, I think of a plan to take care of it." This is a very neat description of a man who, anticipating possible interruptions, lists for himself a variety of alternate behaviors. He says: "If something goes wrong, I can do A or B or C or D." He anticipates the possibility of interruption and subsequent emotional arousal and prepares for bypassing the emotional consequences by having alternate completions immediately available. He *plans* for interruptions.

In discussing frustration tolerance, Drs. Ruff and Korchin noted that the astronauts are easily disappointed. I think this is to be expected. They have well-developed, highly dominant and smoothly operating plans. If these are interrupted, disappointment is an obvious emotional consequence. But disappointment does not grow into disruptive helplessness if good alternate plans are available at the time of interruption. The organism can still complete a relevant sequence. Apart from the availability of alternate responses, I have suggested elsewhere (Mandler 1962, 1964) that frustration tolerance involves the ability to "hold." If one can hold or delay in the face of interruption and rising arousal, then the longer the delay lasts the more likely it is that the situation will change, the more likely it is that one will be able to discover some alternate response that will permit completion. In this sense frustration tolerance is the ability to stop and consider the situation instead of engaging in persistence, for example, which frequently may not produce completion.

* Such availability is, by the way, closely related to Dr. Lazarus' concept of "coping."

The astronauts have this ability; they are practical, they are realistic—which means they have a veridical view of the situation; they can properly evaluate their environment, and they know what could be done if interruptions occur; they are highly adaptive, i.e., they have good alternatives available.

I have mentioned earlier that planning for interruptions is highly adaptive. Sometimes this is difficult; for example when shock is used to interrupt behavior. This stressor, beloved by psychologists, frequently interferes with planning, it does not permit the subject to think about much other than the pain. If, however, the subject has a plan to deal with shock—"When shock occurs, I will do such and such"—then the shock becomes part of the plan, interruption is attenuated, and the degree of disruptive emotional behavior is reduced. I am similarly convinced that when a plan does include the occurrence of and coping with a noxious event, then the *absence* of that noxious event—a new interruption—will also produce arousal and emotional behavior. But in this case the condition under which the arousal occurs is not one of helplessness, and positive emotions, such as euphoria, will be produced. If you expect to be shocked and are not, the interruption will also produce emotional behavior but positive, rather than negative, in tone.

Finally, I would like to relate some of these notions about organization and adaptation to some other problems that were raised by others earlier. Dr. Bovard mentioned that positive reinforcement inhibits stress. Positive reinforcement is the condition that produces consummatory behavior, i.e., well organized responses. Kessen and I (1961) have discussed the role of organized responses in inhibiting distress, and Kessen has demonstrated this phenomenon in the neonate. Positive reinforcement involves the completion and execution of well-organized behavior and is therefore stress inhibiting.

A point that Dr. Sells made earlier fits rather nicely into the picture of adaptive behavior I have drawn here. The confirming outcome of expectations implies that sequences are completed, dissonant outcomes imply their interruption.

Again let me say that I am glad that we are spending some time with the hypernormal astronauts, if for no other reason than that for the counter example to the abnormal hyponormal is so rarely available. I believe that we can learn much that is useful from the individual who has well-developed skills in dealing with stress, maybe more than from those who only show the debilitating effects of interruption.

REFERENCES

BASOWITZ, H., PERSKY, H., KORCHIN, S. J., AND GRINKER, R. R. *Anxiety and stress.* New York: McGraw-Hill, 1955.

CLYDE, D. J. *Manual: Clyde Mood Scale.* Bethesda, Md.: National Institute of Mental Health, 1959.

ELLIOTT, R. Effects of uncertainty about the nature and advent of a noxious stimulus (shock) upon heart rate. *J. personal. soc. Psychol.,* 1966, **3**, 353–356.

HAGGARD, E. A. Some conditions determining adjustment during and readjustment following experimentally induced stress. In S. S. Tomkins (ed.), *Contemporary psychopathology: A source book.* Cambridge, Mass.: Harvard, 1943, pp. 529–532.

KESSEN, W., AND MANDLER, G. Anxiety, pain, and the inhibition of distress. *Psychol. Rev.,* 1961, **68**, 396–404.

KORCHIN, S. J., AND RUFF, G. E. Personality characteristics of the Mercury Astronauts. In G. H. Grosser, H. Wechsler, and M. Greenblatt (eds.), *The threat of impending disaster: Contributions to the psychology of stress.* Cambridge, Mass.: M.I.T., 1964, pp. 197–207.

LEWIN, K. *A dynamic theory of personality.* New York: McGraw-Hill, 1935.

MANDLER, G. The interruption of behavior. In D. Levine (ed.), *Nebraska symposium on motivation: 1964.* Lincoln: University of Nebraska, 1964, pp. 267–343.

————. Emotion. In R. W. Brown et al., *New directions in psychology.* New York: Holt, Rinehart and Winston, 1962, pp. 163–219.

————, AND WATSON, D. L. Anxiety and the interruption of behavior. In C. D. Spielberger (ed.), *Anxiety and behavior.* New York: Academic, 1966, pp. 263–290.

MILLER, G. A., GALANTER, E. H., AND PRIBRAM, K. *Plans and the structure of behavior.* New York: Holt, Rinehart and Winston, 1960.

MORAN, L. J., AND MEFFERD, R. B., JR. Repetitive psychometric measures. *Psychol. Rep.,* 1959, **5**, 269–275.

MOWRER, O. H., AND VIECK, P. An experimental analogue of fear from a sense of helplessness. *J. abn. soc. Psychol.,* 1948, **43**, 193–200.

RUFF, G. E., AND KORCHIN, S. J. Psychological responses of the Mercury Astronauts to stress. In G. H. Grosser, H. Wechsler, and M. Greenblatt (eds.), *The threat of impending disaster: Contributions to the psychology of stress.* Cambridge, Mass.: M.I.T., 1964, pp. 208–220.

————, AND LEVY, E. Z. Psychiatric evaluation of candidates for space flight. *Am. J. Psychiat.,* 1959, **116**, 385–391.

SCHACHTER, S., AND SINGER, J. E. Cognitive, social and physiological determinants of emotional state. *Psychol. Rev.,* 1962, **69**, 379–399.

20

Cerebral Heterostimulation in a Monkey Colony

José M. R. Delgado

Behavioral research based upon stimulation of distinct portions of the subject's brain is relatively new. One of its earliest pioneers was the physiologist José Delgado. In this article he reports on the consequences of extending brain-stimulation techniques from individual to group behavior. In one experiment, a meek monkey learned to control the attacks of another, more aggressive monkey, by pressing a lever. This in turn closed a circuit, thereby stimulating by radio a portion of the brain that inhibited aggression in the attacking monkey.

In another study, one involving a different part of the brain, tone signals that had been regularly paired with stimulation came to elicit (not inhibit) aggressive behavior in the experimental animal. The other monkeys learned to respond to the same tone, but they did so by climbing to the ceiling of the cage, thereby avoiding the tone-elicited aggression of the stimulated monkey.

CEREBRAL HETEROSTIMULATION IN A MONKEY COLONY

Abstract. In an established colony a subordinate monkey repeatedly pressed a lever which stimulated the caudate nucleus of the boss monkey by radio and inhibited his aggressive behavior. In other experiments, timed stimulations of the posteroventral nucleus of the thalamus of the boss monkey, paired with a tone, increased his aggressiveness and established conditioned escape responses of the whole group. Both types of experiments may be useful in neurophysiological and pharmacological investigations.

Electrical stimulation of some areas of the brain induces positive reinforcement, and rats, cats, and monkeys learn to stimulate them-

From *Science* (July 12, 1963), Vol. 141, pp. 161–163. Copyright 1963 by the American Association for the Advancement of Science. Reprinted by permission of the American Association for the Advancement of Science.

FIGURE 1.   Control. Left to right: Sarah, Ali (the aggressive boss, biting his own hand), Lou, and Elsa (hanging from ceiling).

selves by pressing a lever repeatedly for hours or even days (1). This method is very valuable for physiological and pharmacological analysis of the central nervous system. Since animals are capable of self-stimulation, they might stimulate the brain of a cagemate if suitable means were provided.

In a colony of four monkeys (*Macaca mulatta*) the boss, Ali (5.2 kg), was an ill-tempered, powerful male who often expressed his aggressiveness by grimacing and biting his own right hand (Fig. 1). Ali had friendly relations with the female, Sarah (4.0 kg), was hostile toward the other female, Elsa (4.6 kg), who ranked No. 3 in the group, and paid less attention to the male, Lou (3.8 kg), who was lowest in social rank, as determined by the peanut test and by offensive-defensive reactions. The colony was housed for several weeks in a cage 7 by 3 by 3 ft in a soundproof air-conditioned room with constant day and night cycles of 12 hours each. The monkeys were observed through a one-way window from an adjoining room, and their behavior recorded by time-lapse photography (one picture every 2 seconds for 8 hours daily); the data were analyzed with the aid of automation (2). Elsa and Lou were the controls. Multilead electrodes were implanted in the head of the caudate nucleus, thalamus, central gray, reticular substance, and other cerebral areas of Ali and Sarah. Two additional subcutaneous leads made connections between any cerebral contact and a small stimulating device strapped to the back of the animal. This device is a modified radio receiver (3) with a sensitivity of 2 to 4 μv, and it is reliable within a range of several hundred feet. Its only function is to close a switch to activate a transistorized stimulator whose output intensity is adjusted before the experiments. In this way cerebral stimulations are reliable and independent of possible variations, such as antenna orientation and changes in radio signals. Further technical details have been published elsewhere (4).

Controls were established first with the monkey lightly restrained in a chair. Each cerebral point was electrically stimulated; voltage and milliamperage were monitored in an oscilloscope, and bipolar recordings of the electrical activity before and immediately after the stimulations were obtained with an eight-channel Grass electroencephalograph. None of the effects described was accompanied by electrical afterdischarges. In all cases stimulations were monopolar, unidirectional, with exponential fall, 0.5 msec of pulse duration, and 100 cy/sec. The electrode resistance was about 50,000 ohms, and intensities up to 4 ma were used.

After stimulation under restraint, Ali and Sarah were both released in the colony, one wearing a radiostimulator and the other a dummy. In both, telestimulation of the central gray and of the posteroventral nucleus of the thalamus evoked antisocial behavior with increased chasing, jumping, biting, and fighting which was quantified and analyzed (2). Stimulation of the caudate nucleus induced behavioral inhibition (5) and was selected to test possible heterostimulation. In Ali and Sarah caudate stimulation produced similar effects including slight ipsilateral head turning, loss of interest in food, and inhibition of activities, such as drinking, taking of pellets, walking, picking, self-grooming, and diminution of spontaneous aggressiveness. The latter was more impressive in Ali because of his greater size and ferocity. Caudate stimulation did not modify the behavioral categories of nestling (two monkeys embracing each other), balling (one monkey with head down on knees), lying down, or being groomed by another. During caudate stimulation it was possible to touch the animal with one's bare hands, and in this manner the monkeys were caught repeatedly. The animals were not completely inhibited and on occasion withdrew a few steps without attempting to retaliate or bite.

After controls were established a lever was attached to the cage. At any time any monkey could press this bar, which automatically started a tone which was followed 2 seconds later by a 5-second radiostimulation. Tone and stimulation ended simultaneously. In the first series of experiments, the tone was set at 600 cy/sec, and Ali carried the stimulator connected to the caudate nucleus for 4 consecutive days. The lever was located close to a feeding tray, and the first day monkeys exploring the area occasionally touched the lever, starting the tone-simulation cycle. The second day, Elsa pressed the bar 12 times, while each of the other monkeys, including Ali, touched the lever only 0 to 5 times. On the third and fourth days, Elsa pressed the lever 17 and 25 times, and the other monkeys 0 to 7 times. Figure 2 shows one example of Elsa stimulating Ali (6). After the fourth day, radiostimulation was discontinued, but the tone remained connected for 1 week. The next two recorded lever pressings started the tone and produced some head-turning and behavioral inhibition in Ali, but extinction appeared quickly, and successive tones were not effective. The number of lever pressings by Elsa diminished to 9 the first day and to 1 to 8 per day during the following 6 days. No evidence of increased self-stimulation appeared in these studies. Immediately after these experiments the radiostimulator was attached to Sarah for three consecutive days, and the tone was changed to 500 cy/sec. For each monkey, including Sarah, 0 to 6 daily lever pressings were recorded with no significant increase in the number for any animal during the 3 days.

Curiosity probably was not the cause of the increase in lever pressing because fewer were recorded on the first than on the fourth experimental day. Correlation with radiostimulation seems more probable because lever pressings during the third and fourth days were more than twice as many as during any of the seven extinction days when only the tone could be activated. The lever was permanently attached to the cage and competed for the monkeys' attention with padlocks and food on the floor, swings, and other parts of the living quarters. This competition may explain the low number of lever pressings, and it makes more significant the increased pressing resulting when Ali was radiostimulated. Observation of the colony

FIGURE 2. Elsa, pressing the lever, stimulates by radio the caudate nucleus of Ali (on right side of cage), producing behavioral inhibition. Elsa's attitude is significant because her attention is directed not to the lever but to Ali. It is unusual for lower-ranking monkeys to look straight at the boss of the colony because this evokes retaliation.

and analysis of films showed that several times Ali's threatening attitude was followed by Elsa's lever pressing (6).

The studies continued with the radiostimulator again strapped on Ali, this time connected to a contact in the posteroventral nucleus of the thalamus, and with the tone set at 900 cy/sec. Previous radiostimulations of this area had increased Ali's aggressiveness. When the lever was attached to the cage, it was triggered only seven times during three consecutive days. Then the lever was removed and was actuated by a timer once every minute for half an hour. After the fourth trial, signs of conditioning were evident. At the onset of the tone, Ali showed increased aggressiveness, and the other three monkeys grimaced and climbed to the cage ceiling. On several occasions this escape reaction to the tone started before Ali initiated any threat. Later the stimulation was discontinued, and during 30 trials the tone continued to sound once every minute and induced a reaction 25 times in Elsa, 11 times in Ali, and 7 times in both Sarah and Lou. This experiment was duplicated on three different days with results showing similar characteristics and indicates that conditioning may be established through association of the tone with aggressive behavior evoked in Ali. In another series of investigations, there was no individual or social conditioning when motor areas were stimulated in Ali and in Sarah by radio-timed control.

Performance of instrumental responses may be induced by cerebral stimulation and may be conditioned to auditory or visual cues (7). The fact that "spontaneous-like" behavior evoked by brain excitation may also be conditioned to an indifferent stimulus is a relatively new finding. These results have been confirmed in further experiments (8). Behavioral conditioning has also been established on a time basis by programmed stimulations of the superior vestibular nucleus of the thalamus without giving the monkey any cue other than fixed interval of 1 minute between stimulations (9).

Social conditioning may help in the analysis of cerebral stimulation because each member of the colony is an interpreter of the reactions of the stimulated animal. Heterostimulation presents obvious questions about hierarchical control, reciprocal punishment, instrumental self-defense, and other problems related to human behavior (10).

REFERENCES

1. J. V. BRADY, in *Recticular Formation of the Brain,* H. H. Jasper *et al.,* Eds. (Little, Brown, Boston, 1958), p. 689; B. Bursten and J. M. R. Delgado, *J. Comp. Physiol. Psychol.* **51,** 6 (1958); J. Olds and P. Milner, *ibid.* **47,** 419 (1954); J. Olds, *ibid.* **51,** 675 (1958); M. Sidman, J. V. Brady, J. J. Boren, D. G. Conrad, A. Schulman, *Scence* **122,** 830 (1955).

2. J. M. R. DELGADO, in *Pharmacological Analysis of Central Nervous Action,* W. D. M. Paton, Ed. (Pergamon, Oxford, 1962), vol. 8, p. 265; J. M. R. Delgado and R. Rodriguez Delgado, *Phil. Sci.* **29,** 253 (1962).

3. "Venus" frequency-modulated radio receiver modified with miniature coils (Lafayette Radio MS-828) and miniature relays (Elgin National Watch Co. type NMIC-50).

4. J. M. R. DELGADO, in *Bio-Telemetry,* L. Slater, Ed. (Pergamon, New York, 1963), p. 231.

5. N. A. BUCHWALD, E. J. WYERS, C. W. LAUPRECHT, G. HEUSER, *Electroencephalog. Clin. Neurophysiol.* **13,** 531 (1961); J. M. R. Delgado, *Federation Proc.* **16,** 29 (1957); R. G. Heath and R. Hodes, *Trans. Am. Neurol. Assoc.* **77,** 204 (1952); B. W. Robinson and M. Mishkin, *Proc. Intern. Union Physiol. Sci.* **2,** 362 (1962); E. H. Rubinstein

and J. M. R. Delgado, *ibid.* **2**, 366 (1962); J. R. Stevens, C. Kim, P. D. MacLean, *A.M.A. Arch. Neurol.* **4**, 47 (1961).

6. Two months later Elsa and Ali were part of a new colony with three other monkeys. The radiostimulator was then strapped to Ali and connected to his caudate nucleus. Heterostimulation of Ali by Elsa was recorded 22 times in 1 day, and during the bar pressing Elsa's attention was usually directed toward Ali, in a way similar to that shown in Fig. 2. Reproducibility of the phenomenon of heterostimulation was thus demonstrated.

7. J. M. R. DELGADO, W. W. ROBERTS, N. E. MILLER, *Am. J. Physiol.* **179**, 587 (1954); J. M. R. Delgado, H. E. Rosvold, E. Looney, *J. Comp. Physiol. Psychol.* **49**, 373 (1956); D. E. Sheer, Ed., *Electrical Stimulation of the Brain* (Univ. of Texas Press, Austin, 1961).

8. J. M. R. DELGADO, in Symposium on *Pharmacology of Conditioning, Learning and Retention*, 2nd Intern. Congr. Pharmacol., Prague, August 1963.

9. ——, in *Electroencephalog. Clin. Neurophysiol.* Suppl. 24, in press.

10. Supported by grants from the U.S. Public Health Service (M2004-06) and the Office of Naval Research (ONR 609–08).

21

On Cybernetics and the Human Brain

Walter A. Rosenblith

Beginning with the general question, "What is a reasonable model of man's brain?", Rosenblith reviews historical attempts that tried to provide the answer. He suggests that Descartes's views were much more sophisticated than is usually recognized. He continues with an account of Russian conceptions of this issue, particularly those of Sechenov and Pavlov. Finally, the intellectual leap taken by Wiener and his Cambridge colleagues (see Chapter 5) is described.

Rosenblith concludes that although we must avoid the pitfall of assuming on the basis of metaphor that the brain is just a magnificent digital computer we can and should make intelligent use of the computer as a means of studying man's brain.

Man's cultural achievements are largely products of his brain, a biological structure as complex as it is poorly understood. Throughout evolution increasingly powerful nervous systems have permitted the more highly developed species to adapt successfully to relatively stable natural environments. At the present time, at least in the so-called advanced societies, this natural environment is rapidly changing into one that is predominantly man-made. If man is to continue to adapt successfully, he can no longer afford to remain ignorant of the workings and the potentialities of his brain.

Men have certainly tried to gain such understanding. In the Western world, medicine—including pathology, neurology, neurosurgery, and psychiatry—has attempted to give a reasonable account of the most important malfunctions of the brain. Anatomists, physiologists, and more recently biochemists have tried to describe

Reprinted from *The American Scholar*, Vol. 35, No. 2, Spring, 1966. Copyright © 1966 by the United Chapters of Phi Beta Kappa. By permissions of the publishers.

the brain's organization in considerable structural and even chemical detail. Still other disciplines have dealt with human brain functions in terms of sensory and perceptual capacities, in terms of memory, learning, and other types of *higher nervous* (or *mental*) activity. But all these attempts, no matter how successful and instructive, have led to only partial insights. There has emerged no compelling overall view, much less a well-founded theory of the brain's operation. At best, in different modern periods, suggestive metaphors were coined, each related to man's then current and most sophisticated technological achievement: the clock, the telephone, the computer. Each of these metaphors had its day of vogue and glory. When the next ultimate device appeared, specialists and laymen alike wondered how they could have been so naïve as to confuse the workings of as complicated a structure as the brain with that of a clock, for instance. These somewhat ephemeral metaphors, however, left the central question unanswered. What indeed is a reasonable way of describing man's brain and analyzing its *modus operandi?* What is a reasonable model of man's brain?

There exists a broad class of dissimilar devices known as machines. Hence to call something a machine or to compare something to a machine does not yield a great deal of insight into its makeup and function. The simple machines of mechanics (levers, pulleys, *et cetera*) are devices "by which the amount or direction of a force is changed for the sake of gaining some particular end, such as lifting a large weight." The complex machines of the first industrial revolution concerned with forces, motion, and energy are in principle decomposable into elementary simple machines. But this rather narrow technical meaning of the term *machine* acquires new shadings when the machinelike nature of bodily mechanisms is dealt with. According to the relevant part of the dictionary definition, "A person (or organization) acts like a machine in responding automatically and without intelligence or feeling as though responding mechanically to activating stimuli." The dictionary refers also to "the lower animals as mere machines without sense or sensibility." Without taking this set of definitions too seriously, we can see how deeply anchored views derived from Descartes have become in the absence of an up-to-date and comprehensible model of living organisms and, in particular, human brains.

Descartes's views on this subject were surprisingly subtle. He recognized that the concept of a machine carried with it the possibility of constructing a device *ab initio* from specifiable components according to a definite blueprint. Once such a device is built, its performance can be compared with the performance of the biological system whose function it tries to imitate or simulate. Such comparisons are relatively simple in the presence of a clearly defined and easily measurable function, that is, a machine with a special purpose. The more multipurpose the organisms or machines are, however, the more difficult it becomes to establish the criteria for these comparisons. Descartes was much concerned with how such comparisons could be carried out. Given machines or automata capable of simulating faithfully various human actions and even man's appearance, he formulated "two very certain tests" that would distinguish man from brute or more precisely identify those aspects of man's nature that could not be reduced to that of an automaton. The tests relate to (1) the creative use of language and (2) man's enormously varied repertory of actions. It is tempting to contrast Descartes's tests with the research goals of today's students of artificial intelligence: "to construct computer programs which exhibit behavior that we call 'intelligent behavior' when we observe it in human beings." According to Descartes, the human species has certain specific capacities that distinguish it from automata and other biological species and enable it to manipulate a great variety of symbols in the absence of special trigger stimuli. It is thus overall cognitive organization rather than possession of special vocal organs or level of I.Q. that accounts for the use of language in the communication of ideas and for man's ability to cope with many eventualities. As Descartes puts it, "It is morally impossible that there should be sufficient diversity in any machine to allow it to act in all events in life in the same way as our reason causes us to act."

Cartesian views are often oversimplified to such an extent that there may be a tendency to overlook or distort the complex of still perplexing issues he raised. Is there an unbridgeable, qualitative gap between machines and man? Man functions admittedly in part like a machine, but his uniqueness relates presumably to properties that no machine—no matter what its size—can exhibit. At this point one is led to the views of the materialistic philosopher-physician, J. O. de la Mettrie*; to him, man is simply the most intricate of all

---

* In his fascinating essay "L'homme machine" (1748), he tries to marshal both philosophical and observational evidence in favor of such theses as the fol-

animal machines, and human nature can be better understood by precisely comparing the structure of man and of animals.

The nineteenth and the beginning of the twentieth century saw much concern with mechanisms that underlie reflex action. A mechanistic physiology attempted to provide correlative physico-chemical evidence, trying to account for phenomena ranging from neuronal irritability to associative memory. In these researches models of a specific machine were hardly put to use, but the father of Russian physiology, Sechenov (who tried to establish in his *Reflexes of the Brain,* 1863, the physiological basis of psychological processes) wrote that ". . . the idea of the machine nature of the brain is a godsend to every naturalist." Pavlov and others referred to "machine-like, inevitable reactions," but this expression seems to have remained a metaphor without *direct* experimental or theoretical consequences. In these writings the term machine signifies in its generality mainly a commitment to some type of "objective" measurement. This attitude is not too surprising since there was no model of a machine whose functioning was particularly relevant to brain function.

When it became possible to communicate at a distance, the signals of telegraphy, telephony, and broadcasting posed a set of new technical problems to which the conservation laws of physics did not furnish much of an answer. Students of telecommunications became involved in the description and analysis (or even cryptanalysis) of messages, in their structure, their informational content, their resistance to contamination of adventitious noise. They needed to be able to describe the message-carrying capacity of a communication channel, they needed to know how reliably they would be able to control—via appropriate signals—the behavior of faraway power stations, of antiaircraft guns, *et cetera.* As these communication networks became more elaborate, men found themselves increasingly coupled to terminal devices such as telephones and teletype machines, at which messages were either received or sent.

Man first learned how to use tools and language; later on, he

---

lowing: 1. ". . . man is a machine, and . . . in the whole universe there is but a single substance differently modified"; 2. "I believe that thought is so little incompatible with organized matter, that it seems to be one of its properties on a par with electricity, the faculty of motion, impenetrability, extension, etc."; 3. ". . . the brain has its muscles for thinking, as the legs have muscles for walking."

learned how to use machines to increase the power of his muscle with the aid of almost trivial control activities. Now it became obvious that he would be able to extend the scope of operations of his brain. He was able to control and correct in very subtle ways the behavior of complex mechanical devices on the basis of the information fed back to him via the communication channels. The new combination of man and machine seemed to hold the promise of becoming an organic entity, thus constituting a step in the now bio-cultural evolutionary process. To bring such a development about demanded new knowledge about man and his brain, knowledge that would make man's interaction with his machines more than just compatible or efficient. It was to this task of the human use of human beings *and* machines that Norbert Wiener dedicated himself after the publication of *Cybernetics* (1948), three centuries after Descartes.

In the mid-1930's there was formed in Cambridge on the Charles a circle of scientists led by the mathematician Norbert Wiener and the physiologist Arturo Rosenblueth. The latter was an associate—at the Harvard Medical School—of Walter B. Cannon, who is perhaps best known for his work on homeostasis, that is, the error-correcting regulation of the internal environment whose stabilizing influence represents "the wisdom of the body." Norbert Wiener's early education had been in philosophy and mathematics. As a mathematician he had become interested in the analysis of irregularities wherever they are found in nature; such irregularities characterize systems that have many more or less independently varying elements. At the Massachusetts Institute of Technology he worked intimately with colleagues in communications engineering and reflected and speculated on some of the pioneering work on modern computing machines then conducted under the direction of Vannevar Bush. The discussion group conducted monthly meetings on scientific method with particular emphasis upon those areas in science that constituted a no-man's-land between several established fields. In these meetings Wiener succeeded in becoming sufficiently familiar with empirical findings from the fields discussed to enable him to subject some of them to the mathematical techniques he had developed.

During this same period other scientists were concerned with the study of how complex networks made up of very simple elements such as switches or relays might behave—a switch being a device with only two possible states, open or closed. Some treated these problems as problems in electrical circuits, others as problems in logic, and still others as problems in nervous activity because a neuron's activity was presumably an all-or-none process and the neuron therefore another two-state device. These largely theoretical explorations led to some exciting results. It became clear that assemblies made up of a finite number of switches or hypothetical neurons would be able to carry out intricate computations. (Here the word "computation" needs to be taken in a broad sense: it refers not only to numerical calculations but to all those logical operations that such a network can perform.) A computing machine of this type represented a new model for the brain: it was a device capable of symbol manipulation, of, for instance, detecting and recognizing abstract features in a physical environment.

In the middle of World War II there came from the Cambridge group a highly influential paper on the role of purpose in the study and classification of various kinds of behavior. Its authors—Rosenblueth, Wiener and Robert P. Bigelow—contrasted such machines as roulette wheels and clocks, which do not have specific final goals, to machines like target-seeking torpedoes. They subdivided purposeful active behavior into two classes, depending on whether feedback was present or not. When there is feedback, the behavior (called "teleological") is controlled by the margin of error between where the object stands at a given time and its goal. This negative type of feedback prevents objects and organisms from overshooting their goals. All purposeful behavior, which includes voluntary activity, may be considered to require negative feedback to direct it toward its goal.

The authors also state that ". . . uniform behavioristic analysis is applicable to both machines and living organisms, regardless of the complexity of the behaviors." Although there is considerable overlap between the realms of behavior of organisms and machines, there are examples of behavior that are found exclusively in one or the other group. Whether research methods for these two realms can always remain similar depends on whether there are one or several *qualitatively* distinct, unique characteristics present in one group but absent in the other. Rosenblueth and his colleagues hold that such qualitative differences have not appeared so far in any significant area of behavior. This view seems to have been shared by the many designers of artificial animals—"bugs," "tortoises," "homeostats"—that have been built out of hardware parts to illustrate goal-seeking behavior.

Thus in the mid-1940's the stage was set for the emergence of a fairly cohesive complex of ideas that was to become known as "Cybernetics." The actual cauldron from which cybernetics emerged was a series of conferences in Princeton, sponsored by the Macy Foundation, and attended by mathematicians, communications, computer and control engineers, philosophers, and representatives from the various fields of study of the nervous system and social phenomena. The transactions of the later conferences have been published almost verbatim and offer fascinating insights into the personalities of the many colorful participants and, more importantly, into the process of the hammering out of a set of ideas. Most of the participants had been involved in World War II, and the lesson that "machines can't fight alone" had been driven home to them. These war activities rarely corresponded to the lines of traditional academic departments but were instead multidisciplinary, like Macy conferences. The mood of these symposia was one of optimistic and searching reconsideration of many topics that in complexly organized structures relate to communication and control via feedback. To Wiener and his colleagues these key concepts were clearly the cement of the nervous system and of social organization.

They were less concerned with giving a systematic account of how a particular mathematical technique or model related to a set of specific experiments than with suggesting novel ways of looking at old and intractable problems.

Wiener's *Cybernetics, or Control and Communication in the Animal and the Machine* is no scientific treatise, but it remains to this day an imaginative inventory of certain mathematical and conceptual tools from communication and control engineering. The author outlines in addition those topics from the life and social sciences to which these tools may be relevant. Cybernetics can hardly be thought of as a unifying science; it stands in a way between the sciences and philosophy. It suggests certain possible strategies for attacking problems in systems characterized by "organized complexity." It is considerably more, however, than a set of analogies or a convenient language in which one can talk about problems that seem to have something in common. It is an *état d'esprit* that encourages one to analyze biological and social problems not merely by thinking of organisms as machines but by specifying that the most significant *modus operandi* of the brain is that of information-handling under appropriate feedback control.

The particular information-processing machine to which the brain has been compared for the last twenty years is the high-speed electronic digital computer. Computers were more often than not referred to as "electronic" or "giant" brains. Initially these computers were certainly large enough in physical size; vacuum tubes and other electrical parts took up considerably more space than the billions of neurons in a human brain. Depending on his philosophical orientation, the person who set out to compare computers and brains could choose to emphasize similarities or dissimilarities.

In the posthumously published Silliman Lectures, *The Computer and the Brain* (1958), the great mathematician and computer scientist, John von Neumann, dealt with most of the comparisons that had been made and outlined the difficulties standing in the way of an intellectually satisfying resolution. Many of the particular numerical comparisons he himself attempted are a bit outdated in 1966. (Computers evolve rapidly, a generation corresponding to approximately four years!) But von Neumann's general approach remains valid today, whether the emphasis is on physical characteristics and performance of the "componentry" or on organizational features.

We no longer hold the earlier widespread belief that the so-called all-or-none law from nerve impulses makes it legitimate to think of relays as adequate models for neurons. In addition, we have become increasingly impressed with the interactions that take place among neurons: in some instances a sequence of nerve impulses may reflect the activities of literally thousands of neurons in a finely graded manner. In a system whose numerous elements interact so strongly with each other, the functioning of the system is not necessarily best understood by proceeding on a neuron-by-neuron basis as if each had an independent personality. Nor is there any reason to fashion a brain model on the basis of a single type of facts (anatomy, chemistry, electrophysiology). Admittedly the brain's electrical activity represents in convenient form events in the nervous system whose duration ranges from a fraction of $1/1000$ of a second to several seconds; events in the life of an organism that are either much longer or much shorter are not well represented, however, by electrical activity. While there is currently much interest in the phenomena of memory from the viewpoint of molecular biology, it is not yet possible to contrast the componentry of natural and computer memory with respect to such particulars as number of storable items or access time to any particular item.

These very sketchy examples indicate how little specific progress can be expected from gross and overall analogizing. Detailed comparisons of the organization of computer systems and brains would prove equally frustrating and inconclusive. We might be able to identify successfully input and output devices in both. But we would have considerably more difficulty in formally identifying actual neural structures whose primary function is to deal with symbols, or to exercise control over other units, or to act as memory storage devices. And when we ask what type of information processing is genetically "wired in" and what is there potentially that has to be brought out by programmed interaction with environment, the situation is even more difficult.

What conclusions are we to draw from this state of affairs? That the computer is just another, not very appropriate, metaphor? Not quite! Even though detailed structural or functional comparisons may be tantalizing misfits, they have been responsible for many new and penetrating theoretical and experimental questions. Most of these relate to the handling of a commodity that is being called information, even though the formulations of information theory do not directly apply. In the handling of purely abstract or symbolic tasks, where we are as yet unable to point to any specific chain of relevant events in the brain, computer programs are the best systematic descriptions of the way in which men solve such problems; beyond this, these programs contribute significantly to an emerging cognitive technology.

But this is not all. Computers have become indispensable tools in the study of man's brain. They assist in detecting significant patterns of neuronal activity, and they permit us to simulate the possible modes of behavior of networks made up of quite realistic neuron-like elements. These few tasks can do no more than illustrate the generality of computers as logical instruments. No matter how important the clock, the telephone, and all the technological inventions that have enlarged man's sensory capacities, computers represent an effect of a different magnitude: man's ability to handle symbols promises to be many times magnified. The enormous development of man's cortex—both in size and richness of potential organization—is commonly considered the most significant aspect of the evolutionary jump man represents. By coupling the capacities of man's brain with the capabilities of computers in a manner that will make them supplement each other, we may achieve a significant jump in the individual's and society's ability to deal with problems that are now too complex to be handled by the unaided brain.

In our present state of ignorance with regard to the ultimate potentialities of both computers and brains, to ask whether computers are good models for human brains and whether man's uniqueness is a matter of quantity rather than quality, is hardly to ask the right questions. Instead we must ask ourselves how we can make wise use of the enormously enhanced logical capability that lies ahead and how we can achieve a wise division of labor between the bio-logical and the purely logical.

Extensions
to the
Individual

22

A General Introduction to Psychoanalysis: First Lecture

Sigmund Freud

In this, the first of a series of twenty-eight lectures given by Freud to medical students, he warns in simple language of the key problems involved in their study and acceptance of psychoanalysis. These issues include: (1) the absence of any structural defect in the nervous system to which neurosis can be ascribed; (2) the difficulty in admitting that mere discourse between patient and therapist can be a genuine form of treatment; (3) the fact that no possibility exists for public demonstration of psychoanalytic therapy—the patient becoming "mute" if an onlooker is present; (4) the proposition that most behavioral processes take place without awareness; and (5) the further proposition that these unconscious processes originate largely in sexual impulses.

I do not know what knowledge any of you may already have of psychoanalysis, either from reading or from hearsay. But having regard to the title of my lectures—Introductory Lectures on Psychoanalysis—I am bound to proceed as though you knew nothing of the subject and needed instruction, even in its first elements.

One thing, at least, I may pre-suppose that you know—namely, that psychoanalysis is a method of medical treatment for those suffering from nervous disorders; and I can give you at once an illustration of the way in which psychoanalytic procedure differs from, and often even reverses, what is customary in other branches of medicine. Usually, when we introduce a patient to a new form of treatment we minimize its difficulties and give him confident assurances of its success. This is, in my opinion, perfectly justifiable, for we thereby increase the probability of success. But when we

Reprinted from *A General Introduction to Psychoanalysis*, sixth edition (1957), pp. 19–28; reprinted by permission of Liveright Publishing Company.

undertake to treat a neurotic psychoanalytically we proceed otherwise. We explain to him the difficulties of the method, its long
duration, the trials and sacrifices which will be required of him;
and, as to the result, we tell him that we can make no definite
promises, that success depends upon his endeavours, upon his
understanding, his adaptability and his perseverance. We have, of
course, good reasons, into which you will perhaps gain some insight
later on, for adopting this apparently perverse attitude.

Now forgive me if I begin by treating you in the same way as I
do my neurotic patients, for I shall positively advise you against
coming to hear me a second time. And with this intention I shall
explain to you how of necessity you can obtain from me only an
incomplete knowledge of psychoanalysis and also what difficulties
stand in the way of your forming an independent judgment on the
subject. For I shall show you how the whole trend of your training
and your accustomed modes of thought must inevitably have made
you hostile to psychoanalysis, and also how much you would have
to overcome in your own minds in order to master this instinctive
opposition. I naturally cannot foretell what degree of understanding
of psychoanalysis you may gain from my lectures, but I can at least
assure you that by attending them you will not have learnt how to
conduct a psychoanalytic investigation, nor how to carry out a
psychoanalytic treatment. And further, if any one of you should feel
dissatisfied with a merely cursory acquaintance with psychoanalysis
and should wish to form a permanent connection with it, I shall not
merely discourage him, but I shall actually warn him against it. For
as things are at the present time, not only would the choice of such
a career put an end to all chances of academic success, but, upon
taking up work as a practitioner, such a man would find himself in a
community which misunderstood his aims and intentions, regarded
him with suspicion and hostility, and let loose upon him all the
latent evil impulses harboured within it. Perhaps you can infer from
the accompaniments of the war now raging in Europe what a countless host that is to reckon with.

However, there are always some people to whom the possibility
of a new addition to knowledge will prove an attraction strong
enough to survive all such inconveniences. If there are any such
among you who will appear at my second lecture in spite of my
words of warning they will be welcome. But all of you have a right

to know what these inherent difficulties of psychoanalysis are to which I have alluded.

First of all, there is the problem of the teaching and exposition of the subject. In your medical studies you have been accustomed to use your eyes. You see the anatomical specimen, the precipitate of the chemical reaction, the contraction of the muscle as the result of the stimulation of its nerves. Later you come into contact with the patients; you learn the symptoms of disease by the evidence of your senses; the results of pathological processes can be demonstrated to you, and in many cases even the exciting cause of them in an isolated form. On the surgical side you are witnesses of the measures by which the patient is helped, and are permitted to attempt them yourselves. Even in psychiatry, demonstration of patients, of their altered expression, speech and behaviour, yields a series of observations which leave a deep impression on your minds. Thus a teacher of medicine acts for the most part as an exponent and guide, leading you as it were through a museum, while you gain in this way a direct relationship to what is displayed to you and believe yourselves to have been convinced by your own experience of the existence of the new facts.

But in psychoanalysis, unfortunately, all this is different. In psychoanalytic treatment nothing happens but an exchange of words between the patient and the physician. The patient talks, tells of his past experiences and present impressions, complains, and expresses his wishes and his emotions. The physician listens, attempts to direct the patient's thought-processes, reminds him, forces his attention in certain directions, gives him explanations and observes the reactions of understanding or denial thus evoked. The patient's unenlightened relatives—people of a kind to be impressed only by something visible and tangible, preferably by the sort of "action" that may be seen at a cinema—never omit to express their doubts of how "mere talk can possibly cure anybody." Their reasoning is of course as illogical as it is inconsistent. For they are the same people who are always convinced that the sufferings of neurotics are purely "in their own imagination." Words and magic were in the beginning one and the same thing, and even to-day words retain much of their magical power. By words one of us can give to another the greatest happiness or bring about utter despair; by words the teacher imparts his knowledge to the student; by words

the orator sweeps his audience with him and determines its judge-
ments and decisions. Words call forth emotions and are universally
the means by which we influence our fellow-creatures. Therefore let
us not despise the use of words in psycho-therapy and let us be
content if we may overhear the words which pass between the
analyst and the patient.

But even that is impossible. The dialogue which constitutes the
analysis will admit of no audience; the process cannot be demonstrated. One could, of course, exhibit a neurasthenic or hysterical
patient to students at a psychiatric lecture. He would relate his case
and his symptoms, but nothing more. He will make the communications necessary to the analysis only under the conditions of a special
affective relationship to the physician; in the presence of a single
person to whom he was indifferent he would become mute. For
these communications relate to all his most private thoughts and
feelings, all that which as a socially independent person he must
hide from others, all that which, being foreign to his own conception of himself, he tries to conceal even from himself.

It is impossible, therefore, for you to be actually present during
a psychoanalytic treatment; you can only be told about it, and can
learn psychoanalysis, in the strictest sense of the word, only by
hearsay. This tuition at second hand, so to say, puts you in a very
unusual and difficult position as regards forming your own judge-
ment on the subject, which will therefore largely depend on the
reliance you can place on your informant.

Now imagine for a moment that you were present at a lecture
in history instead of in psychiatry, and that the lecturer was dealing
with the life and conquests of Alexander the Great. What reason
would you have to believe what he told you? The situation would
appear at first sight even more unsatisfactory than in the case of
psychoanalysis, for the professor of history had no more part in
Alexander's campaigns than you yourselves; the psychoanalyst at
least informs you of matters in which he himself has played a part.
But then we come to the question of what evidence there is to
support the historian. He can refer you to the accounts of early
writers who were either contemporaries or who lived not long after
the events in question, such as Diodorus, Plutarch, Arrian, and
others; he can lay before you reproductions of the preserved coins
and statues of the king, and pass round a photograph of the mosaic
at Pompeii representing the battle at Issus. Yet, strictly speaking, all

these documents only prove that the existence of Alexander and the reality of his deeds were already believed in by former generations of men, and your criticism might begin anew at this point. And then you would find that not everything reported of Alexander is worthy of belief or sufficiently authenticated in detail, but I can hardly suppose that you would leave the lecture-room in doubt altogether as to the reality of Alexander the Great. Your conclusions would be principally determined by two considerations: first, that the lecturer could have no conceivable motive for attempting to persuade you of something which he did not himself believe to be true, and secondly, that all the available authorities agree more or less in their accounts of the facts. In questioning the accuracy of the early writers you would apply these tests again, the possible motives of the authors and the agreement to be found between them. The result of such tests would certainly be convincing in the case of Alexander, probably less so in regard to figures like Moses and Nimrod. Later on you will perceive clearly enough what doubts can be raised against the credibility of an exponent of psychoanalysis.

Now you will have a right to ask the question: If no objective evidence for psychoanalysis exists and no possibility of demonstrating the process, how is it possible to study it at all or to convince oneself of its truth? The study of it is indeed not an easy matter, nor are there many people who have thoroughly learned it; still, there is, of course, some way of learning it. Psychoanalysis is learnt first of all on oneself, through the study of one's own personality. This is not exactly what is meant by introspection, but it may be so described for want of a better word. There is a whole series of very common and well-known mental phenomena which can be taken as material for self-analysis when one has acquired some knowledge of the method. In this way one may obtain the required conviction of the reality of the processes which psychoanalysis describes, and of the truth of its conceptions, although progress on these lines is not without its limitations. One gets much further by submitting oneself to analysis by a skilled analyst, undergoing the working of the analysis in one's own person and using the opportunity to observe the finer details of the technique which the analyst employs. This, eminently the best way, is of course only practicable for individuals and cannot be used in a class of students.

The second difficulty you will find in connection with psychoanalysis is not, on the other hand, inherent in it, but is one for which

I must hold you yourselves responsible, at least in so far as your medical studies have influenced you. Your training will have induced in you an attitude of mind very far removed from the psychoanalytical one. You have been trained to establish the functions and disturbances of the organism on an anatomical basis, to explain them in terms of chemistry and physics, and to regard them from a biological point of view; but no part of your interest has ever been directed to the mental aspects of life, in which, after all, the development of the marvellously complicated organism culminates. For this reason a psychological attitude of mind is still foreign to you, and you are accustomed to regard it with suspicion, to deny it a scientific status, and to leave it to the general public, poets, mystics, and philosophers. Now this limitation in you is undoubtedly detrimental to your medical efficiency; for on meeting a patient it is the mental aspects with which one first comes into contact, as in most human relationships, and I am afraid you will pay the penalty of having to yield a part of the curative influence at which you aim to the quacks, mystics, and faith-healers whom you despise.

I quite acknowledge that there is an excuse for this defect in your previous training. There is no auxiliary philosophical science that might be of service to you in your profession. Neither speculative philosophy nor descriptive psychology, nor even the so-called experimental psychology which is studied in connection with the physiology of the sense-organs, as they are taught in the schools, can tell you anything useful of the relations existing between mind and body, or can give you a key to comprehension of a possible disorder of the mental functions. It is true that the psychiatric branch of medicine occupies itself with describing the different forms of recognizable mental disturbances and grouping them in clinical pictures, but in their best moments psychiatrists themselves are doubtful whether their purely descriptive formulations deserve to be called science. The origin, mechanism, and interrelation of the symptoms which make up these clinical pictures are undiscovered: either they cannot be correlated with any demonstrable changes in the brain, or only with such changes as in no way explain them. These mental disturbances are open to therapeutic influence only when they can be identified as secondary effects of some organic disease.

This is the lacuna which psychoanalysis is striving to fill. It hopes to provide psychiatry with the missing psychological foundation, to discover the common ground on which a correlation of bodily and mental disorder becomes comprehensible. To this end it must dissociate itself from every foreign preconception, whether anatomical, chemical, or physiological, and must work throughout with conceptions of a purely psychological order, and for this very reason I fear that it will appear strange to you at first.

For the next difficulty I shall not hold you, your training or your mental attitude, responsible. There are two tenets of psychoanalysis which offend the whole world and excite its resentment; the one conflicts with intellectual, the other with moral and æsthetic prejudices. Let us not underestimate these prejudices; they are powerful things, residues of valuable, even necessary, stages in human evolution. They are maintained by emotional forces, and the fight against them is a hard one.

The first of these displeasing propositions of psychoanalysis is this: that mental processes are essentially unconscious, and that those which are conscious are merely isolated acts and parts of the whole psychic entity. Now I must ask you to remember that, on the contrary, we are accustomed to identify the mental with the conscious. Consciousness appears to us as positively the characteristic that defines mental life, and we regard psychology as the study of the content of consciousness. This even appears so evident that any contradiction of it seems obvious nonsense to us, and yet it is impossible for psychoanalysis to avoid this contradiction, or to accept the identity between the conscious and the psychic. The psychoanalytical definition of the mind is that it comprises processes of the nature of feeling, thinking, and wishing, and it maintains that there are such things as unconscious thinking and unconscious wishing. But in doing so psychoanalysis has forfeited at the outset the sympathy of the sober and scientifically minded, and incurred the suspicion of being a fantastic cult occupied with dark and unfathomable mysteries.* You yourselves must find it difficult to understand why I should stigmatize an abstract proposition, such as "The psychic is the conscious," as a prejudice; nor can you guess yet what evolutionary process could have led to the denial of the unconscious, if it does indeed exist, nor what advantage could have been achieved by this denial. It seems like an empty wrangle over words to argue whether mental life is to be regarded as co-extensive

---

* [Literally: "that wishes to build in the dark and fish in murky waters."—Tr.]

248

with consciousness or whether it may be said to stretch beyond this limit, and yet I can assure you that the acceptance of unconscious mental processes represents a decisive step towards a new orientation in the world and in science.

As little can you suspect how close is the connection between this first bold step on the part of psychoanalysis and the second to which I am now coming. For this next proposition, which we put forward as one of the discoveries of psychoanalysis, consists in the assertion that impulses, which can only be described as sexual in both the narrower and the wider sense, play a peculiarly large part, never before sufficiently appreciated, in the causation of nervous and mental disorders. Nay, more, that these sexual impulses have contributed invaluably to the highest cultural, artistic, and social achievements of the human mind.

In my opinion, it is the aversion from this conclusion of psychoanalytic investigation that is the most significant source of the opposition it has encountered. Are you curious to know how we ourselves account for this? We believe that civilization has been built up, under the pressure of the struggle for existence, by sacrifices in gratification of the primitive impulses, and that it is to a great extent for ever being re-created, as each individual, successively joining the community, repeats the sacrifice of his instinctive pleasures for the common good. The sexual are amongst the most important of the instinctive forces thus utilized: they are in this way sublimated, that is to say, their energy is turned aside from its sexual goal and diverted towards other ends, no longer sexual and socially more valuable. But the structure thus built up is insecure, for the sexual impulses are with difficulty controlled; in each individual who takes up his part in the work of civilization there is a danger that a rebellion of the sexual impulses may occur, against this diversion of their energy. Society can conceive of no more powerful menace to its culture than would arise from the liberation of the sexual impulses and a return of them to their original goal. Therefore society dislikes this sensitive place in its development being touched upon; that the power of the sexual instinct should be recognized, and the significance of the individual's sexual life revealed, is very far from its interests; with a view to discipline it has rather taken the course of diverting attention away from this whole field. For this reason, the revelations of psychoanalysis are not tolerated by it, and it would greatly prefer to brand them as æsthetically offensive, morally reprehensible, or dangerous. But since such objections are not valid arguments against conclusions which claim to represent the objective results of scientific investigation, the opposition must be translated into intellectual terms before it can be expressed. It is a characteristic of human nature to be inclined to regard anything which is disagreeable as untrue, and then without much difficulty to find arguments against it. So society pronounces the unacceptable to be untrue, disputes the results of psychoanalysis with logical and concrete arguments, arising, however, in affective sources, and clings to them with all the strength of prejudice against every attempt at refutation.

But we, on the other hand, claim to have yielded to no tendency in propounding this objectionable theory. Our intention has been solely to give recognition to the facts as we found them in the course of painstaking researches. And we now claim the right to reject unconditionally any such introduction of practical considerations into the field of scientific investigation, even before we have determined whether the apprehension which attempts to force these considerations upon us is justified or not.

These, now, are some of the difficulties which confront you at the outset when you begin to take an interest in psychoanalysis. It is probably more than enough for a beginning. If you can overcome their discouraging effect, we will proceed further.

23

Some Applications of Operant Conditioning to Behavior Therapy

Arthur J. Bachrach

Beginning with the 1950s, there has been increasing application of operant conditioning techniques to the treatment of mental illness. Wolpe, Salter, and Reyna—who have been among the leaders in these efforts—have pulled together the story of progress and failure of various investigations in their book, *The Conditioning Therapies*. Bachrach's contribution provides a clear, detached, informative survey of the field.

He starts by noting how psychoanalysis and behaviorism have points of agreement as well as disagreement. He then reviews certain more fundamental characteristics of operant conditioning, and in the process gives a concise description of its central features.

Bachrach next goes on to give resumés of a few experiments with mental patients; the results collectively show that operant techniques can be used to reinforce socially desirable, and to extinguish socially undesirable, behavior (see also Chapter 9 and 24).

INTRODUCTION

Before I get into the consideration of some of the applications of operant conditioning to behavior therapy I would like to make a few general comments about behaviorism and psychoanalysis, in particular, the areas of agreement and disagreement, as I view them. I do not intend to dwell on the scientific and metaphysical aspects of the difference between these two systems, but will content myself with presenting a brief comparison and comments. I think the major differences are in *methodology*. Among these are the following: Psychoanalysis deals with inferences about "inner" behavior, interprets, and symbolizes. Behaviorism deals with ob-

From *The Conditioning Therapies* by Joseph Wolpe, Andrew Salter, and L. J. Reyna. Copyright © 1964 by Holt, Rinehart and Winston, Inc., pp. 62–75.

servable motor activity, minimizes interpretation, and demands specification of operations. To place these in a tabular form, let me first present the points of departure between psychoanalysis and behaviorism and then the points of agreement.

Points of Departure

PSYCHOANALYSIS
> Philosophical heritage:
> > ideas, will, personality; dualistic (mind as distinct from body), mental apparatus
> Emphasis on inner causes of behavior
> Inferential and interpretative symbols
> Emphasis on individual

BEHAVIORISM
> Biological heritage:
> > muscles, glands, effectors; monistic (mind as physiological response), observable action
> Emphasis on environmental events controlling behavior
> Operational response
> Study of individual but emphasis on general laws of behavior

Points of Agreement

> Importance of observing behavior
> Acceptance of cause-effect relationship (behavior not whimsical)
> Lawful determinism of behavior
> Importance of understanding history of individual and his learning experiences
> From this, relation of past events to current behavior
> Acceptance of genetic, constitutional factors as relevant

Some Characteristics of Operant Conditioning as a Behavioral System

Behavioristic systems, in general, rely on an emphasis on the accurate description of behavior and of the methodologies involved in the manipulation of behavior. Of the characteristics fairly specific to operant conditioning, there are two which I believe are of major importance; these are, first, the *emphasis on the individual* and, second, the *free operant*. The emphasis on the individual is in contrast with the most frequently used approach in psychological research—the use of group data. In the experimental analysis of behavior, as represented by operant conditioning, the individual is the subject of systematic research. Operant conditioning, originally propounded by Skinner (1938), has developed along these lines. Sidman (1956), in a discussion of Skinner's work, offers the following comment:

> Skinner's rejection of "confidence level statistics" derives from his clearly stated interest in the behavior of the individual. This interest dictates an experimental design different from that generally used in psychology. Instead of running groups of animals and averaging their data, it becomes necessary to run individual animals through all of the experimental manipulations. Each animal thus constitutes a replication of the experiment, which not only affords an opportunity for detecting differences among animals, but also actually imposes the obligation to report them and, where possible, to *explain* them. The procedure of treating differences among animals as lawful, rather than as examples of the capriciousness of nature or of the experimental techniques, provides Skinner with one of his substitutes for statistical treatment. Experimentation is continued until the variables responsible for "deviant" behavior are identified. A corollary of this point of view is that any behavioral effect repeatedly demonstrated in the same animal is a lawful phenomenon.

Inasmuch as the central focus of behavior therapy is with the individual, the systematic replication with the single individual provides more information and more control than grouping data can possibly do. This is not an argument against group data, but merely a suggestion that behavioral manipulation occurs most reliably and most systematically with individuals. It also does away with a mythical average, a concept which is not entirely useful in clinical behavioral manipulation.

The concept of the *free operant* tends to differentiate operant conditioning from classical, or respondent, conditioning in that it works with an organism theoretically free to respond or not to respond under certain environmental conditions. As Ferster (1953) observes, "the use of the free operant is a method of wide generality; it refers to any apparatus that generates a response which takes a short time to occur and leaves the animal in the same place ready to respond again. The free operant is used in experiments when the main dependent variable is the frequency of occurrence of behavior." He further observes that almost all the problems encountered in a science of behavior fit this paradigm when one asks the questions, What is the likelihood of a piece of behavior occurring on this particular occasion? How strong is the tendency to behave on this occasion relative to another occasion? The concept of response frequency will be considered in more detail below. At the moment, I would like only to observe that when an animal is free to respond it allows for a *shaping* of behavior, beginning with perhaps diffuse and exploratory responding. We might also suggest that it helps eliminate some of the artifacts engendered by apparatus in a classical conditioning experiment. Liddell and Gantt have pointed out in their writings that one of the crucial factors in the development of experimental neuroses in the Pavlovian conditioning techniques was the harness in which the animal was strapped. By keeping the organism free-moving the problems engendered by immobilization and restriction of activity are minimized or eliminated.

The Specification of Response and Stimulus

Fundamental to any behavioristic system is the recognition of the necessity for the clear specification of the behavior to be studied and controlled. As I have suggested earlier, one of the difficulties with a "psychodynamic" approach to behavior is that it does not clearly specify the responses demanded of the individual, because its terminology is couched in the abstract and uses indirect behavioral descriptions or inferences such as "ego-strength" or "depression." Whereas the psychoanalytic therapist may attempt to "build up the ego-strength of his patient," the conditioner, in his experimental manipulations, must be more specific about the responses with which he is working. So we begin with the specification of the response. The experimenter must indicate what he wishes the individual, whose behavior he is manipulating, to do. In animal experimentation, for example, this may be simply set in terms such as the requirement that a pigeon peck at a translucent plastic key a total of 50 times before he is rewarded by the presentation of food. On a more complex human level the demands for specification are no less real and no less important.

An example of this may be drawn from a recent case of *anorexia nervosa* treated by operant conditioning techniques by W. J. Erwin, Jay Mohr, and myself. A complete report of the medical and experimental psychological aspects of this case is in press (1964) [published in 1965]. For the moment, let me draw upon one illustration from this individual's situation. By definition, this patient was a person who ate with a frequency significantly below her usual frequency, and certainly, in group terms, critically below normal frequency. Without resorting to such unproved explanatory concepts as the "fear of oral impregnation" or, indeed, without any primary consideration of factors which had been involved in her initial cessation of eating, we specified the response we desired simply as an increase in the frequency of food intake, with its concomitant increase in the amount of ingested food. Inasmuch as it was obvious that the eating response and food did not have their expected reinforcing characteristics for this individual, the case was studied to learn what reinforcement *would* be significant to her. We found that she enjoyed visits from people, music, reading, and television, and was accordingly placed on deprivation for all of these. She was put in a barren room and the presentation of visitors, records, television, or books was made contingent upon eating and weight gain. Time does not permit a full account of this case but, as I have noted, such an account is in preparation. The main point to be drawn from this illustration is that there was no need to resort to inferential explanations of her behavior, but there *was* a clear need to specify what it was we demanded of her, as well as the conditions under which the eating response could be manipulated and increased in frequency. I might add that after a little over a year of such operant conditioning control of her behavior both in and out of the hospital situation, she has more than doubled her initial experimental weight of 47 pounds and is continuing to add weight. I think this emphasis on the specification of behavior is central to the system of psychotherapy based on the principle of reciprocal inhibition expounded by Wolpe (1958).

Although the specification of the response may be a relatively simple matter in the experimental control of behavior, the specification of the *stimulus* is not so simple. Indeed, it may become inferential. We can usually only guess as to the stimuli which evoke or set the occasion for behavior, and so one of the tenets of operant conditioning is that it is more effective to start with a response which is observable, measurable, and manipulable and to consider that the realationship of

$$\text{Response} \longrightarrow \text{Reinforcement}$$

is the critical one.

We may begin with the assumption that stimulating conditions are always involved in an organism's response, but by far the clearer datum with which we can work is the response itself, and those consequences upon the response which alter the future likelihood of that response's recurrence. "Reinforcement" is the term generally applied to the consequences of a response; one of the best definitions of reinforcement is that offered by Sidman (1960): "Any event, contingent upon the response of the organism that alters the future likelihood of that response." By definition, positive reinforcement (usually termed loosely a "reward") is any event likely to increase the probability of the response's recurring, whereas a negative reinforcement (loosely a "punishment") is any event that tends to decrease the probability of that response's recurrence, although some procedural differentiation must be made.

Beginning with a suggestion of Goldiamond's, Thompson (1962) has developed a model to differentiate types of reinforcement and their relationship to response probability (or its empirical counterpart, response frequency).

Stimulus event / *Response probability*	Presentation		A) *Termination* B) *Postponement*
	Contingent upon response	Noncontingent upon response	Contingent upon response
Increase	Positive reinforcement Fixed interval Fixed ratio Variable interval Variable ratio	Superstitious behavior	Negative reinforcement A) Escape B) Avoidance
Decrease	Punishment	Conditioned suppression	A) Extinction B) Differentiated reinforcement of low rates (DRL)

The reinforcement contingencies in a free-operant situation are those conditions (temporal, intensive, and topographical) under which a response is closely followed by an environmental consequence. Schedules of reinforcement, or programmed contingencies, may be *procedurally* delineated into six classes on the basis of response probability as a function of stimulus events.

To illustrate, using the above schema, "punishment" is defined as the *presentation* of a *stimulus event, contingent upon the response,* which produces a *decrease* in *response probability.* Conversely, "negative reinforcement" (escape) is defined as the termination of a stimulus event, contingent upon the response, which produces an increase in response probability. Thus, punishment might be a shock that is delivered to a rat only when he presses a bar. Similarly, if the shock is on all the time, except when a bar press terminates it for a specific duration, an escape contingency is in effect. The remaining schedules may be differentiated in a similar fashion.

Using the concept of response frequency allows us to approach our data with greater clarity. An example of this is found in the work on brain stimulation reported by Olds and Milner (1954). They discovered that electrical stimulation of the septal area of the brain was reinforcing to a rat. The original and quite logical hypothesis was that if electric shock delivered to a rat's feet through a grid on the floor of the cage was "punishing," then electric shock delivered directly to the rat's brain would, perhaps, be more punishing. This did not prove to be the case. A rat punished for entering a certain corner of a box, by the delivery of a shock to his septal area, increased his movement toward that corner. Using our definition of positive reinforcement as any event that increases the probability of a response's recurring, then we must say that electrical stimulation of the brain was positively reinforcing; hence it was not at all punishing, but, on the contrary, rewarding. The excellent work of the last few years reported by other investigators, such as Brady (1962), supports the evidence that electrical stimulation of the brain under certain conditions is positively reinforcing. Although it is certainly possible to use an explanatory fiction such as "masochism" to explain why a rat or other animal (cats, dogs, monkeys, and other organisms have been used in these experiments) will deliver electrical stimulation to his own brain when given an opportunity to operate a manipulandum to do this, it is simpler and much more effective to note the relationship of electrical stimulation and increased responding, and to work from there.

Response Frequency

Throughout this paper I have been referring to the concept of response frequency, which is basic to operant conditioning. The frequency with which a response is emitted is the clearest datum with which a psychologist can work, and, as noted above in the use of the free operant, experiments are designed to allow the animal to make a response and be ready to respond again. Elsewhere (1962a) I have referred to the fact that descriptions of behavior are very often expressed in terms which have an underlying response frequency, referring to the observations of Skinner (1953) that to describe a person as "hostile" or as "an enthusiastic skier" or as "an inverterate gambler" is clearly to denote the frequency of a particular response class. The "enthusiastic skier" skis a lot. The "inveterate gambler" gambles with frequency. In short, what is often used as a "personality" description is simply a reference to a particular frequent response class as observed by others.

Shaping

If the operant conditioner, approaching an organism in an experimental space, specifies the response he desires from the organism and the frequency with which he wishes this response emitted, he is in a position to shape the organism's behavior. In the establishment of behavior the experimenter begins with the mass of responses available to the organism he is manipulating. Sidman (1960) offers an example of shaping behavior:

> Shaping is accomplished by reinforcing successively closer approximations to the behavior with which the experimenter ultimately wants to work. The experimental situation, for example, may be one in which a monkey is to be reinforced with food for pressing a lever. If the monkey just sits quietly at first, the experimenter will wait until the animal moves and will then immediately deliver the food. By continuing to reinforce all movements, the experimenter will soon have an active animal with which to work. He then reinforces only those responses which bring the animal closer to the lever, as if drawn by an invisible string. The experimenter now directs his attention to the animal's hand. He delivers the food whenever the hand moves closer to the lever, and it is not long before the animal places its hand on the lever and depresses it. The experimenter can then turn the rest of the job over to his automatic apparatus, which

will deliver the food only when the animal actually depresses the lever.

We may modify some of the rules suggested by Sidman in the establishment of behavior through shaping. A basic rule is to reinforce the behavior immediately. "If the reinforcement is delayed even by a fraction of a second, it is likely to be preceded by some behavior other than that which the experimenter intended to reinforce." It is also critical that the experimenter not give too many or too few reinforcements for an approximation of the desired final response. As Sidman observes, "Behavior that is initially reinforced must ultimately be extinguished as we move closer to the end point. If we reinforce intermediate forms of behavior too much, these once-reinforced but now-to-be-discarded responses will continue to intrude and will unduly prolong the shaping process." And, from the other standpoint, there is the risk that an experimenter may abandon a response "before he has reinforced it enough and, as a consequence, both the response and the variations which stem from it extinguish before he can mold the next closer approximation to the final behavior. The subject may then return to his original behavior, as if he had never gone through a shaping process at all." Sidman notes, at this point, that it is often tempting to refer to an animal who does not respond "correctly" as being "stupid." It is tempting also for us to consider that the therapist may refer to a patient as being "resistant" if his therapeutic manipulations prove unsuccessful. Many proponents of the experimental analysis of behavior feel that "the organism is always right," and that if we were able to know the reinforcement history of the subject, his physiological condition, and the environmental stimulus conditions under which he is performing we could probably assume that his behavior (while perhaps maladjusted in the eyes of others) is appropriate to his own situation.

A final rule which Sidman suggests is one basic to the present discussion:

> *Carefully specify the response to be reinforced in each successive step.* Before abandoning one response and reinforcing the next approximation to the final behavior, the experimenter must watch the subject closely to determine what behavior is available for reinforcement. He should then specify that behavior as quantitatively as possible and adhere rigorously to the specification he has established.

Otherwise he may inadvertently reinforce a slightly different but highly undesirable form of response and unnecessarily prolong the shaping process.

Let me turn now to an example of the shaping of complex behavior, with an illustration drawn from laboratory work.

COMPLEX BEHAVIOR

Several years ago a team of psychologists at Barnard College, under the direction of Drs. Rosemary Pierrel and J. Gilmour Sherman, set up a demonstration of complex behavioral chaining in a white rat. We have modified this demonstration for the same purpose, to demonstrate that complex behavior may be conditioned, response by response, to form a final "fluid" response chain. Our rat, S. R. Rodent, is reinforced by the presentation of food in a tray following bar pressing. But before he can get to press the bar to receive his pellets, Rodent has to climb a spiral staircase, run across a drawbridge, climb a ladder, get into a cable car and pull himself across a gap a couple of feet above the floor of his box, climb another stairway, play a toy piano (hitting two keys of eight which activate a switch, the switch opening a crossing gate from a model railroad), run through the tunnel when the crossing gate is open, climb into an elevator, pull a chain to release the elevator, ride down to the bottom floor and then press his bar to receive his pellets. . . . I might add, parenthetically, that this behavior is extremely reinforcing to the experimenter.

But we did not set up this demonstration purely for our own amusement. We did it because we wished to show that at each particular stage the behavior of the organism is specifically conditioned. The impression while watching S. R. Rodent run through all these paces (which he does in approximately 15 seconds) is that his is a fluid single motion, but he wasn't trained that way. For one thing he was trained "backward." First, he was trained to the tray approach, i.e., to become accustomed to eating his pellets in the tray of the food magazine. Then he was trained to press the bar to deliver the pellet. Next he was shaped to elevator riding to get down to the bar to press it for the pellet. Next, to pull the chain to release the elevator so that he could ride down, and so on. At each individual stage of the shaping, the desired response was achieved by approximation techniques. For example, to oversimplify one illustration, the most difficult response of getting him to pull the chain to release the elevator was accomplished by getting him to make movements toward the chain—to sniff it, to touch it with his nose, then his paws, and finally to pull it. Each one of these was an approximation toward the final desired response of chain pulling. The obvious advantage of training "backward" is that each response becomes not only a cue (or discriminative stimulus) for the immediate and succeeding response, but also a secondary reinforcement for the preceding one. Pressing the piano key, for example, sets the occasion for a click associated with the opening of the crossing gate, making the tunnel accessible to his running.

There are, of course, implications for human learning in S. R. Rodent's behavior. In the shaping of skills, for example, such as tennis strokes or the operation of a motor vehicle, the final fluidity of the action is not like the original training in which a chain of separate responses was individually shaped. Admittedly leaping generalizations, I think that there are implications also for psychotherapy. I don't believe that the abstract conceptual approach to psychotherapy is as effective as the clear delineation of therapist and patient behavior, involving the responses of both persons in the interaction, and the cue or discriminative stimuli occasioning these responses. It is for this reason, I think, that Hans Strupp (1962), who is certainly a good psychodynamic therapist, has said that he feels that the outcome studies are probably not as useful in psychotherapy as process studies which help focus on what is actually occurring in the immediate therapeutic situation. Learning the significant discriminative stimuli and the differentiated responses clearly specified at each appropriate step should provide a great deal more information about psychotherapy than will abstract theoretical formulations of psychodynamics.

I would like now to report two experiments that have been accomplished using operant conditioning techniques on psychiatric patients. What happens, obviously, is that we no longer have complete control of the experimental subjects as we do with S. R. Rodent, or as we have with pigeons or monkeys in an experimental situation. With our animals we can control deprivation and reinforcement, we can control the actual manipulation of the organism in the experimental space; but in the "real life" situation on a psychiatric ward such control is necessarily limited. I've always liked a term proposed by Egon Brunswik—"representative design" —which suggests that the ideal experiment is one that has a minimum of artificiality and a maximum of control. Ideally, if we can get a cross-over point where experimental controls are still rigorous, and yet the problem with which we are working is close to the real-life situation, we would have representative design. This problem has been attacked in some detail in recent volumes (Bachrach, 1962b, 1962c).

I would like to report first an experiment accomplished by Ayllon and Michael (1959), who analyzed the ward behavior of psychiatric patients and concluded that many of the ward problems presented by these patients resulted directly from the reinforcement setting in the hospital. They concerned themselves primarily with the behavior of the patients on the ward that might become "so persistent that it engages the full energies of the nurses, and postpones, sometimes permanently, any effort on their part to deal with the so-called basic problem." They were referring to such behaviors as "failures to eat, dress, bathe, interact socially with other patients and walk without being led, hoarding various objects, hitting, pinching, spitting on other patients, constant attention-seeking actions with respect to the nurses, upsetting chairs in the dayroom, scraping paint from the walls, breaking windows, stuffing paper in the mouth and ears. . . ."

As an example of the extinction of such undesirable behavior, the nurses were able to withhold reinforcement of patients' responses of habitually entering the nurse's office. Such behavior had obviously been reinforced by the nurse's responding (even though it might have been with annoyance) to patients entering the nurse's office. By ignoring this behavior the nurses were able to reduce the incidence to a point where it was no longer disturbing their routine duties.

Another technique used in the study is reminiscent of Wolpe's reciprocal inhibition. They reinforced incompatible behavior in a patient who was violent. In two patients, who consistently refused to eat unless they were aided by the ward nurses, escape and avoidance conditioning techniques were used. Both patients were also extremely concerned with neatness and with keeping their clothes clean, and the nurse began the practice of spilling food on the patients' clothing whenever they insisted on being spoon-fed. This negatively reinforcing spilling could be avoided if the patients fed themselves. In both cases the result was the desired response of self-feeding.

In a similar series of experiments, conducted by Ayllon and Haughton (1962), the experimenters found that approximately 50 percent of the schizophrenic patients on a ward presented food problems. The subject population consisted of 45 psychiatric patients, 91 per cent of whom were long-term schizophrenics. The eating behavior of the approximately 50 percent of this population that had a history of refusal to eat had remained relatively unaffected by one or more of these techniques: spoon-feeding, tube-feeding, intravenous feeding, and electroshock. All aids to feeding the patients were discontinued. The patients in one experiment were left alone at mealtimes, and had to go into the dining room to eat. Next the level of complexity was raised so that the patient could not eat unless she appeared in the dining room within thirty minutes after a nurse called dinner (a discriminative stimulus). The doors would then be locked and the patient would miss that particular meal. Successful establishment of self-feeding in the social dining room situation was achieved.

In another related experiment the investigators set up a chain of responses after the eating was under control.

> The patients were required to drop a penny into the slot of a collection can to gain entrance to the dining room. In addition, access to the dining room was limited to 5 minutes from the time of meal call. The development of the coin as S^D [discriminative stimulus] for entering the dining room was begun by having a nurse distribute a penny to each of the patients congregated outside the dining room at meal time.

By other shaping techniques the motor response required to obtain food reinforcement was learned by all the schizophrenic patients. Other experimental controls were used and the authors conclude that

> studies using schizophrenics attribute their frequently impaired performance to underlying intellectual, perceptual or sensory deficits. The data reported in this paper demonstrate that the control of psychotic behavior depends largely on the use of strong reinforcers.

Evidence is clearly presented in these experiments that the schizophrenic "out of touch with reality" can be controlled behaviorally if the environmental conditions and manipulations are properly established.

There have been other experimental programs, such as Lindsley's (1960), in which more experimentally controlled techniques were used with psychotic patients, and Ellis, Barnett, and Pryer's (1960) work on mental defectives. All the experiments with the patients have followed the general principles of operant conditioning, with necessary modifications. Accepting the principle of the lawfulness of behavior, we can be confident and hopeful that the techniques of operant conditioning developed in the laboratory can ultimately be applied to behavior therapy with as much success as is demonstrated in experimental animals.

REFERENCES

AYLLON, T., AND MICHAEL, J. The psychiatric nurse as a behavioral engineer. *J. exp. Anal. Behav.*, 1959, **2**, 323–334.

———, AND HAUGHTON, E. Control of the behavior of schizophrenic patients by food. *J. exp. Anal. Behav.*, 1962, **5**, 343–352.

BACHRACH, A. J. An experimental approach to superstitious behavior. *J. Am. Folklore*, 1962, **75**, 1–9(a).

——— (Ed.) *Experimental foundations of clinical psychology.* New York: Basic, 1962(b).

———. *Psychological research.* New York: Random House, 1962(c).

———, ERWIN, W. J., AND MOHR, J. P. The control of eating behavior in an anorexic by operant conditioning techniques. In L. Ullman and L. Krasner (Eds.) *Case studies in behavior modification.* New York: Holt, Rinehart and Winston [1965].

BRADY, J. V. Psychophysiology of emotional behavior. In A. J. Bachrach (Ed.) *Experimental foundations of clinical psychology.* New York: Basic, 1962.

ELLIS, N. R., BARNETT, C. D., AND PRYER, M. W. Operant behavior in mental defectives: Exploratory studies. *J. exp. Anal. Behav.*, 1960, **3**, 63–69.

FERSTER, C. B. The use of the free operant in the analysis of behavior. *Psychol. Bull.*, 1953, **50**, 264–274.

LINDSLEY, O. R. Characteristics of the behavior of chronic psychotics as revealed by free-operant conditioning methods. *Dis. Nerv. Syst.* (Monograph Supplement), 1960, **21**, 66–78.

OLDS, J., AND MILNER, P. Positive reinforcement produced by electrical stimulation of septal area and other regions of rat brain. *J. comp. physiol. Psychol.*, 1954, **47**, 419–427.

SIDMAN, M. Verplanck's analysis of Skinner. *Contemp. Psychol.*, 1956, **1**, 7–8.

———. *Tactics of scientific research: evaluating experimental data in psychology.* New York: Basic, 1960.

Skinner, B. F. *The behavior of organisms: an experimental analysis.* New York: Appleton, 1938.

————. Some contributions of an experimental analysis of behavior to psychology as a whole. *Amer. Psychologist,* 1953, 8, 69–78.

Strupp, H. Patient-doctor relationships: psychotherapist in the therapeutic process. In A. J. Bachrach (Ed.) *Experimental foundations of clinical psychology.* New York: Basic, 1962.

Thompson, D. A schema of response probability as a function of stimulus events. *Technical Report, ONR, Contract Nonr* 474 (8), University of Virginia, 1962.

Wolpe, J. *Psychotherapy by reciprocal inhibition.* Stanford: Stanford U. Press, 1958.

24

Some Implications of Psychotherapy Research for Therapeutic Practice

Allen E. Bergin

The serious student of human behavior must sooner or later come to grips with the question of whether experimental psychology has much to add to our understanding of psychopathology. In this survey of the relation between psychotherapeutic research and actual practice, Bergin provides the reader with a broadly based critique of the effectiveness of different research approaches and types of therapy. The author holds that such evidence as is available indicates that Rogers' "client-centered" or "nondirective" therapy is most successful. This approach emphasizes the therapist's acceptance of the patient as he is, thereby reducing the latter's need to be defensive.

Although the article is somewhat technical, relatively few terms require definition, because the general meaning is usually clear from the text. The "MMPI" referred to in Table 1 is the Minnesota Multiphasic Personality Inventory. The coded scales ("L" through "Es") represent different personality characteristics examined in the MMPI. "Variance" is a statistic equivalent to the square of the standard deviation, and is a measure of variability. "F" is the ratio of one variance to another; it indicates whether the variances are significantly different. Finally, "TAT" stands for Thematic Apperception Test.

A survey of psychotherapy research findings is digested into 6 broad conclusions, and implications for practice and research are drawn from them. They are: (a) Psychotherapy causes clients to become better or worse adjusted than controls, (b) Control Ss improve with time as a result of informal therapeutic encounters, (c) Therapeutic

From the *Journal of Abnormal Psychology* (1966), Vol. 71, No. 4, pp. 235–246; Copyright 1966 by the American Psychological Association, and reproduced by permission.

progress varies with therapist warmth, empathy, adjustment, and experience, (d) Client-centered therapy is the only interview-oriented method that has been validated by research, (e) Traditional therapies are seriously limited in effectiveness and are relevant for a small minority of disturbances, and (f) Behavior therapies have considerable promise for enhancing therapeutic effectiveness and should be utilized or experimented with more widely.

The material to follow is a digest of research findings which have implications for practice and research in psychotherapy. It has been formulated in terms of six conclusions and implications which appear justifiable and defensible. This catalogue of conclusions is based upon a comparative handful of research reports which have been carefully selected from the present empirical chaos for their relative adequacy of conceptualization, design, and outcome. Conclusions have been drawn only in those areas where the results appear to have substance and where they have been replicated; consequently, many areas of study are excluded.

THE DETERIORATION EFFECT

Conclusion 1

Psychotherapy may cause people to become better or worse adjusted than comparable people who do not receive such treatment.

Recently, a curious and provocative finding occurred in the preliminary results of the Wisconsin schizophrenia project conducted by Rogers, Gendlin, and Truax (Rogers, 1961; Truax, 1963; Truax and Carkhuff, 1964). It was that the patients in psychotherapy tended to become either better or worse in adjustment than their matched control-group counterparts.

At that time two earlier studies were analyzed (Barron and Leary, 1955; Cartwright, 1956; Cartwright and Vogel, 1960) in which similar findings had occurred; but being incidental to other results, they had not been emphasized in proportion to their true import (Bergin, 1963). Since then, four additional studies with similar findings have been discovered (Fairweather, Simon, Gebhard, Weingarten, Holland, Sanders, Stone, and Reahl, 1960; Mink, 1959; Powers and Witmer, 1951; Rogers and Dymond, 1954). In all seven studies, although there tends to be no difference in the average amount of change between experimentals and controls, there does tend to be a significant difference in *variability* of change. The criterion, or change, scores for treatment groups attain a much wider dispersion than do those of control groups, even though the mean change in both groups is quite similar. Typically, control subjects (Ss) improve somewhat, with the varying amounts of change clustering about the mean. On the other hand, experimental Ss are typically dispersed all the way from marked improvement to mark deterioration. Now frequently documented, this information is alarming to say the least. Psychotherapy can and does make people worse than their control counterparts! Because of the controversial nature of this conclusion, the following material is presented as detailed substantiating evidence in its support.

Table 1 is reproduced from Cartwright's (1956) reanalysis of the well-known Barron and Leary study (1955).

Table 1. Variances of Discrepancy Scores on MMPI Scales for Individual Psychotherapy and Nontreatment Groups

SCALE	INDIVIDUAL PSYCHOTHERAPY ($N = 42$) V[a]	NONTREATMENT GROUP ($N = 23$) V	F
L	19.89	23.43	1.18
F	215.21	22.94	9.38**
K	55.95	31.70	1.76
Hs	127.46	64.16	1.99*
D	244.30	93.32	2.62**
Hy	113.21	87.80	1.29
Pd	155.00	89.68	1.73
Pa	111.94	68.06	1.64
Pt	208.51	73.27	2.85**
Sc	272.91	74.13	3.68**
Ma	126.79	75.34	1.68
Es	43.56	14.82	2.94**

[a] Variances computed from *SD* data reported by Barron and Leary (Table 2, p. 243).
* $p < .05$.
** $p < .01$.

Cartwright comments on the data as follows:

/ For many scales the variance results suggest that mean differences between the groups are absent because differences of two kinds, opposed in sign, are present. It seems that some therapy patients *deteriorated* to a greater extent than did the waiting-list

> controls, while some therapy patients *did improve* significantly more
> than the controls [pp. 403–404].

It should be noted that this occurred only for individual and not for
group therapy.

It is a fascinating fact that Cartwright's observation has lain
unattended in the literature for years, while implicit in his statement
is a clear means of resolving much of the controversy over negative
results in therapy-outcome studies. It is even more fascinating that
Cartwright himself participated in a study (Rogers and Dymond,
1954) in which a similar phenomenon occurred, but just as with the
data in the Barron and Leary study it was never emphasized in
proportion to its true import. The classic features in this study apparently overshadowed the passing references to a *client-deteriora-
tion phenomenon.* While the study is properly famous for other
reasons, it provides supporting bits of evidence for the thesis that
negative change in therapy is not an isolated or chance occurrence.
A careful reading of the report indicates that of 25 therapy Ss, 6 or
24%, declined in self-ideal correlation between pretherapy and
follow-up testing. A quick computation of the mean change in self-
ideal correlation indicates that those who increased averaged an
increment of .49 in their correlations, whereas those who declined a
decrement of $-.40$, a difference that is striking considering the fact
that the mean pretherapy correlations were not different for these
two subgroups. While some chance fluctuations in scores are to be
expected, these changes in both directions can hardly be attributed
to the effects of imperfect test reliability. While Butler and Haigh
(1954) do not examine these possibilities in the data, they do allude
to them in passing: "It is of interest, though it does not bear directly
upon the hypothesis, that there has also been a marked increase in
the degree of variation of correlations (self-ideal) over this period
[p. 63]."

It may be argued, of course, that decline in self-ideal correlation can be an indication of improved adjustment, particularly when
the correlation is extremely high as in the case of some paranoid Ss.
However, the pretest correlations of all six Ss who declined in this
study were low, ranging from .28 to $-.12$. The question of whether
self-ideal correlations actually measure adjustment at all is still a
subject of some debate, so it would seem unwise to draw conclusions about psychotherapy in general from data based on this

measure alone. In another section of Rogers and Dymond, an analysis of behavior observations made of the clients independently of therapist progress ratings yielded results similar to those found with the self-ideal measure:

> During the whole period from pre-therapy to follow-up, observers saw a definite increase in the maturity of behavior of those clients whose therapy was rated as successful and a sharp decrease in the maturity of behavior of those clients rated as unsuccessful. The relationship was statistically significant [p. 228].

While there are additional fragmentary evidences of deterioration phenomena in the book, these suffice to illustrate the point.

In a controlled study of counseling with high school students, Mink (1959) observes the same phenomenon: "Counseling affected the expression of social adjustments on the California Test of Personality. The forms of expression indicate both improvement and recession [p. 14]."

The excellent multifactor design executed by Fairweather et al. (1960) yielded similar results:

> Generally, significantly different variances occurred on most instruments between treatments and diagnoses. The control group usually had the smallest variance and the three psychotherapy groups the largest [p. 24]. In these three interactions, one or all of the three long-term psychotic groups in psychotherapy demonstrated changes in the maladaptive scale direction [MMPI] while the controls remain[ed] relatively the same or change[d] in the adaptive direction [p. 9].

Cartwright and Vogel (1960) discovered the same type of differential effect in a neurotic sample using different criterion measures:

> Thus, as measured by the Q score, adjustment changes, regardless of direction, were significantly greater during a therapy period than during a No-Therapy period [p. 122]. The Post-therapy tests showed those in therapy with experienced therapists to have improved significantly on both tests, whereas those in therapy with inexperienced therapists not to have improved . . . , in fact they bordered on a significant decrease in health on the TAT [p. 127].

Turning back several decades to the Cambridge-Somerville youth study (Powers and Witmer, 1951) which was initiated in 1937, the same phenomenon is found with a group of predelinquent boys:

When the Study Services were effectual most of the boys did function better than their C-twins. This conclusion can be accepted, however, only if its opposite is also accepted: that some of the boys who were not benefited may have been handicapped in social adjustment by the organization's efforts. If this is true, we can conclude that the apparent chance distribution of terminal adjustment ratings . . . was due to the fact that the good effects of the Study were counterbalanced by the poor [p. 455].

Elsewhere the authors indicate that in a significant proportion of cases where the counselor's efforts were judged as poor, the boys "were more socially maladjusted than their control twin [p. 509]." It is unfortunate that this excellently designed and executed study is one leaned upon most heavily by Eysenck (1960, 1965) in his bold denial of the usefulness of psychotherapy, for while the study shows no difference between experimentals and controls, it demonstrates the efficacy of treatment as well as its deteriorative effect.

Finally, to cite the recent Wisconsin project on therapy of schizophrenia which has been published (Truax, 1963) thus far only in tempting bits and pieces:

High levels of therapist-offered conditions during therapy are related to patient improvement, but . . . low levels . . . are related to patient deterioration, so that if all the therapy combined is indiscriminately compared to control conditions there is little average change. Thus, psychotherapy can be for better or for worse [p. 256].

Since the length of therapy varied in these seven studies from a few months to several years, it seems doubtful that the observed deterioration can be accounted for by the temporary regression that sometimes occurs during treatment. The views of most writers would indicate that the average deterioration due to this effect for a treatment group would be small after brief and lengthy periods of therapy but large in between; whereas the findings reported here suggest a consistent, rectangularly distributed, amount of regression, regardless of the length of time transpired prior to obtaining outcome estimates. Unfortunately, so little controlled empirical work has been done with analytic therapies, which are presumably the richest sources of such data, that it is difficult to compare the findings reported here with what might be found if research were done on them.

Fortunately, these various data indicate that psychotherapy can make people considerably better off than control Ss. Therefore, contrary to the notions of some critics, psychotherapy can produce improvement beyond that which may occur due to spontaneous remission alone. Consistently replicated, this is a direct and unambiguous refutation of the oft-cited Eysenckian position (Eysenck, 1960, 1965).

A general paradigm is suggested by the double-edged effect observed in the studies cited which may be schematized as shown in Figure 1. Such a startling phenomenon certainly deserves a name, and *The Deterioration Effect* is suggested here.

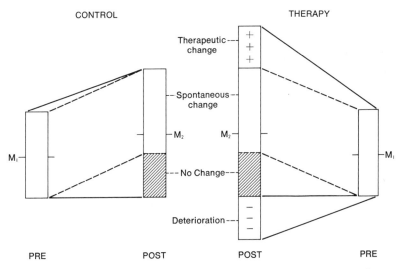

FIGURE 1. The Deterioration Effect. (Schematic representation of pre- and posttest distributions of criterion scores in psychotherapy-outcome studies.)

It is interesting to note that a phenomenon similar to the great variability in the quality of therapeutic effects noted here has also been observed in relation to the accuracy of diagnostic evaluations (Garfield, 1963). Apparently, even well-known diagnosticians vary greatly in the accuracy of their judgments. When all of these judgments are pooled, average predictions or discriminations often are not different from chance estimates; but some individuals appear to far exceed chance predictions while others actually do worse than chance.

Implication 1

(a) The practice of psychotherapy should not be given up as some have advocated. (b) Those engaged in this field should be more cautious and critical of their own practices, carefully eliminating any ineffective or harmful therapeutic techniques. They should find out whom they are making worse or better, and how, with all due speed. (c) They should find out if some therapists make people better and if some make them worse, or if individual therapists do both. After that, comes the ticklish business of making changes in technique, personality, or personnel as may be necessary to eliminate negative influences and accentuate positive ones.

NATURAL THERAPEUTIC CONDITIONS

Conclusion 2

(a) It has been frequently replicated, and is now a well-established fact, that control Ss who do not receive psychotherapy change positively as a group with the passage of time. This is the so-called "spontaneous remission" effect (Eysenck, 1952, 1960, 1965). (b) Three studies (Frank, 1961; Gurin, Veroff, and Feld, 1960; Powers and Witmer, 1951) indicate that many of these disturbed persons who receive no formal psychotherapy seek and obtain help from various professional and nonprofessional sources such as friends, clergymen, physicians, teachers, and occasionally even psychotherapists (Bergin, 1963).

All this has typically been unknown to the researchers who were depending upon these so-called controls to be a baseline for comparison with their treatment cases. It seems clear that this aid has an ameliorative effect, as the people improve, although it would be impossible to substantiate this fully without further study of the influences upon control Ss in their "natural" habitat. To the extent that this position is correct, it further undermines the Eysenck-type position, because it shows that control Ss often change due to the influence of therapy or therapy-like procedures. Thus, "spontaneous remission" is just another name for the effects of informal therapy.

Implication 2

(a) Researchers who utilize control groups should carefully ascertain that these groups are indeed controls, or, if necessary, should directly measure the effects of nonexperimental influences which they cannot control. (b) The fact that some of these previously uncontrolled influences are much like therapy, but frequently occur outside of a professional setting, implies that nonprofessional help can stimulate positive personality change. This may consist partly of individuals with "therapeutic personalities" who are sought out for counsel and catharsis by many people. It may be also that unrecognized, but powerful, therapeutic agents exist naturally in everyday life. Just as cures for various physical disorders have been discovered by studying health, so it may be possible to discover antidotes for some of the mental disorders that confront us by discovering conditions already existing in "nature" which support or promote personality integration.

INGREDIENTS OF THERAPY

Conclusion 3

Therapeutic progress varies as a function of therapist characteristics such as warmth, empathy, adequacy of adjustment, and experience.

In a recent review, Gardner (1964) cited a smattering of positive results to the effect that the more a therapist has an attitude of *liking and warmth* the more likely he is to obtain positive change in his clients. While some of the studies enumerated are of questionable design or generalizability, they are relatively consistent when compared with many other areas of research.

A recent questionnaire study of patients' retrospective reports regarding their therapeutic experience (Strupp, Wallach, and Wogan, 1964), which was not reported by Gardner, further confirms this general finding. While the study is uncontrolled and appears to be contaminated by artifactually inflated correlations, it is of interest that it strongly emphasizes the importance of therapist warmth and genuineness in relation to patient-perceived outcome ($r = .53$).

Additional data on this point come from the client-centered group in a series of studies with neurotics and psychotics. It should be noted that some of the therapists studied were *not* client-centered. These studies are consistent in discovering a significant relationship between operational measures of Rogers' concept of positive regard and independent indices of therapeutic progress or outcome (Truax and Carkhuff, 1964, 1965a; Barrett-Lennard, 1962). Measures of the therapist's attitudes have included ratings by both the therapist himself and the patient. Three types of analysis have resulted in similar findings and in different studies with different samples of clients and therapists. It has thus become increasingly clear, within the limits of these studies, that a therapist's ability to be warm and positively inclined toward his patient is an effective therapeutic ingredient. The effects of intentional authoritarian demands or other forms of planned therapist aggression which are sometimes advocated have not been studied and thus cannot be compared with these findings.

Acknowledging the past confusion and contradiction involved in studies of *empathy*, it is suggested that the recent data summarized at Chicago (Barrett-Lennard, 1962), Wisconsin (Truax, 1961b; Truax and Carkhuff, 1964), and Kentucky (Dickenson and Truax, 1965; Truax and Carkhuff, 1965a; Truax, Carkhuff, and Kodman, 1965; Truax and Wargo, 1965) offer promising leads. Analyses of recorded therapist behavior and ratings by clients of their therapists during the process of treatment have yielded consistently positive relationships between empathic understanding and outcome.

The strength of these findings lies in careful design (Rogers, 1961) and in the analysis of therapist behavior *in vivo*, which is unusual in empathy research. A new empathy measure has been operationalized by Truax (1961b) and is defined by Truax and Carkhuff (1964) as accurate "sensitivity to current feelings *and* the verbal facility to communicate this understanding in a language attuned to the patient's current being [p. 8]." While the scale is still crude and might not be accepted by analysts as measuring their "kind" of empathy, its usefulness has been relatively substantial in these studies.

The third characteristic, *adequacy of adjustment*, has not been studied as thoroughly as the others, but thus far the data are relatively consistent. Those therapists who are more anxious, conflicted, defensive, or "unhealthy" are least likely to promote change in their cases.

Several studies have indicated that supervisor and client ratings of the therapists' competence are negatively related to his degree of anxiety or maladjustment (Arbuckle, 1956; Bandura, 1956; Bergin and Solomon, 1963). Other studies have yielded similar findings when the therapist's actual in-therapy behavior and the patient's response to it was evaluated and used as criteria of competence. For example, Bandura, Lipsher, and Miller (1960) found that therapists' hostility anxiety was directly associated with avoidance responses to patients' expressions of hostility toward them. The more hostility conflict a therapist had, the more likely he was to avoid his patients' hostility and consequently the patient's self-exploration in this area diminished and his conflicts remained unresolved. A practically identical result was found by Winder, Ahmad, Bandura, and Rau (1962) with regard to dependency anxiety.

In another study (Bergin and Solomon, 1963) it was found that measures of the therapists' degree of personal disturbance correlate negatively with his level of empathy as measured by ratings of tape-recorded psychotherapy interviews. Independent measures of personality strength, on the other hand, correlated positively with degree of "live" empathy. In addition, ratings of therapist anxiety level correlated negatively with independent ratings of therapeutic competence.

Additional data come from the client-centered studies already cited with regard to warmth and empathy, in their examination of therapist congruence. Congruence (Rogers, 1957, 1959) means essentially the healthiness of the therapist in his relationship with his client—his spontaneity, nondefensiveness, openness, or genuineness. Like positive regard and empathy, this variable has also been related to therapeutic progress, and further confirms the general finding of a direct connection between level of therapist adjustment and therapeutic effectiveness.

The three elements of warmth, empathy, and congruence have been found, in the Wisconsin studies, to vary directly with outcome in both negative and positive directions. That is, when these therapist characteristics were at a low level, the patients were getting worse; when they were high, the patients improved (Truax and Carkhuff, 1964). These studies thus provide a partial answer to the question raised earlier as to how negative change occurred in the outcome studies reviewed, although they are limited in that the observed differences were not large, and there is also some question as to whether the division into high and low conditions was done before or after the fact. The other studies cited here in the same realm further clarify the point, although none of the data are precise enough to make practical selection decisions possible.

With regard to the much debated variable of therapist experience, it may be asserted that, in general, more experienced therapists are more effective and successful. This is based on four studies (Barrett-Lennard, 1962; Cartwright and Vogel, 1960; Chance, 1959; Fiedler, 1950a, 1950b, 1951), one of which suggests that highly inexperienced therapists may actually cause patient deterioration (Cartwright and Vogel, 1960).

Implication 3

(a) Since psychotherapists are effective partly as a function of personal adjustment, they should be selected for this quality and not solely on the basis of academic and intellectual abilities. Future practice of therapy should therefore be modified by new selection procedures which will bring healthier personalities to bear upon problems of pathology, and by closer self-scrutiny and exposure of one's work among present practitioners.

There is presently no evidence that personal therapy for a disturbed therapist can qualify him for practice and should not be depended upon to perform that function until such evidence is provided. This does not, of course, prove that the experience of being treated cannot be useful to a student therapist whose functioning is within a relatively normal range. There are no studies in which treated neurotics have improved to a level of functioning which is similar to that of control normals even though they do change in level of adjustment; therefore, treatment should not be counted upon to take care of errors in selection. The behavior ratings and personality inventories used in the studies reviewed could provide a beginning in research geared specifically toward the selection problem.

(b) Given the necessary personal attributes, therapists should develop their abilities in the realm of warmth and empathic communication, particularly in the case of empathy which is known to be subject to training and experience influences. Further study should be conducted so that clear, measurable standards of performance can be required of aspirants to professional status before they are permitted to practice. As an example, the Truax Empathy Scale (Truax, 1961b) could be used as a beginning to assess one's level of functioning via analysis of recorded interviews.

(c) Inexperienced potential therapists should be very carefully introduced to practice with clients, perhaps with much more stringent care than is now commonly exercised. Since all beginners make many mistakes, it may be useful and ethical to have them see more resilient, normal people until they reach a criterion level of interview performance, measured perhaps on dimensions such as warmth and empathy which appear to be accepted by most schools of therapy as vital though not necessarily sufficient for successful treatment.

Conclusion 4

To date, the only school of interview-oriented psychotherapy which has consistently yielded positive outcomes in research studies is the client-centered approach (Rogers and Dymond, 1954; Shlien, Mosak, and Dreikurs, 1962; Truax and Carkhuff, 1964).

The fact that other schools have not subjected their methods to systematic study of this sort is important but it should not deter one from accepting the fact that client-centered treatment has some positive value when properly conducted according to Rogers' (1957) paradigm. The implications for practice seem quite clear, particularly in view of the consistently dismal reports on percentages of improvement in psychoanalytic therapy (Eysenck, 1965; Wolpe, 1964b).

It appears from these reports that the poorest results were obtained with more classical, long-term psychoanalysis, namely a lower percentage of improved cases than the 67% "spontaneous" remission rate. Briefly, analytically oriented eclectic psychotherapy was more promising in that the percentage improvement equaled the spontaneous remission figure. This type of therapy was also used in some of the studies cited in this paper on the deterioration effect; therefore, despite the generally negative evidence, some analytically oriented therapists must be having a positive effect beyond that occurring in control groups.

It should also be noted that the technique of "moderate interpretation" (Speisman, 1959), which derives from the analytic tradition, has potential therapeutic significance. Its definition is very similar to that given for "good" interpretation by various analysts (Fenichel, 1941) and it is related to productive patient self-exploration. It consists of responding to client affect just below the surface and labeling, identifying, or emphasizing it. This does not involve making connections between past and present, being diagnostic or theoretical, nor telling the patient about feelings he "really has" when he's not experiencing them. It is, rather, an instance of good empathy. If one looks carefully at the definitions and operations for identifying accurate empathy and moderate or good interpretation, it is very difficult to distinguish between them. Truax and Carkhuff (1964) refer to this notion in an interesting comment:

> "accurate empathy" has much in common with the "good psychoanalytic interpretation," in that it makes use of both verbal and nonverbal cues presented by the patient. It differs from some good psychoanalytic interpretations in its insistence that the therapist's empathic response focuses upon feelings and experience of the patient from the patient's own unique viewpoint.

The importance of these observations should not be underestimated, for if they are accurate it appears that effective variables cut across schools of treatment and thus provide the basis for applying techniques on the basis of known effects rather than on doctrines promulgated by warring factions. This also indicates that titles, degrees, or years of training should not define the psychotherapist, but rather what the individual can do. Thus one might call himself "client-centered" and espouse the teachings of that school while at the same time presenting the low level of therapist empathy found to result in client deterioration. On the other hand, a psychoanalyst might be functioning at a high level according to the client-centered empathy scale.

Conclusion 5

In spite of all so far stated about the possibilities for substantially improving consulting-room effectiveness, some stubborn facts still require confrontation. One is that even when the various sources of slippage and inadequacy are accounted for, interviews still do not generally produce very dramatic changes in people. Another is the now well-known fact that many types of people simply are not helped at all by this procedure.

Studies of the relationship between client qualities and therapeutic outcome indicate consistently and clearly that positive outcome is limited or nil with many personality types. It is common for private practitioners and even clinics either to refuse to treat, or reluctantly to accept for treatment, cases that do not fit their conception of psychotherapy. To a great extent this is realistic because traditional methods do not work with these cases. These "rejects," as compared with "accepted" cases, tend to be less intelligent, less anxious, less educated, less verbal and insightful, more concrete and action-oriented, more severely disturbed, more impulsive in the sociopathic sense, and often find the typical consulting-room procedure rather meaningless (Barron, 1953; Cartwright, 1955; Fulkerson and Barry, 1961; Garfield and Affleck, 1961; Hollingshead and Redlich, 1958; Kirtner and Cartwright, 1958a, 1958b). This general observation has been made fairly frequently by various clinicians and is currently rather well-substantiated by the research literature.

Implication 5

The implication of these data, which only confirm an already widely believed idea, is that novel or modified techniques must be developed for dealing with a vast population whose problems are not amenable to standard methods. The importance of novel approaches is further emphasized by the fact that standard methods are not dramatically effective even in those cases where they are applicable, except in rare instances. The latter unusual cases would be a proper subject of study in themselves and may actually suggest innovation even though they arise in "traditional" therapy.

There are three primary sources of possible innovation that might alleviate this predicament. One is creative work in the clinical setting; another is naturally existing conditions in society; and another is that general area of research which is concerned with personality and behavior change such as studies of learning, attitude change, and personality development.

THE PROMISE OF BEHAVIOR THERAPY

Conclusion 6

Studies of learning have thus far been very fruitful in generating principles and methods for promoting personality change. The work by Wolpe (1958), Lazarus (1963), Lang and Lazovik (1963), Lindsley (1963), and others has been both provocative and fruitful. The cases presented and research studies reported provide more positive evidence of the usefulness of these methods than is the case in any form of traditional interview or dynamic psychotherapy, including client-centered therapy.

They involve clinical adaptation of learning principles, such as counterconditioning or extinction of anxiety symptoms, positive reinforcement in shaping adaptive responses and developing appropriate discriminations, aversive conditioning of maladaptive approach responses, and modeling. It is the effects of these methods which are important here. Wolpe (1964a) cites over 200 cases of neurosis in 89% of which he has obtained substantial recovery. Lazarus (1963), in England, reports 408 cases with a similar improvement rate. The striking aspect of these results is that they have been achieved with difficult symptom pictures in brief periods of time. Unfortunately, these are clinical reports by individual therapists who rate their own case outcomes. Independent criteria and control Ss are completely lacking, and it is difficult to discern how comparable their cases are with those reported in other studies. Still, it is rare to find such high rates of claimed cure even in the clinical literature.

A number of well-designed studies appear to substantiate the clinical reports of Wolpe and Lazarus. Lang and Lazovik (1963) were able significantly to alter snake phobias with brief desensitization procedures. Effects of testing and training in relaxation were controlled, and no symptom substitution occurred during 6 months of follow-up. Lazarus (1961) demonstrated substantial and rapid change of phobic symptoms and impotence by group desensitization methods. A comparison group being treated by traditional interpretive group therapy showed considerably less improvement, only 2 of 17 cases becoming symptom free after 22 sessions. These same cases were subsequently treated by group desensitization and after a mean of 10 sessions each, two thirds were symptom free. Paul (1966) found that desensitization procedures were far more effective in eliminating speech anxieties than brief insight therapy, an attention-placebo condition, and a no-therapy control condition.

In a study of operant conditioning methods, which are different from Wolpe's techniques, King, Armitage, and Tilton (1960) found that substantial changes could be effected even in schizophrenic cases. They were able to produce clinically observable improvement in cases so treated which was greater than the changes occurring in conventional interview therapy, recreational therapy, or no therapy. Ayllon and Michael (1959) effected substantial positive changes in ward behavior of psychotics by programing the reinforcements of their hospital environment according to operant principles. Lovaas, Schaeffer, and Simmons (1966) appear to have induced important changes in the social behavior of difficult cases of childhood autism by systematic use of negative reinforcement. In a review, Lindsley (1963) argues for the general promise of operant techniques; although the evidence thus far pertains primarily to simple motor and verbal behaviors. Conceivably, this approach will prove to be more useful with the more primitive behaviors of psychotics and small children than with the more complex, symbolically involved adult neuroses.

A most interesting development in behavior therapy involves the systematic application of principles of imitative or observational learning. Bandura (1965b) argues persuasively from the vantage point of extensive experimental work (Bandura, 1965a, 1965c) that modeling procedures provide powerful conditions for the acquisition of new responses and the modification of old ones. Though controlled clinical applications have just begun, they already lend considerable substance to Bandura's view (Berberich and Schaeffer, 1965; Frank, 1965; Hoehn-Saric, Frank, Imber, Nash, Stone, and Battle, 1965; Krumboltz and Thoreson, 1964; Krumboltz and Schroeder, 1965; Krumboltz, Varenhorst, and Thoreson, 1965; Nelson and Bijan, 1965; Thoreson and Krumboltz, 1965; Truax and Carkhuff, 1965b).

Several extensive reviews further substantiate the generality of Conclusion 6 (Bandura, 1965b; Bandura and Walters, 1963; Eysenck and Rachman, 1965; Franks, 1964; Grossberg, 1964; Krasner and Ullmann, 1965; Ullmann and Krasner, 1965; Wolpe, 1964b).

In spite of the fact that the evidence is favorable, these techniques have been criticized by clinicians as removing symptoms without changing basic pathology and as being limited to very simple neuroses. Neither criticism, however, fits the evidence. Wolpe (1964a) cites data on 88 cases which indicate that a high proportion of complex neuroses can be successfully treated (89%) and in a much briefer time than is typical of traditional methods (Table 2).

Table 2. Comparison of Numbers of Sessions in Complex and Simple Neuroses

NEUROSES	N	MDN NO. SESSIONS	M NO. SESSIONS
Complex	65	29	54.8
Simple	21	11.5	14.9
Total	86	23	45.4

Note.—The total is only 86 because 2 cases that turned out to be schizophrenic are excluded.

The more telling critique of this work is Breger and McGaugh's (1965) point regarding the uncontrolled case reports, which are the basis for the high cure rates, and the rater bias in estimating outcomes encountered in many of the experimental studies. Faulty as a proportion of these reports are, the overall record still represents the best there is in the field of psychotherapy.

In addition to the fact that difficult cases show improvement in a short time, these reports indicate that significant relapses are rare. This is perhaps the most persuasive evidence that behavior therapists are right when they assert that "symptoms" are not symptoms of psychoanalytic-style pathology, but that they are learned behaviors subject to modification via relearning.

Some learning theorists have criticized Wolpe in particular, claiming that his techniques do not derive directly and logically from learning principles and thus do not have the scientific base he claims (Breger and McGaugh, 1965; Mowrer, 1963). While this may be true to some extent, it is irrelevant to the question of the technique's effectiveness and ignores the possibility that these clinical phenomena may eventually become the basis for reformulating learning theories in terms of complex, socially significant human behavior. In this case, one would not expect principles of behavior therapy to conform rigorously to conceptions derived largely from animal research.

Implication 6

The implications of this work seem quite clear. Since these techniques are effective with many types of symptomatology, they should be used. With regard to some of the more complex and difficult problems, behavior therapists argue that it would be better to spend time developing more complex social learning paradigms for treatment than to expend equal energy modifying less promising traditional interview methods. It appears that special effort should be devoted to integrating these methods with others and in some cases substituting them for the other methods. It would seem important to avoid a current tendency to isolate behavior therapies from the mainstream of treatment and thus create another rigid "school" which will gradually become as impervious to new ideas as the traditional schools already are.

CONCLUSION

In conclusion, it is only regrettable that comment upon so many topics of research has had to be excluded. Suffice it to say that the results in many of those not mentioned are not as yet amenable to synthesis. A good example is the material on the patient-therapist relationship. Nearly all of this research actually pertains to therapist qualities and has nothing to do with an analysis of interactional factors. An unusual exception is the work of Barrett-Lennard (1962) which was cited briefly in the discussion of therapist qualities. The few other useful facts in this domain were also included in that section. Another promising line of investigation is that on patient-therapist similarity; but the meaning of the data is still quite ambiguous (Sussman, 1964).

In spite of the fact that much of what is called psychotherapy research is appalling in its inadequacy, to have found a handful of reliable conclusions is gratifying. The groundwork seems well laid by these studies for initial steps at productive innovation in therapeutic treatment.

REFERENCES

ARBUCKLE, D. S. Client perception of counselor personality. *Journal of Counseling Psychology*, 1956, **3**, 93–96.

AYLLON, T., AND MICHAEL, J. The psychiatric nurse as a behavioral engineer. *Journal of the Experimental Analysis of Behavior*, 1959, **2**, 323–334.

BANDURA, A. Psychotherapist's anxiety level, self-insight, and psychotherapeutic competence. *Journal of Abnormal and Social Psychology*, 1956, **52**, 333–337.

————. Behavioral modification through modeling procedures. In L. Krasner and L. Ullmann (Eds.), *Research in behavior modification*. New York: Holt, Rinehart and Winston, 1965. Pp. 310–340. (a)

————. Psychotherapy conceptualized as a social-learning process. Paper read at the Kentucky Centennial Symposium on Psychotherapy, University of Kentucky, April 1965. (b)

————. Vicarious processes: A case of no-trial learning. In L. Berkowitz (Ed.), *Advances in experimental social psychology*. Vol. 2. New York: Academic Press, 1965. Pp. 3–48. (c)

————, LIPSHER, D. H., AND MILLER, P. E. Psychotherapists' approach-avoidance reactions to patients' expressions of hostility. *Journal of Consulting Psychology*, 1960, **24**, 1–8.

————, AND WALTERS, R. H. *Social learning and personality development*. New York: Holt, Rinehart and Winston, 1963.

BARRETT-LENNARD, G. T. Dimensions of therapist response as causal factors in therapeutic change. *Psychological Monographs*, 1962, **76** (43, Whole No. 562).

BARRON, F. Some test correlates of response to psychotherapy. *Journal of Consulting Psychology*, 1953, **17**, 235–241.

————, AND LEARY, T. Changes in psychoneurotic patients with and without psychotherapy. *Journal of Consulting Psychology*, 1955, **19**, 239–245.

BERBERICH, J., AND SCHAEFFER, B. Establishment of verbal behavior through imitation. Paper read at American Psychological Association, Chicago, September 1965.

BERGIN, A. E. The effects of psychotherapy: Negative results revisited. *Journal of Counseling Psychology*, 1963, **10**, 244–250.

————, AND SOLOMON, S. Personality and performance correlates of empathic understanding in psychotherapy. *American Psychologist*, 1963, **18**, 393. (Abstract)

BREGER, L., AND McGAUGH, J. L. Critique and reformulation of "learning-theory" approaches to psychotherapy and neurosis. *Psychological Bulletin*, 1965, **63**, 338–358.

BUTLER, J. M., AND HAIGH, G. Changes in the relation between self-concepts and ideal concepts consequent upon client-centered counseling. In C. R. Rogers and R. F. Dymond (Eds.), *Psychotherapy and personality change.* Chicago: University of Chicago Press, 1954. Pp. 55–75.

CARTWRIGHT, D. S. Success in psychotherapy as a function of certain actuarial variables. *Journal of Consulting Psychology,* 1955, **19,** 357–363.

———. Note on "changes" in psychoneurotic patients with and without psychotherapy. *Journal of Consulting Psychology,* 1956, **20,** 403–404.

———, AND VOGEL, J. L. A comparison of changes in psychoneurotic patients during matched periods of therapy and no-therapy. *Journal of Consulting Psychology,* 1960, 24, 121–127.

CHANCE, E. *Families in treatment.* New York: Basic Books, 1959.

DICKENSON, W. A., AND TRUAX, C. B. Group counseling with college underachievers: Comparisons with a control group and relationship to empathy, warmth, and genuineness. Unpublished manuscript, University of Kentucky, 1965.

EYSENCK, H. J. The effects of psychotherapy: An evaluation. *Journal of Consulting Psychology,* 1952, **16,** 319–324.

———. The effects of psychotherapy. In H. J. Eysenck (Ed.), *Handbook of abnormal psychology.* New York: Basic Books, 1960. Pp. 697–725.

———. The effects of psychotherapy. *International Journal of Psychiatry,* 1965, **1,** 97–178.

———, AND RACHMAN, S. *The causes and cures of neurosis.* San Diego: Knapp, 1965.

FAIRWEATHER, G. W., SIMON, R., GEBHARD, M. E., WEINGARTEN, E., HOLLAND, J. L., SANDERS, R., STONE, G. B., AND REAHL, J. E. Relative effectiveness of psychotherapeutic programs: A multicriteria comparison of four programs for three different patient groups. *Psychological Monographs,* 1960, **74** (5, Whole No. 492).

FENICHEL, O. *Problems of psychoanalytic techniques.* Albany: Psychoanalytic Quarterly, 1941.

FIEDLER, F. E. A comparison of therapeutic relationships in psychoanalytic, nondirective, and Adlerian therapy. *Journal of Consulting Psychology,* 1950, **14,** 436–445. (a)

———. The concept of the ideal therapeutic relationship. *Journal of Consulting Psychology,* 1950, **14,** 239–245. (b)

———. Factor analyses of psychoanalytic, nondirective, and Adlerian therapeutic relationships. *Journal of Consulting Psychology,* 1951, **15,** 32–38.

FRANK, J. D. *Persuasion and healing.* Baltimore: Johns Hopkins Press, 1961.

———. The role of hope in psychotherapy. Paper read at the University of Kentucky Centennial Psychotherapy Symposium, April 1965.

FRANKS, C. (Ed.) *Conditioning techniques in clinical practice and research.* New York: Springer, 1964.

FULKERSON, S. D., AND BARRY, J. R. Methodology and research on the prognostic use of psychological tests. *Psychological Bulletin,* 1961, **58,** 177–204.

GARDNER, G. G. The psychotherapeutic relationship. *Psychological Bulletin,* 1964, **61,** 426–437.

GARFIELD, S. L. The clinical method in personality assessment. In J. Wepman and R. Heine (Eds.), *Concepts of personality.* Chicago: Aldine, 1963. Pp. 474–502.

————, AND AFFLECK, D. C. Therapists' judgments concerning patients considered for psychotherapy. *Journal of Consulting Psychology,* 1961, **25,** 505–509.

GROSSBERG, J. M. Behavior therapy: A review. *Psychological Bulletin,* 1964, **62,** 73–88.

GURIN, G., VEROFF, J., AND FELD, S. *Americans view their mental health.* New York: Basic Books, 1960.

HOEHN-SARIC, R., FRANK, J. D., IMBER, S. D., NASH, E. H., STONE, A. R., AND BATTLE, C. C. Systematic preparation of patients for psychotherapy: I. Effects on therapy behavior and outcome. *Journal of Psychiatric Research,* 1965, **2,** 267–281.

HOLLINGSHEAD, A. B., AND REDLICH, F. C. *Social class and mental illness.* New York: Wiley, 1958.

KING, G. F., ARMITAGE, S. G., AND TILTON, J. R. A therapeutic approach to schizophrenics of extreme pathology. *Journal of Abnormal and Social Psychology,* 1960, **61,** 276–286.

KIRTNER, W. L., AND CARTWRIGHT, D. S. Success and failure in client-centered therapy as a function of client personality variables. *Journal of Consulting Psychology,* 1958, **22,** 259–264. (a)

————, AND ————. Success and failure in client-centered therapy as a function of initial in-therapy behavior. *Journal of Consulting Psychology,* 1958, **22,** 329–333. (b)

KRASNER, L., AND ULLMANN, L. (Eds.) *Research in behavior modification: New developments and implications.* New York: Holt, Rinehart and Winston, 1965.

KRUMBOLTZ, J. D., AND SCHROEDER, W. W. Promoting career planning through reinforcement. *Personnel and Guidance Journal,* 1965, **44,** 19–26.

————, AND THORESON, C. E. The effect of behavioral counseling in group and individual settings on information-seeking behavior. *Journal of Counseling Psychology,* 1964, **9,** 324–333.

————, VARENHORST, B., AND THORESON, C. E. Non-verbal factors in the effectiveness of models in counseling. Paper read at American Personnel and Guidance Association, Minneapolis, April 1965.

LANG, P. J., AND LAZOVIK, A. D. Experimental desensitization of a phobia. *Journal of Abnormal and Social Psychology,* 1963, **6,** 519–525.

LAZARUS, A. A. Group therapy of phobic disorders by systematic desensitization. *Journal of Abnormal and Social Psychology,* 1961, **63,** 504-510.

————. An evaluation of behavior therapy. *Behavior Research and Therapy,* 1963, **1,** 69–79.

LINDSLEY, O. R. Free-operant conditioning and psychotherapy. In J. H. Masserman (Ed.), *Current psychiatric therapies.* Vol. 3. New York: Grune & Stratton, 1963. Pp. 47–56.

LOVAAS, O. I., SCHAEFFER, B., AND SIMMONS, J. Q. Building social behavior in autistic children by use of electric shock. In J. O. Palmer and M. J. Goldstein (Eds.), *Perspectives in psychopathology: Readings in abnormal psychology.* New York: Oxford University Press, 1966. Pp. 222–236.

MINK, O. G. A comparison of effectiveness of nondirective therapy and clinical counseling in the junior high school. *School Counselor*, 1959, **6**, 12–14.

MOWRER, O. H. Freudianism, behavior therapy, and "self-disclosure." *Behavior Research and Therapy*, 1963, **1**.

NELSON, K., AND BIJAN, G. Teaching social behaviors to schizophrenic children through imitation. Paper read at American Psychological Association, Chicago, September 1965.

PAUL, G. L. *Effects of insight, desensitization, and attention placebo treatment of anxiety.* Stanford: Stanford University Press, 1966.

POWERS, E., AND WITMER, H. *An experiment in the prevention of delinquency.* New York: Columbia University Press, 1951.

ROGERS, C. R. The necessary and sufficient conditions of therapeutic personality change. *Journal of Consulting Psychology*, 1957, **21**, 95–103.

———. A theory of therapy, personality, and interpersonal relationships, as developed in the client-centered framework. In S. Koch (Ed.), *Psychology; a study of a science.* Vol. 3. New York: McGraw-Hill, 1959. Pp. 184–256.

———. A theory of psychotherapy with schizophrenics and a proposal for its empirical investigation. In J. G. Dawson and N. P. Dellis (Eds.), *Psychotherapy with schizophrenics.* Baton Rouge: Louisiana State University Press, 1961. Pp. 3–19.

———, AND DYMOND, R. F. *Psychotherapy and personality change.* Chicago: University of Chicago Press, 1954.

SHLIEN, J. M., MOSAK, H. H., AND DREIKURS, R. Effect of time limits: A comparison of two psychotherapies. *Journal of Counseling Psychology*, 1962, **9**, 31–34.

SPEISMAN, J. C. Depth of interpretation and verbal resistance in psychotherapy. *Journal of Consulting Psychology*, 1959, **23**, 93–99.

STRUPP, H. H., WALLACH, M. S., AND WOGAN, M. Psychotherapy experience in retrospect: Questionnaire survey of former patients and their therapists. *Psychological Monographs*, 1964, **78** (11, Whole No. 588).

SUSSMAN, A. Patient-therapist similarity as a factor in psychotherapy. Unpublished manuscript, Teachers College, Columbia University, 1964.

THORESON, C. E., AND KRUMBOLTZ, J. D. Relationship of counselor reinforcement of selected responses to external behavior. *Journal of Counseling Psychology*, 1966, in press. 229

TRUAX, C. B. A scale for the measurement of accurate empathy. *Psychiatric Institute Bulletin*, Wisconsin Psychiatric Institute, University of Wisconsin, 1961, **1**, No. 10. (a)

———. The process of group psychotherapy: Relationships between hypothesized therapeutic conditions and intrapersonal exploration. *Psychological Monographs*, 1961, **75** (7, Whole No. 511). (b)

————. Effective ingredients in psychotherapy. *Journal of Counseling Psychology*, 1963, **10**, 256–263.

————, AND CARKHUFF, R. R. For better or for worse: The process of psychotherapeutic change. In *Recent advances in behavioral change*. Montreal: McGill University Press, 1964.

————, AND CARKHUFF, R. R. Experimental manipulation of therapeutic conditions. *Journal of Consulting Psychology*, 1965, **29**, 119–124. (a)

————, AND CARKHUFF, R. R. Personality change in hospitalized mental patients during group psychotherapy as a function of the use of alternate sessions and vicarious therapy pretraining. *Journal of Clinical Psychology*, 1965, **21**, 225–228. (b)

————, AND CARKHUFF, R. R., AND KODMAN, F. Relationships between therapist-offered conditions and patient change in group psychotherapy. Unpublished manuscript, University of Kentucky, 1965.

————, AND WARGO, D. G. Human encounters that change behavior: For better or for worse. Unpublished manuscript, University of Kentucky, 1965.

ULLMANN, L., AND KRASNER, L. (Eds.) *Case studies in behavior modification*. New York: Holt, Rinehart and Winston, 1965.

WINDER, C. L., AHMAD, F. Z., BANDURA, A., AND RAU, L. Dependency of patients, psychotherapists' responses, and aspects of psychotherapy. *Journal of Consulting Psychology*, 1962, **26**, 129–134.

WOLPE, J. *Psychotherapy by reciprocal inhibition*. Stanford: Stanford University Press, 1958.

————. Behavior therapy in complex neurotic states. *British Journal of Psychiatry*, 1964, **110**, 28–34. (a)

————. The comparative clinical status of conditioning therapies and psychoanalysis. In J. Wolpe, A. Salter, and L. J. Reyna (Eds.), *The conditioning therapies*. New York: Holt, Rinehart and Winston, 1964. Pp. 5–20. (b)

25

How People Change

Allen Wheelis

Wheelis is a published novelist, as well as a practicing psychoanalyst. The combination is fortunate, because he is able to draw upon both talents in order to emphasize a cardinal principle of psychoanalytic treatment; that is, the patient must want to change, if therapy is to be successful.

He begins his essay by distinguishing between two types of suffering: imposed and elected. The latter is the kind that commonly characterizes the inner feelings of the man on the street; he may not have any obvious reason for being unhappy, but he is. Wheelis then confronts the issue of psychotherapy vis-à-vis medical practice. He observes not only that many patients go to psychiatrists as they would to a surgeon but that many psychiatrists act as though they were, indeed, "psychic surgeons." It is at this juncture that therapy requires philosophy, and the philosophy of importance is that of the will to choose.

Insight, as such, *may* be necessary for change, but it is not sufficient. A major problem, for both patient and therapist, is that of establishing whether circumstances which appear to prevent change—even though the need for change is acknowledged—are actual or self-imposed.

We have not far to look for suffering. It's in the streets, fills the air, lies upon our friends. Faces of pain look at us from newspaper, from TV screen. We know them: black man swinging in the warm wind, sealed cattle cars rumbling through the bitter cold, the glare of Auschwitz at midnight, the sweet smell.

And then there's always the suffering inside. But that's different. It may be very bad, this private misery, but different.

For many people pain is imposed, there's no escape. It may be impersonal, unavoidable, as by fire, flood, cancer; or man-made, as

"How People Change" is to be published in 1970 as part of a larger work, *The Desert*, by Allen Wheelis. Reprinted with permission of Basic Books, Inc., Publishers, New York. This article originally appeared in *Commentary* (1969), Vol. 47, No. 5, pp. 56–66.

in wars, sack of cities, rape of girls. Victims still have choice; there's always a little corner of freedom. They may throw spears at the bombers or bow in prayer, may curse or plead; but they may not choose to suffer or not suffer. That choice has been foreclosed. Starving blacks of Biafra scrounge for roots, fight each other for rats; Vietnamese children with melted flesh wander homeless, orphaned, across a lunar desert.

Many of us have never known this kind of misery, have never felt a lash or club, never been shot at, persecuted, bombed, starved —yet we suffer too. Wealth and intelligence and good fortune are no protection. Having had good parents helps but guarantees nothing; misery comes equally to high-born and low, comes with the gold spoon, to prince and princess and ladies in waiting, to groom and gamekeeper, to the mighty and the humble. We feel our suffering as alien, desperately unwanted, yet nothing imposes it. We eat, often exceedingly well; the roof over our head is timber and tile; deep carpets, thin china, great music, rare wine; a woman looks at us with love; we have friends, families; our needs are met. In some way, unnoticed, unknown, we must elect our suffering, create it. It may be quite intense.

Some of it is public knowledge—madness, suicide, running amuck. Some of it is visible only to a few, to family and friends who see the withdrawal, depression, the sense of rejection, the clawing competitiveness, the bitter frustration, bafflement, and anger, year after year after year. At the concert or opera, walking about in the lobby, they bow, they smile, they glitter—show nothing of the misery inside. And some of our suffering is altogether private, known to no one but him who suffers, not even his wife, is borne with shame as some indescribable awkwardness in living, a kind of disloyalty to be in despair in the lap of plenty.

Imposed suffering has priority over elected suffering, as material needs take precedence over spiritual. "First feed the belly, then talk right and wrong," says Mac the Knife. Or Sartre: "The exploitation of men by other men, undernourishment—these make metaphysical unhappiness a luxury and relegate it to second place. Hunger—now that *is* an evil." Imposed suffering, therefore, protects from the elected kind, crowds it out. We simply cannot create despair from subjective roots if we are forced into despair by persecution. In the concentration camp, states of created despair are remembered vaguely, as if from a different life, discontinuous with the present one in which despair issues from the SS truncheons.

To those whose suffering is imposed, elected suffering seems unreal. Lacking in measurable circumstance, in objective explanation, it seems illusory, made up, "in the head." Victims of the whip feel envy of those so sheltered from pain as to be able to dream up states of misery; contempt when such fortunate ones have the arrogance to elegize their torment; a hateful mirth at existential despair hatching in a nest of IBM stock certificates.

We who compose our own misery are ambivalent toward victims of imposed suffering. We feel a subtle pride—secret, never expressed, unknown often even to ourselves—that our misery is more complicated, spiritual; as if we whispered, "The pain of being hungry, of being beaten, is very bad, we sympathize, will make a contribution to CARE; but it is, after all, a primitive suffering; anyone can feel it; just leave them alone, give them enough to eat, and they'd be happy—whereas only a poet could feel what I feel." At the same time, more openly felt, more easily expressed, we feel shame, judge our created misery to be petty in comparison.

In fact they are equally bad: depression or starvation is a hard choice; the terror of the ledge ten floors up matches the terror of the firing squad. In felt experience, that is: in worthiness we cannot call them equal. We who compose our own misery are ashamed at Babi Yar, at Nagasaki, on the slave ships from Africa, in the arena at Rome. They were innocent of their suffering, we are guilty of complicity with ours; they had no choice in theirs, we bear responsibility for ours.

Created suffering, except where precluded by imposed pain, affects us all. The well-adjusted lie: listen to them at your risk; listen to them long enough, declaiming the official view, being serious with their slogans, and you lose contact with your own heart. Poets tell the truth: the sadness of Greece and Gethsemane, of Sodom and Gomorrah, of the Pharaohs and their minions and their slaves, was as our own. It's part of being human, we differ from one another only in more or less. A few tranquil ones, with little conflict, suffer less; at the other extreme, stretched by despair to some dreadful cracking point, one goes berserk. In between are the rest of us, not miserable enough to go mad or jump off the bridge, yet never able if we are honest to say that we have come to terms with life, are at peace with ourselves, that we are happy.

The older I get the less I know, the darker the well of time. The enigma grows more bleak. I seek. I am concerned with suffering and with change, and I write equally for patient and therapist. What one should know will be useful, also, to the other. Here psychotherapy parts company with medicine.

The book for the surgeon is not the book for the surgical patient. One delivers one's ailing body—with its abscess or tumor or broken bone—into the hands of the surgeon, and his most elementary information and skill will transcend anything the patient need know. The patient must cooperate—one green capsule three times a day, keep the leg elevated, force fluids—but need not understand how or why. The responsibility lies with the surgeon, the problem is his, his the accountability for failure, the credit for success. Patient and surgeon do not learn from the same text.

Many patients go to psychiatrists as if to surgeons, and many psychiatrists regard themselves as psychic surgeons. When such a patient comes to such a therapist a relationship of considerable length may result, but little else. For the job can be done, if at all, only by the patient. To assign this task to anyone else, however insightful or charismatic, is to disavow the source of change. In the process of personality change the role of the psychiatrist is catalytic. As a cause he is sometimes necessary, never sufficient. The responsibility of the patient does not end with free-associating, with being on time, with keeping at it, paying his bills, or any other element of cooperation. He is accountable only to himself and this accountability extends all the way to the change which is desired, the achieving of it or the giving up on it.

So—consider one who suffers. Perhaps a woman with a warm heart but frigid. What can she do? Perhaps a mother who wants to love her children but does not. Maybe a homosexual living an endless series of hostile transient encounters. Perhaps a man in his middle fifties with a depressive character, normal to his friends, but constantly brushing away cobweb thoughts of suicide, one who is bored, finds no meaning in life, is ashamed. Consider one who suffers—anyone you know well. Consider perhaps yourself.

I live in a desert. Hour by hour feel myself dying. Surely I believe in something. Not much perhaps, but a little. What?

We are what we do . . . Identity is the integration of behavior. If a man claims to be honest we take him at his word. But if it should transpire that over the years he has been embezzling, we unhesitatingly discard the identity he adopts in words and ascribe to him the identity defined by his acts. "He claims to be honest," we say, "but he's really a thief."

One theft, however, does not make a thief. One act of forthrightness does not establish frankness; one tormenting of a cat does not make a sadist, nor one rescue of a fledgling a savior. Action which defines a man, describes his character, is action which has been repeated over and over, and so has come in time to be a coherent and relatively independent mode of behavior. At first it may have been fumbling and uncertain, may have required attention, effort, will—as when one first drives a car, first makes love, first robs a bank, first stands up against injustice. If one perseveres on any such course it comes in time to require less effort, less attention, begins to function smoothly; its small component behaviors become integrated within a larger pattern which has an ongoing dynamism and cohesiveness, carries its own authority. Such a mode then pervades the entire person, permeates other modes, colors other qualities, in some sense is living and operative even when the action is not being performed, or even considered. A young man who learns to drive a car thinks differently thereby, feels differently; when he meets a pretty girl who lives fifty miles away, the encounter carries implications he could not have felt as a bus rider. We may say, then, that he not only drives a car, but has *become* a driver. If the action is shoplifting, we say not only that he steals from stores but that he has *become* a shoplifter.

Such a mode of action tends to maintain itself, to resist change. A thief is one who steals; stealing extends and reinforces the identity of thief, which generates further thefts, which further strengthens and deepens the identity. So long as one lives, change is possible; but the longer such behavior is continued the more force and authority it acquires, the more it permeates other consonant modes, subordinates other conflicting modes; changing back becomes steadily more difficult; settling down to an honest job, living on one's earnings, becomes ever more unlikely. And what is said here of stealing applies equally to courage, cowardice, creativity, gambling, homosexuality, alcoholism, depression, or any other of the myriad ways of behaving, and hence of being. Identity comprises all such modes as may characterize a person, existing in varying degrees of integration and conflict. The greater the conflict the more unstable the identity; the more harmonious the various modes the more durable the identity.

The identity defined by action is present and past; it may also foretell the future, but not necessarily. Sometimes we act covertly, the eye does not notice the hand under the table, we construe the bribe to have been a gift, the running away to have been prudence, and so conceal from ourselves what we are. Then one day, perhaps, we drop the pretense, the illusion cracks. We have then the sense of an identity that has existed all along—and in some sense we knew it but would not let ourselves know that we knew it—but now we do, and in a blaze of frankness say, "My God! I really am a crook!" or "I really am a coward!" We may then go too far and conclude that this identity is our "nature," that it was writ in the stars or in the double helix, that it transcends experience, that our actual lives have been the fulfilling of a pre-existing pattern.

In fact it was writ only in our past choices. We are wise to believe it difficult to change, to recognize that character has a forward propulsion which tends to carry it unaltered into the future, but we need not believe it impossible to change. Our present and future choices may take us upon different courses which will in time comprise a different identity. It happens, sometimes, that the crook reforms, that the coward stands to fight.

. . . *And may do what we choose.* The identity defined by action is not, therefore, the whole person. Within us lies the potential for change, the freedom to choose other courses. When we admit that those "gifts" were bribes and say, "Well, then, I'm a crook," we have stated a fact, not a destiny; if we then invoke the leopard that can't change his spots, saying, "That's just the way I am, might as well accept it," we abandon the freedom to change, and exploit what we have been in the past to avoid responsibility for what we shall be in the future.

Often we do not choose, but drift into those modes which eventually define us. Circumstances push and we yield. We did not choose to be what we have become, but gradually, imperceptibly became what we are by drifting into the doing of those things we now characteristically do. Freedom is not an objective attribute of life; alternatives without awareness yield no leeway. I open the door of my car, sit behind the wheel, and notice in a corner of vision an ant scurrying about on the smooth barren surface of the concrete parking lot, doomed momentarily to be crushed by one of the thousand passing wheels. There exists, however, a brilliant alternative for this gravely endangered creature: in a few minutes a woman will appear with a picnic basket and we shall drive to a sunny, hilltop meadow. This desperate ant has but to climb the wheel of my car to a safe sheltered ledge, and in a half hour will be in a paradise for ants. But this option, unknown, unknowable, yields no freedom to the ant, who is doomed; and the only irony belongs to me who observes, who reflects that options potentially as meaningful to me as this one to this ant may at this moment be eluding my awareness; so I too may be doomed—this planet looks more like a parking lot every day.

Nothing guarantees freedom. It may never be achieved, or having been achieved may be lost. Alternatives go unnoticed; foreseeable consequences are not foreseen; we may not know what we have been, what we are, or what we are becoming. We who are the bearers of consciousness but of not very much, may proceed through a whole life without awareness of that which would have meant the most, the freedom which has to be noticed to be real. Freedom is the awareness of alternatives and of the ability to choose. It is contingent upon consciousness, and so may be gained or lost, extended or diminished.

Modern psychiatry found its image in the course of dealing with symptoms experienced as alien. A patient so afflicted seeks no alteration of character or personality, would be offended if the physician suggested such or pretended to any competence in that area. Nothing is felt to be wrong with the patient as a person, his self is not presented for examination or treatment. He is a patient only because he's sick, and his sickness consists of an ailment of which he wishes to be relieved. If the trouble is of recent onset and condenses a specific conflict of impulse and inhibition the medical model may be tenable: insight may function as medicine and dispel the symptom. On those exceedingly rare occasions when we still see such a case, we can be real doctors again and cure someone. The following is an example.

A thirty-five-year-old woman suddenly, and for the first time in her life, develops a spasm of the right foot and a left-sided migraine. Brain tumor is suspected but neurological examination is normal. On psychiatric consultation it is learned that she has been married fifteen years, no children, is devoutly religious, cannot tolerate hostile feelings, but in fact despises her alcoholic husband. At a party, on the evening before her trouble began, she went upstairs looking for a bathroom and chanced upon her husband with a woman on his lap, the two of them in deep, prolonged kissing. She watched for a few moments, then backed out without being seen. On leaving the party, as her husband was drunk, she drove the car. Reaching home he stumbled out to open the garage door and for a moment was caught in the headlights. Just beyond him was a concrete wall. The motor was idling fast. She felt dizzy, passed a hand over her face. Upstairs, a few minutes later, her right foot began to twitch; during the night she waked up with a headache.

In this case, properly prepared, the interpretation, "You wanted to kill your husband," may effect a cure. No will is necessary, no action, no change in being. Insight is enough.

Most psychiatrists know such cases only from reading examples like this one. The patients who actually appear in their offices—whatever their symptoms—suffer problems of being. When the symptom is migraine it has occurred not once but hundreds of times, over many years. It is not the somatic expression of a specific conflict, but a response to any conflict, any tension, a way of running from whatever seems too much; it has become a mode of being in the world. The patient may feel it as alien, want to be rid of it, but it has become useful in a thousand unnoticed ways; its removal would not be simple relief but would expose the patient to conflicts which he has no other way of handling. The symptom does not afflict the patient, it *is* the patient.

This headache will not dissolve with insight, and here the medical model breaks down. What is called for is not cure of illness but change in what one is. Insight is not enough. Effort and will are crucial.

The most common illusion of patients and, strangely, even of experienced therapists, is that insight produces change; and the most common disappointment of therapy is that it does not. Insight is instrumental to change, often an essential component of the process, but does not directly achieve it. The most comprehensive and penetrating interpretation—true, relevant, well expressed, perfectly timed—may lie inert in the patient's mind; for he may always, if he be so inclined, say, "Yes, but it doesn't help." If a therapist takes the position, as many do, that a correct interpretation is one that gets results, that the getting of results is an essential criterion for the correctness of an interpretation, then he will be driven to more and more remote reconstructions of childhood events, will move further and further from present reality, responding always to the patient's "Yes, but why?" with further reachings for more distant antecedents. The patient will be saying, in effect, "Yes, but what are you going to do about it?" and the therapist, instead of saying, as he should, "What are *you* going to do about it?" responds according to his professional overestimate of the efficacy of insight by struggling toward some ever more basic formulation. Some patients don't want to change, and when a therapist takes up the task of changing such a one he assumes a contest which the patient always wins. The magic of insight, of unconscious psychodynamics, proves no magic at all; the most marvelous interpretation falls useless—like a gold spoon from the hand of a petulant child who doesn't want his spinach.

An anguished woman enters our office, sits down, weeps, begins to talk, and we listen. We are supposed to know what's up here, what the problem *really* is, and what to do about it. But the theories with which we have mapped the soul don't help, the life she relates is unlike any other. We may nevertheless cling to our map, telling ourselves we know where we are and all is well, but if we look up into the jungle of her misery we know we are lost. And what have we to go on? What to cling to? That people may change, that one person can help another. That's all. Maybe that's enough.

The suffering is a given, but the problem is a choice, is subjective and arbitrary, rests finally upon nothing more than the patient's will, upon his being able to say "This . . . is what I want to change."

Those psychiatrists who regard themselves in the manner of medical men would disagree, would hold that a psychic problem—homosexuality, for example, or compulsivity—is objectively verifiable, that a panel of competent therapists would concur. This view would hold that the problem "emerges" from the "material," is recognized and defined by the therapist who then presents it to the patient along with his recommendation for treatment.

But since the problem is something for which a solution is sought, only the patient can designate it. The therapist may perceive that a certain conflict leads regularly to such and such situations which cause suffering. But a cause of suffering is not a problem unless it is taken as such by the patient.

Likewise the goal of treatment must be determined by the

patient. The only appropriate goal for the therapist is to assist. If the therapist cannot in good faith help to the end desired he is free to decline, but he cannot reasonably work toward goals of his own choosing. Even so benign a therapeutic aim as to "help the patient realize his potential" may be too much. It is too much if that is not what the patient wants. Sometimes, indeed, the patient may want the opposite, may feel that his trouble comes from having begun to realize incompatible potentialities, and that he must now turn away from some of them.

Freedom is that range of experience wherein events, courses of action, attitudes, decisions, accommodations, are seen as elective. It may be more or less, so we need to ask how much we want. In small things we always want choice. What color to paint the house? buy an Olds or a Buick? go to the Bergman film or the Ozawa concert? It would be onerous to be constrained here. In deeper matters we want to be held back. We might choose to live or die, but prefer *not* to choose, want to believe rather that we *have* to live. A kind man does not ponder becoming a sadist, an honest man does not consider whether to become a bandit; we prefer to consider such matters settled, removed from choice and hence from freedom.

In between such minor and major issues lies the middle ground of decision and action wherein some find freedom and choice while others find constraint and necessity. One man sees himself inextricably stuck in a marriage, a career, in obligations to children, relatives, colleagues, bound to his way and place of life, unable to change. Another in the same circumstances finds it possible to resign as judge of the circuit court, divorce a Philadelphia Mainline wife after twenty-four years of marriage and three children, move to Italy, live with an actress, take up painting, If we forgo the moral condemnation we generally visit upon those of greater scope and daring than ourselves, we are likely to discover great envy.

Necessity is that range of experience wherein events, courses of action, attitudes, decisions are seen as determined by forces outside ourselves which we cannot alter. A bored woman says, "I'd like to take a job, but can't leave home because of the children." With that "can't" she alleges necessity: staying home or leaving home is not open, the decision is imposed, runs counter to her wants; she designates her children's need as her necessity. Her prerogative to do this is clear, is granted, but it must be noted that nothing external to herself requires this view. Certainly her children's needs do not require it: within the same block other mothers manage somehow with baby-sitters and so hold jobs. The necessity that constrains her does not contrain them; it is of a different order from that which would derive from locked doors and barred windows.

The realm of necessity, therefore, must comprise two categories: the subjective or arbitrary, and the objective or mandatory. Mandatory necessity—like natural law which cannot be disobeyed—is that which cannot be suspended. It derives from forces, conditions, events which lie beyond the self, not subject to choice, unyielding to will and effort. "I wish I had blue eyes," ". . . wish I were twenty again," ". . . wish I could fly," ". . . wish I lived in the court of the Sun King." Such wishes are irrelevant, choice is inoperative; the necessity impartially constrains. And since it cannot be put aside there's not much arguing about it. "If you jump you will fall—whether or not you choose to fly." There is consensus, we don't dwell on it, we accept.

Arbitrary necessity derives from forces within the personality, but construed to be outside. The force may be either impulse or prohibition: "I didn't want to drink, but couldn't help it." That is to say, the impulse to drink does not lie within the "I." The "I," which is of course the locus of choice, does not "want" to drink, would choose otherwise, but is overwhelmed by alien force. "I want to marry you," a woman says to her lover, "want it more than anything in the world. But I can't divorce my husband. He couldn't take it . . . would break down. He depends on me. It would kill him." Here it is loyalty, caring for another's welfare, which is alleged to lie outside the deciding "I," which therefore cannot choose, cannot do what it "wants," but is held to an alien course. As though she were saying, "I do not here preside over internal conflict, do not listen to contending claims within myself to arrive finally at an anguished, fallible decision, but am coerced by mandates beyond my jurisdiction; I yield to necessity." The issue is not one of conscious versus unconscious. The contending forces are both conscious. The issue is the boundary of the self, the limits of the "I."

Arbitrary necessity, therefore—like man-made law—is that which may be suspended, disobeyed. When dealing with ourselves the constraining force seems inviolable, a solid wall before us, as though we really "can't," have no choice; and if we say so often enough, long enough, and mean it, we may make it so. But when we then look about and observe others doing what we "can't" do we must conclude that the constraining force is not an attribute of the surrounding world, not the way things are, but a mandate from within ourselves which we, strangely, exclude from the "I."

The lady who "wants" to marry her lover but "can't" divorce her husband might here object. "When I said 'can't,'" she might say, "it was just a way of speaking, a metaphor. It meant that staying with my husband represents duty, not desire, that's all. In a theoretical way I could choose . . . I know that. But it's just theoretical. Because . . . you see, the conflict is so terribly unequal, the considerations that make me stay, that absolutely demand I stay with my husband . . . they're so overwhelmingly strong, there's really no choice. That's all I mean."

We make serious record of her objection. In passing we note with surprise that the inequality of the conflict leads her to conclude there is "really no choice," whereas this same circumstance would have led us to say rather that the choice is easy, one she might arrive at promptly, with the conviction of being right.

It's only a metaphor, she says. In some theoretical way, she says, she is aware of choice. Perhaps. But we have doubt. In any event we must point out that she specifically denies this choice for which she now claims oblique awareness, that she locates the determining duty outside the "I" and its "wants." And we might add that if she continues such metaphorical speech long enough she will eventually convince even herself; her "theoretical" choice will become more and more theoretical until, with no remaining consciousness of option, it will disappear. She then will have made actual something that may once have been but a metaphor. Nothing guarantees our freedom. Deny it often enough and one day it will be gone, and we'll not know how or when.

Objective necessity is not arguable. My lover dies, I weep, beat my fists on the coffin. Everyone knows what I want; everyone knows that nothing will avail, no prayer, no curse, no desperate effort, nothing, that I shall never get her back. When there is argument about necessity, the alleged constraint is arbitrary, subjective. A house in flames, a trapped child, a restraining neighbor: "You can't go in! It's hopeless." I see it differently: I *can* go in—if I have the nerve. There may be a chance. It's not clear whether the situation permits or proscribes; the difference of opinion indicates that the necessity at issue is arbitrary. My neighbor's statement is more plea than observation; he asks me to perceive that the contemplated action is precluded, to see that there is no choice. By so deciding I can make it so. If I agree it is impossible, then—even if mistaken—my having arrived at that judgment will, in a matter of moments, make it true. Our judgments fall within the field of events being judged, so themselves become events, and so alter the field. We survey the course of history and conclude, "Wars are inevitable." The judgment seems detached, as if we observed from a distant galaxy; like all judgments, it may be mistaken. In any event it is not inert, it has consequences, shapes actions, moves interest and behavior from, for example, the politics of dissent to the connoisseurship of wine; it chips off one more fragment of the obstacle to war, and thereby makes more likely the war which, when it comes, will vindicate our original judgment and the behavior which issued from it. So we create the necessity which then constrains us, constrains ever more tightly day after day, so vindicating ever more certainly our wisdom in having perceived from the outset we were not free. Finally we are bound hand and foot and may exclaim triumphantly how right we were!

The areas of necessity and of freedom vary in proportion to each other and in absolute measure. They vary, also, from person to person, and, within the same person, from time to time. Together they comprise the total extent of available experience the range of which is a function of awareness and concern.

Adolescence, traditionally, is the time of greatest freedom, the major choices thereafter being progressively made, settled, and buried, one after another, never to be reopened. These days, however, an exhumation of such issues in later life has become quite common, with a corresponding increase in freedom which makes life again as hazardous as in youth.

Throughout our lives the proportion of necessity to freedom depends upon our tolerance for conflict: the greater our tolerance the more freedom we retain, the less our tolerance the more we jettison; for high among the uses of necessity is the pursuit of tranquility. What we can't alter we don't have to worry about; so the enlargement of necessity is a measure of economy in psychic housekeeping. The more issues we have closed the fewer we have to fret about. For many of us, for example, the issues of stealing and of homosexuality are so completely buried that we no longer have consciousness of option, and so no longer in these matters have freedom. We may then walk through Tiffany's or go to the ballet without temptation or conflict. For one to whom these are still live issues, and for whom the choice depends upon a constantly shifting balance of fallibly estimated rewards of gain or pleasure as against risks of capture or shame, such exposure may cause great tension.

Tranquility, however, has risks of its own. As we expand necessity and so relieve ourselves of conflict and responsibility, we are relieved, also, in the same measure, of authority and significance. When a crisis arises which does not fall within our limited routine we are frightened, without resources, insignificant.

For some people necessity expands cancerously, every possibility of invention and variation being transformed into inflexible routine until all freedom is eaten away. The extreme in psychic economy is an existence in which everything occurs by law. Since life means conflict, such a state is living death. When, in the other direction, the area of necessity is too much diminished we become confused, anxious, may be paralyzed by conflict, may reach eventually the extreme of panic.

The more we are threatened, fragile, vulnerable, the more we renounce freedom in favor of an expanding necessity. Observing others then who laugh at risk, who venture on paths from which we have turned back, we feel envy; they are courageous where we are timid. We come close to despising ourselves, but recover quickly, can always take refuge in a hidden determinism. "It's all an illusion," we say, "it looks like their will and daring as against my inhibition and weakness, but that *must* be illusion. Because life is lawful. Nothing happens by chance. Not a single atom veers off course at random. My inhibition is not a failure of nerve. We can't see the forces that mold us, but they are there. The genetic and experiential dice are loaded with factors unknown, unknowable, not of our intending, are thrown in circumstances over which we have no vision or control; we are stuck with the numbers that turn up. Beware the man who claims to be captain of his soul, he's first mate at the very best."

The more we are strong and daring the more we will diminish necessity in favor of an expanding freedom. "We are responsible," we say, "for what we are. We create ourselves. We have done as we have chosen to do, and by so doing have become what we are. If we don't like it, tomorrow is another day, and we may do differently."

Each speaks truly for himself, the one is just so determined, the other is just so free; but each overstates his truth in ascribing his constraint or his liberty to life at large. These truths are partial, do not contend with each other. Each expresses a quality of experience. Which view one chooses to express, to the exclusion of the other, better describes the speaker than the human condition.

In every situation, for every person, there is a realm of freedom and a realm of constraint. One may live in either realm. One must recognize the irresistible forces, the iron fist, the stone wall—must know them for what they are in order not to fall into the sea like Icarus—but, knowing them, one may turn away and live in the realm of one's freedom. A farmer must know the fence which bounds his land, but need not spend his life standing there, looking out, beating his fists on the rails; better he till his soil, think of what to grow, where to plant the fruit trees. However small the area of freedom, attention and devotion may expand it to occupy the whole of life.

Look at the wretched people huddled in line for the gas chambers at Auschwitz. If they do anything other than move on quietly, they will be clubbed down. Where is freedom? . . . But wait. Go back in time, enter the actual event, the very moment: they are thin and weak, and they smell; hear the weary shuffling steps, the anguished catch of breath, the clutch of hand. Enter now the head of one hunched and limping man. The line moves slowly; a few yards ahead begin the steps down. He sees the sign, someone whispers "showers," but he knows what happens here. He is struggling with a choice: to shout "Comrades! They will kill you! Run!"— or to say nothing. This option, in the few moments remaining, is his whole life. If he shouts he dies now, painfully; if he moves on silently he dies but minutes later. Looking back on him in time and memory, we find the moment poignant but the freedom negligible. It makes no difference in that situation, his election of daring or of inhibition. Both are futile, without consequence. History sees no freedom for him, notes only constraint, labels him victim. But in the consciousness of that one man it makes great difference whether or not he experiences the choice. For if he knows the constraint and nothing else, if he thinks "Nothing is possible," then he is living his necessity; but if, perceiving the constraint, he turns from it to a choice between two possible courses of action, then—however he chooses—he is living his freedom. This commitment to freedom may extend to the last breath.

Sometimes in therapy profound change occurs spontaneously,

without effort or intention. It is a rare experience—anytime, any-where—to be known and understood without being judged, to be regarded with affection and respect, without being used. No thera-pist can feel this way about all his patients, though he must try. When he does genuinely so feel, he creates a nurturing context in which the patient may take in and make his own the therapist's way of thinking about problems, a certain reflectiveness about suffering, a tendency to hold conflicting motives in suspension while looking for connections, meanings, significance.

Such identification leads to slight, subtle, often unnoticed changes in action and behavior, in one's way of dealing with one's self and others; and over a period of time these changed actions may achieve a change of being. One then feels one's self to be profoundly different without knowing how or why. If one is asked, "Well, what did you learn? What was the main insight?" one may stumble about, fabricate some inadequate answer, yet may know certainly that one is a better person, more able to love.

This sort of change is rare. We can't count on it, can't make it happen; when it occurs it is great good fortune, a bonus. Usually change—when it occurs at all—follows long and arduous trying.

Neurotic suffering indicates inner conflict. Each side of the conflict is likely to be a composite of many partial forces, each one of which has been structured into behavior, attitude, perception, value. Each component asserts itself, claims priority, insists that something else yield, accommodate. The conflict therefore is fixed, stubborn, enduring. It may be impugned and dismissed without effect, imprecations and remorse are of no avail, strenuous acts of will may be futile; it causes—yet survives and continues to cause—the most intense suffering, humiliation, rending of flesh. Such a conflict is not to be uprooted or excised. It is not an ailment, it is the patient himself. The suffering will not disappear without a change in the conflict, and a change in the conflict amounts to a change in what one is and how one lives, feels, reacts.

Personality is a complex balance of many conflicting claims, forces, tensions, compunctions, distractions, which yet manages somehow to be a functioning entity. However it may have come to be what it is, it resists becoming anything else. It tends to maintain itself, to convey itself onward into the future unaltered. It may be changed only with difficulty. It may be changed from within, spontaneously and unthinkingly, by an onslaught of physiological force, as in adolescence. It may be changed from without, again spontaneously and unthinkingly, by the force of unusual circumstance, as in a Nazi concentration camp. And sometimes it may be changed from within, deliberately, consciously, and by design. Never easily, never for sure, but slowly, uncertainly, and only with effort, insight, and a kind of tenacious creative cunning.

Personality change follows change in behavior. Since we are what we do, if we want to change what we are we must begin by changing what we do, must undertake a new mode of action. Since the import of such action is change, it will run afoul of existing entrenched forces which will protest and resist. The new mode will be experienced as difficult, unpleasant, forced, unnatural, anxiety-provoking. It may be undertaken lightly but can be sustained only by a considerable effort of will. Change will occur only if such action is maintained over a long period of time.

The place of insight is to illumine: to ascertain where one is, how one got there, how now to proceed, and to what end. It is a blueprint, as in building a house, and may be essential, but no one achieves a house by blueprints alone, no matter how accurate or detailed. A time comes when one must take up hammer and nails. In building a house the making of blueprints may be delegated to an architect, the construction to a carpenter. In building the house of one's life or in its remodeling, one may delegate nothing; for the task can be done, if at all, only in the workshop of one's own mind and heart, in the most intimate rooms of thinking and feeling where none but one's self has freedom of movement or competence or authority. The responsibility lies with him who suffers, originates with him, remains with him to the end. It will be no less his if he enlists the aid of a therapist; we are no more the product of our therapists than of our genes: we create ourselves. The sequence is suffering, insight, will, action, change. The one who suffers, who wants to change, must bear responsibility all the way. "Must" because as soon as responsibility is ascribed, the forces resisting change occupy the whole of one's being, and the process of change comes to a halt. A psychiatrist may help perhaps crucially, but his best help will be of no avail if he is required to provide a kind or degree of insight which will of itself achieve change.

Should an honest man wish to become a thief the necessary action is obvious: he must steal—not just once or occasionally, but frequently, consistently, taking pains that the business of planning and executing thefts replace other activities which in implication might oppose the predatory life. If he keeps at it long enough his being will conform to his behavior: he will have become a thief. Conversely, should a thief undertake to become an honest man, he must stop stealing and must undertake actions which replace stealing, not only in time and energy, and perhaps also excitement, but which carry implications contrary to the predatory life, that is, productive or contributive activities.

If a homosexual should set out to become heterosexual, among all that is obscure, two things are clear: he should discontinue homosexual relations, however much tempted he may be to continue on an occasional spontaneous basis, and he should undertake, continue, and maintain heterosexual relations, however little heart he may have for girls, however often he fail, and however inadequate and averse he may find himself to be. He would be well advised in reaching for such a goal to anticipate that success, if it be achieved at all, will require a long time, years not months, that the effort will be painful and humiliating, that he will discover profound currents of feeling which oppose the behavior he now requires of himself, that emerging obstacles will each one seem insuperable yet each must be thought through, that further insight will be constantly required to inform and sustain his behavior, that sometimes insight will precede and illumine action, and sometimes blind dogged action must come first, and that even so, with the best of will and good faith and determination, he still may fail. He should beware of beckoning shortcuts, such as drug therapy or hypnosis. They falsify the reality with which he must most intimately deal, that of his own thought, feeling, drive; they undermine his commitment of internal resources by encouraging him to feel that there is an easier way. There is no short-cut, no safe conduct, no easier way. He must proceed alone, on nerve. He is not entitled to much hope—just that he has a chance. He may take some bleak comfort only in knowing that no one can be sure at the outset that he will fail, and that it is his own unmeasured and unmeasurable resources of heart and mind and will which have most bearing on the eventual outcome.

This is self-transcendence and is not to be confused with a type of coercive treatment in which the therapist acts as agent for society, and the goal is adjustment. Punishment, brainwashing, and lobotomy fall in this category. Less extreme varieties are known variously as operant conditioning, behavior therapy, or conditioned reflex therapy. All such treatment takes the person as object and seeks to achieve the desired change by manipulation. The alcoholic may be so rigged with wires as to receive an electric shock each time he takes a drink. The homosexual man may be provided with male partners who insure that sexual experiences will be exceedingly unpleasant, while concurrently gently seductive ladies, without demands of their own, introduce him to the delights of polarized sexuality. Such things may be arranged for a fee.

We are in no position to comment on the efficacy of behavior therapy as generally practiced, but in principle we know it works. People may indeed be treated as objects and may be profoundly affected thereby. Kick a dog often enough and he will become cowardly or vicious. Men who are kicked undergo similar changes; their view of the world and of themselves is transformed. The survivors of Hitler's concentration camps testify that the treatment received did have an effect. Nor do we find any reason to doubt the alleged results of Chinese throught-control methods. People may indeed be brainwashed, for benign or exploitative reasons.

Behavior therapy is not, therefore, being contrasted to self-transcendence in terms of efficacy; the contrast is in terms of freedom. If one's destiny is shaped by manipulation one has become more of an object, less of a subject, has lost freedom. It matters little whether or not the manipulation is known to the person upon whom it acts. For even if one himself designs and provides for those experiences which are then to affect him, he is nevertheless treating himself as object—and to some extent, therefore, *becomes* an object.

If, however, one's destiny is shaped from within then one has become more of a creator, has gained freedom. This is self-transcendence, a process of change that originates in one's heart and expands outward, always within the purview and direction of a knowing consciousness, begins with a vision of freedom, with an "I want to become . . .," with a sense of the potentiality to become what one is not. One gropes toward this vision in the dark, with no guide, no map, and no guarantee. Here one acts as subject, author, creator.

Sometimes a process of character change may proceed with increasing momentum and finality to solid completion. The honest man becomes the complete thief; the thief becomes the completely honest man. When character change proceeds to such radical conclusion it is likely, not only that the old way of life has been given up, but also that a new way of life, directly opposite in implication, has been adopted. Such a change is experienced, not as a deflection of course, but as an absolute turning around, a conversion, may even call for a change of name. Saul of Tarsus had such an experience on the road to Damascus and—having been the chief persecutor of Christianity—became its greatest exponent. Malcolm X had such an experience in prison with the teaching of Elijah Muhammad, and changed not simply from thief to non-thief, but from thief to social reformer; the completeness and finality with which he transcended the old identity owed as much to his having undertaken to correct injustice with passion and commitment as it did to his giving up stealing. Had he simply "learned his lesson," decided not to steal any more, and taken an indifferently-regarded job as gas station attendant, he might never have altogether ceased being a thief. Some of the temptation, bitterness, and envy, something of the way of thought, the attitude, and outlook of a thief might have remained.

Such change as occurred in Saul or Malcolm X is rare, seems so far beyond anything we might achieve by our own efforts that, when it occurs, we usually ascribe credit—to a mystic force, to a revelation, to the hand of God. The changes we achieve with ourselves, with or without therapy, are likely to be partial and provisional. The homosexual gets married, has children, but never feels entirely safe with women; the frigid woman becomes capable of climax, but not easily and not always; the impotent man becomes able usually to make it, but can never be sure; the depressive character can work, may occasionally feel glad to be alive, but is not likely ever to be described as of sunny disposition; the phobic woman becomes less anxious, no longer has to decline invitations, but always has sweaty palms at cocktail parties. Such changes must be counted success; far more frequent in outcome, even with considerable effort, is no change at all. He who undertakes to transform himself, therefore, should think not of all or none, sick or well, miserable or happy, but of more or less, better or worse. He should undertake only to do what he can, to handle something better, to suffer less. The kingdom of heaven need not concern him.

When the thief takes a job and determines to go straight, when the homosexual gets a girl and renounces sexual relations with men, he does so with a vision of what he will become. Rarely may such direct action, in the course of time and of great effort, succeed without further insight and with no change of plan. More often the course upon which one has embarked entails so much anxiety, uncertainty, confusion, that reappraisal becomes necessary. One finds that his entire self was not known, that submerged aspects of self now rise up in terror, threat, and subversion, screaming outrage, demanding revocation. One is forced to a halt, sometimes driven back. The whole issue has to be rethought. "What I'm giving up is more important than I knew." "Maybe I don't want to change." "Am I going at it the wrong way?" Newly emerging feelings and reactions must be explored in relation to other known elements and to one's now threatened intention.

Here therapy may offer insight into bewildering experience, help with the making of new connections, give comfort and encouragement, assist in the always slippery decision of whether to hang on and try harder or to look for a different way to try. That person gains most from therapy, and gains it most quickly, who has the heart and will to go it alone in the event that therapy does not help; whereas he who clings to therapy as drowning man to ship's timber is more likely to burden therapy with a weight it can't support, and so take himself and therapy down together.

Sometimes we suffer desperately, would do anything, try anything, but are lost, find no way. We cast about, distract ourselves, search, but find no connection between the misery we feel and the way we live. The pain comes from nowhere, gives no clue. We are bored, nothing has meaning; we become depressed. What to do? How to live? Something is wrong but we cannot imagine another way of living which would free us.

Yet there must be a way, for no sustained feeling can exist as a thing in itself, independent of what we do. If the suffering is serious and intractable it must be intimately and extensively connected, in ways we do not perceive, with the way we live. We have to look for such connections. Sometimes there is nothing to be done until they are found.

Therapy may help. One may discover, for example, a simmering hatred of one's wife, not consciously felt, not expressed, but turned against one's self, experienced as depression. Such a finding may still not indicate what one should do; for that will depend on yet other feelings, connections, implications. Should one begin to express the anger? Perhaps, if the grievance is reasonable and if there is also affinity and love. Should one get a divorce? Perhaps, if there is not even that minimum affection necessary for trying to work out differences. Sometimes there is no love, and good reason for hatred, and still one does not want a divorce: then one must be struck by this curious thing, that one clings to a source of frustration and torment, must ask why, and perhaps only then may begin to uncover a profound dependence which has been both well hidden by, and fully expressed in, the hostile tie. One hates her but can't leave her because one is afraid. Afraid of what? And why? What one should do may come to be known only after this dependence is examined in its relations with various other feelings and experiences. Sometimes there is no grievance and much love, and so, gradually, one may learn that he scapegoats his wife and may realize that he must, therefore, need to feel hatred, that he is using it for ulterior purposes—perhaps to cover up feelings of inadequacy, so avoiding the awareness of what he might want to do if he weren't afraid.

Much of our suffering is just so obscure as this. Frigidity, social anxiety, isolation, boredom, disaffection with life—in all such states we may see no correlation between the inner feeling and the way we live. Yet no such feeling can be independent of behavior; and if only we find the connections we may begin to see how a change in the way we live will make for a change in the way we feel.

Since freedom depends upon awareness, psychotherapy may, by extending awareness, create freedom. When in therapy a life story of drift and constraint is reworked to expose alternatives for crucial courses of action, asking always "Why did you do that?," attaching doubt to every explanation which is cast in the form of necessary reaction to antecedent cause, always reminding the patient that "Even so . . . it was possible to have acted otherwise"— in all this one is rewriting the past, is taking the story of a life which was experienced as shaped by circumstance and which was recounted as such, and retelling it in terms of choice and responsibility. As a court may remind a defendant that ignorance of the law is no excuse, so a therapist may remind a patient that blindness to freedom does not justify constraint. And insofar as it may come to seem credible to rewrite one's life in terms of ignored choice, to assume responsibility retrospectively for what one has done and so has become, it will become possible likewise to see alternatives in the present, to become aware that one is free now in this moment to choose how to live, and that what one will become will follow upon what he now does.

When, however, in therapy a life story is reworked to expose the forces which "drove" one to do as he did, emphasizing traumas which twisted him and shaped defenses, hidden constraints, situational and libidinal, which required that he react in the way he did and in no other—in all this, too, one is rewriting the past, is taking a story which must have contained some elements of freedom and responsibility and retelling it in terms of causes lying outside one's control, so teaching the patient to see himself as the product of inner and outer forces. Where he feels himself to be the author of action, his analysis will reveal him as an object being acted upon. He then comes to regard himself as being lived by unknown and largely unknowable forces. As consolation prize he may acquire the capacity to guess at the nature of those obscure forces that move him. But only guess. He must not attempt seriously to bear witness to that which, by definition, he cannot know. He must remain forever the dilettante, making modest conjecture at the gusts which blow him this way and that. He becomes not only an object but opaque, most necessarily to himself.

A "completely analyzed" person is one who has been treated for many years by an orthodox analyst. When such a one breaks down and is hospitalized we are surprised; if he is himself a psychoanalyst we are shocked. Our reaction bespeaks the assumption that thorough analysis resolves all serious inner conflict, that thereafter—though one may expect times of sadness, uncertainty, and unrest—these will derive from reality conflicts and so will not lead to breakdown. There is little to support such a view; indeed, the most cursory glance at three generations of analysts leaves it in tatters. The surprise we feel when a "well analyzed" person breaks down derives from the wish to view man as a machine. Very delicate and complicated, to be sure, like a fine watch, and liable therefore to subtle, tricky problems of adjustment which may require the lengthy services of an expert; but when finally we get rid of all the bugs we may expect smooth and reliable function. Such an image of man is at odds with what we know life to be. If we seriously regard our private thought and feeling, our visions at night when the wind blows, when rain falls on a deserted island, then—though fine adjustments have been made by a great watchmaker—we find so much conflict, misery, confusion that we know we are never through and never safe. The suffering and the danger cannot be left behind. They are what we are.

In reconstructing a life story truth is necessary but not sufficient. Truth does not demarcate, cannot determine whether we should dwell upon cause or choice. Two histories of the same life may be radically different, yet equally true. If we have failed an examination we may say, "I would not have failed if the teacher had not asked that question on Cromwell—which, after all, had not come up in class," or "I would not have failed if I had studied harder." Both statements are addressed to the same experience, in the same effort to understand; both claim to answer the question "Why did I fail?" and both may be true. Truth does not here provide the criterion for selection; the way we understand the past is determined, rather, by the future we desire. If we want to excuse ourselves we elect the former view; if we want to avoid such failures in the future we elect the latter. (If we believe our aim to be the passing of such exams in the future, and if we nevertheless elect the former view of the present failure, then we are confused.)

Likewise in addressing ourselves to the failure of a lifetime, and asking why, we may arrive at answers significantly different but equally true. In the life most free and most aware, so much defining action still occurs without choice that it is always feasible to compose an accurate and cogent account in terms of genes, drives, and circumstance. Conversely, in the life most crushed by outside force, there nevertheless exists the potentiality for actions other than those in fact taken. With the noose around our neck there still are options—to curse God or to pray, to weep or to slap the executioner in the face.

Of two equally true accounts of the same life the one we choose will depend upon the consequences we desire, the future we intend to create. If the life is our own or one of our patients', if it involves suffering and there is desire to change, we will elect a history written in terms of choice; for this is the view that insists upon the awareness of alternatives, the freedom to make one's self into something different. If the life in question is one we observe from a distance, without contact or influence, for example a life which has ended, we may elect a history written in terms of cause. In reconstructing a life that ended at Auschwitz we usually ignore options for other courses of individual behavior, locate cause and responsibility with the Nazis; for our intent is not to appraise the extent to which one person realized existing opportunity, but to examine and condemn the social evil which encompassed and doomed him. In considering the first eighteen years in the life of Malcolm X few of us would find much point in formulating his progress from delinquency to rackets to robbery to prison in terms of choice, holding him responsible for not having transcended circumstance; most of us would find the meaning of his story to lie in the manner in which racism may be seen as the cause of his downward course.

Conflict, suffering, psychotherapy—all these lead us to look again at ourselves, to look more carefully, in greater detail, to find what we have missed, to understand a mystery; and all this extends awareness. But whether this greater awareness will increase or diminish freedom will depend upon what it is that we become aware of. If the greater awareness is of the causes, traumas, psychodynamics that "made" us what we are, then we are understanding the past in such a way as to prove that we "had" to become what we are; and, since this view applies equally to the present which is the unbroken extension of that determined past, therapy becomes a way of establishing why we must continue to be what we have been, a way of disavowing choice with the apparent blessing of science, and the net effect will be a decrease in freedom. If, however, the greater awareness is of options unnoticed, of choices denied, of other ways to live, then freedom will be increased, and with it greater responsibility for what we have been, are, and will become.

Extensions
to
the
Group

26

American Personality Tests In Cross-Cultural Research—a Caution

Leonard V. Gordon · Akio Kikuchi

The note of caution struck by Gordon and Kikuchi serves to remind Americans that their cultural values are not universally distributed, let alone accepted.

These authors make the point that mere translation of a personality test from English to another language hardly assures that test results based upon the translated version will have any valid meaning. They reason that the same values may be represented by different behaviors in the two cultures, or even discrepant values by identical behaviors.

The term "factor analysis" refers to a statistical procedure frequently used to determine whether a mixture of responses can be sorted out into a set of categories or factors, each of which contributes in some measure to the whole matrix.

In a large number of cross-cultural studies, paper-and-pencil personality tests originally developed in the United States have been translated and administered within some other culture. Typically, the translation is reported as having been made with care by a psychologist or other professional fluent in both English and the foreign language employed, and as having been checked by obtaining a back-translation from an individual other than the original translator. Rarely does an evaluation of the translation progress beyond this point. Comparisons then are made between mean scores of the foreign sample and mean scores of a counterpart American group, with both samples selected so as to be similar in characteristics, such as socioeconomic status, sex, educational background, and vocational orientation. Differences on test variables are interpreted as reflecting differences between the two cultures.

From *The Journal of Social Psychology* (1966), Vol. 69, pp. 179–183; reprinted by permission of *The Journal Press,* Copyright 1966.

Translations developed solely in this manner and not further evaluated may not be usable for making valid cross-cultural comparisons. It is the purpose of this paper to discuss certain problems associated with the translation of personality tests for use in cross-cultural research, and with the interpretation of cross-cultural findings obtained through the use of such translations. While these problems have been noted in connection with the translating of American tests, the present discussion will have a more general applicability.*

Paper-and-pencil personality tests typically are developed by one of two approaches: (a) by an empirical or criterion-oriented approach, in which items are selected on the basis of their relationship to a criterion of interest or on the basis of their ability to discriminate between criterion groups; and (b) by a construct-oriented approach, in which some method of internal analysis serves as the basis for item selection, and in which scale validity is established in terms of relationships to a variety of relevant external criteria.

Criterion-developed tests should not be used for making cross-cultural comparisons. Any meaning that this type of instrument might have is derived from the nature of the criterion used in its development. Since what constitutes favorable criterion performance often differs across cultures, and since quite different characteristics may be required to achieve a given level of criterion performance in different cultures, cross-cultural results based on empirical keys may be uninterpretable. For example, a valid predictor of leadership behavior, developed by empirical methods with U.S. Army officers and applied in translation to Korean officers, would permit us to conclude little, if anything, about the leadership potential of the latter group. Behavior which is judged to be effective leadership performance for U.S. Army officers differs from that which is judged to be effective for Far Eastern officers. For the latter group, leadership effectiveness is defined to a large extent in terms of the officer's relationship with his superiors, rather than with his subordinates. Similarly, a sales interest key derived by empirical methods in the United States would tell us little about the sales interest of subjects in certain Near East areas, such as Egypt, where sales encounters differ in character from those in this country.

* For example, where American tests are used in other English-speaking cultures.

Personality tests most appropriately and widely used in cross-cultural research are those which measure particular constructs. The items in such tests represent samplings from a universe of items that help define the constructs, and test results are interpreted in terms of the constructs rather than the specific items that happen to be used. When an American test and a translation are to be used for making cross-cultural comparisons, both forms must measure the same construct. Also, they should be comprised of a comparable sampling of items, in the sense that both sets of items should reflect the same level or strength of the construct *within* each culture. This is best accomplished by including as many identical items as possible in both forms. When modifications or replacements are made, the new items should be similar to the original items in factor structure and preference value. If the two forms measure somewhat different constructs or differ materially in content or level of item sampling, it may not be possible to determine whether obtained differences are due to differences in culture or to the lack of a common metric.

Thus, before a translation is undertaken there should be good reason to believe that the construct, as measured by the items in the American instrument, is meaningful within the second culture. This belief, based on a thorough understanding of both cultures, should be treated as an hypothesis to be tested in the development and construct-validation of the translated instrument. The judgment that the items in the American instrument are easily translatable is not sufficient to establish the construct within the second culture. An instrument developed on this basis may provide uninterpretable measurement within the second culture. If the American construct as measured does not appear to be applicable to the second culture, a determination will have to be made as to whether a common construct, measurable by similar item content, is identifiable in the two cultures. If so, the development of new parallel instrumentation can be undertaken.*

The above suggests that considerable thought should be given

---

* The present discussion uses the American paper-and-pencil personality test as a point of departure only because practically all such instruments used in cross-cultural research are of American origin. The same cautions would apply where a non-American instrument is to be translated. In those rare instances where a construct relevant test has already been developed within the second culture, the development of parallel instruments should, of course, fully utilize this test and the data available for it.

to the original selection of an instrument for possible translation. Not only must the constructs and items be evaluated in terms of cross-cultural relevance, but such matters as (a) the acceptability of particular types of items, (b) the meaningfulness of test format and directions, and (c) the susceptibility to response sets within the second culture must also be considered.

The nature of the construct must be kept clearly in mind during the process of translation. The translator should be alert to the possibility that items that are readily translatable may carry a connotation different from that of the original. For example, it was noted that, while "Conformity" as measured by the Survey of Interpersonal Values (3) is a meaningful construct for Italian subjects, certain items would be interpreted as reflecting the type of adherence to regulations prescribed under the Fascist regime and would assume a political meaning. Minor item modification avoided this problem.* A further check on the meaning of the translated items may be obtained by having a back-translation performed by a person unfamiliar with the original instrument or the constructs contained therein. This is a rather commonly used procedure.

A statistical evaluation of the translated items, by factor analysis or some other scaling method, often will provide new information regarding the meaning that certain items have for the respondent population. For example, in a factor analysis of items translated into Japanese from the Survey of Interpersonal Values, it was found by Kikuchi (4) that the item "To have people think of me as being important," which had been judged to be a good Recognition item, loaded on the Leadership factor. The idea of valuing Recognition is very poorly regarded in Japan, and this item appears to have been interpreted by Japanese subjects as the individual's valuing the holding of an important position or office. Similarly, what had been considered to be a Benevolence item—"To do things for other people"—apparently was interpreted by Japanese subjects as representing a desire to be in a role subordinate to a superior, as indicated by a negative loading on Leadership.†

* Luigi Meschieri, Instituto Nazionale Di Psicologia, Rome; personal communication.

† This type of evaluation is useful in the development of American personality tests. For example, it was found that the item "*Anxious* to make new acquaintances" loaded on the Emotional Stability factor, while the modified item "*Eager* to make new acquaintances" loaded on the Sociability factor (2).

Once a translated form has been prepared, it is essential to obtain reliability information on the individual scales. Without reliability information, meaningful interpretation of cross-cultural (or within-cultural) results is not possible. For example, statistically significant cross-cultural differences may result from a comparison of reliable scores in one culture with chance scores in another, or no significant differences may be found between groups within the second culture solely because of the unreliability of the scales.

Bilingual subjects within the second culture have been administered original and translated forms by some investigators in order to assess the comparability of the two forms. This type of analysis will provide useful information only (a) if the subjects are sufficiently fluent in their second language to understand nuances in item meaning, and (b) if bilingualism is not in itself related to the characteristics measured in such a way as to make them unrepresentative of their culture or to bring about an undue restriction in range. Cross-language correlations for bilingual groups should not be expected to approach the reliabilities of the scales, since language of presentation is known to exert a significant influence on the responses of the subjects (1, 6).

Parallel instruments, consisting of identical or near-identical items that fully and reliably measure a particular construct within two cultures, still may not provide sufficient data for making cross-cultural comparisons. Constructs, in any culture, do not stand alone. They bear particular relationships to other constructs for particular subgroups, and these relationships help define the meaning of the construct as much as the items through which they are measured. For example, "Benevolence" as a value is a very different matter for an army officer and for a college student (members of two American subcultures). Correlational data show that for the officer "Benevolence" is directly related to his power drive, while for the college student it is quite independent (3). Army officers and college students, for whom this value has equal strength, may try to satisfy it in very different ways, and from a very different motivational basis. Thus, it would be advisable to include, as part of the cross-cultural instrumentation, measures of constructs that are likely to be related, in some meaningful way, to those of primary interest. Information regarding the interrelationships among the constructs within each culture will be important for the interpretation of cross-cultural results.

The fact that a given construct is not readily translatable into the second culture is in itself an important cross-cultural datum. The modifications required in item translation, or the nature of the content that must be excluded from the American or other-cultural construct to establish a common construct, may provide information regarding cross-cultural differences as valuable as that which is obtained from measures of the common construct. Such information should be considered fully in the interpretation of cross-cultural findings.

Finally, a battery of parallel personality tests, no matter how inclusive, will not necessarily provide a comprehensive comparison of important personality characteristics of the populations of the two cultures. Such instruments will measure only those characteristics that are common to both, while characteristics that are salient only in one culture will be neglected. For example, none of the published American tests would measure the very important Japanese value "Giri" or "Filial Piety" (5). Investigators who plan to use only translated American tests, or specially devised tests which measure aspects common to the two cultures, must keep this limitation in mind. Again, it may be that the very characteristics that are significant in one culture and not in the other represent more important cross-cultural data than those characteristics that are relatively significant in both.

REFERENCES

1. GARSEE, J. W. A study of Samoan interpersonal values. Unpublished Master's thesis, University of Oklahoma, Norman, 1965.
2. GORDON, L. V. Gordon Personal Profile. New York: Harcourt, 1953.
3. ———. Survey of Interpersonal Values and Manual. Chicago: Science Research Assoc., 1960.
4. KIKUCHI, A. Measuring interpersonal values. *Bull. Faculty of Liberal Arts, Fukushima University,* 1964, 36–41.
5. ———. A survey of Japanese interpersonal values. *Jap. Ann. Soc. Psychol.,* 1964, **5**, 161–177.
6. LAMBERT, W. R. The role of language and accent variations in person perception. In *Proceedings, XVII International Congress of Psychology.* Amsterdam: North-Holland Pub. Co., 1964. Pp. 190–191.

27

Social and Cultural
Backgrounds of Mental Illness

Marvin K. Opler

Social psychiatry is a relatively new field. It takes the position that neurotic tensions can neither be understood nor treated in the absence of knowledge of the social context in which the conflicts originate. In this, the introductory chapter to his book, *Culture and Social Psychiatry*, Opler urges a middle course between the strictly biological and the strictly sociocultural extremes that have been offered in explanation of the etiology of mental illness. To follow this course, he believes, one must study and amalgamate the findings of anthropologists, psychiatrists, and biologists.

The impact of social and cultural environment upon the development of personalities is the central concern of social psychiatry. While this environment is in no sense a fixed form of pattern into which personality falls and is moulded, neither is it simply a mere extraneous influence added to inevitable results determined by the child-rearing practices of a culture. The attempts to exaggerate the socio-cultural setting to a global and inclusive mould effect are daily belied by the variations in personalities encountered by observers, scientific or otherwise, in any given setting. On the other hand, even the most cursory acquaintance with psychiatric case histories individually considered indicates the crudity of beginning with the Freudian basic disciplines and inferring therefrom the total contours of adult personality configurations. Both methods, the grossly cultural and the rigidly psychogenic, are only partly useful as formulae and only partly true to individual and cultural realities.

These theoretical opposites fail in that they do not assess, beyond the one-way causal scheme either for psychiatry or anthro-

From *Culture and Social Psychiatry*, pp. 5–24; reprinted by permission of the Publishers, Atherton Press, Inc. Copyright © 1967, Atherton Press, Inc., New York. All rights reserved.

pology, the exact relationship that environmental experiences bear *throughout* the life history to individual adjustment. As Edward Sapir once said, "The worlds in which different societies live are distinct worlds, not merely the same world with different labels attached." In connection with Princeton's Perception Demonstration Center, Hadley Cantril has shown how the nature of the individual's experience in life, even upon the perceptual level, depends on his prior assumptions, how these in turn are built from past experiences; and how attitudes, opinions and percepts change only when the individual is blocked and feels frustration. No doubt, turning to psychiatry, a building up of cognitive, attitudinal and perceptual patterns has also an organic, metabolic and hormonal basis since the organism, as such, is the reactive mechanism; however, personality is more than mechanism, and the individual is more than an autonomous system, self-propelled and self-motivated.

Ordinarily, a person's experiences are in the normal course interpreted along lines laid down by his culture, even though the channels cut by culture thread through such more familiar terrain as family structure and functioning, a system of values and beliefs, a range of social and economic statuses, certain practices and taboos, attitudes towards health and illness, and such features as the characteristic styles of interpersonal relationships. All of these features are the coin of the realm of personality formation, affecting marital, parent-child, sibling, peer, and other group relations. They vary with culture, and with degree and pace of acculturation or culture change. Among the basic orientations provided by culture, A. I. Hallowell has recently listed self- and object-orientation, spatio-temporal orientation, a motivational orientation, and a sense of normative standards and values.[1] The kinds of relationships set up within a culture and defining its age-groups, its sex behavior and attitudes, its statements of the individual position in the family and in the social group are no doubt ramifications of these basic categories. They may be seen also in what Ruth Benedict once called the continuities and discontinuities of the life history pattern.

This life span, or life cycle, is lived in a constant homeostatic relationship with this total environment, parts of which become internalized and implicit in an individual's responses and reactions as well as external and explicit. On the individual level of responses in actions and symbols, unique though these are, no life is lived alone and apart from interpersonal patterns of communication and interaction. All personality formation, or the psychodynamics of well or ill alike, rely in the last analysis upon symbolic forms of communication and self-expression in which what is human *and* cultural is shared, while that which is bizarre and autistic is closer to raw impulse or guarded illusion. A psychiatry, or a behavioral science, which credits a human being with a dynamic life biography and with conditions of existence in communicated and felt socio-cultural settings, but which ends by denying reality of the social and cultural groups, cannot move from case A to case B, or indeed fully assess the impact of other people on either A or B.[2]

In his recent posthumous work, *The Interpersonal Theory of Psychiatry,* Harry Stack Sullivan has stated that progress toward a "psychiatry of peoples" can emerge only from improved understanding of significant patterns of living in the modern world coupled with the discovery of important details in personality development by which persons of different socio-cultural background "come to manifest more or less adequate behavior in their given social settings." Each of these lines of inquiry, the first in anthropology and the second in social psychiatry, he regarded as a "necessary supplement to the other." Seen from this vantage point, not merely the often unrecallable earlier stages of childhood confusion, but any appropriate and less dereistic or painful points in the life cycle are equally important in their own right "in the unfolding of possibilities for interpersonal relations in the progression . . . toward mature competence for life in a fully human world." The importance of families, communities, socio-political entities, group cultures and sub-cultures as the settings for these progressive efforts of the individual are all alluded to by Sullivan. He also stresses the special skills in the study of interpersonal relationships, participant observation and interviewing techniques using the operational approach and field theory concepts of psychiatric and anthropological science. Finally, we learn that, ideally, the psychiatrist as "participant observer" uses concepts derived from the anthropologist's analyses of other cultures.[3]

This concordance of interests in the fields of psychiatry and anthropology in three areas, the individual personality, the cultural background, and family or social group participation is a convergence in broadly integrative behavioral science. That it should appear in the consolidating and synthesizing phases of each discipline in the Twentieth Century is not surprising. If, as has been known for some time, there are intimate connections between the organization of personality and its socio-cultural background, then the study of either is revealing of outlines, demarcations and significances of conduct in the individual.

The increasing use of projective test methodologies in the study of cultures is instructive at this juncture, since it was Rorschach himself who first studied psychotic patients from two different Swiss cantons and who reported that the results obtained seemed to indicate variation in the actual form of psychoses which could be attributed to distinct cultural backgrounds. The ease with which the Rorschach, and other projective techniques, could be administered even to nonliterate peoples, and the objective criterion of "blind analyses" by psychologists who did not know the informant, opened the way for on-the-spot ethnologists to gather reasonably unbiased personality data. It is no wonder that psychologists, interpreting such materials with scoring systems which were not even well-established in our culture, found these to fall short of adequate quantitative establishment of norms elsewhere and were consequently guided by intelligent use of the raw materials and by general principles governing the use of the total instrument.

The underlying Rorschach principles, or assumptions, that the individual had no way of knowing what was expected in terms of performance and therefore characteristically responded in the way in which he handled every life situation seemed true enough if one further assumed inherent grouping principles in the perception of form, as promulgated by Gestalt psychology, and secondly, recognized the possibility of cross-cultural differences and comparisons. Indeed, Hallowell showed that certain responses were popularly given despite strongly divergent cultural backgrounds.[4] On the other hand, Laura Thompson, in a study of three different Hopi communities with variance in economic security and social organization, demonstrated through projective material the importance of cultural background and varying social organization in the personalities of members of each group.[5] Hallowell, even earlier, found significant Rorschach differences among acculturated and unacculturated Salteaux.[6]

The techniques of separate or blind analyses, initiated by the anthropologist, Cora DuBois, and Oberholzer in DuBois' *The People of Alor,* were continued with inclusion of the Thematic Apperception Test by the anthropologist Thomas Gladwin and the clinical psychologist, Seymour B. Sarason, in their joint work, *Truk; Man in Paradise*.[7] In such blind interpretations, there is remarkable similarity in interpretations given by ethnologists and clinicians, as where, in the last example, Sarason was able to draw conclusions, similar to Gladwin, about the concentration of Trukese on rigid suppression of feelings and impulses, and on the development of conformance and concreteness of thinking in these subjects. Actually, the anthropological data on the all-important lineage relationships proved to be of crucial significance in explaining the development of conforming, inhibited, suppressing personalities. On the other hand, the psychological data revealed a dominance of women and forced an ethnological re-examination of the material wherein, though seemingly more submissive, they did indeed occupy the truly pivotal position in social organization because of their primary role in the handling of food allocations. With these basic orientations in mind, purely descriptive data including male and female sexual conduct, family organization and even child-rearing practices fall in line. Equally, records examined by Oberholzer, and revealing kinds of reaction typical of patients suffering brain injury in our culture, were adequately understandable only when cultural themes and organization were explicit. In the Trukese study, an important sexual problem of women was missed in Rorschach interpretations of the psychologist by merely not knowing the female sexual symbol.

Jules Henry has pointed out that the use of rare detail in Rorschachs of a jungle people of South America is a function of their need to observe their surroundings in order to survive. Similarly, Cook's finding of "overuse" of space-responses in Samoa reflected simply the special cultural value attached to the color white. The point is clear that in two sciences related to social psychiatry, in cultural anthropology and clinical psychology, there is increasing awareness that in order to understand both culture and personality adequately, one must ascertain how the personality of the members of a given society finds expression *within a social and cultural framework*. Three-dimensional social psychiatry, involving the techniques of social science and psychology, would likewise require as a necessary parameter of scientific observation the notion of a socio-cultural frame of reference for normative and aberrant; for gauging the intensities of affect; the types and degrees of human expressivity in different cultures; the choice of cultural symbols used in human communication; or in short, the varying cognitive, perceptual and attitudinal interpretations of any cultural human being.

Awareness of these generalized, or cultural, symbolic functions in individual psychodynamics is not limited to psychology. The fact that human communication and expression are based on symbols to which meanings are assigned was discovered, so to speak, independently in psychiatry once the notion of an inevitable course of illness and rigid diagnostic categories, as in the classical descriptive work of Kraepelin, gave way to a more dynamic view of variables in typology, illness progression, and environmental influences as in the work of Adolf Meyer. With the gradual death of the notion of a "unit psychosis," the ideological importance of longitudinal case history grew, relying at first on relating the organic and metabolic functioning to unique symbolic functioning of personality. Gradually, the hospital as a therapeutic milieu, "push therapy," the phenomena of transference and countertransference, and explorations into symbolic content and dynamics came into purview. The movement was from hospitalized to ambulatory treatment where possible; from custodial care and descriptive analysis to devices aimed at gradual socialization and improved environment; from cross-sectional symptomatology to assessment of the longitudinal course of illness; and from random exploration and probing to carefully guided support and re-education.

Increasingly the psychosocial position required a knowledge of the cultural setting and background of each patient to the end that his world of meanings and experiences be assessed in therapy, and his organic and symbolic functioning understood in terms of the contexts or milieus of family, community, social and sub-cultural groups in which he had played a role. Independently, in the social sciences, the areas of social action and interactive process were explored in social systems and social roles. The social statuses and their functions in the social structure, and the manner in which that structure was systematized were all important ingredients in defining an individual's relationships to his fellows, and his activities, to be sure, in relation to theirs. Nevertheless, the anatomy and physiology of a social system and its functioning related ultimately to a further system of meanings, at once cultural and personal in essence. This was to say that roles were, by and large, culturally defined; that social structures varied with cultural backgrounds and identities, and that whole social systems were built on foundations supplied by what Kluckhohn called implicit (Sapir's "unconsciously patterned") and explicit (consciously followed) cultural symbols.

In the work of Adolf Meyer, the challenge to an oversimplified and rigid typology and labeling process was to construct new typologies having greater range and also greater reference to the variability of process in the adaptation, or maladaptation, to environment. In therapy, too, one of his contributions was to point to possibilities of adaptation to a milieu, or to point up positive relationships which a patient was in a position to utilize. In the same intellectual period, John Dewey in philosophy was noting that a social existence was a necessary condition for the development of normative mentation processes in any individual. Physical anthropologists like Boas were pointing out the mutational plasticity of humans under environmental changes; social biologists like Hogben were documenting environmental effects in the statistical incidence of mental deficiency; and H. S. Jennings was initiating the studies of human behavior and genetics which have led ultimately to our present knowedge that of the more than five hundred single gene substitutions for which there is good evidence, only a minor few determine behavioral resultants. The psychoanalytic movement, least "organicist" of all, was at the same time enjoying a growth of popularity in the United States while giving rise to sharply varying systems like those of Horney, of Roheim, of Rado, Kardiner and Ferenczi, which like Sullivan's were directly influenced by anthropologists such as Sapir and Linton, Kluckhohn, Benedict and Mead.

In none of this transfer of interest to total life span, to situational context or milieu, to relationships within a social system, and to cultural background, were the sacred precincts of any one science inviolable. Multidisciplinary research recognized that the pathology of a society reflects its general conditions, and conversely offered important clues to an understanding of the culture. Galen's ancient phrase, "Man is a whole with his environment," found epidemiological confirmation not in the least from carefully designed public health inquiries in which the epidemiology (*how much* illness in time periods of incidence) soon came to mean *how much* illness emerged in relation to age, sex and finally social and cultural strata. Why these problems of incidence and prevalence mean very little for certain kinds of illness such as mental disorder, unless at the same time etiological problems of the same illness groups are attacked, is a matter which will be discussed below. Suffice it to say the scenes were set for interest in the *how and why* of mental illness by a study of the incidence or occurrences of different psychopathological states in persons of specific socio-cultural background.

Psychiatry, par excellence, is a science which specializes in a knowledge of the way human experience is utilized in the total economy of personality; psychiatrists soon realized that as a generalizing behavioral science it must press beyond individual case formulations to psychosocial typologies. Indeed, J. L. Halliday in his *Psychosocial Medicine*[8] defines illness in general as "a reaction, or mode of behavior, or vital expression of a living unit in response to those forces which he encounters as he moves and grows in time." Etiology of mental illness is studied in terms of dual, relational causes which lie both in the nature of the individual and in the nature of his environment, *but in both at the same time.* While a culture is, at any point in time, more massive and imposing than any individual participant and must be distinguished from the individual, the great danger in multidisciplinary research involving relational causal systems, is to so abstract the individual from his meaningful cultural background that he ceases to be a responsive or live subject for diagnosis, case formulation or psychotherapy. There are simply no individuals apart from specific socio-cultural background.

By culture we then mean an imposing and conditioning variable which always becomes internalized, in one way or another, in the psychic systems of human beings. Far from being a mere matter of the artifacts and social organization of a people, culture also contains their range of expressive symbolism, whether in art, language, dance or song, or in the non-verbal communication patterns involved in gestures, interpersonal emotional contacts, and the rules governing relationships of age groups and of sexes. It[9]

> consists of patterns, explicit and implicit, of and for behavior acquired and transmitted by symbols, constituting the distinctive achievement of human groups, including their embodiments in artifacts; the essential core of culture consists of traditional (i.e., historically derived and selected) ideas and especially their attached values; culture systems may, on the one hand, be considered as products of action, on the other as conditioning elements of further action.

More specifically, it includes the patterned family and social influences, the means of symbolic communication forged into a way of life, affirmed and reaffirmed in the common currency of custom, and most importantly, always having a significant discernible meaning and value for the individual.

That these traditional ideas, or themes of culture influencing patterns of behavior; the prevailing ethics, the child-rearing practices, the notions of social integration, the taboos, religious values, and attitudes toward health and illness; that these leitmotifs of a culture were precipitates of history or could influence history was probably not the main fact about them. Surely the dynamic interplay of factors within culture influenced history. But equally important, at least for behavioral science, was the manner in which these elements in a way of life became incorporated in individual functioning, how much or to what extent ego involvements became dependent on them, and why they had much to do, positively or negatively, with super-ego functioning.

The tendency, in the Freudian view, to equate culture and super-ego, as in *Totem and Taboo,* was a needless oversimplification. Not all in culture, except in Dr. Pangloss' "best of all possible worlds" is positive, sublimated, humanly helpful and real achievement. Even more serious, human impulses, perceptions, emotionalized attitudes and knowledge are dependent upon cultural circumstances. The tendency to regard "normal" or "social" behavior as the sublimated, cultural achievement, and "culture" as due to successful repression or identity of feelings with others (both formulated in *Totem and Taboo*) begs two questions. May there not be what Jahoda has called "indiscriminate adjustment through passive acceptance of environmental conditions" as distinct from inability to adjust, or different from active mastery and adjustment? Secondly, the negative, destructive experiences likewise felt by the organism and interpreted on perceptual, cognitive and attitudinal levels (Rado's destructive emotions as opposed to welfare emotions) are, no matter how far from personal self-fulfillment, still caught in the same web of cultural circumstances.

If psychosomatic responding to stress or psychic distorting reactions to frustration are found, they are nevertheless referable to felt experience within a cultural framework. It has been suggested that emotion *is* bodily change plus attitudes stemming from experience, in the cumulative work of men like W. B. Cannon, Harold Wolff, or William Grace.[10] Animal experimentation on emotional conditioning has also, even in a non-cultural setting, led to similar conclusions.[11] It remains to relate emotionally charged attitudes in humans to the cultural settings and contexts, stressful or beneficial, in which they eventuate.

Therefore, while cultures are not to be confused with unique clinical cases, or with negative clinical formulations, they do contain *stress systems* of a generalized character which are capable of differentiation, one from another, and which have considerable clinical importance. Attempts to define these in terms of social structure alone, or by rates of interaction of persons in a social structure, may be misleading. Indeed, in anthropology, whole schools or systems have been developed and abandoned, on the premise that types of social structure and interactional systems may be studied alone and apart from the psychological qualifications of the *meanings of cultural conduct for individuals*. Such a system was Radcliffe-Brown's at Chicago in the 1930's, or the Chapple and Coon equilibrium-disequalibrium theories of social interaction at Harvard in the 1940's.

But if culture, social system and personality are functional variables, they are interdependent and interrelated. As concerns the always unique and personalized systems of affect and thought in any individual, it is always the *individual* who hopes, thinks, acts, dreams and aspires. Nevertheless, each individual has a particular place in social structure of a definable sort and a particular set of cultural beliefs and conditions in his background. There is no longer serious doubt as to the overwhelming importance of life history in mental illness, but the relevance of social and cultural background in furnishing guide lines to this personalized life cycle remains to be explored.

Beginning with Kraepelin, it has been known that psychopathological illness varies in content and in type with culture. Ziehen noted variations in Holland and in German Thuringia. Bleuler, in Switzerland, remarked upon differences in English and Irish cases, Bavarians and Saxons; speaking of his own hospital, he wrote: "Indeed, in our hospital, it is easy to note the difference between the reactions of the Bernese as compared with the Zurichois who are quite closely related racially."[12] P. M. Yap has described the Latah reaction in Malaya, Arctic Hysteria in Siberia, and Imu in Hokkaido.[13] In the same British journal of psychiatry, E. H. Hare reports on variations in the Congo, Papua and India; while J. Carothers in 1947 compared incidence data among Africans of

Kenya with those of American Negroes.[14] An analysis of the possible significance of these patterns of cross-cultural variances will be given below. To date, they have largely followed a rather euphoric pattern: Faris in 1934 finding no schizophrenias in Belgian Congo; Seligman in 1929 finding no protracted mental disorders in Papua, merely brief attacks; unless acculturated to the west, Seligman and Dhunjibhoy's data (1930) locating no schizophrenias, unless like Parsees, the people were highly advanced in "Western civilization"; Carothers' Kenya colonists having low incidence or disorder and with freedom from most of our social, sexual and economic problems "in consequence" having no "obsessional neuroses"; the Okinawans, unexposed to concepts of sin and guilt, being reported as notably free of anxiety and all neuroses.

For the United States, the best known statistics are of a different order. Of all persons hospitalized, psychiatric disorder equals the number of cases for all other illnesses combined; of these mental illnesses, more than half are nonorganic schizophrenias, depressive states or severe psychoneuroses. Beyond this are those ambulatory, in private care or receiving no treatment whatsoever. The probably conservative estimate of one out of twelve infants suffering from mental disease in his later life course, or one out of sixteen Americans ill now, does not include the psychological components in psychosomatic ailments (asthma, allergies, migraine, rhinitis, urticaria, neurodermatitis, ulcerative colitis, peptic ulcer, nonglandular obesity, essential hypertension, etc.), nor does it include the 20,000 suicides per year, the accident-prone, that part of crime and delinquency described by Wertham and Redl, marital discord and divorce, and such problems as impotence and frigidity. Further, there are countless cases of minor compulsions, private phobias, and transient hysteriform simulations of certain diseases. A sardonic wit has called this The Aspirin Age of the Atomic Era in Urban America.

Before the ethical or philosophic questions that this problem raises, there are first the scientific, methodological ones. The psychosocial position has supplanted what Felix and Bowers call "the older assumptions of geographic or biological determinism of human behavior . . . the product of climate, heredity or original sin."[15] In place of the solitary individual governed by such somewhat fateful and extraneous forces, Jahoda speaks of a human need for "active adjustment," "attempts at mastery of environment," "the ability to perceive correctly the world and himself," and mental health as a dynamic concept, not simply a state of being.

Human energies which utilize symbolic human constructs in interpersonal communication may do so for better or worse, but they will not act solely on behalf of a biological unit, or emotionalized *id* impulses except in the most poorly integrated personalities. What Freud interpreted as raw impulse, basic need and earliest cathected orientations are better seen in the continuum of adaptive adjustment in which impulse, need and cathexis are always modified, early in life to be sure, in the area of interpersonal communication. That integration of "mental" and emotional functions, or even cognitive adequacy, or personal insight, may be won or lost in discrete personal histories should not blind us to the fact that real, interpersonal contacts in a common, workaday world always help to define the limits of the normative and the aberrant. Within this framework, the nonintegration or the thought disturbance, or lack of judgment implied in any disorganizing illness is not there as nonconformity in the narrow sense of majority tastes and aspirations. It is the result of communicated and felt emotionality that is destructive, that is a part of no normative group, however small, no positive social force, and no tradition of a sustaining sort. Even bohemian literary and artistic movements have been aimed accurately at lace-curtained salons of dead art. There should be no confusion of regimentation with functional movements, or with principles of positive conformance. Aberration is not innovation.

It is no longer believed in most quarters that the circumstances which lead the individual inexorably into some tortured world "of his own making" are really of his making. Nor is the determinism of today one which stresses such isolated events as nursing or weaning, or the various swaddling or swathing practices of Czech, Slovak, Italians, Russians, or Polish to be read off as modal personality determinants. The individual as a psychosocial unit, capable of tremendous emotional expression, is subject to adaptive adjustment in such a way that while his experience, to be sure, is always felt and motivated, ordinarily that pattern of experience has itself context and meaning, integration, and considerable reaffirmation before it may achieve any emotional hue. If psychological field theory and anthropological behavior studies have proved anything, they have taught that while it is always the individual who functions adequately (or who may otherwise despair, hallucinate, hate, compensate, fear, or withdraw) he is nevertheless one, in either case, whose experiences are largely imposed from without, become immediately involved in an integration of sorts, are felt within and interpreted along lines laid down by a whole series of social and cultural events. Before styles of interpersonal relationship reach individual "minds and hearts," they are subject to the greater statistical weight and frequency of socio-cultural group phenomena.

As Benedict, Horney, and Redlich have noted, each in separate ways,[16] the cultural norms and standards are present to help define both normal and aberrant. While psychiatry has noted a certain patterning, or typology, in certain disease processes, it remains to investigate specific cultural scenes and the pathology within them, to locate the effectively charged points in the cultural stress systems. There is no reason to feel that a culture may not be studied and diagrammed for ambiguities, conflicts, discontinuities in life course, obvious stress features, and handicaps to maturation and healthy development. Reaction formations, premised from one case to the next on typical anxieties, fears, hates, confusions and lack of positive communication within such systems may be balanced against studies of "normals" from matched circumstances within a culture to learn what readings of the cultural map develop the well and ill. When this is done, the functions (and limits) of both destructive and welfare emotions will be fully understood within the systems of human communication in which they alone have meaning.

This connection of culture and social group, not with modal personality constructs of dubious value clinically, but with statistically oriented epidemiology and psychiatrically valid studies of the etiology of health and illness, is the course suggested for social psychiatry. At this point, no other course, it is felt, can link experience with expression in human symbolic communication systems, or deal adequately in the triadic systems of culture, social group and personality, with such related patterns as values and attitudes; the same linkage exists between world outlooks and personal horizons, the social position of the sexes and actual sexual behavior, the status system and characteristic styles of interpersonal behavior, or in brief, between culture and personality. Since these relationships are already well known in anthropological monographs across the earth's surface, the obvious need is application to psychiatric phenomena. Let us therefore plot the course, theoretically, which marks the normative, usual experience in relation to that which marks out the aberrant.

Since both courses are functionally important, or operationally used, by the individual, a dynamic and graphic analogy may be apposite. It is suggested as an alternative to the individually centered (and limited) theory of id, ego and super-ego.

The normal, usual experience is the road most people, representing the creative aspects of a culture at its best, can follow. They take it, not simply as individuals but in groups, each with a life span and with certain age, sex and organic attributes. The line of persons and of families following the course are only in unusual systems, rigid and restrictive, in a tight line. Instead there are all the alternative routings, the by-passes, the room for occasional choice and the variant speeds, stops, impediments and hazards. The vehicles to such accomplishment are culturally designed and constructed. Generally, they vary in age within automotive or historical limits, in aspects of design and purpose, the truck and town sedan even in functional class reference. Beyond the "cultural" make and construction, denoted by name, and the "class" or usage functions, denoted by structure, there are the differentiated motives of drivers. (In view of the penchant for making individual motivational systems "basic" to some systems of social psychology, we shall add that the make or construction, the cultural label on any car, together with age, implies much, realistically considered, as to what pure motivation can really accomplish in the driver's seat.)

The road hazards or conditions, and the make or type of car, we prefer to think of as the different conditions of culture. The former might be called, in this metaphor, the cultural stress system; the latter, the vehicle intended for human accomplishment of purposes and goals, we mean to be the cultural modalities, or means, for such achievement. But some drivers, some motivational systems as it were, doubtlessly because of the hazards and stresses, the inadequacies of the vehicle and its continuing strain on the adjustive motivational system, abandon the trip and set off—presumably afoot and with certainly less efficiency—on the pathways and trails with no certain markings, armed only with their primitive energies and impulses, and with only remnants of their original purpose. We submit that the topography, the strains, the barriers, impediments and roadblocks have something to do, even as to their place of location in the journey, with the points that mark out the by-paths, the impractical shortcuts, and the meandering lonely trails.

Note one fact about the lonely trails, the ten percent of mental disorder. Epidemiologically considered, they are not wholly unique pathways, as clinical experience on similar cases, or statistics on given nosological entities indicate. As history changes and cultures vary, new styles of mental illness arise and are described. The phrase, "worlds of their own making," has little meaning in view of the Dancing Mania, or Tarantism, of Thirteen Century Italy, described by Ferdinandus and Baglivi and redescribed by Sigerist. The imagined tarantula bite felt in the dull slack of hot summer seasons sent people to streets and market places to dance together in gay, almost ceremonial attire, until insensate or carried away. The Mania, which spread in Europe for a few centuries reads strangely like the Vailala Madness of New Guinea, reported by F. E. Williams for the dislocated, acculturated areas of that island; it is reminiscent also of certain aspects of the Ghost Dance of the Plains, described by Cora DuBois, or the Ute Indian Ghost Dance (M. K. Opler). Studies like Cantril's of the invasion from Mars, or the Mattoon, Illinois hysteria; the Beloi cult of the BaThonga or the Vada sorcery of the Trobiands; or Latah and Imu reactions demonstrate that there is little about mental illness which is immutable in time or hard to duplicate cross-culturally in special times and places. Yet if we are not hopelessly to chronicle the cross-cultural phenomena in separate, unrelated studies, the study of well and ill within the settings of modern, populous cultures and sub-cultures, including our own, is next in order.

Psychopathological differences may be expected in modern cultures. As Parsons and Shils have recently pointed out, *all* cultures regulate social and sexual behavior, control organized activities, and affect traditional behavior of any sort through processes of symbolic communications.[17] This means, at the very least, that all areas of perception, feeling and evaluation are culturally differentiated during the period when a child first experiences meaningful contacts with adults by the learning of language or by the development of what Piaget might call a social sense. Wayne Dennis' studies of infancy differentiation among Navajo and Hopi children in the Thirties and Forties, or those of Rene Spitz and John Bowlby showing the importance of maternal figures in early maturation, lend support. A variety of anthropological data points to a continuing process of differentiation, through life span. The full-length biography and a variety of personal documents were proposed early by Sapir and Kluckhohn as a firm way of testing the impact of culture upon personality.

In social psychiatry, and in ethnopsychiatric surveys such as J. C. Carothers' *The African Mind,* the study of individual patients, or of symptomatology and psychodynamics of individual disorders, has broadened into concern for the ambulatory patient and, finally, to consideration of the person in his community and socio-cultural setting. As yet, few studies have been made in the kind of modern scene, marked by ethnic and status constrasts, which assure us that modernized urban cultural heterogeneity has been studied at all. A total stock-taking of methodological problems involved in epidemiological study in the United States and Europe is required. . . .

REFERENCES

1. HALLOWELL, A. I. The self and its behavioral environment. *Explorations: Studies in Culture and Communication,* **2,** 106–165, 1954.
2. OPLER, M. K. Psychoanalytic techniques in social analysis. *J. of Social Psychol.,* **15,** 91–127, 1942 (*Vide,* p. 115).
3. SULLIVAN, HARRY STACK. *The Interpersonal Theory of Psychiatry.* New York, Norton, 1953 (*Vide,* pp. xi, 365, 371, 376).
4. HALLOWELL, A. I. *Popular Responses and Cultural Differences,* Rorschach Research Exchange, **IX,** 1945.
   ———. The Rorschach technique in the study of personality and culture. *Am. Anthropologist,* **47,** No. 2, 1945.
5. THOMPSON, LAURA. *Culture in Crisis: A Study of the Hopi Indians:* or, Attitudes and acculturation. *Am. Anthropologist,* **50,** No. 2, 1950.
6. HALLOWELL, A. I. *Acculturation Processes and Personality Changes as Indicated by the Rorschach Technique,* Rorschach Research Exchange, **VI,** 1942.
7. DuBOIS, CORA. *The People of Alor.* Minneapolis, Univ. Minnesota Press, 1944.
   GLADWIN, THOMAS, AND SARASON, S. B. *Truk: Man in Paradise.* New York, Wenner-Gren Foundation Publications in Anthropology, No. 20, 1953.
8. HALLIDAY, J. L. *Psychosocial Medicine: A Study of the Sick Society.* New York, Norton, 1948.
9. KROEBER, A. L., AND KLUCKHOHN, C. *Culture.* Papers of the Peabody Museum, **47,** 1952 (*Vide,* p. 118).
10. CANNON, W. B. *Bodily Changes in Pain, Hunger, Fear and Rage.* New York, Appleton, 1929.

WOLFF, HAROLD G. Protective reaction patterns and disease. *Ann. Int. Med.*, **27**, 1947.

GRACE, WILLIAM. Relationship of specific attitudes and emotions to certain bodily diseases. *Psychosom. Med.*, **14**, No. 4, 1952.

11. LIDDELL, HOWARD S. Conditioning and emotions, *Scient. Am.*, **190**, No. 1, 1954. (Reference is also made to current work of Horsley Gantt.)

12. BLEULER, EUGEN. *Dementia Praecox or The Group of Schizophrenias.* New York, Internat. Univ. Press, 1950 (*Vide*, pp. 336, 463). See also ZILBOORG, G., AND HENRY, G. W. *A History of Medical Psychiatry.* New York, Norton, 1941.

13. YAP, P. M. The Latah reaction. *J. Men. Sc.*, **98**, 515–564, 1952.

14. HARE, E. H. The ecology of mental disease, *J. Men. Sc.*, **98**, 579–594, 1952.

15. FELIX, R. H. AND BOWERS, R. V. Mental hygiene and socio-environmental factors. *Milbank Mem. Fund Quart.*, **26**, 125–147, 1948.

16. BENEDICT, RUTH. Anthropology and the abnormal. *J. Genet. Psychol.*, **10**, 59–82, 1934. Cf., HORNEY, KAREN, *New Ways in Psychoanalysis.* New York, Norton, 1939. Also, Redlich, F., The concept of normality. *Am J. Psychotherapy*, **6**, 551–576, 1952.

17. PARSONS, TALCOTT. *The Social System.* Glencoe, Illinois, Free Press, 1951.

28

Whose Strength, Whose Weaknesses

Robert Coles

Coles, who is a psychiatrist, poignantly describes the hardships encountered in the daily routine of a typical sharecropper's family.

Ruth, the mother, emerges as the central figure. The writer marvels at her ability to compartmentalize her existence. She and her family barely survive on federal food subsidies (mostly lard and flour); yet she manages her white mistress' domestic affairs (including the preparation of menus, and the cooking of Southern delicacies) with skill, and without apparent resentment.

Coles is sympathetically critical of the educated person's efforts to understand how Ruth manages to live in these two different worlds. He observes that such attempts too often result in specifying appropriate psychological categories and placing people in them, at the expense of losing concern for the people themselves. It is perhaps uneducated Ruth who possesses the strengths, and the intellectual, the weaknesses.

They would be sitting or standing there in front of the cabin, or peering at me from the inside; and I would start slowing myself down. I always needed the extra seconds that a few more steps provide. I would hold my head bowed or pretend to notice something up there in the sky, or over toward the plantation proper. That way their eyes and mine didn't connect, and I didn't have to smile and start saying hello before they could really hear me. That way I could get my mind set for the purpose of my visit, the discovery of certain things, the unearthing of information I thought I ought to possess.

In the beginning ritual masked fear on both sides. I noticed

Reprinted from *The American Scholar*, Vol. 37, No. 4, Autumn, 1968. Copyright © 1968 by the United Chapters of Phi Beta Kappa. By permission of the publishers. "Whose Strengths, Whose Weaknesses" by Robert Coles, delivered in part as the Commencement Address at Haverford College in May, 1968, will be included in Volume II of *Children of Crisis*, to be subtitled "Migrants, Sharecroppers and Mountaineers."

how quiet they all were. My car's noise was a signal to them. They usually heard the car before they saw it because of a sudden turn in the road that made us visible to one another only at the very end of a milelong unpaved, dusty road. By the time I was in sight they had taken up their positions. They seemed rooted. They never looked at me. Or rather, they looked at me when I would not notice. At times I thought them wooden, impassive—and, of course, frightened. When the day came that *I* was not so frightened, their eyes caught mine. I remember being close to grateful that I had someone else's nervousness to observe. Fear has power; power seeks to affirm itself by exertion. And so the edgy, responsive dark irises and white eyeballs belied the calm, the silence. I looked on feet crossed, making still circles out of many legs, and knees crossed, enabling worn, mud-caked shoes to point, but not move an inch. Hungry for the truth, I found it in movement. The eyes did, after all, move and the eyes, my mother told me, were the "windows of the soul." What is more, I thought (or had to think) I saw dilated pupils, which every doctor knows to be a telltale sign that all is not well inside, below, underneath, wherever. (And haven't we learned in this century that any worthwhile truth has to be buried, concealed, and apparent only to the well-trained, in contrast to the well-educated or the desperately or necessarily or naturally sensitive?)

I now realize that my movements and postures underwent the same careful scrutiny that theirs did. Five years later we could reminisce: "I don't believe we knew what you were after. I thought maybe you was here to spy on us, or to sell something. But my sister, she said there was nothing around here to spy, that they didn't already know, the bossman and all. And we don't have the money to buy nothing, so no one could be wasting his time every week for that, to sell. Well, we thought there was no harm just waiting to see. Before long you find out everything you ask about— that's what my daddy used to tell me, and he's right.

"Now, with you we figured you was too slow to be with the sheriff, and not sure of yourself, not enough. And my little boy, James it was, he said, 'Mama, the man doesn't always know what to say.' I think maybe that was the first time any of us, we'd seen a man in a suit be shy—I mean be shy himself and be shy with words, too. Then, when you switched to regular clothes, the summer pants, and no more of the tie and like that, well then we decided you might be from up there in Washington, and the government. You know, they're trying to be for us, on our side. I tried to tell people you are a doctor with a college, but they said doctors don't go around the country sitting and talking here and there.

"No, I can't say I ever been to a doctor's office. They ask you to pay first, and we can't, not first or later. So, it's just as well. They'd give us medicine, if they agreed to see us, and then the next thing you knew there'd be the sheriff here, and we'd be hauled off to jail for not paying the doctor's bill."

But before we came to that kind of mutual confession—in which I replied in kind, about my thoughts about their thoughts, and finally, about my thoughts period—there had to be one long stretch of coming and going, of sly and bewildered talk, of muscles relaxed a bit, quickly tightened up, then once again allowed to slacken, now for a little more time. They began to realize that I was in fact an oddball—who belonged to no recognizable part of their world. And after much too long a period of time I began to realize—an important first step—that they were not the helpless, pitiable objects of study I have to admit I predominantly felt them to be. Oh, it was never necessary to be that blunt. Instead of calling them the wretched of the Southern earth, I could lash out at the South itself: the region's blacks are terribly poor people; they are mercilessly exploited by the individual bossmen, often "managers" or "foremen" who do the rough and tough work, the squeezing dry of lazy bodies, the extraction of ergs from machines that are running at a caloric loss. (But aren't millions of people in other countries and continents even worse off?) And finally, they are badly educated people, barely literate or for all practical purposes illiterate.

All that is true, I thought to myself in the beginning, but someone has to be hardheaded enough to document what oppression does to its victims, how degraded they actually become. Cannot relentless psychological scrutiny turn into the sharpest kind of social criticism? Romantics may speak of a "culture" that peasants have, or include them in some "agrarian tradition"; but I came to them armed with both Marx and Freud, and so in a way any desire to cover up their "condition" and my account of it with soft, understated, merely allusive or (worst of all) ambiguous language was doubly suspect. I knew to ask myself whether I was beholden to the "power structure"—perhaps one I simply don't care to recognize myself, let alone acknowledge to others. I knew to ask myself whether sharecroppers, simple sharecroppers, vulnerable sharecroppers, made me feel scared and to blame for something. And of course I knew that we are all afraid; we all feel at fault; everyone has "work" to do, fears and guilts to understand and "resolve."

So, it is better to be blunt, I decided as I started visiting them. They are "deprived" and "disadvantaged" and all the rest. They need "higher horizons." They should go North. They need "enrichment programs." They are eligible for every "title" in every federal law; and they need more laws with more "titles." *Headstart* is only a beginning. *Leap* is a drop in the bucket. *Upward Bound* is not "relevant," not to people so badly off, so out of things, so firmly, almost intractably part of—what is it called?—the *lumpen-proletariat*. The only things that will help them, change them, make them part of America, are "massive programs," a "frontal assault" on their poverty, a "basic restructuring" of our society, a "planned attack" on—well, everything "socioeconomic" and "psychosocial" and "sociocultural" that amounts to their very bad lot.

And here are some of the things I found—in one family from the Mississippi Delta—that go to make up that bad lot. The cabin has no heat, no running water, although three miles away there is a faucet and "all the water you can tote." (Not every family in the "area" is that lucky.) And the children, the seven children: none was born in hospitals; none was delivered by doctors; none has ever seen physicians; none has taken vitamin "supplements" as infants or vitamin pills as children; none is without evidence of illness; and none has any clothes that can be called his, his alone.

"The children, they're the most trouble when they're by theirselves. Most of the time they're together, though. And then I know it's okay." They are indeed together. They sleep together: four in one bed, three in another, all in one room. The other room belongs to their parents, and also serves as the kitchen—and living room and dining room. They share not only space and time but clothes and plates and forks. There are three pairs of shoes to go around, so only certain children can fight their way into them, or fight to fill them up—and then go to church, or, yes, to school. (And, naturally, it is the absence from school that bothers us secular, twentieth-century Americans, for whom education is sacred, a way to virtually everything, at least on this earth.) As for the children in that cabin, church wins over school hands down. They fight to go with their parents on Sunday, "to walk with them" as one boy put it, and to sit there and see and hear "everyone get to talking, and have a real good time." Those who stay at home are sad, but they turn happy on Monday if spared school because they still don't have those shoes, or because they feel tired and sick, or because they have to mind the younger ones and help around the house—which means in the fields or around "the place." (It is no mansion. It has no columns, not even a magnolia tree. It is a substantial house, nondescript in style, painted white with green shutters and a green door.)

I don't know what the United States Census Bureau did with the information they obtained from the parents of those seven children. (Such families are sometimes overlooked and not counted at all.) Are they classified sharecroppers or tenant farmers or field hands or employees or retainers or servants or just plain slaves? Are they listed as educated up to this grade or that one? Are they called citizens of this country, or aliens? The questions, the questions you and I answer every decade, can be very embarrassing, although not to "us." They weren't the questions I first had in mind when I started my "study," and they may seem a bit simpleminded to serious social scientists. But they are questions that I rather think no psychoanalytic study of sharecroppers ("in depth," of course) can quite afford to ignore.

"No, sir, I can't say I've ever voted," said the father one day when I got around to that issue. "Yes sir, I think I know what you mean. [He knew damn well what I meant.] They have the law now, that says we can go vote. Some are trying it, and some aren't. I'm afraid I haven't got around to it, yet. But I hope to, before I die I hope to. Right now I guess I've got some other things to do."

Well, what other things? (Those are the good moments, when the observer is practically invited to ask something.) "I don't know—things like where to live, you know. We're thinking of going North. My sister is up there, in Chicago, and she keeps telling us to leave. But we're afraid to. They don't need a lot of us here, but I hear they don't need us there, either. We don't know what to do. We work on the crops part of the time, but the machines do more and more. There's some cotton they can't get, and there's the cattle and a few vegetables we have. I've got the chores to do. And my wife helps out in The House."

His father "worked on shares." Put differently, his father produced cotton and gave it over to the present bossman's father, and in return they continued to live side by side, the sharecropper and the bossman—on the latter's land. The bossman gave the sharecropper a few hundred dollars to spend during the course of the year, and The House sent over some food and some outgrown and secondhand clothes. The man I know grew up and became a field hand. There was no point getting credit for seed and tools and living quarters and food, and then working the land and receiving a share of the crop's value, minus charges for all the credit advances, including the money required for drainage, for irrigation, for fencing: "The bossman, he came and told me that with my daddy it was one thing, but times are changing, and a lot of the sharecroppers, they're not needed, and he was switching. I could work for him and in return I could live in the house and he would make sure that I never starve to death. And even with the machines coming, we could stay, because my wife is such a good help and especially her cooking."

His wife's cooking: until then I thought I knew everything about her cooking. In the morning she makes breakfast. She fries up some grits and they are washed down with either a coke or some coffee. There is no such thing as lunch. The children have another coke, and some very cheap candy like licorice or sugarcoated gum, which they chew and chew, and chew dry, and take out of their mouths and stretch and tear into fragments and laugh over and play with and stick upon one another. The parents also have another coke and some candy, which they eat with greater reserve. Supper is the main meal. It is served early, about half past four or five, and includes without exception fried potatoes and more grits and greens; and bread with peanut butter sometimes, and fatback sometimes. Every once in a while a stew appears, made of potatoes and gravy and pork. Even more unusual is a soup, the product of boiled bones and potatoes and greens. For dessert there is another coke, and maybe more candy.

I asked about cooking and I heard this: "We have practically no money, so it's hard to get by. We grow a little, but we haven't much land to do it on, and the bossman wouldn't want us spending too much time on that. My kids grow some flowers, the zinnias. You can't eat zinnias, I know it, but you can like them—just like you can rest beside a sunflower. We get our greens from the yard, and some tomatoes, though they don't last long. We don't have the money to buy the foodstamps. We get the commodities, and that's how we live. We'd be dead right now without the lard and flour they give, the government. Yes sir, everyone of us would be dead. I try to fill my kids' stomachs up as best I can. I figure if they doesn't hurt them too much, their stomachs, well then, that's good. They gets their energy from the candy and the coke. They take a drink and bite on the licorice, and I know they've got their sugar in them and can keep going."

But her husband was talking about the cooking she did for the bossman. I asked her about that and she told me: "Oh, yes. I've been helping her out for years. I go up there and do what she tells me. I don't plan anything. She always says to me: 'Ruth, I've planned today's menus out.' Then she lists what I've got to do and I go ahead and get to work there."

She gets to work in a spacious, well-equipped kitchen. The sink is stainless steel. The stove is an electric range. The refrigerator is huge, and next to it stands a freezer, and next to *it* stands a washing machine and then a dishwasher. ("I do the dishes and some laundry, too.") Obviously, she has a few minutes to relax, because there is a small television set on one counter—and also a waffle iron, and a toaster, and a mixer for "working up" cakes, and an electric knife sharpener, which also takes care of pencils. I never would have seen all those electrically run gadgets had I not decided to compare her place of work with her place of residence. I knew her bossman well, and, in fact, once heard him say this about Ruth: "She's a fine woman, and so is her husband a fine man. They do an honest day's work, and we'll never let them go without a roof over their heads. I'm going to build them a new place, as a matter of fact. We're letting a lot go, though a lot of them don't want to. I tell them they may as well go North. We can't use them here. One by one they slip away; but you know, we have quite a few still here, right on our land. Eventually I suppose we'll only have maybe five families left here. Imagine that! It's hard for me to believe, after all these years with about a hundred or more. But I sure hope Ruth never leaves. I told my wife I think we'd near starve to death. She's the best cook in this county, easily."

I discovered what he meant. I had lunch with him and his wife. I had a big lunch, that started with a glass of tomato juice and a neatly cut piece of lemon. Then Ruth served us hot diced chicken and rice with raisins mixed in and peas and chutney on the side. And finally we had deep-dish apple pie and ice cream and coffee. It was all tasty, all neatly and attractively presented. The rice was fluffy and warm and covered with butter and seasoned just right. The chicken was cut perfectly, not too small and not too large. The peas were not overcooked; they were fresh, not frozen or canned, and like the rice, delicately salted. The pie had a light crust, and inside were warm tart apples, neither too syrupy nor dry. I was afraid I was going to be told that the ice cream was homemade, but no, it was store-bought: "It used to be we'd make our ice cream here, when I was a child. But you know it's too easy to buy it, and I think Ruth has enough to do as it is." I had commented on how good the ice cream was, and on how good the ice cream was at a nearby (and larger) plantation, where it was a bit ostentatiously, if generously, handed over with the hostess' advice from across the table that "Mary-Jean makes it, fresh every day." Ruth's mistress had been there many times—and clearly regretted the unfavorable comparison that I suppose I had unwittingly made.

When I left the house my stomach was filled with Ruth's food, and my mind was finally brought up short, the way it should have been months before. I kept on thinking of Ruth and that kitchen and of all the Ruths in America. I was there in that county to "study" her and her family, to get to know how they *really* live and think and feel. I had spent months visiting them and being observed by them and taking stock of all sorts of things they said and did. I was really rather proud of myself; and I was ashamed, too. I had made the effort to reach Ruth's family; and in so doing found out once again how awful their kind of American experience is—in contrast, say, to mine.

But guilt masks many things, one of which is pride. The guilt I easily knew about was the kind I easily notice in both myself and in patients. We have so much; others have so little. We feel ashamed of ourselves because we know the inadequacy of whatever good deeds we have done, whatever goodwill we feel. The guilt I began to feel for the first time after that lunch was something else, though; it had to do with the recognition of a willful kind of ignorance and blindness—mine. For a long time I had known that Ruth worked for the bossman's wife—cooked and cleaned and dusted for her, looked after her clothes and her dishes and her bedroom and bathroom. I knew all that, but I never really allowed myself to go any further; in fact, to bridge the two worlds that Ruth did every day. It was all right, of course, for *me* to bridge those two worlds; but Ruth in my mind had to be a sharecropper's wife, pure and simple. (And don't thousands of them work in those big houses in one capacity or another?)

Perhaps—to be generous to myself—I was merely a pedantic, unimaginative, anxious "investigator," who was slightly overwhelmed by all he was meeting up with. The search for order and clarity can often help a case of the nerves, can help a person come to terms with his worries and fears as well as his "methodology." Somehow a confusing, ambiguous, irony-filled world becomes a little more manageable when this man is distinguished from that one; and if they both can be placed on a graph or two and made part of a few percentages and made to possess a few "attitudes" and "beliefs" and "habits" and "problems"—well then, all the better. Ruth and her mistress live worlds apart on that plantation. I was busy finding out precisely how far apart; and every liberal bone in my body, I assure you, was full of the proper mixture of outrage and pity and sadness. In my cool, farsighted, evenhanded moments I felt sorry not only for Ruth but for her mistress, a kind, soft-spoken woman who speaks ill of no one and at moments can challenge my stereotypes as significantly as Ruth eventually did: "I have a lot of respect for Ruth, and you know we have many like her in Mississippi. She is a good person, and we have never had cause to complain about her. I never made this world, but I'll admit there are times when I say to myself that there but for the grace of God go I. What I mean is that I do believe Ruth has the same intelligence we do, and if things were different—well, I think she could be, well, I think she could be just like me, more or less. She could run the house, I'm sure, and plan things and make sure everything goes according to schedule."

When I heard that, I was in danger of being a very smug listener. I felt like getting up and screaming at the polite and honorably frank speaker. I felt like telling her that Ruth already was running her house, that without Ruth the house would be messy and disorganized, and its occupants would find mealtimes a lot less pleasant. But I was really agitated because I was hearing from someone else a very familiar kind of condescension, one that I fear is all too much the property of people like me rather than of Southern white ladies who "favored" Barry Goldwater and refer to themselves as "of conservative disposition." Neither she nor I— although I have to say, she at least a little better than I—seemed able to talk about the extent of Ruth's social and cultural achieve-ment. Yes, we know that she is a good cook; and her mistress *senses* (and perhaps does not dare let her mind become more explicit) that without such "nigra help" life would be far different; and all along I knew, prided myself on knowing, that Ruth is a fine, hard-working, reliable person who is exploited and only appreciated in ways that don't cost a cent. But in the last analysis (the commend-ably unsparing one) I had to conclude that Ruth lacked dignity, even as her mistress knows that Ruth is only potentially capable of being dignified. And, needless to say, I had set out to study the consequences of the indignity America has visited upon people like Ruth: what happens to a woman who is stripped of her legal rights, her rights as a citizen, and kept socially apart as well as miserably poor.

I think it was the array of electric appliances in the kitchen that first made me stop and think and realize how much had been escap-ing my notice. Ruth was the master of all those machines. She was a gracious hostess, who served fine meals. She knew better than I where on the table a lot of those extra forks or spoons go. She knew her spices. She knew how to take care of the finest, most expensive clothes. She knew which plants needed a lot of water, which very little. She knew how to care for flowers. I remember my mind latching on to that last fact. I remember deciding to ask Ruth about those flowers: "Well, she likes her flowers. She grows a lot of them, and there will be times when she has to send for them, from the store, you know. I fix them up. I know which vases to use for which flowers, and how she likes them. She used to say 'good'; but now she just expects it, I guess—that I'll do right. You see what I mean?"

Of course I hadn't been seeing; that is the point. I had been figuring out how Ruth lives, and how her mind deals with "reality" and what psychological "defenses" she used. I had been developing a very clear idea of the hardships she faces every day, and even the stubborn persistence she possesses. I had declared her in my mind a desperate but inventive woman who somehow, beyond all explana-tion, endured. I was not so sure that she would, as Faulkner pre-dicted, prevail; but I was prepared to say it was possible. I had at least shaken off the simpleminded view that the poor and even persecuted people are *only* hurt, sad, beaten down in spirit, deraci-nated, and branded with the unforgettable "mark of oppression." I was not going to become a "romantic" about Ruth and her family, but I would no longer be a slobbering, so-called reformer who needs the people whose cause he espouses to be as down-and-out, wretched and shattered as possible. Life is hard and even brutal for Ruth, and to survive has cost her a lot. But she is shrewd and ingenious, I had gradually persuaded myself; in the words of contemporary psychoanalysis, her mind has learned to be "adaptive"—and so has her overworked, tired body.

For all that generosity, for all the evolution my mind had been going through before I ate Ruth's lunch in her mistress' home, I had failed miserably to realize that Ruth is a *cultured lady*, a woman who knows her cuisine and her horticulture. Her manners are impeccable; her sense of timing in polite company faultless. She knows what people want and need and deserve and she gives it all to them. She is intuitive and sensitive. Her sensibilities are refined; and she even is at ease with our reigning technology. Her hands deal with the racks of the dishwasher, the shelves of the freezer, the clocks and pointers of the stove—and that pencil sharpener. ("The mister, he taught me how, and now missus gives me the pencils every once in a while, from all over the house. She says the noise of the machine gets to her; it makes her nervous. So she has to leave the room before I start.")

I am not saying that suddenly my mind came to its senses and fought its way to a more accurate and honorable picture of Ruth and her family. But over time, starting with that lunch, I did come to see more and more of Ruth's life, and the more I saw the harder put I was to fit her into convenient categories I had brought with me when I first met her. She is still poor. She is still disenfranchised. She continues to speak ungrammatical English, and so I have to edit her remarks. To this day she needs a doctor, a lawyer, a teacher—as do her children and her husband. She has no more money now than she ever did. And *she* would like a different life—so who am I to wax ecstatic over the countryside of the lovely Delta, the trees and flowers near her cabin, the rich, productive land, the mighty and almost mythic river that she can see by taking a good long walk for herself. Yet, who am I to do something else, deny her life its achievements and its ironies and its ambiguities, refuse her mind the sense of style and the subtlety it surely demonstrates all the time?

At times I am pleased with my own ability to leave Cambridge, Massachusetts, and somehow come to a reasonably strong and valuable "relationship" with a family like Ruth's. I am not so pleased, however, when I remind myself how long it took me as an anthropologist or psychiatrist or whatever, to recognize *Ruth's* experience and competence. She, too, goes back and forth between two worlds; every day she does. She, too, watches others and tries to help them out. She, too, takes away burdens from people and makes them feel less harried, less at the mercy of this and that. Like a "trained mental health professional" (as they rather ponderously call themselves), she adjusts herself to the lives, the problems, the needs of others. She doesn't get "overinvolved," though. When she and they part company, she knows how to go back to her own life and live it. If she has any "fantasies" about life over there in The House, she controls them, buries them or, more likely, lets them quietly come and quickly go. ("Oh, every once in a while I ask myself why God did things the way he did, and made me me and her her; but pretty soon there's the next thing I have to tend to.") Ignorant and barely literate, she is sophisticated and worldly; and as the bossmen in my profession say about precious few of us, she has "very good ego-defenses." She has taught me a lot I rather expected to find out; but most of all she has taught me about the weaknesses in my way of thinking that prevented her various strengths from being immediately and properly obvious to me. The arrogant man wants to make his world the whole world. He pushes himself ahead of anyone in sight and blinds himself to all sorts of things that he might see in others. When he is safely up front he may mellow, and here or there grant a few favors; but without prodding, I fear, only a few.

Epilogue
and
Prologue

29

Relations of Biological and Social Homeostasis

Walter B. Cannon

In this, the epilogue to his famous volume, *The Wisdom of the Body,* published in 1932, Cannon reveals an avant-garde approach to social phenomena —one that might well surprise some of his more conservative, biologically oriented disciples.

He conjectures that the problems of division of cellular labor, blood transportation, and lymph distribution found in the intact biological entity are representative of fundamental laws concerning system "organization." Appropriate organization assures homeostatic control, or the correction of system perturbation. Cannon argues by analogy that social processes, in much the same way that physiological processes operate are also subject to homeostatic principles. Cannon then offers some of his own thoughts on how the body politic might better function, if more deliberate use were made of homeostatic governing techniques.

Are there not general principles of stabilization? May not the devices developed in the animal organism for preserving steady states illustrate methods which are used, or which could be used, elsewhere? Would not a comparative study of stabilizing processes be suggestive? Might it not be useful to examine other forms of organization—industrial, domestic or social—in the light of the organization of the body?

These are tempting questions. Many times in the history of philosophy and sociology similar questions have led to an examination of the analogies between the body physiologic and the body politic. The biologist is as subject to temptation in respect to these

Reprinted from *The Wisdom of the Body,* pp. 287–306, by Walter B. Cannon, M.D., SC.D. By permission of W. W. Norton & Company, Inc. Copyright 1932 by Walter B. Cannon. Copyright renewed 1960 by Cornelia J. Cannon. Revised Edition Copyright 1939 by Walter B. Cannon. Copyright renewed 1966, 1967 by Cornelia J. Cannon.

analogies as are the philosophers and sociologists! He may lack the philosophers' broad outlook and the sociologists' knowledge of the complex details of the social system. But as a unit of that system he is interested in it. And he looks on the analogies from the biological point of view. May not the new insight into the devices for stabilizing the human organism, which we have been examining in the foregoing chapters, offer new insight into defects of social organization and into possible modes of dealing with them? The details of bodily homeostasis are, of course, available to anyone who cares to see whether they offer any suggestions for the study of social conditions. As a stimulus to such suggestions it might not be amiss to consider some features of their apparent analogies.

In an earlier chapter I pointed out that the single-cell organism, living in a flowing stream, is dependent immediately on its surroundings; it has no means of controlling the environment and must submit wholly to what the environment imposes upon it. Only when cells grow in masses do they acquire the possibility of developing an internal organization, capable of separating them from the disturbances due to shifts of external circumstance.

We must not overlook the fact that when cells grow in masses they still remain living units. Like the isolated single cell each cell in a complex organism has its own life processes. In our discussion of homeostasis we have considered the environment—the internal environment—which is provided for this living units. We have not, however, regarded the events occurring within the units themselves. Each one takes in from its fluid contact water and salts and oxygen; it takes in food which it uses to build up or repair its own structure, or to elaborate new substances for special secretions, or to secure the energy needed in performing other special services for the organism as a whole; and finally it discharges the waste resulting from the wear and tear and from the débris of its own activities. All these complicated functions the cell normally carries on in a nicely adjusted manner, with not too much and not too little of either intake or output. And throughout the multitudes of exchanges which are involved it preserves in a marvelous manner its intimate texture and precise action.

In the one-cell organism all the vital functions—digestion, motion, reproduction—are performed by it alone. As cells grow in masses the phenomenon of division of labor appears. The cells are arranged in separate structures or organs for special services—

muscles for pulling, nerves for conducting impulses, glands for secreting. Of course, these organs are not always active. For long periods, even in the waking state, many muscles and their controlling nerves may be idle. The digestive organs do not work steadily except when given work to do. Only the respiratory organs and the heart must keep persistently at their tasks; and the heart, when beating at the moderate rate of seventy pulses per minute, is actually contracting only nine hours in the twenty-four—rest periods after each contraction amount to fifteen hours every day. Even in the parts of an organ activity is not continuous; muscle fibers take turns in keeping up a long pull, capillaries are closed down when blood is not needed, and the glomeruli of the kidneys operate in shifts. The labor of internal organs (the viscera) is, as a rule, so well regulated by inherent automatisms that the phenomena of fatigue rarely appear—the waves course over the stomach at their routine rate, the kneading movements of the intestines cannot be made to go faster than their wont. The central nervous system alone can force activities to such a degree as to bring about the limitations and inefficiencies resulting from fatigue—and that system is almost wholly limited to a control of the muscles which pull on the bones. Furthermore, fatigue itself is a check on excessive activity. It is clear, then, that the processes going on in individual cells, as well as those going on in organs, are accompanied by a large amount of local self-regulation.

The centrally important fact is that with the division of labor, which is implicit in the massing of cells in great multitudes and their arrangement in specific organs, most of the individual units become fixed in place so that they cannot forage for themselves. Far removed from the sources of essential supplies, these segregated and specialized units would necessarily cease their activities and would soon die unless there was developed, at the same time with their development, a means of transportation and distribution which would assure these supplies. This transporting and distributing system we recognize as the fluid matrix of the organism—the rapidly flowing blood and the more slowly moving lymph. The existence of the fluid matrix at once simplifies the problem of the remotely situated cells engaged in particular tasks. Having that provision they need not be concerned with getting food, water and oxygen, avoiding too great heat or cold, and keeping clear of the dangers of accumulating waste. All these conditions are attended to by a special organization, which, as we have seen, holds the fluid matrix constant. So long as that constancy is preserved, the various kinds of cells in the different organs are free to give full time to their special services. The fluid matrix, therefore, is a prime requisite for the more complex organization of living units. It makes such organization possible. It gives such organization stability. And insofar as the constancy of the fluid matrix is evenly controlled it is not only a means of liberating the organism as a whole from both internal and external limitations, as we have repeatedly noted, but it is an important measure of economy, greatly minimizing the need for separate governing agencies in the various organs.

We may remark in passing that the cells in the organs which control the constancy of the fluid matrix are themselves part of the total organization of the body. They do not act by imposing conditions from the outside. In maintaining steady states in the blood and lymph they work both for the welfare of the cells in other organs essential to the body, and also for their own welfare. In short they well illustrate the arrangements for mutual dependence; in spite of generous provision for factors of safety, the integrity of the organism as a whole rests on the integrity of its individual elements, and the elements, in turn, are impotent and useless save as parts of the organized whole.

In primitive conditions, small human groups living by the chase and by simple agriculture encountered circumstances not unlike those which prevail in the life of isolated single cells. Individuals were free, free to move about over wide ranges and to forage for themselves, but they were dependent on what their immediate environment at the moment could furnish. They had little control over that environment. Of necessity they had to submit to the conditions which it determined.

Only when human beings are grouped in large aggregations, much as cells are grouped to form organisms, is there the opportunity of developing an internal organization which can offer mutual aid and the advantage, to many, of special individual ingenuity and skill. But with the development of larger and more complex social communities, just as with the evolution of the larger and more complex organisms, the phenomenon of division of labor becomes more and more pronounced. The list of special types of workers in a civilized society is almost unlimited. Again, like the division of labor in the animal organism, the division of labor in a complex social group has two noteworthy effects—it leads gradually to relative fixation of the individual members of the group in places where they perform their peculiar labor, and they may then be far removed from the sources of supply necessary for their continued existence. The expert mechanic in a large urban industry, for example, can neither grow his food, make his clothing, nor procure his fuel directly. He must rely on members of other groups for these things. He can do his part only so long as the others do theirs. Each one finds security in the general coöperation. Once more, just as in the body physiologic, so in the body politic, the whole and its parts are mutually dependent; the welfare of the large community and the welfare of its individual members are reciprocal.

It is obvious that at present the nation has not yet achieved a full measure of success in maintaining constancy of the routine of its existence or in assuring to its human elements a continuous provision for their essential needs. There is widespread search for the conditions which would diminish the anxieties and distress which are caused by the great ups and downs of economic fluctuations. Stability would free mankind from a vast amount of pain. In our own individual bodily organization we have an example of methods of successful achievement. By storage and release of material supplies, by altering the rate of continuous processes, by natural defenses against injury, and by a wide margin of safety in its functional arrangements, the normal organism protects itself for decades against perturbations. Through myriads of eons of experience our bodies, though composed of extraordinarily labile material, have developed these devices for maintaining stability. What have they to suggest?

At the outset it is noteworthy that the body politic itself exhibits some indications of crude automatic stabilizing processes. In the previous chapter I expressed the postulate that a certain degree of constancy in a complex system is itself evidence that agencies are acting or are ready to act to maintain that constancy. And moreover, that when a system remains steady it does so because any tendency towards change is met by increased effectiveness of the factor or factors which resist the change. Many familiar facts prove that these statements are to some degree true for society even in its present unstabilized condition. A display of conservatism excites a radical revolt and that in turn is followed by a return to conservatism. Loose government and its consequences bring the reformers into power, but their tight reins soon provoke restiveness and the desire for release. The noble enthusiasms and sacrifices of war are succeeded by moral apathy and orgies of self-indulgence. Hardly any strong tendency in a nation continues to the stage of disaster; before that extreme is reached corrective forces arise which check the tendency and they commonly prevail to such an excessive degree as themselves to cause a reaction. A study of the nature of these social swings and their reversal might lead to valuable understanding and possibly to means of more narrowly limiting the disturbances. At this point, however, we merely note that the disturbances are roughly limited, and that this limitation suggests, perhaps, the early stages of social homeostasis.

As an analogous condition of affairs, we may recall that in the evolution of vertebrate animals, and also in the development of the individual organism, the physiological devices which preserve homeostasis are at first not well developed. Only among forms which show other signs of being highly evolved do we find the automatic processes of stabilization working promptly and effectively. I would point again to the strikingly greater control of the internal environment by the complex mammalian than by the relatively simple amphibian creatures; and associated therewith the much greater freedom and independence in the presence of disturbing conditions. Is it not possible that social organization, like that of the lower animals, is still in a rudimentary stage of development? It would appear that civilized society has some of the requirements for achieving homeostasis, but that it lacks others, and because lacking them it suffers from serious and avoidable afflictions.

For the present adhering fairly strictly to physiological considerations (i.e., to the supplies of food, shelter, etc.) we are forced to recognize that the homeostasis of the individual human being is largely dependent on social homeostasis. There are certain essential needs which must be satisfied in order to preserve our personal health and efficiency. Some of the needs are satisfied gratuitously. Oxygen, and sometimes water also, we may have at will, without cost. It is noteworthy that in cities a supply of water is obtained only by community action and at public expense. There are other needs, however, which in the long run are quite as urgent as the needs for water and oxygen, and which at times cannot be satisfied because of the lack of social stability. These are the elementary requirements of food and of shelter (clothing, housing and warmth), and the benefits of medical care. To specialized workers in the social organization, limited and segregated as they are by their specialization, so that they must rely almost wholly on social homeostasis, disburbances of that homeostasis may be seriously harmful. Not only may the bodily needs be inadequately supplied, but in addition there may be suffering because of a loss of the sense of security. In the animal organism, as we have learned, the device which preserves homeostasis, which protects the cells in all parts from perturbations whether from within or without, is the controlled fluid matrix. What is the agency in civilized society which corresponds to that feature of our bodily arrangements?

In a functional sense the nearest equivalent to the fluid matrix of animal organisms that is found in a state or a nation is the system of distribution in all its aspects—canals, rivers, roads and railroads, with boats, trucks and trains, serving, like the blood and lymph, as common carriers; and wholesale and retail purveyors, representing the less mobile portions of the system. In this vast and intricate stream, whose main channels and side branches reach more or less directly all communities, goods are placed, at their source, for carriage to other localities. These other localities are also sources of goods which likewise are placed in the stream. Thus the products of farm and factory, of mine and forest, are borne to and fro. But it is permissible to take goods out of the stream only if goods of equivalent value are put back in it. Ordinarily, of course, this immediate exchange does not occur. It would be highly awkward. To facilitate the process of exchange, money, which has generally recognized value, is employed. Or credit may temporarily be its substitute. By means of his money or his credit any individual can take from the stream whatever he needs or desires. Money and credit, therefore, become integral parts of the fluid matrix of society.

To assure the same degree of stability in the social organism that has been attained in the animal organism the latter suggests such control of the fluid matrix that its constancy would be maintained. That would involve, in the first instance, the certainty of continuous delivery by the moving stream of the necessities of existence. Food, clothing, shelter, the means of warmth, and assistance in case of injury or disease are naturally among these necessities. Stability would involve also the assurance of continuous remuneration of individual labor—labor which would produce exchangeable goods and which would be paid a wage sufficient to allow the laborer to take from the stream the necessary things which he and those dependent on him require. I have stated the situation, for the present, in the lowest terms. *At least* these conditions should be met if stabilization of the social organism is to be achieved. In the light of biological experience social stabilization should be sought, not in a fixed and rigid social system, but in such adaptable industrial and commercial functions as assure continuous supplies of elementary human needs.

The social organism like the animal organism is subject to disturbances, some imposed from without, some due to its own activities. Droughts, floods, earthquakes, fires and pestilence may destroy immense accumulations of goods—crops and cattle, homes and workshops—and leave great numbers of men, women and children not only destitute of the prime requirements of life, but without the means of getting them, either directly or by going to the common stream. A new machine may be invented which, because it can do the work of thousands of laborers, throws thousands of laborers out of their jobs. Thus they lose for a time the opportunity to earn the money which they must have in order to take from the stream what they require. Or there may be excessive production of certain goods so that they do not move in the stream but accumulate; or such goods have a value so much reduced that they bring little in exchange, and consequently other exchangeable goods accumulate; or men may become apprehensive of future security so that money is not used to take goods from the stream but is hoarded, and again goods accumulate; or credit may be withdrawn, which has the same effect of retarding the usual processes of trading. In whatever way the movement of goods may be checked or hindered, the result is the same. The common stream becomes clogged, its rate of flow becomes slower, manufacture becomes hazardous, workmen are therefore unemployed, and being unemployed they cannot earn the wherewithal to secure what they must have. In these various types of disaster the individual members of the social organization are not responsible for the ills which circumstance forces them to endure. As more or less fixed units, performing specialized tasks in a complex system of tasks, they are incapable of making quick adjustments to new conditions as they arise. In the emergency they are impotent to modify the system to the advantage of all. Either type of remedy—new individual adjustments or modification of the general system—requires time and thoughtful planning.

What does the stability of the organism suggest as to modes of solving the problem? Here we must be careful not to extend the principles of homeostatic orderliness at first to large and unwieldy administrative regions. If we assume a limited and fairly self-sufficient administrative region, we may suppose that the suggestions of the organism would be somewhat as follows.

The organism suggests that *stability is of prime importance*. It is more important than economy. The organism throws away not only water and salts, but also sugar, if they are present in excess in the fluid matrix. This rejection is uneconomical. The organism is driven into convulsions if the sugar supply runs too low, and the convulsions mark the acme of the manoeuvres which bring forth extra sugar from the hepatic reserves to restore the normal glycemic percentage. Violent shivering may be induced to develop the additional heat which prevents a fall of body temperature. All these extreme activities, which are wasteful of energy, are not ordinarily employed, because milder measures suffice; but they are ready, whenever they are needed, to keep uniform the internal environment. This evidence that in critical times economy is secondary to stability is supported by the generous provisions of factors of safety in the body. The status of blood volume, lung capacity, blood pressure and cardiac power, for example, is not set by economy, but by the chance of having to meet unusual demands which would disturb the fluid matrix of the body if they were not met.

The organism suggests, also, that there are early signs of disturbance of homeostasis which, if sought, can be found. These warning signals are little known in the social organism, and yet their discovery and the demonstration of their real value would make contributions to social science of first-rate importance. In the complexity of modern social interrelations the strategic control would appear to reside in the devices for distributing goods, in commerce and the flow of money rather than in manufacture and production. Our bodily devices would indicate that the early warning signals, pointing to social and economic danger, should perhaps be sought in sensitive indicators of fluctuations of the commercial stream, though the causes of these fluctuations may be found in industry.

The organism suggests, furthermore, that the importance of

stability warrants a specially organized control, invested by society itself with power to preserve the constancy of the fluid matrix, i.e., the processes of commerce. Does not this imply that when there is prospect of social perturbation there should be power to limit the production of goods to a degree which would reasonably adjust the supply to the demand? power to lay aside stores of goods which could be released if crises arise? power to require the accumulation of wage reserves which could be used at times of temporary unemployment? power to arrange emergency employment or training for new types of labor skill? and power to accelerate or retard the routine processes of both the production of goods and their distribution, in accordance with desirable adaptations to internal or external disturbing factors? It is noteworthy that in the bodily organism such powers as storing or releasing material reserves, hastening or checking continuous processes, are exercised not by the cerebral cortex, where adaptive intelligence is mediated, but by lower centers of the brain which work in an automatic manner when appropriate signals call upon them to act.

The development of organisms indicates that the automatic devices which keep steady the internal environment have resulted from a long course of experience, possibly of experimental trial, error and correction. It seems reasonable to expect that the modes of assuring social stability, that may develop, will be the resultant of a similar evolution. Intelligence, and the example of successful stabilizing processes already in action, however, may make the evolution in society relatively rapid.

If cells of the bodily organism are injured, or are attacked by disease germs, the fluid matrix at once sets up procedures which are favorable to the restoration of the normal state. The conditions in the organism, therefore, point to the assurance of expert protective and restorative attention, through arrangements in the social group, so that the group shall not be weakened by the incapacity or ill health of its members.

We must take account of the fact that the adult organism represents a fairly fixed number of constituent cells, i.e., it is the equivalent of an adjusted population. It has no provision for any process which would be the equivalent of immigration into the social community. Nor has it any provision for unlimited growth, either as a whole or in its parts. Indeed, when some cells reproduce themselves in an uncontrolled manner they form a malignant disease, endangering the welfare of the organism as a whole. Against such pathology the body has no protection. It appears, therefore, that any wisdom which the human organism has to offer to the social organism would be based on the proviso of a population which is adjusted to reasonably assured means of subsistence and which is undisturbed by large increases from either local or foreign sources.

A noteworthy difference between the social and the biological organism is the certainty of death in the latter. In the course of existence the cells lay down intracellular substance which becomes obstructive, or they become injured by accident in irreparable ways, or they degenerate with age, until finally an essential organ of which they are members fails to play its rôle and the failure of that organ ends the activities of the whole organism. Death is a means of ridding society of old members in order to yield places for the new. A state or a nation, therefore, does not need to contemplate its own end, because its units are ceaselessly refreshed. The stabilizing processes in a body politic, therefore, when once discovered and established, might be expected to continue in operation as long as the social organization itself, to which they apply, remains fairly stable in its growth.

It is of considerable significance that the sufferings of human creatures because of lack of stability in the social organism have more and more stimulated efforts directed towards improvement. Various schemes for the avoidance of economic calamities have been put forth not only by dreamers of Utopias but also by sociologists, economists, statesmen, labor leaders and experienced managers of affairs. In all such proposals a much greater control of credit, currency, production, distribution, wages and workmen's welfare is anticipated than has been regarded as expedient or justifiable in the individualistic enterprises of the past.

Communists have offered their solution of the problem and are trying out their ideas on a large scale in Soviet Russia. The socialists have other plans for the mitigation of the economic ills of mankind. And in the United States, where neither communism nor socialism has been influential, various suggestions have been offered for stabilizing the conditions of industry and commerce. Among these suggestions are the establishment of a national economic council or a business congress or a board of industries or of trade associations, representing key industries or the more highly concentrated industries, and endowed (in some of the schemes) with mandatory power to coördinate production and consumption for the benefit of wage earners; provision for regularity and continuity of employment, with national employment bureaus as an aid, with unemployment insurance as a safety device, and with planned public works as a means of absorbing idle workmen; incentives for the preservation of individual initiative and originality in spite of the dangers of fixed organization; shortening of the working time and prohibition of child labor; the raising of the average industrial wage; and the assuring of the general public through governmental regulation that in any arrangements which are made its interests will be protected.

The multiplicity of these schemes is itself proof that no satisfactory single scheme has been suggested by anybody. The projection of the schemes, however, is clear evidence that in the minds of thoughtful and responsible men a belief exists that intelligence applied to social instability can lessen the hardships which result from technological advances, unlimited competition and the relatively free play of selfish interests.

By application of intelligence to medico-social problems, destructive epidemics such as the plague and smallpox have been abolished; fatal afflictions, e.g., diphtheria and tuberculosis, have been greatly mitigated and largely reduced; and vast areas of the earth's surface, formerly dangerous to man, have been made fit for safe and sanitary habitation because of the conquest of malaria, yellow fever and hookworm disease. These achievements all involve social organization, social control, and a lessening of the independence of the individual members. Economic and sociological programs, in which emphasis is laid on the well-being of the human elements in production as well as on material profits, have purposes similar to the medical programs just mentioned. They recognize that the social organism, like the bodily organism, cannot be vigorous and efficient unless its elements are assured the essential minimal conditions for healthful life and activity. And the possession of a mind by the human elements would require that these conditions include not only provision for the elementary needs which we have been considering, but also reasonable satisfaction of desires.

In our study of the effects on the organism of a controlled stability of the fluid matrix we noted that just insofar as the stability is preserved the organism is released from the limitations imposed by internal and external disturbances. Is it not probable that similar results will flow from control and stabilization of the fluid matrix of the social organism? The hope is not unreasonable that the distress arising from catastrophes can be greatly mitigated, and that the suffering due to lack of necessary things which is attendant on great economic fluctuations can be obviated, by carefully planning and by intelligently regulating the processes of production and distribution. Banishment of this distress and suffering would bring freedom from fears, worries and anxieties concerning livelihood, which now may fill men with dark despair. As a Lord Chancellor of England has declared, and his declaration has been approved by a Justice of the United States Supreme Court, "Necessitous men are not, truly speaking, free men." The assurance of freedom *to men who are willing to work* would justify a larger control of economic processes, repugnant though that may seem, for it would be a sacrifice of lesser for greater values.

Bodily homeostasis, as we have learned, results in liberating those functions of the nervous system that adapt the organism to new situations, from the necessity of paying routine attention to the management of the details of bare existence. Without homeostatic devices we should be in constant danger of disaster, unless we were always on the alert to correct voluntarily what normally is corrected automatically. With homeostatic devices, however, that keep essential bodily processes steady, we as individuals are free from such slavery—free to enter into agreeable relations with our fellows, free to enjoy beautiful things, to explore and understand the wonders of the world about us, to develop new ideas and interests, and to work and play, untrammeled by anxieties concerning our bodily affairs. The main service of social homeostasis would be to support bodily homeostasis. It would therefore help to release the highest activities of the nervous system for adventure and achievement. With essential needs assured, the priceless unessentials could be freely sought.

There might be apprehension that social stabilization would tend towards dull monotony, that the excitements of uncertainty would be lacking. That would be true, however, only for the fundamental requirements of existence. There would still be the social disturbances of new inventions, the social interest in renowned exploits, in the discords of human nature, in reports of fresh ideas, in the intrigues of love and hate, and in whatever other events there may be that make life varied and colorful. Above all there might be apprehension that social stabilization would too greatly interfere with the free action of individuals. As repeatedly emphasized, however, steady states in society as a whole and steady states in its members are closely linked. Just as social stabilization would foster the stability, both physical and mental, of the members of the social organism, so likewise it would foster their higher freedom, giving them serenity and leisure, which are the primary conditions for wholesome recreation, for the discovery of a satisfactory and invigorating social *milieu,* and for the discipline and enjoyment of individual aptitudes.

30

At a Choice Point

William Seeman · Philip A. Marks

In a whimsical account of how Herman, a white rat, might view psychology, Seeman and Marks pose some serious questions. Among them are the following: Do psychologists tend to attack data-producing, but trivial, problems? Where do the professional rewards lie—are they given to the thinkers, or to the technicians? Is our educational system designed to reinforce the intellectual conformist, or the dissenter? Where can the line be drawn between "scientific" and "nonscientific" disciplines?

The authors' purpose is not to provide answers; they are far too sophisticated to make the attempt. Rather, their goal is merely to puncture academic pomposity.

This is a story about a white rat who wanted to be a psychologist. His name was Herman. As Herman was at the upper end of the rat-intelligence continuum, and was, in fact, the very, very brightest member of a "bright" strain which had been developed over many generations, he was able to secure entrance to a graduate school.

One of the first things he learned (which he had, of course, known all along) was that there was a vast amount of experimental literature about the behavior of the white rat at a choice point. (To be sure, there were a few Skinnerians who occasionally had some unkind words to say about the T-maze as an instrument of experimentation, but in the main the maze was accepted as shedding light on the "dynamics" of choice behavior.) What surprised our white rat, Herman, however, was that very little knowledge was available about the behavior of the *psychologist* at a choice point. Except for a few major efforts, such as the Michigan study of clinical psychology students, there had not been much time available for the investigation of the investigative behavior of psychologists and of the choices involved therein. He did find that E. K. Strong had

From *American Scientist* (1962), Vol. 50, pp. 538–547; reprinted by permission.

demonstrated quite a while back that professional choices were not likely to be wholly accidentally determined. And thinking about this it occurred to him (let us face it—our rat, Herman, had a taint of the "clinician" somewhere about him) that the psychoanalysts might be right, and that it might be true, as Roy Schafer had said, "Interests themselves must be regarded as . . . expressions . . . of major dynamic trends." So he was not in the least surprised when he found that Strong and Tucker had demonstrated that four rather distinctive profiles could be derived respectively for surgeons, internists, pathologists, and psychiatrists. He would have been surprised if it were *not* so, if these different specialists were *not* "different kinds of people."

Then, in diligent pursuit of his course assignments, Herman began to read the long "methodological" discussions which dotted the pages of the *Bulletin,* the *Review,* and, to a lesser extent, the pages of some of the other journals. In a short time he was able to distinguish between "theory" and "meta-theory," although it must be admitted that he occasionally confused these with "methodological considerations." One thing he found: psychological theorizing being what it was, it seemed terribly easy for some psychologists to yield to the temptation of telling *other* psychologists what, as theorists and/or methodologists and/or meta-theorists they *had* to do in order to remain members-in-good-standing of the "scientific" club. The rules of the game called "science" as they pertained to the domain called "behavior" were sometimes laid out with enviable precision, neatness, and order. The more our Herman thought about this, the more puzzled he became; puzzled then worried, then haunted. He pursued an elusive idea and an elusive word—*choice.* It disrupted his chain of associations, became obsessively omnipresent in his thoughts, and punctuated his dreams in a shamelessly unsymbolic and undisguised form. It seemed to him that there were a number of instances in which important but implicit choices were being made; instances in which it was not quite explicit, always, *that* there were choices being made. For example, he happened one day upon two graduate doctoral students who were just completing experiments, one on secondary reinforcement, the other on changes in the "self-concept" with psychotherapy. The student with the secondary-reinforcement problem was taunting the other with his lack of "rigor." Either you were rigorous, said the former, or you were not. If you were, you could call yourself a "scientist"; if you were not, you couldn't.

That evening Herman worked far into the night, digging deep into the philosophy of science. He read, he thought; he thought, he read, and then he thought harder and harder. The more he read and the deeper he immersed himself in thought, the more perplexed he became. It was clear that rigor was a great idea, as it was clear, most psychologists would agree, that any and every area of psychology ought to be made as rigorous as possible, although writers on projective techniques occasionally contrived to give a contrary impression. But he wondered why, if rigor were the absolutely exclusive criterion, the student had not done an experiment in classical mechanics! What looked like the beautiful precision and control of secondary reinforcement (like "rigor," in short) began to look like sloppy lack of controls as compared with the precision and rigor of classical physics. This particular experiment, as he recalled, had been executed in the absence of any knowledge about the life history of the rat subjects before they had been purchased at the institute. And, being a white rat himself, he knew this might not be an irrelevant variable. It must be, then (so our Herman ruminated) that there was an element of *choice* here; the psychologist took what rigor he could get and took it in something he happened to be *interested* in. To the psychologist's credit it had to be said that rigor was largely devised, evolved, invented, or discovered as a result of blood, sweat, tears, thought, and the ingenuity of his efforts. All in all, considering the psychology of the investigator, it seemed to Herman that this constituted an interesting bit of behavior at a choice point. It made him sad, though, to think of the poor thanks the psychologist sometimes got for his efforts at rigor, for he remembered the graduate student in physics who had asked scornfully: "Tell me, are there any *laws* in psychology?"

Then too the methodological papers puzzled him in another way. He seemed to recall that somewhere MacFarlane had written that the centralist doctrine which was given substantial meaning by the work of Freud had somehow got distorted (in the projective techniques) into "Your unconscious is you." He wondered whether, comparably, the doctrine of operationism hadn't got distorted into "seeing is believing." Thus, in a discussion of intervening variables *versus* hypothetical constructs, he was informed that while one was

permitted (if he *must*) to resort to hypothetical constructs, temporarily, he had nevertheless better cash these in at the earliest market
opportunity for intervening variables. What looked like a methodological *must* to one psychologist seemed to Herman on closer
examination, to be a doctrinal preference. If he were a clinician
(which thank heavens, he was not!) he might even have said that
this was an *interest* choice being smuggled in (quite unconsciously)
as formal methodological doctrine. Such a methodological dictum, if
adopted, would make it impossible to suggest that things might not,
in fact, be what they seem, and that skimmed milk could conceivably
masquerade as cream. It would, for example, make it impossible to say that observed behavior such as a persistent and hyper-
kinetic pursuit of women by a man could be a "defensive reaction-
formation," a means of defending against "unconscious homoerotic
impulses." He had read somewhere that Meehl had referred to this
as sometimes giving the appearance of having a heads-I-win-tails-
you-lose flavor. But here, too, there was a choice. Some psychologists might be made uncomfortable by the mere mention of such a
possibility, and had every right to avoid it and to work in another
theatre of operations. Those who elected to work this area would
just have to be content with a little less rigor, less elegance, less
precision, and perhaps a good deal more discouragement.

One October morn our Herman walked into his statistics course
and sat down. The instructor was a well-known statistician with a
widely-respected book in the field. He began the lecture (the instructor, that is) by announcing that he had spent the summer
reading all the psychology journal articles he could (including the
experimental journals) and these had depressed him. Of the whole
lot, there were only two satisfactory papers; just two papers in
which the researchers had been careful to see that all the assumptions underlying the statistical procedures used were actually met
by the data. The statistician then proceeded to present to the class
as an illustrative instance a study which *did* meet the requirements.
It was a study in tossing pennies. Now Herman had no objection to
tossing pennies, and he certainly felt that people who enjoyed
tossing pennies ought to be permitted to do so. (He had himself
once made a brief but disastrous visit to Las Vegas and the roulette
tables.) But as a white rat he had (he felt) a certain natural interest
in the *human organism*. He thought that he should be permitted to
choose between a precise estimate of something he was not the least

interested in and a less precise estimate of something he passionately wanted to know.

Herman was made saddest of all by the constant guerilla warfare carried on by the "clinical" and "experimental" students. He thought the clinicians sometimes had a tendency to fuzziness about the "clinical method," "dynamics," and "clinical validation." He especially wondered what the latter might mean, and he counted seven different definitions of the word "dynamic." (On the other hand he had just read Gibson's seven different definitions of the word "stimulus.") But, thinking again in terms of choice and in the psychology of the investigator, it occurred to him that some of the more solid clinicians were making much the same *kind* of choice when they elected to research "countertransference," "identifica-

Table 1. Qualifying Examination.

1. MATHEMATICS	STATISTICS
2. H-CONSTRUCT	I-VARIABLE
3. ARISTOTLE	GALILEO
4. S-O-R LAWS	S-R LAWS
5. RORSCHACH	MMPI
6. FACTOR ANALYSIS	PSYCHOANALYSIS
7. PSYCHOPHYSICS	BEHAVIORISTICS
8. PREDICTION	EXPLANATION
9. S-R LAWS	R-R LAWS
10. LOGIC	MEASUREMENT
11. CONSTRUCT VALIDITY	CONCURRENT VALIDITY
12. HOCKHEIMER	SEDLITZ

tion," and "self-concept" in preference to secondary reinforcement, pursuit rotor tasks, and reactive inhibition—the same kind of choice as were those psychologists who elected to research secondary reinforcement, pursuit rotor tasks, and reactive inhibition in preference to the capture probability of electrons, magnetic field, and hydrodynamics; all of which latter could, beyond all shadow of doubt, be stated with more exact and elegant mathematical precision and with greater generality than the "laws" of secondary reinforcement, pursuit rotor tasks, and reactive inhibition. At least it appeared to our rat that the same logic which would compel the psychologist to turn from the disturbing messiness and lack of controls in research on "countertransference," "identification," and the "self-concept" to the more rigorous controls of secondary reinforcement, pursuit rotor tasks, and reactive inhibition should compel the psychologist to turn from the messiness and lack of controls in research on secondary reinforcement, pursuit rote tasks, and reactive inhibition to the more elegant, more general, more precise research on capture probability, magnetic fields, and hydrodynamics.

Troubled by this unprecedented and heretical view, Herman's advisor recommended that he (Herman) schedule his doctoral qualifying examination at once. Passively Herman acquiesced. The examination, reproduced in Table 1, was given in three parts.

The instructions for each part were simple and straightforward, and were these.

Part I: "Select the member of each pair having the highest personal *interest* value"; Part II: "Select the member of each pair having the highest '*rigor*' value"; Part III: "Select the member of each pair having the highest *theory* value" (i.e., the one that is more theoretical than empirical).

Separate answer sheets were used for each part, and in no instance was Herman informed of the precise nature of the required tasks or permitted to see the instructions until he had completed the preceding part (e.g., he had to complete Part I before he could even be informed that there was to be a Part II, etc.). Herman's Interest, Rigor, and Theory scores are given in Table 2.

Table 2. Herman's Interest, Rigor, and Theory Scores.

PART I: INTEREST		PART II: RIGOR		PART III: THEORY	
A	B	A	B	A	B
1. (X)	( )	1. (X)	( )	1. (X)	( )
2. ( )	(X)	2. ( )	(X)	2. (X)	( )
3. ( )	(X)	3. ( )	(X)	3. ( )	(X)
4. (X)	( )	4. ( )	(X)	4. (X)	( )
5. ( )	(X)	5. ( )	(X)	5. (X)	( )
6. (X)	( )	6. (X)	( )	6. ( )	(X)
7. ( )	(X)	7. (X)	( )	7. ( )	(X)
8. (X)	( )	8. (X)	( )	8. ( )	(X)
9. (X)	( )	9. (X)	( )	9. (X)	( )
10. (X)	( )	10. (X)	( )	10. (X)	( )
11. ( )	(X)	11. (X)	( )	11. ( )	(X)
12. (X)	( )	12. (X)	( )	12. (X)	( )

Herman's advisor, and indeed his entire department, were extremely delighted with the results. A comparison of Herman's interests with his notions of rigor revealed a congruency of 75.0%—he was, so they reasoned, a rigorous-rat. A comparison of his interests with his notions of theory revealed a congruency of 66.7%—Herman was a theoretically-oriented-rigorous-rat. Yet, upon *Herman's* closer inspection, such results were, for him, scarcely cause for rejoicing. What saddened him was the state of affairs represented by his low rigor-theory item overlap (41.7%). He wondered how a theoretically-oriented-rigorous-rat like himself could have actually obtained a higher rigor-empirical percentage (58.3%). Was he conflicted? It occurred to him that quite possibly he was—that, being infra-human, of course he was—"I am," he mused, "a theoretically-oriented-rigorous-conflicted-rat!"

In his second year of graduate study Herman became fascinated with the problems presented by learning theory. After surveying the various theories as presented in Hilgard, he tackled reinforcement theory more systematically, studying Hull with great care. One night he fell asleep whilst ruminating over the problem of extinction and stimulus-response asynchronism. Suddenly, he sat bolt upright, waking from a dream in which he had been pursuing Hull's idea of developing a unit of habit strength, the "hab." Why not a unit of rigor—the "rig?" Well, why not? (The *definition* of rigor was, at least implicitly, very easy. It could be found in Mendelssohn's opening sentence in the paper "Probability Enters Physics": "Physics—or, if you like, experimental philosophy—is a philosophical method which differs from others in that it relies on rigorous quantitative relations between observations.")

In a burst of creative excitement and activity he burrowed into the works of Norbert Wiener and Anatol Rapaport: into cybernetics, into information theory, into James Miller's general systems theory. Armed with this constellation of information he then set to work building a machine, a rigometer, which like an ammeter or a voltmeter, would register values directly on a dial. In this manic burst of imaginative activity, Herman hardly ate or slept; it was too exciting. He knew that if the circuits could be made to reverberate properly, if enough circuits could be provided to obviate information overload, and if the programing mathematics could be mastered, the most complex theories and experimental designs could be fed into the machine and a precise measure of their rigor obtained in "rig" units.

At last the machine was ready. Would it work? With trembling paws and much trepidation Herman fed into the machine a number

of theories: Newton's gravitational theory, Maxwell's and Boltz-
mann's equations expressing pressure and temperature of a gas as
average energy of motion of gas molecules, Schrödinger's mathematical representation of de Broglie's theory of matter waves. The
indicator swept over the face of the dial registering extraordinarily
high values in "rigs." So far so good! Feeding in the various theories
of learning, Herman saw the indicator move downward on the dial;
lower and lower "rigs," as was to be expected. As he fed in the theories
of transference and countertransference the dial plummeted ever
lower. Herman was delighted. His rigometer was an indubitable
success!

Nothing succeeds like success, and nothing breeds success
more than the proliferation of previous success. Herman had run
across some of Flesch's measures of readability and across some
measures of interest. Why not, though, a more *precise* measure of
interest, so that various problems could be assessed for their interest
value? He decided to build another machine, an intometer, based
upon certain statistical facts: The listed interests of the APA membership; the rated interest value of certain questions (e.g., How
long does it take an ameba to locate food in a T-maze? How can we
devise methods to prevent mutual annihilation by the hydrogen
bomb? etc.); the nature and extent of subscriptions to professional
journals; and a number of other variables. Only after he had completed this piece of apparatus did it occur to Herman to investigate
the relationship between the rigor value (in "rigs") and the interest
value (in "ints") of certain questions. What he found disturbed him
not a little, and is presented in Figure 1.

He found that if he plotted on the abscissa the interest values
of some of the problems randomly sampled from the universe of
problems, and along the ordinate the rigor values of the tightest
experimental designs which could be devised to study those problems—he found that an inverse relationship turned up. One could
say either that high rigor problems had low interest values or that
high interest problems had low rigor values as measured by the
instrumentation. With this Herman was not at all happy.

But degree-getting is not a process which waits on the personal
happiness of the student, human or infra-human. The dissertation
hurdle had now to be cleared. Herman selected as his problem "the
prediction of daydreams in a gravitational field" and set up the
problem in the following manner: He first surveyed a number of

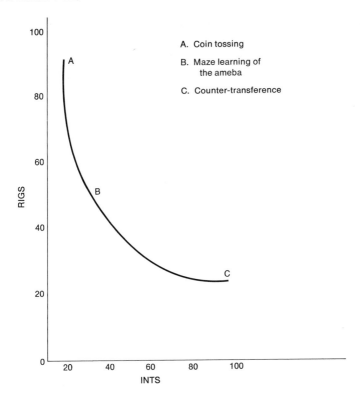

FIGURE 1. Relationship between rigor values (RIGS) and interest values (INTS) for a random sample of problems.

college samples to determine the incidence of certain daydreams types, and established with astonishingly high reliability (with rank-order correlations of the magnitude of .95) the incidence of these daydreams types under twenty-five separate conditions. This was a purely empirical study, involving nothing more than frequency counts of daydreams. The dissertation problem proper was designed to answer the question: What kinds of theories could maximally predict these twenty-five daydream frequencies? To answer this question Herman selected five physicists, five chemists, five zoologists, five physiologists, five learning theorists and five clinical psychologists, and asked each of these to select any available theory in his chosen domain. These theories were then fed into the rigometer and their mean value in "rigs" thus determined. The next step was to require each selected theory to deduce logically (i.e., predict) the daydream outcomes, and the total number of "hits" (successful predictions) was computed for the theories in the chosen domains described above. The results of the experimental procedure are presented in Figure 2.

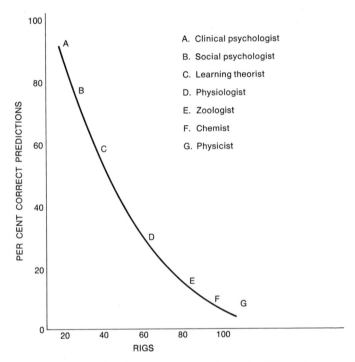

A. Clinical psychologist

B. Social psychologist

C. Learning theorist

D. Physiologist

E. Zoologist

F. Chemist

G. Physicist

FIGURE 2. Relationship between rigor values (RIGS) and per cent of correct predictions of daydreams for a selected number of theories (correct predictions for all 25 daydreams would yield 100%; for 24 daydreams 96%, etc.).

Herman's committee confronted these experimental results with dismayed incredulity, and were thrown into pandemonium. (Notable exceptions to this reaction were to be observed in the committee member representing the philosophy of science and the honorary committee member from physics, both of whom inspected the curve representing the results with imperturbable equanimity. Having examined the experimental results with minute and corrosive care and being unable to locate any errors in the design, procedure, and data analysis, the committee members concluded that Herman's thesis was not quite cricket. It was simply inadmissible, on logical-theoretical-methodological-meta-theoretical grounds, that any theory of lower rig value could effect more successful predictions in *any* scientific domain. Surely, to take any other position was to throw a wrench into the machinery of science.

However heretical the doctrine presented by our theoretically oriented rigorous-conflicted-rat, that doctrine, he maintained, had its validity credentials firmly anchored to the experimental results of his thesis. His committee remained unimpressed and unconvinced.

Herman then confronted them with yet another piece of experimental evidence. This was a little problem he had worked out just for the fun of it, at the time he had done his major survey of daydreams. At that time he had asked the chairman of each of the following departments in the university graduate school to suggest a problem of current interest in his own domain. Indicated here are the departments and the problems set forth:

A. Physics (The capture probability of electrons)
B. Chemistry (The molecular structure of crystals)
C. Zoology (Tonic labyrinthine reflexes of the crawdad)
D. Physiology (Muscle action potentials)
E. Learning (Gradient of secondary reinforcement)
F. Clinical psychology (Outcomes of psychotherapy)
G. Sociology (Delinquency prediction and control)
H. Anthropology (Cultural evolution of mankind)
I. Political science (Avoidance of mutual annihilation by the H-bomb)

The rig values attached to the methods of inquiry designed to investigate these questions are given in Figure 3.

Herman then challenged the committee to draw a line dividing the "scientific" from the "non-scientific" disciplines. (Naturally, to avoid contamination with respect to inter-rater agreement he politely requested them to do this independently.) The committee quite naturally refused to comply with such a highhanded request on the part of a graduate student, especially when he was infra-human. Herman then inquired whether the people at position A should expel from the scientific brotherhood (on the grounds of low rig value) all people at position E; or whether the people at position

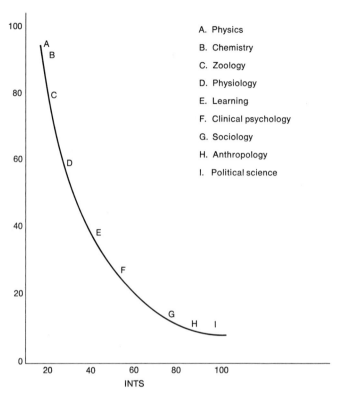

A. Physics
B. Chemistry
C. Zoology
D. Physiology
E. Learning
F. Clinical psychology
G. Sociology
H. Anthropology
I. Political science

FIGURE 3. Relationship between interest values (INTS) and rigor values (RIGS) as a function of departmental problems.

E should (on the same grounds) expel all people at position F; etc. The committee stared stonily and silently first at each other and then at Herman. *They* knew right from wrong, doctrinal sin from doctrinal truth. They politely but firmly suggested that such heretical doctrine (and such experimental results) could not be embraced under the rubric of "science." Equally firmly, they suggested Herman might be in the wrong school. Moreover, they left him no choice!

Index

Accommodation, in Piaget's theory, 176–77

Adams, D. K., 83, 97

Adaptation: behavioral, vii; cybernetics, 229–38; homeostasis, 355–68; and Hull's view, 30–31, 40; and language, 160; and Piaget's theory, 171–79; purpose and teleology, 45–54; race relations, 340–51; stress, 205–21

Albright, W. F., 154, 161

Animal psychology, evaluated, 369–89

Anxiety, *see* Conditioning, classical; Stress

Asch, Solomon, 140

Assimilation and accommodation, in Piaget's theory, 175–77

Associationism, 58, 73

Avoidance, *see* Conditioning

Azrin, N. H., 105–16

Bachrach, Arthur J., 250–64

Bavelas, Alex, 162–70

Beach, Frank A., 183–98

Behavior, 27–44, 45–54; adaptive, 30–31; a classification of, 50–51; genes and, 191–92; instinctive, 188–92; language and, 153–61; ontogeny of, 193–95; operant, 80–98; predictive, 49–50; purposeful, 46–49

Behavior: A Systematic Approach (Notterman), 99

Behavior of Organisms, The (Skinner), 100, 104

Behavior theory, 27–44; anthropomorphism in, 36

Behavior therapy, 250–64; promise of, 280–83

Behavioral processes, 86–90

Behavioral sciences (U.S.S.R.), 74–76

Behaviorism, compared with psychoanalysis, 251

Behavioristic method of study, 46

Bekhterev, V. M., 69–70, 74, 78, 79

Benedict, Ruth, 324, 339

Bergin, Allen E., 265–88

Bernatowicz, A. I., 84, 97

Bigelow, Julian, 45–54, 80, 171

Bleuler, Eugen, 332, 339

Bower, T. G. R., 179

Brain stimulation, 223–28

See also Cybernetics, and the brain

Bridgman, P. W., 42, 44

Cannon, Walter B., 233, 331, 338, 355–68

Carothers, J. C., 338

Causality, and teleology, 54

Cognition and cognitive processes, 71–73, 151–79

Cohn, Robert, 153–61

Coles, Robert, 340–51

Communism and psychology, *see* Union of Soviet Socialist Republics

Concepts (concept formation): of velocity, 171–73; and verbal behavior, 153–61

Conditioned reinforcement, *see* Secondary reinforcement

Conditioning, classical (or respondent), 57–79; escape and avoidance, 199–202; instrumental (or operant), 80–98, 251–59

About the Author

JOSEPH M. NOTTERMAN is Professor of Psychology at Princeton University. He has been a member of its faculty since 1956. He has also held teaching and research appointments at Columbia University and at the William Alanson White Institute of Psychiatry, Psychoanalysis, and Psychology.

Professor Notterman has served as Visiting Lecturer and Visiting Scientist in educational programs sponsored jointly by the American Psychological Association and the National Science Foundation. He was a member of the National Institute of Health's Experimental Psychology Research Review Panel during 1964–1969. Among other affiliations, he is a Fellow of the American Association for the Advancement of Science, a Scientific Associate of the Academy of Psychoanalysis, and a Fellow of the American Psychological Association.

His published works include the book DYNAMICS OF RESPONSE (Wiley, 1965), written with D. E. Mintz, the book BEHAVIOR: A Systematic Approach (Random House, 1970), and articles which have appeared in *Science*, the *Journal of Experimental Psychology*, the *Journal of the Experimental Analysis of Behavior*, the *Journal of Abnormal and Social Psychology*, the *Journal of Comparative and Physiological Psychology*, and other periodicals.

ACM-1
64
1 5 3 7 1   9